THE CHINESE MADHYAMA ĀGAMA AND THE PĀLI MAJJHIMA NIKĀYA

VOLUME 15

The Chinese Madhyama Āgama and The Pāli Majjhima Nikāya

A Comparative Study

BHIKṢU THICH MINH CHAU

MOTILAL BANARSIDASS PUBLISHERS
PRIVATE LIMITED • DELHI

*Reprint: Delhi, **2009***
First Indian Edition: Delhi, 1991

ISBN: 978-81-208-0794-5

MOTILAL BANARSIDASS
41 U.A. Bungalow Road, Jawahar Nagar, Delhi 110 007
8 Mahalaxmi Chamber, 22 Bhulabhai Desai Road, Mumbai 400 026
236, 9th Main III Block, Jayanagar, Bangalore 560 011
203 Royapettah High Road, Mylapore, Chennai 600 004
Sanas Plaza, 1302 Baji Rao Road, Pune 411 002
8 Camac Street, Kolkata 700 017
Ashok Rajpath, Patna 800 004
Chowk, Varanasi 221 001

Printed in India
BY JAINENDRA PRAKASH JAIN AT SHRI JAINENDRA PRESS,
A-45 NARAINA, PHASE-I, NEW DELHI 110 028
AND PUBLISHED BY NARENDRA PRAKASH JAIN FOR
MOTILAL BANARSIDASS PUBLISHERS PRIVATE LIMITED,
BUNGALOW ROAD, DELHI 110 007

FOREWORD

Students of Buddhism and Buddhist culture all over the world must be thankful to Dr. Thich Minh Chau for the most laborious and meritorious work he has produced. His work is concerned with a meticulous, detailed and incisive comparative treatment of the Pāli Majjhima Nikāya with the Madhyama Āgama, the canon of the Sarvāstivādins, now preserved in the Chinese translation. For want of detailed treatment, the old Āgama was almost a sealed book to the majority of scholars interested in Buddhism for their lack of knowledge of Chinese. Dr. Minh Chau's work is replete with many a surprising discovery. He has shown that this Āgama and the Pāli Nikāya have a good deal in common and the divergences are also revealing. He is correct, to my mind, in his assertion that both the recensions of the Sarvāstivādins and the Theravādins are based upon a common heritage. Though an uninformed admirer of Pāli may claim in consonance with the orthodox commentators such as Buddhaghosa that Pāli tradition preserves the original doctrine in its strict purity and represents the actual Teachings of the Master, scholars now are critical of this tall claim. The general consensus of opinion among the scholars, both western and eastern, veers round to the proposition of Dr. Thich Minh Chau that both the versions are based upon one original text which is lost now.

This work was submitted as a Doctorate thesis by the author and received unanimous recommendation of the Board of Adjudicators. His work has really extended the horizon of our knowledge He has approached the subject from the scholar's point of view and detached attitude to promote the cause of truth and not with a set purpose to bolster up a pet dogma or the fad of sectaries. Our knowledge of Buddhism alike in doctrinal, philosophical and disciplinarian aspects, is still condemned to be narrow and sectional for want of materials. Unfortunately, the almost major part of Buddhism enshrined in Sanskrit is lost, but for the few fragments brought to light by the explorers and researchers. Though the quantum of Sanskrit works available is bound to compare unfavourably with that of the Pāli literature, the intrinsic value of the former, and its penetrating insight and logical appraisal of problems demonstrate the fallacy of developing the mediaeval attitude of hatred and jealousy, which undermined the vitality of Buddhism in the Past. So far as loyalty to the central doctrine and tenets of the Buddha, the fountainhead of all these Buddhist Scriptures, is taken into account, it cannot now be supposed that Sanskrit Buddhism is an aberration from the pristine doctrine. These small fragments and the original Sanskrit works discovered in Nepal and Tibet have shown the invincible vitality of the Buddhist faith. Our insight into the secret of expansion of Buddhism in the countries of Asia is deeper and stronger by reason of our acquaintance with these treasures. It has been a puzzle to scholars how Buddhism attained to the status of world religion without the extensive backing of royal patronage and the munificence of rich mercantile magnates. Of course, such patronage came in all the same because Buddhism represented the divine in man and showed the way to transcend the animal instincts. Royal patronage was rather the result and not the condition. By its insistent stress on the transitoriness of worldly prosperity and adversity alike, it strenghtens the spiritual fortitude both of the monks and laymen. It chastens the powerful and encourages the poor and down-trodden.

Both mediaeval and modern history show that worldly prosperity and power are indispensable to protect spiritual advance and national tradition. Foreign conquests have devitalised the conquered people all over the world and the result was an avalanche in apostasy. The power and glory of Buddhism stem from its universal love and friendship. The Buddha conquered by love and mercy and so also his followers. The world now badly requires this philosophy of love and it is unsurprising that scholars and intellectuals are looking forward to Buddhism for the light in the darkness caused by this mad race of armaments and military power. The world is in the grip of fear and nothing can be more demoralizing than loss of self-confidence. The Buddha's life is a vivid example of *Viriya* (energy) and vigilance (*appamāda*). If we can imbibe even fractions of these virtues in our humdrum course of life, the world will turn to a better and nobler career.

Dr. Minh Chau has not done anything which indirectly aimed at this objective. His work is that of a scholar, critical, cautious and faithful to the truth. But the Madhyama Āgama and the Majjhima Nikāya consist of rich dialogues and parables which ennoble the soul and put us in the right path. A student who devotes his time to this work will be naturally goaded to the study of the original works which will instil in him the virtues which Buddhism puts in the forefront. The immediate result of scholarship may not be pragmatic in the broad sense. But it is not sterile. It produces results which are more powerful and permanent on account of their foundation on objective study. The application of theoretical values to life is an aftermath. Viewed in this perspective, Dr. Minh Chau's work will reward the labour of his students both in the short and in the long run. I am hopeful that Dr. Minh Chau will not rest on his oars or relinquish this line of research. We want a complete discovery of Buddhism and he may by his personal effort and example inspire a band of scholars to undertake the prodigious task in spite of the drudgery involved. Buddhism must be restored to its pristine glory and vitality and this can be achieved only by following up the line of work undertaken by the present author in true missionary spirit.

It causes me immense gratification that this work was undertaken and finished in the premises of the Nava Nalanda Mahavihara ; we shall always be proud of what has been done by Dr. Minh Chau and his fellow-workers. When he goes back to his native home, he will, like Hsuan-tsang whose life and activities have been the subject of one of his books, devote the rest of his life to the fulfilment of his mission of propagating the perennial truths of Saddharma for the well-being of many, for the happiness of many and for generating love and friendship by showing up the futility and fatuity of ego-centric bias.

S. MOOKERJEE
Director,
NAVA NALANDA MAHAVIHARA
23 - 3 - 64

ABBREVIATIONS

A.M.R.H. Aspects of Mahāyāna and its relation to Hīnayāna.

C Chinese.

C.A.P.N. The Comparative catalogue of Chinese Āgamas and Pāli Nikāyas.

CMA Chinese Madhyama Āgama.

C N° 30, vi, 18 b, 3–4 : Chinese sūtra N° 30, Case Tse vi, page 18 b, lines 3 and 4.

C.S. N° Comparative study N°

D.P.P.N. Dictionary of Pāli Proper Names.

E.M.B. Early monastic Buddhism.

F.H.T.T.T. Fu-hsüeh-ta-tzu-tien (佛學大字典).

H.I.L. History of Indian literature, Vol. II, Winternitz.

JRAS. Journal of the Royal Asiatic Society.

M.A. Majjhima Nikāya commentary (PTS).

M.L.S. Middle Length Sayings.

M.R.E.T. Manuscript remains of Buddhist literature found in Eastern Turkestan.

Ms. Madhyama Āgama Sanskrit.

Mv. Mahāvagga, PTS Edition.

P Pāli.

P.E.D. Pāli English Dictionary (PTS).

PMN Pāli Majjhima Nikāya.

P N° 2, (i, 89, 7–32) : Pāli sutta N° 2, Vol. i, page 89, line 7 to line 32.

PTS Pāli Text Society.

Q.A. Question and Answer.

Rev. fr. Reverend friend.

Sarv. Sarvāstivāda or Sarvāstivādin.

Sk. Sanskrit.

S.L. The Sarvāstivāda Literature.

Ther. Theravāda or Theravādin.

ThigA. Therīgāthā Commentary (PTS).

T.M.N. Pāli Majjhima Nikāya (PTS).

Tse Case Tsê (昃), Hsü-ts'ang (續藏), Japanese Edition.

Ven. Venerable.

W.H. One : The World Honoured One.

CONTENTS

PART ONE

INTRODUCTION.

PART TWO

SIMILARITIES AND DIFFERENCES BETWEEN THE CHINESE AND THE PĀLI VERSIONS.

B. — Samādhi or Concentration :

C. — Paññā or Wisdom :

PART THREE

15 SPECIMENS OF COMPARATIVE STUDY OF CHINESE AND PĀLI CORRESPONDING SŪTRAS.

PART FOUR

APPENDIXES.

PART ONE

INTRODUCTION

I. — INTRODUCTION

About one century after Lord Buddha's parinibbāna, the Buddhist community was split into 18 schools or more ; and two schools, the Theravāda and the Sarvāstivāda put into shade all other schools by the voluminous bulk of their Canon and by the extensive area of their influence.

But if the Ther. Canon came down to us almost in its entirety, the same cannot be said of the Sarv. Canon, the Sanskrit originals of which were almost all lost, except for some fragments discovered in Central Asia, some remains brought back from Nepal, the recent discoveries of the Gilgit manuscripts and its Chinese and Tibetan translations. A comparative study of both Tripitakas would throw a lot of light on the origin of the ancient Canon and on the similarities and differences between the tenets of the Sarv. and of the Ther.. Attempts by some noted scholars had been made in this direction ; but mostly they confined their activities to the Vinayapiṭaka. Thus Dr. W. PACHOW in his « A COMPARATIVE STUDY OF THE PRĀTIMOKṢA » and Dr. A. C. BANERJEE in his « THE SARVĀSTIVĀDA LITERATURE » dealt mainly with the monastic rules to be followed by the monks and the nuns. Dr. BAPAT had opened a new vista in his ARTHAPADASŪTRA by comparing the Chinese Arthapadasūtra with the Pāli text, but his work is confined only to one portion of the Suttanipāta. Thus a systematic comparative study of the Sūtrapiṭaka of the Ther. and of the Sarv. canons is still a desideratum. My present work : « A COMPARATIVE STUDY OF THE CHINESE MADHYAMA ĀGAMA AND THE PĀLI MAJJHIMA NIKĀYA » is an attempt to fill this lacuna.

Importance of the work :

In this present work, efforts are made to introduce one important section of the Sarv. Canon, the MADHYAMA ĀGAMA, almost in its entirety. This Āgama, hitherto known in its Chinese translation, is dealt with very extensively, starting with the composition of the whole work in its division into vargas, fasciculi, days of recital and sūtras (1), setting forth its doctrinal division of Sīla, Samādhi and Paññā with all their minute subdivisions (2), we have also taken into account the Buddha's life (3), the Sangha with its daily routine (4), the similes, the gāthās or verses and the conclusions of sūtras (5). No details are neglected in order to give a clear vision of the essentials of the Madhyama Āgama of the Sarv. Canon. While dealing with

(1) See infra.
(2) See infra.
(3) See infra.
(4) See infra.
(5) See infra.

the tenets of the Sarv. School, some internal and external evidences are collected with a view to proving that the CMA really belongs to the Sarv. School, this finding was only guessed at or alluded to by previous scholars (1).

The high percentage of similarities between the Chinese and the Pāli versions and the presence of many literally identical passages show that there existed a basic stock, not only of doctrines, but also of texts, agreeing in all essentials with both the Chinese and the Pāli versions. Thus among the 98 C and P corresponding sūtras, there are 45 sūtras with similar titles and 15 sūtras with nearly similar titles, 62 sūtras of the same locations and 15 sūtras of almost the same locations (2). The treatment of the fundamental doctrines such as the Satipaṭṭhāna, the eightfold Path, the Jhānas of the rūpa and arūpa worlds, the 4 Noble Truths etc. (3) is almost similar and the wording of some passages can be said to be identical in both versions. All this proves the existence of an ancient Canon, probably the lost Magadhi Canon referred to by WINTERNITZ in his HISTORY OF INDIAN LITERATURE (4). Prof. ANDRÉ BAREAU accepting the existence of such Canon writes : « L'hypothèse selon laquelle cette identité serait due, non à l'existence de ce Proto Canon, mais à des emprunts mutuels entre Canons tardifs me paraît pratiquement insoutenable, due moins pour l'ensemble des textes, car elle a pu se réaliser dans certains cas particuliers » (The hypothesis asserting that that identity is due, not to the existence of this Proto Canon, but to mutual borrowing between late Canons seems to me practically untenable, at least for the whole of the Canon ; because this identity can be achieved in some particular cases).

The whole Part Two, from Chapter I to Chapter IX, is entirely devoted to a minute comparative study of the Sarv. and the Ther. doctrines and traditions, and thus it serves to show on the one hand to what extent the similarities go, and on the other hand, what the marked differences between the two traditions are.

The Chapter on the Sarv. and the Ther. characteristics (5) can be said to be the summary of the whole work, in which pecularities of each school are assembled together and explained. It aims also at explaining some differences in practices actually followed by the people of some Buddhist countries in modern times. The high percentage of the similarities testifies to the high authority and reliable fidelity of the Pāli transmission as aptly expressed by WINTERNITZ : « The more this Buddhist Sanskrit literature is opened up, and the more minutely it is compared with the Pāli Canon, the more it is proved that Oldenberg is right when he says : « The Pāli copy, though naturally not of infallible accuracy, must still be

(1) See infra.
(2) See infra.
(3) See infra.
(4) *H.I.L. ii*, pp. 232-233.
(5) See infra.

judged as eminently good ». (1) The divergences thus collected, when scanned with sufficient attention, would show the deliberate hands of the compilers who added texts, portions of texts and details which suited the tenets of their respective school and suppressed those which were found antagonistic to them. Thus for instance, the C deliberately dropped the Jīvakasutta in which the Buddha was reported to allow the monks to partake of the 3 kinds of meat (2), while the Pāli omits reference to the existence of the suffering in the Past, in the Present and in the future (3). This shows how rightly Dr. N. DUTT observed : « The Pāli Piṭakas undoubtedly passed through several redactions with accretions and omissions till the texts reached the form in which we have them now. The artificial and stereotyped form of each sutta takes away the original freshness of the sayings and distinctly reveals the clipping and shaping hands of the redactors of a time far away from the time of the Teacher ». (4) Of course the same should be said of the Sarv. Canon. The present works serves also to illustrate the magnificient and pioneering work done by Sanghadeva, an Indian monk from Kashmir to spread Buddhism in China. On Prof. André Bareau's suggestion, I have collected enough Pāli and Chinese equivalents so as to compile a small glossary of Pāli-Chinese-English equivalents. But the lack of space in this work compels me to reduce it to a minimum.

Review of previous works :

While going through this comparative study of the CMA with the PMN, I cannot resist having the impression of treading on an almost virgin soil, as few systematic works have been done so far in this field of Buddhist literature.

CHIZEN AKANUMA in his « THE COMPARATIVE CATALOGUE OF CHINESE ĀGAMAS & PĀLI NIKĀYAS » made the first attempt to compare the Chinese Āgamas and the Pāli Nikāyas ; but his work although greatly impressive and of vital importance, is confined only to cataloguing the titles of corresponding sūtras, and does not go into the details of the work itself. A. F. RUDOLF HOERNLE in his « MANUSCRIPT REMAINS OF BUDDHIST LITERATURE FOUND IN EASTERN TURKESTAN » has tried to make a systematic comparative study of the Sanskrit fragments found in Central Asia with their Pāli corresponding suttas ; but as far as the Madhyama Āgama is concerned, only fragments of two sūtras, the Upālisūtra and the Śukasūtra are found and they are too fragmentary and too scanty to allow of a comparative evaluation. To my enquiry whether any Western Scholars have done anything on my subject, Prof. ANDRÉ BAREAU, a noted French scholar wrote that there was a group of German scholars under the leadership of Prof. WALDSCHMIDT of Berlin, who have been working on the remains only of the Dīrgha Āgama and of

(1) *H.I.L.* ii. 19-20.
(2) See infra.
(3) See infra.
(4) *F.M.B.* i, Preface.

the Samyukta Āgama, but not of the Madhyama Āgama. As far as the Japanese scholars are concerned, I learned frcm Prof. SAKURABE that from time to time, some Japanese scholars had written articles on the CMA, such as Prof. SAKURABE himself, Prof. CHIZEN AKANUMA, Dr. MOCHIZUKI etc... But their wokrs which are mostly in Japanese cannot reach all the readers at large and are confined to one or two aspects of the CMA only. Thus a work which deals with a systematic comparative study of the CMA and the PMN as a whole has remained yet a desideratum.

Method adopted:

In the present work, I have selected the text of the CMA, translated by SANGHADEVA to compare with the PMN. I am compelled to neglect some sūtras of the Madhyama Āgama translated by other authors as the scope of my work does not allow me to incorporate them in. I have confined my comparative study to only 98 Chinese sūtras with their Pāli corresponding suttas as selected and classified in CHIZEN AKANUMA'S *C.A.P.N.*, the remaining sūtras with corresponding suttas in other Āgamas or in other Nikāyas are omitted. The comparative study is made in respect of such subjects as titles, location of sūtras, classification of vargas, sīla, samādhi, paññā etc... But the comparative study sūtra by sūtra is also not neglected and fifteen such specimens are also given. When a passage is compared, the Chinese passage is translated as faithfully as possible, while only the gist of the correspon-ding Pāli passage is given and the points of similarity and difference with the Chinese passage are noticed ; the Pāli text being well and widely known needs not much elaboration. For every passage compared, the number of volume, page and lines of both the Chinese and the Pāli texts are given for easy reference. When necessary some remarks are added to the passages compared. In the romanisation of the Chinese letters, I have followed the Wade-Giles' system adopted by the MATHEWS'CHINESE ENGLISH DICTIONARY as it is universally known. For the Chinese text of the Madhyama Āgama, I have followed the Hsü-ts'ang edition, case Tsê (昃), as it is handy and as the T'ai-sho edition is not available at Nālandā. As for the Pāli text, I have selected the MAJJHIMA NIKĀYA edited by the Pāli Text Society.

Structure of the thesis:

The present work is divided into four main parts :

Part One : Introduction which covers the introduction itself along with some evidences to prove that the CMA belongs to the Sarv. school, some characteristics of the Sarv. and the Ther. schools, and mutual relations between the CMA and the PMN along with a list of 98 common sūtras selected for comparative study.

Part two deals mainly with the similarities and differences of the two versions in respect of the arrangement of vargas and sūtras, the titles, location of the sūtras, and roles played by diverse personages in the sūtras, doctrinal tenets under their division into Sīla, Samādhi and Paññā, the Buddha and the Sangha, similes, verses and conclusions of the sūtras.

Part three comprises fifteen selected comparative studies out of 98 sūtras common to the two versions. The comparative study of all the 98 common sūtras has been completed in my manuscript, but 15 specimens only are printed for lack of space in the present work.

Part four comprises APPENDIXES, which cover among other things, a biography of Sanghadeva, some remarks on his translation, some remarks on Miss Horner's Middle Length Sayings, a list of 222 sūtras of the CMA classified according to vargas, fasciculi and days of recital, corresponding titles and places of occurrence of the Chinese and Pāli corresponding sūtras, a glossary of Pāli-Chinese-English equivalents, fragments of 2 Sanskrit sūtras of the Madhyama Āgama, etc...

I may hope that the comparative study of the CMA with the PMN, will be looked upon as a humble and new contribution to the field of Buddhist knowledge and literature.

II. — EVIDENCES TO PROVE THAT THE CMA BELONGS TO THE SARV. SCHOOL:

Modern scholars are almost unanimous on the existence of a Sanskrit Canon, parallel to if not more extensive than the Pāli Canon, and there is great agreement among them in regarding the Sanskrit canonical texts as belonging to the Sarv. school. Thus Prof. WINTERNITZ in his H. I. L. (1), writes: « The Nikāyas of the Pāli Canon find their parallel in the Āgamas of the Sanskrit Canon; the Dīrghāgama corresponding to the Dīghanikāya, the Madhyama Āgama to the Majjhima Nikāya, the Samyuktāgama to the Samyutta Nikāya and the Ekottarāgama to the Aṅguttara Nikāya ». And further he writes that the Sarv. had a Sanskrit Canon of its own, and although no complete copy of that canon had come down to us, we know it firstly from many fragments, large and small, which had been discovered in Eastern Turkestan and secondly from quotations in other Buddhist Sanskrit works, such as Mahāvastu, Divyāvadāna and Lalita-Vistara, and lastly from Chinese and Tibetan translations (2). Dr. N. DUTT shared the same view when he catalogued the 4 Āgamas as belonging to the Sarv. literature (3). He further writes: « The Tibetan traditions corroborated by the recent finds of manuscripts in Eastern Turkestan, leave no room for doubt about the fact that the Sarv. adopted grammatical Sanskrit (and not mixed Sanskrit) as the medium of their literature and that they possessed a complete canon of their own in 3 divisions sūtra, vinaya and abhidharma » (4). Dr. A.C. BANERJEE in his THE SARVĀSTIVĀDA LITERATURE, quoting Nanjio's Catalogue writes: « Nanjio's Catalogue under caption « sūtras of the Hīnayāna » mentions besides the 4 Āgamas, a few other works, in all about 56, which appear to be distinct translations of the different sūtras of the various Āgamas. It is however to be noted that the 4 Āgamas and other Chinese works included in the Catalogue under the heading, sūtras of Hīnayāna, almost all belong to the Sarv. or the Vaibhāṣika school » (5). We are not so optimistic as to affirm that all the 4 Āgamas belong to the Sarv. school. But the present comparative study of the CMA with the PMN helps us, with the assistance of a series of internal and external evidences to declare with certainty that the CMA represents the tenets of the Sarv. school.

---

(1) Vol. ii, p. 234.
(2) Vol. ii, p. 231-232.
(3) *E.M.B.* ii, p. 125.
(4) *E.M.B.* ii, p. 124.
(5) *S. L.*, p. 23.

1. — *The term Āgama and Nikāya.*

The Chinese uses the term Chung-a-han, Chung for Madhyama and A-han is a transliteration for the term Āgama. But the Pāli prefers the expression Majjhima Nikāya. As far as the terms Nikāya and Āgama are concerned, according to the SANSKRIT ENGLISH DICTIONARY OF MONIER WILLIAMS (1), the former in its sense of « collection of sacred texts » seems very appropriate to Buddhism, while the latter in its sense of « traditional doctrine, collection of such doctrines, sacred works » refers to works perhaps several centuries earlier than the advent of Buddhism. It is evident that the two terms are almost synonymous and the Pāli Canon uses the term Nikāya in the particular sense of collection of suttas, while other Canons, Prākrit and Sanskrit, adopted the term Āgama for their own texts. An inscription of Nāgārjunikoṇḍa (Pillar C 2) mentions that the Aparamahāvinaseliya (probably identical with Aparaśaila, Andhraka sect) possessed Dīgha, Majjhima and Saṃyutta-Nikāyas and not Āgama (2). This sect has apparently its Canon written in Prākrit with some affinities with but clearly different from the Pāli. It seems that there was a geographical repartition of these two terms, the term Āgama being used in the North and the Centre of India, and the term Nikāya being used in the Deccan and in Ceylon ? (3). But the proofs are too slender to be conclusive on this point. We find also the term Āgama used in the Pāli Canon. Thus, the PĀLI ENGLISH DICTIONARY (4) mentions the use of the term *Svāgamo* « versed in the doctrine » and *Āgatāgamo* « one to whom the Āgama or the Āgamas have been handed down ». Thus the distinction between the two terms is far from being clear cut. As the Ther. use the term Nikāya for their Canon and the term Āgama is adopted by the Sarv. and by some other sects for their texts, we have reason to believe that the term Āgama was used to design the Sarv. Canon, because so far no other Canons have been discovered, except some portions of the Sanskrit Sarv. Canon.

2. — *The Sanskrit Canon :*

Among the fragments of the Āgamas found in Eastern Turkestan, two fragments of two sūtras in the Madhyama Āgama are found : the Upālisūtra and the Śukasūtra (5).

A comparative study of the fragments of Upālisūtra with its corresponding Chinese passages shows a great deal of similarities between the Chinese and the Sanskrit texts ; though they cannot be affirmed to be identical in every respect.

(1) P. 129 and p. 544.
(2) H. Sastri, Epigraphia Indica Vol. xx, 1929-30, Delhi, p. 20.
(3) Supplied by Prof. André Bareau.
(4) *P.E.D.* p. 95.
(5) See infra Appendix N° 9.

The following Chinese and Sanskrit passages which are quoted from C N° 133, Yu-p'o-li-ching (vi, 30b, 20; 39a, 19) and from the *M.R.E.T.* (1) show pronounced similarity between the Chinese passage and the Sanskrit text.

C 2a : Of the great Noble One, with self-training (completed)
With holiness obtained, with mastery of speech.

Sk 2a : *Āryasya bhāvitâtmanaḥ prâpa*tipraptasya vyākaraṇeṣu/

C 2b : With good mindfulness, with subtle and right contemplation/Not high and also not low/

Sk 2b : Smṛtimato vipaśyasya anabhinata*sya no apanatasya*/

C 2c : Impassible, always having mastery of oneself,
Of the Buddha, Yu-p'o-li is the disciple//

Sk 2c : *Aniñjyasya yaśiprâptasya Bhagavatas tasya śrāvaka Upālī*//

C 5a : Of Him who is a great dragon, (2) delighted in dwelling high, with fetters extinguished, with emancipation obtained/

Sk 5a : Nāgasya prântasayānasya kṣīṇasamyojanasya mu*ktasya*/

C 5b : Clever in discussion, pure,
Wisdom born, sorrow and grief removed/

Sk 5b : Pratimantrakasya dhantasya prajñā-dhvajasya vītarāgasya/

C 5c : No returner to existence, the Sakya,
Of the Buddha, Yu-p'o-li is the disciple//

Sk 5c : *Anāvṛtta*kasya Śakrasya Bhagavatas tasya śrāvaka Upālī// (3)

Dr. BAPAT is of the opinion that the C version is nearer to the P text than to the Sanskrit one and it might have a Prakrit canon as its original source. Thus in the Upālisutta, the C 5c (4) mentions the Sakya, the same with the P interpretation, while the Sanskrit text refers to Śakrasya. In the Śukasūtra (C N° 170, Ying-wu-ching = P. N° 135, Cūlakamma-vibhaṅgasutta), the C text agrees more with the Pāli. There is very little common ground between the Sanskrit text and the C which does not mention the ten Dharmas as detailed in the Sanskrit text (5). So he asserts that the C original might be a kind of Prakrit, older than the Sanskrit text. Anyhow, in this sūtra, the order of the C verses runs parallel to that of the Sanskrit text, and not to that of the P text (6) and some differences between the C and the Sanskrit passages might occur due to some editing mistakes or to faulty interpretation ; such as C : Delighted in dwel-ling high = S : Prāntaśayānasya ; C : Sorrow and grief removed = S: Vītarāgasya.

(1) P. 30-31.
(2) It should be translated as elephant.
(3) The underlined lines are restituted passages done by R. HOERNLE.
(4) See Sk 5c
(5) See M.R.E.T. pp.48-50.
(6) See infra.

3. — *The Ācariyaparamparā or patriarchal succession :*

In the chart given on p. 18 of the book « ASPECTS OF MAHĀYĀNA AND ITS RELATIONS TO HĪNAYĀNA », Mahākassapa is shown as the first and foremost ācariya of the Sarv. sect, while Sāriputta is considered to be the first ācariya of the Ther. sect. This fact is corroborated by BUSTON and TĀRANĀTHA (1), who tell us that Mahākassapa entrusted the guardianship of the Sangha to Ānanda, while Buddhaghosa (2) gives a list of ācariyas of the Abhidhamma, tracing it from Sāriputta. We see in *C. S.* N° 26 that Shê-li-tzu (P : Sāriputta) addressed Ta-chia-yeh (P : Mahākassapa) as *Tsun-che* (尊者 : Respected Sir = P : Bhante), and Ta-chia-yeh addressed Shê-li-tzu as *Hsien-che* (賢者 : The Good One = P : Āvuso) (C N° 184, vii, 35a, 10-11). But in its Pāli counterpart, Sāriputta called Mahākassapa as *Āvuso*, and Mahākassapa replied to Sāriputta also as *Āvuso* (P N° 32, i, 213, 33-37 ; 214, 1-2). This difference in the terms of address shows that the CMA belongs to the Sarv. tradition which accepts Mahākassapa as the foremost and highest patriarch ; while the PMN belongs to the Ther. tradition which considers Sāriputta as the foremost and highest Ācariya, higher even than Mahākassapa. The above fact is further corroborated by the omission of the Pāli sutta N° 111, Anupadasutta in all the Āgamas (3). In this sutta, the Buddha extolled elder Sāriputta as follows :

(*iii*, 29, 10-15) : « Sāriputtaṃ eva taṃ sammā vadamāno vadeyya : Bhagavato putto oraso mukhato jāto dhammajo dhammanimmito dhammadāyādo no āmisadāyādo ti. Sāriputto, Bhikkhave, Tathāgatena anuttaraṃ dhammacakkaṃ pavattitaṃ sammad eva anuppavattetīti ». (Of Sāriputta, it can be rightly said : He is the Blessed One's son, born of his mouth, born of dhamma, shaped by dhamma, an heir to dhamma, not an heir to material things. Sāriputta, oh monks, rightly rolls on the supreme wheel of dhamma set in motion by the Tathāgata). As the Buddha is said to have extolled elder Sāriputta so highly, the Sarv. might drop this sutta from their Canon or it might be interpolated by the Theravadins in their Canon. This difference in the position of Mahākassapa and Sāriputta in the Ācariyaparamparā between the Ther. and the Sarv. serves to explain why even now-a-days, the worship of the sacred relics of Sāriputta and Moggallāna is very popular in the Ther. countries, while in the Buddhist temples of China, Korea, Japan and Viet-Nam, the Buddha's statue is attended on either side by the statues of Mahākassapa and Ānanda, but not of Sāriputta and Moggallāna.

---

(1) BUSTON ii, p. 108.
(2) *ATTHASALINI* p. 32.
(3) Appendix : N° 6, p. 533.

4. — 9 *aṅgas and* 12 *aṅgas :*

Another prominent difference between the Chinese and the Pāli versions is the adoption by the Chinese version of the 12 divisions or aṅgas, and by the Pāli version of the 9 divisions of the Scriptures.

In C. S. N° 19, the Chinese (C N° 200, vii, 64b, 4-5) adopts the following division and order : 1) *Chêng-ching* (正 經 : principal sermons) ; 2) *Ko-yung* (歌 詠 : metrical pieces) ; 3) *Chi-shuo* (記 說 : prophecies) ; 4) *Chieh-t'a* (偈 他 : verses) ; 5) *Yin-yüan* (因 緣 : introductory parts) ; 6) *Hsüan-lu* (撰 錄 : selections, quotations) ; 7) *Pên-ch'i* (本 起 : stories of the Past) ; 8) *Tz'u-shuo* (此 說 : This is said) ; 9) *Shêng-ch'u* (生 處 : birth-places) ; 10) *Kuang-chieh* (廣 解 : detailed explanations ; 11) *Wei-ts'êng-yu-fa* (未 曾 有 法 : wonderful dharmas) ; 12) *Shuo-i* (說 義 : explanation of meaning). The Pāli (P N° 22, i, 133, 24-25) follows a different enumeration and order : 1) suttaṃ, 2) geyyaṃ, 3) veyyākaraṇaṃ, 4) gāthā, 5) udānaṃ, 6) itivuttakaṃ, 7) jātakaṃ, 8) abbhutadhammaṃ, 9) vedallaṃ.

First, if we compare the Pāli list with the Nieh-p'an-ching list (1), we find the two lists almost the same, except that the Nieh-p'an-ching list interchanges the order of the last two. We notice also that in the Nieh-p'an-ching list, the 3rd dharma, Chi-shuo (Sk. vyākaraṇa) has the meaning of prophecies while the Pāli veyyākaraṇa conveys the meaning of answer, explanation, exposition. If we compare the Chinese list of our text with the Pāli list, we can safely propose the following corresponding terms : C 1 = P 1 ; C 2 = P 2 ; C 3 = P 3 (not of the same meaning) ; C 4 = P 4 ; C 8 = P 6 ; C 9 = P 7 ; C 10 = P 9 ; C 11 = P 8. It remains P 5 udānaṃ which can be compared with C 6 Hsüan-lu, meaning selection, quotation. This correspondance is not a happy one as the Chinese usually translates udānaṃ by Wu-wên-tzu-shuo (無 問 自 說), meaning spoken voluntarily without being asked, while here the Chinese means selection, quotations. Now there remain three Chinese terms not available in Pāli : C 5 : Yin-Yüan (Sk. Nidāna) : introductory matter ; C 7 : Pên-ch'i (Sk. Avadāna) : stories of the past ; and C 12 : Shuo-i (Sk. Upadeśa) : explanation of meaning. Dr DUTT rightly observes : « But this division of scriptures into 12 aṅgas was not the work of the Mahāyānists. It had been made by the Sarv. and the Mahāsanghikas and followed by some of the other Hīnayānic schools. The 3 additional aṅgas are nidāna, avadāna and upadeśa » (2). This passage is important in the sense that it shows that the CMA belongs to the Sarv. school. Dr. ANESAKI was of the opinion that the division into 12 pravacanas characterised by Nāgārjuna in his *Prajñā-paramitā śāstra* as being the Mahāyānistic classification in constrast with the 9 of the Hīnayānist-was in no way exclusively Mahāyānistic, because the 4 Āgamas were hīnayānistic (3).

(1) *Fu-hsüeh-ta-tzu-tien*, vol. ii, p. 64c.
(2) *A. M. R. H.* p. 9.
(3) *JRAS* 1902, p. 897.

5. — *Past, present and future dharmas :*

In *C. S. N*° 95, there is one passage dealing with the five aggregates, which shows a distinctive feature of the Sarv. as represented in the CMA :

C N° 31 : (*v*, 42*b*, 11–13) : « There are the growing aggregates of material forms, of feeling, of perception, of activities and of consciousness. In brief, these 5 growing aggregates are suffering. Thus this noble truth of suffering has existed in the past, is existing in the present and will be existing in the future ; this is real truth, not false truth, not moving away from reality, obtained by the Noble Ones, known, seen, understood, attained and fully and rightly realized by the Noble Ones, that is why this is called the noble truth of suffering ».

P N° 141 : (*iii*, 250, 26–31) : « Katame c'āvuso, saṅkhittena pañcupādānakkhandhā dukkhā ? — Seyyathīdaṃ : rūpūpādānakkhandho vedanūpādānakkhandho saññūpādānakkhandho saṅkhārūpādānakkhandho viññāṇūpādānakkhandho ; ime vuccant', āvuso, saṅkhittena pañcupādānakkhandhā dukkhā. Idaṃ vuccat', āvuso, dukkhaṃ ariyasaccaṃ ».

Thus the Pāli omits totally the stress on the existence of suffering in the past, in the present and in the future. This passage serves to explain the doctrine « sabbam atthi » of the Sarv. who maintain the existence of the 5 dharmas in their essence (dravyasāt) at all times, whether in the past, present or future. This doctrine of the Sarv. is explained as follows : « All (sarvaṃ) exists (asti). The past (atīta) and the future (anāgata) exist really and substantially. This is their fundamental tenet. The Blessed One has said in one sūtra : « Oh monks, if the past rūpas did not exist, the learned disciple would not « take into account » the past rūpas... If the future rūpas dit not exist, the learned disciple would not, « would not delight » in the future rūpas. Because of the existence of the future rūpas that the learned disciple... ». Again, the vijñāna comes into existence owing to two causes. What are the two ? cakṣurindriya and rūpa, manas and dharmas ». It is impossible that in the same person (pudgala), there exist at the same time two cittas, especially that of the object (ālambana) to be known and that of the *agent of knowledge*. Therefore, one will be already in the past when the other appears, and the latter will be still in the future when the former appears. If the past and the future things did not exist, there will be no meeting between the agent of knowledge and its object, and all knowledge would be impossible. There is knowledge of things, past and future, such as memory and anticipation, which occur as a matter of course. If things of the past and the future did not exist, this knowledge would be impossible, because it would have no object ; every knowledge should possess an object which really exists. Moreover, the same person cannot simultaneously accomplish an action (karman) and receive the fruit (vipākaphala) of this action. When the action is accomplished, its fruit is still a thing of the future ; and when the agent receives this fruit, the action which has generated it is a thing of the past. If things of the past and future did not exist, the past actions, being non-existant, would not be able to produce fruits» (1).

The omission of any reference to this real existence of suffering in the past, in the present and in the future in the Pāli version is significant, as it shows that the Ther. deny any such existence. Prof. STCHERBATSKY, referring to the passage : « *Everything exists means that the 12 āyatanas exist* » (2) which cannot be traced in the Pāli Canon, said that evidently the Ther. suppressed it, because it did not agree with their particular tenet (3). The existence of the above passage in the Chinese version and its omission in the Pāli version is another proof that the CMA belongs to the Sarv. school.

6. — *On the Madhyama Āgama quoted in Śamathadeva's commentary :* (4)

The work of Prof. SAKURABE (mentioned above) serves as another proof to assert that the CMA belongs to the Sarv. school. The ABHIDHARMAKOŚOPĀYIKA-NĀMA-ṬĪKĀ, is a commentary by ŚAMATHADEVA on Vasubandhu's Abhidharmakośa. This commentary is preserved only in Tibetan version and quotes a number of passages from the Āgama sūtras. The learned professor came to the conclusion that they are far more akin to the CMA than to the PMN. As the *Abhidharmakośopāyika-nāma-ṭīkā* is a commentary on Vasubandhu's Abhidharmakośa, which deals mainly with the Sarv. doctrine, it belongs to the Sarv. school and it is but natural that it quotes Sarv. works.

The following reasons help to show that the Madhyama Āgama passages quoted in the *Abhidharmakośopāyika-nāma-ṭīkā* are nearer to the CMA than the PMN :

a) Most of the titles of sūtras in the Madhyama Āgama quoted by Śamathadeva (Ms) coincide with those in the CMA even though they are sometimes different from those in PMN :

Ms : BhikṣunīdharmadinnāS. = CMA N° 210 Fa-lo-pi-ch'iu-ni-ching (Sk. BhikṣunīdharmanandīS.). Not the same with PMN N° 44, Cūḷavedalla-sutta. *Notes :* Dharmadinnā is sometimes written as Dharmanandī, hence Fa-lo.

Ms : AvarabhāgīyaS. = CMA N° 205, Wu-hsia-fên-chieh-ching (Sk. Pañca avarabhāgīyaS.) ; not the same with PMN N° 64, Mahā-Maluṅkya-sutta.

---

(1) Translated from « Les sectes bouddhiques du Petit véhicule » of André Bareau, p. 137.
(2) Samyukta xiii, p. 16, Mc Govern.
(3) *The Central conception of Buddhism*, p. 4, foot-note N° 13.
(4) Supplied by Prof. Sakurabe.

b) Arrangement of sūtras in Ms is very similar to that in CMA and that in PMN is quite different. Thus the Ms MahānidānapariyāyaS and the CMA N° 97 Ta-yin-ching are included both in the Madhyama Āgama, while their Pāli corresponding sutta N° 15, Mahānidānasutta is included in the Dīgha-nikāya. The Ms Sūryasaptakasūtra and the CMA N° 8, Ch'ih-jih-ching are both included in the Madhyama Āgama but their Pāli corresponding sutta N° 62 is included in the Aṅguttara Nikāya, vii, 63. The Ms Saptasatpuruṣagatis and the CMA N° 6, Shan-jên-wang-ching are both included in the Madhyama Āgama while their Pāli corresponding sutta belongs to Aṅguttara Nikāya, vii, 52.

7. — *Teachings found in CMA coincide with those found in Sarv. Abhidharma Śāstras :*

Another proof of the CMA belonging to the Sarv. school is that the teachings in the CMA are taken up and developed in the Sarv. Abhidharma works.

a) The four Paths and the four Fruits :

A Chinese sūtra named *Yu-ch'ieh-chang-che-ching* (N° 39, v, 54a, 6-7) contains the following passage : « This one is an A-la-han-hsiang (Sk. Pratipannaka arhat), this one is an A-la-han ; this one is an A-na-han-hsiang (Sk. Pratipannaka anāgāmī) ; this one is an A-na-han ; this one is a Ssu-t'o-han-hsiang (Sk. Pratipannaka sakṛdāgāmī) ; this one is a Ssu-t'o-han ; this one is a Hsu-t'o-yüan-hsiang (Sk. Pratipannaka srota-āpanna), this one is a Hsu-t'o-yüan. Thus this division into 2 kinds of A-la-han, 2 kinds of A-na-han, 2 kinds of Ssu-t'o-han, 2 kinds of Hsu-t'o-yüan is well developed and commented on in the Vasubandhu's *Abhidharmakośa*, Chapter vi, *Aryamārganirdeśa* (1). We quote the following passage where are described the practice and the attainment of the Pratipannaka Srota-āpanna and of the Srota-āpanna :

Laukikebhyo'gradharmebhyo dharmakṣāntir anāsrava//25//
Kāmaduḥkhe ; tato'traiva dharmajñānam tathā punaḥ/
Śeṣaduḥkhe'nvayakṣānti jñāne ; satyatraye tathā//26//
Evam ṣoḍaśacitto'yam satyābhisamayaḥ ;/

This passage explains the practice and the attainment of a Pratipannaka Srota-āpanna and of a Srota-āpanna. When one attains the following fifteen moments, one is called a Pratipannaka Srota-āpanna : 1) duḥkhe dharma-jñāna-kṣānti, 2) duḥkhe dharmajñāna, 3) duḥkhe anvayajñānakṣānti, 4) duḥkhe anvayajñāna, 5) samudaye dharmajñānakṣānti, 6) samudaye dharma-jñāna, 7) samudaye anvayajñānakṣānti, 8) samudaye anvayajñāna, 9) nirodhe

(1) *L'Abhidharmakosa de Vasubandhu*, iv, p. 119-302.

dharmajñānakṣānti, 10) nirodhe dharmajñāna, 11) nirodhe anvayajñānakṣānti, 12) nirodhe anvayajñāna, 13) mārge dharmajñanakṣānti, 14) mārge dharmajñāna, 15) mārge anvayajñānakṣānti. When the last and 16th moment or mārge anvayajñāna is attained, one is called a *Srota āpanna*. The other three fruits are dealt with in the subsequent pages. The above quotation in the Abhidharmakośa which is a Sarv. Śāstra tends to testify that the CMA in which the above sūtra is included, belongs to the Sarv. school.

b) *The 62 dhātus or elements :*

In *C.S. N°* 72, the Chinese version (N° 181, vii. 31b, 15-20 ; 32a, 1-4) enumerates in all 62 elements while the Pāli version counts only 41 elements. The Abhidharmakośa of Vasubandhu in its commentary on kārika N° 27 as to the way of classification of the elements into skandhas, āyatanas and dhātus takes this division of 62 elements from the CMA, but not the division of 41 dhātus of the Pāli texts, as seen under :

« Evam Bahudhātuke'pi dvāṣaṣṭirdhātavo deśitāḥ ».

This passage is rendered in French in the « Abhidharmakośa de Vasubandhu » (1) as follows : « De même les 62 dhātus énumérés dans le Bahudhātuka doivent être rangés dans les 18 dhātus en tenant compte de leur nature » (In the same way, the 62 dhātus enumerated in the Bahudhātuka should be classified into 18 dhātus in accordance with their nature).

c) *The 8 hsüeh-jên or sekha :*

In the CMA C N° 127, *Fu-tien-ching* (vi, 46a, 7-9), 2 kinds of fields of merit are mentioned, the 18 learners or śaikṣas and the nine non-learners or aśaikṣas. The 18 śaikṣas are as follows : 1) *Hsin-hsing :* Śraddhānusārin, 2) *Fa-hsing :* Dharmānusārin, 3) *Hsin-chieh-t'o :* Śraddhādhimukta, 4) *Chien-tao :* Dṛṣṭiprāpta, 5) *Shên-chêng* : Kāyasākṣin, 6) *Chia-chia* : Kulamkula, 7) *I-chung* : Ekavījika, 8) *Hsiang-hsü-t'o-yüan* : Pratipannaka Srota āpanna, 9) *Tê-hsü-t'o-yüan* : Srota āpanna phala, 10) *Hsiang-ssu-t'o-han* : Pratipannaka Sakṛdāgāmī, 11) *Tê-ssu-t'o-han* : Sakṛdāgāmī phala, 12) *Hsiang-a-na-han* : Pratipannaka anāgāmī, 13) *Tê-a-na-han* : Anāgāmī phala, 14) *Chung-pan-nieh-p'an* : Antarāparinirvāyin, 15) *Shêng-pan-nieh-p'an* : Upapadyaparinirvāyin, 16) *Hsing-pan-nieh-p'an* : Sābhisaṃskāraparinirvāyin, 17) *Wu-hsing-pan-nieh-p'an* : Anabhisaṃskāraparinirvāyin, 18) *Shang-liu-sê-chiu-ching* : Ūrdhvasrota-rūpantimāt. The Abhidharmakośa (2) writes : « The W.H. One told Kei-ku-tu (P : Anāthapiṇḍika) : « Oh householder, you should know, the field of merit is of 2 kinds : learners and non-learners. Learners are 18 : 1) Pratipannaka Srota āpanna, 2) Srota āpanna, 3) Pratipannaka Sakṛdāgāmin, 4) Sakṛdāgāmin, 5) Pratipannaka Anāgāmin, 6) Anāgāmin, 7) Pratipannaka arhat, 8) Śraddhānusārin, 9) Dharmānusārin, 10) Śraddhādhimukta, 11)

(1) i, p. 49.
(2) *Fu-hsüeh-ta-tzu-tien*, vii, p. 1020.

Dṛṣṭiprāpta, 12) Kulamkula, 13) Ekavījika, 14) Antarāparinirvāyin, 15) Upapadyaparinirvāyin, 16) Sābhisaṃskāraparinirvāyin, 17) Anabhisaṃskāraparinirvāyin, 18) Ūrdhvasrota ». Thus the Abhidharmakośa quotes also the 18 śaikṣas but does not follow the same order, drops the kāyasākṣin and adds the Pratipannaka arhat. Curiously enough, the Abhidharmakośa seems to quote the very sūtra mentioned in the CMA. Unfortunately the Fu-hsüeh-ta-tzu-tien does not mention the source of this sūtra.

d) *The* 9 *Wu-hsüeh or aśaikṣas*

In the same Chinese sūtra N° 127, *Fu-tien-ching,* 9 *Wu-hsüeh* or Aśaikṣas are mentioned as follows : 1) *Ssu-fa* : Cetanādharman, 2) *Shêng-chin-fa* : Prativedhanādharman, 3) *Pu-tung-fa* : Akopyadharman, 4) *T'ui-fa* : Parihāṇadharman, 5) *Pu-t'ui-fa* : Aparihāṇadharman, 6) *Hu-fa* : Anurakṣaṇādharman, 7) *Chu-fa* : Sthitākampya, 8) *Hui-chieh-t'o* : Prajñāvimukta, 9) *Chü-chieh-t'o* : Ubhayatobhāgavimukta. But the « Abhidharmakośa de Vasubandhu » (1) quotes : « 6 kinds of arhats are recognised : Arhantaḥ ṣaṇ matāḥ ». The Sūtra (Madhyama, 30, 4 : Samyukta, 33, 10) says that there are 6 kinds of arhats : 1) Parihāṇadharman, 2) Cetanādharman, 3) Anurakṣaṇādharman, 4) Sthitākampya, 5) Prativedhanādharman, 6) Akopyadharman. On the contrary, the Fu-hsüeh-ta-tzu-tien (2) quotes the Abhidharmakośa vol. xxv as mentioning 6 kinds of arahants as above, then 7 kinds of arahants, adding Aparihāṇa arahā ; then 9 kinds of arahants adding Prajñāvimukta & Ubhayatobhāgavimukta. Thus we cannot say that the quotations in both the CMA and the Abhidharmakośa are identical. But the dharmas quoted are almost the same in the Sarv. śāstras and in the CMA, but do not agree with those in the PMN.

8. — *Arahat is liable to fall from arahanthood :*

In the division into 9 Asekhas as seen above, the Chinese version mentions a class of Arahats called *T'ui-fa* : Parihāṇadharman, and thus admits that a class of arahats is liable to fall from arahanthood. This is another proof of the CMA being of the Sarv. school, as testified by the following passage : (3) « In Vasumitra's treatise as well as in the Kathāvatthu, it is stated that the Sarv. believed that the Arhats were liable to fall from arahanthood. On this point, the Ther. hold a different opinion. They believe that the Arhats are as pure as Buddhas, and cannot fall down from that position. The Mahāsaṅghikas also do not support the Sarv. in regard to this point (4).

All these internal and external evidences enumerated above give us ample reasons to believe that the CMA belongs to the Sarv. School.

(1) iv, p.251.
(2) xvi, p.2844.
(3) *A.M.R.H.* p.25, note 3.
(4) Masuda, Origin etc.,p.27 ; Kathavatthu, i, 2.

III. — SOME SARV. AND THER. CHARACTERISTICS :

As the CMA belongs to the Sarv. tradition and the PMN, to the Ther. tradition, a general comparative study of the 98 common sūtras reveals many distinctive features peculiar to each school ; and these characteristics help to explain some different traditions actually followed by some Saṅghas even at the present time. These features serve also to reveal the forces already at work at a very carly time, and which were responsible for the future divergence between the Sarv. and the Ther. as testified by the contradictory accounts of the Third Council.

1. — *Annual retreat :*

The monks are required to observe 3 months'retreat every year. But the Chinese version refers to *summer-retreat* and the Pāli version speaks of *rainy-season retreat.* Thus in *C. S. N°* 20, the retreat is referred to as summer-retreat (C N° 9, v, ii b, 4-6), while its Pāli corresponding passage (P N° 24, i, 145, 12-15) speaks of rainy season retreat. In « THE LIFE OF HSÜAN TSANG » published by the Chinese Buddhist Association, Peking, there is reference also to summer-retreat. Thus it writes : « As it was just at the time when the monks had spent their *summer-retreat,* a number of several thousand people congregated at the place from far and near » (1) In the account of the first Council, this passage is recorded by Hsüan Tsang : « During the three months of *summer retreat,* the Tripiṭaka was collected and written on palm leaves for circulation (2). This explains the difference in date in the observance of retreat in the Ther. countries and in China and in Vietnam. Thus in Ceylon for example, the monks start their rainy season retreat from the day next to the full-moon of Āṣādha (June-July) or a month later and end it on the day after the fullmoon of the 9th month or of the 10th month. But the monks in Vietnam now-a-days begin their summer-retreat on the 16th of the 4th month of the lunar calendar and their pavāraṇā is celebrated on the 16th of the 7th month of the lunar calendar, that is 2 months earlier than the Pāli tradition. Hsüan-Tsang in his Records of the journey to the west (3) recorded that the observance of the summer-retreat from the 16th of the 4th month of lunar calendar was wrong because the translators were not expert in the customs and traditions of the Western countries (India) ; the retreat should begin on the 16th of the 3rd month not of the 4th month, that is one month still earlier. If we take into consideration this remark of Hsüan-Tsang, we

(1) p. 102.
(2) p. 113.
(3) Hsi-yü-Chi, Book II.

find a difference of 3 months between the 2 traditions. Thus we can safely assume that, because the rainy season in Magadha corresponds to the summer season in North West India and in China as well, the C translation used the term summer-retreat instead of the term rainy-season retreat.

Thus this difference as to the exact season of retreat shows that each version represents a different school and tradition. The summer-retreat has been followed by the Northern School represented by the monks in North India, Central Asia, China, Korea, Japan and Vietnam ; while the rainy-season retreat has been followed by the monks of Ceylon, Burma, Thailand, Cambodia and Laos.

2. — *The nisīdana or sitting mat :*

One more difference which shows the different tradition of each version, is the use of *nisīdana* or *sitting mat*. The C version always mentions the Buddha and the monks putting a sitting mat on their shoulder and spreading it on the ground when they went to the forest for meditation, while the P mostly ignores this detail. Thus in *C.S.* N° 15 (1), the W. H. One, when night was over, in the morning, put on the robe, took the begging bowl and entered Chia-wei-lo-wei (P: Kapilavatthu) for alms. Having finished his meal, in the after-noon, having put back bowl and robe, washed his hands and feet, he put the sitting mat on his shoulder, went to the Sakyan Bamboo grove Temple, entered that Great Forest, came to a tree, spread his sitting mat and sat down crosslegged... » And its P corresponding passage (N° 18, i, 108, 15-18) is almost the same, but omits the act of putting the sitting mat on the shoulder... spread his sitting mat (2).

This difference explains why now-a-days, the practice of the nisīdana is lost in the Ther. countries ; but in China and Vietnam, this practice is still in existence. When a monk receives high ordination, he is given besides a set of 3 robes and a begging bowl, an extra nisīdana, a rectangular piece of cloth, mostly of dim colour, with 4 patches of cloth pasted at four corners to destroy its beauty. The monk, in his daily use of the nisīdana, is asked to recite the following gāthā :

« Ni-shih-t'an, the sleeping mat helps the mind-seed germinate and grow up/

Develop, open up and ascend the land of the Noble Ones,

And thus abide by the Tathāgata's admonition.//

---

(1) C N° 115, vi, 35b, 15-17.

(2) See infra for more details.

There is probability in the supposition that the observance of this nisīdana shows that the Sarv. were forest-dwellers and prescribed this practice to their followers. But now-a-days, as the practice of going into the forest for meditation is almost lost, the use of the nisīdana is confined only within the Temple and thus loses its effectiveness. Anyhow the preservation of this tradition testifies to the fact that the Chinese and the Vietnamese Sangha inherit the traditions represented in the CMA.

3. — *The Buddha's deportment and Ven. A-nan's attendance :*

In C.S. N° 3, there is a passage in the Chinese sūtra N° 88 (vi, 9a, 3-5) describing the Buddha folding up into four, his Yü-to-lo-sêng (P : Uttarāsaṅga), spreading it over the bed, rolling his Sêng-chia-li (P : Saṅghāṭi), to make it a pillow and lay down on his right side, with one leg resting on the other, meditating on the light sign, with right mindfulness, right understanding and constantly thinking of wanting to get up. This passage is omitted in the Pāli corresponding passage (1). Among the 19 Chinese sūtras not found in the Nikāyas, the omission of the Chinese sūtra N° 80, Chia-ch'ih-na-ching is significant, as this sūtra depicted the Buddha as actively lending a helping hand in making robes for Ven. A-na-lü-t'o (P : Anuruddha) and after the work, lying down in front of the monks to take rest, in the same way as described above. There is every likelihood that the Pāli compilers were not happy over these attitudes of the Buddha and dropped the sūtra. Again in *C.S. N°* 15, *N°* 22, *N°* 42, *N°* 67 etc... Ven. A-nan was frequently described as standing behind the Buddha and fanning him with a fan or attending upon him with a duster. These details are wanting in the Pāli version (2). It might be that the Ther. looked upon these activities as unbecoming of a Buddha and of a monk as these attitudes might elicit criticism from other sects, so the Ther. referred to these details very rarely. But the Sarv. might consider these deportments as perfectly natural and justified, as relation between the Buddha and his disciples, especially with Ven. A-nan was nothing but that between father and son and the dignified way which the Buddha adopted in lying down in front of the monks had nothing questionable to deserve reproach of any kind. These considerations justified the Sarv. in preserving these details.

4. — *Stress on compassion.*

The comparative study of the practice of the 4 illimitables (P : Brahmavihārā) of the 2 versions shows a more or less identical approach between the Ther. and the Sarv. traditions, but the Chinese text lays more stress

(1) This pattern is found in P. N° 3, Sekhasutta.

(2) In mahaparinibbanasuttam, Digha Nikaya, ii, p. 138, Roman edition, elder Upavāno is described as fanning the Blessed One.

on this practice than its counterpart in Pāli. Thus in *C.S. N°* 25, *N°* 21, *N°* 64, the Chinese enumerates the practice of the 4 illimitables while the Pāli ignores this kind of meditation (1). Again in *C. S. N°* 89, the Chinese refers to poor people, orphans and beggars as among people who should be given charity while the Pāli prefers to ignore them.

C N° 170 : (*vii*, 17*b*, 2–8) : « There are people who are not givers, who do not give charity to recluses, brāhmaṇas, poor people, orphans and beggars coming from afar ; they do not give food...»

P N° 135 : (*iii*, 205, 6–15) : Almost the same. But it mentions charity to be given only to recluses and brāhmaṇas and omits poor people, orphans and beggars coming from afar.

Thus this tendency towards compassion which was already latent in the early texts of Sanskrit Buddhism might account for the stress on MAITRĪ or compassion taken by the Mahāyānists who put Maitrī almost on the same footing with Prajñā or wisdom. This tendency serves also to explain the cult of Avalokiteśvara or Kuan-shih-yin, which is considered as the Goddess of Compassion so popularly worshipped in Korea, China, Japan and Vietnam. In Tibet, the Dalai Lama is reported to be the incarnation of Avalokiteśvara.

5. — *Vegetarianism versus non-vegetarianism :*

Among the precepts to be observed by a monk in his training, the Pāli *N°* 112 (*iii*, 34, 12–13) adds this precept « *āmakamaṃsapaṭiggahaṇā paṭivirato ahosiṃ* », abstinence from accepting raw meat, implying thereby that cooked meat is allowed. But the Chinese corresponding passage *N°* 187 (*vii*, 39*b*, 14–20 ; 40*a*, 1–10) drops this precept, thus impliying that all kinds of meat are prohibited. Again the dropping from all the Chinese Āgamas of the Pāli sutta *N°* 55, *Jīvakasutta* (1), in which the Buddha was reported to allow the monks to take three kinds of meat, confirms the Sarv.'s : attitude against meat-eating. The Pāli passage is as follows... « Tīhi kho ahaṃ Jīvaka ṭhānehi maṃsaṃ aparibhogan ti vadāmi : diṭṭhaṃ sutaṃ parisaṅkitaṃ... Tīhi kho ahaṃ Jīvaka ṭhānehi maṃsaṃ paribhogan ti vadāmi : adiṭṭhaṃ asutaṃ aparisaṅkitaṃ ». (I, Jīvaka, declare that in three cases, meat is not to be used: when it is seen, heard and suspected... I, Jīvaka, declare that in three cases, meat may be used, when it si not seen, heard, suspected). In the LIFE OF HSÜAN TSANG (3), the famous Chinese pilgrim is reported to observe the vegetarian diet as follows : « On the following day, the king invited the Master to his palace and offered him food. But the food contains three kinds of pure meat and the Master would not accept it. The king thought it strange, so the Master explained that it was allowable according to the

(1) For more details, see infra para B, Samadhi, 4, the Brahmavihara.

(2) See Appendix N° 6, about Suttas not to be found in C. Agamas.

(3) p. 39.

Gradual Teaching, but he followed Mahāyāna Buddhism which prohibited the eating of meat. Thus he took some other kinds of food ». We find also in the LAṄKĀVATĀRASŪTRA (1) a Mahāyānic canonical text, a chapter which severely condemns meat-eating.

This difference in attitude towards meat-eating in the two versions serves to explain why now-a-days, meat-eating is allowed for the monks of countries following the Ther. tradition, while the monks of such countries as China, Korea, Vietnam observe vegetarianism faithfully.

6. — *Expressions of wonder :*

After the Buddha's speech, his listeners used to express their wonder or delight. But their expressions are not the same in both versions, as seen in *C.S.* N° 68 :

C N° 144 : (*vi*, 76*a*, 5) : « Suan-chu-mu-chien-lien said : Oh Ch'ü-t'an, I have already known ; Oh Ch'ü-t'an, I have already understood. » Then he ended by declaring to take refuge in the Triple Gem and his asking the Buddha to accept him as a disciple.

P N° 107 : (*iii*, 7, 3-9) : « Abhikkantaṃ, bho Gotama, abhikkantaṃ, bho Gotama. Seyyathāpi, bho Gotama, nikkujjitaṃ vā ukkujjeyya, paṭichannaṃ vā vivareyya, mūḷhassa vā maggaṃ ācikkheyya, andhakāre vā telapajjotaṃ dhāreyya : cakkhumanto rūpāni dakkhintīti ; — evaṃ eva bhota Gotamena anekapariyāyena dhammo pakāsito ».

The same can be said of *C.S.* N° 39 in which the *C* N° 133 : (*vi*, 57*a*, 12) and the *Pāli* N° 56 : (*i*, 378, 30-35) resort to their respective way of expressing the wonder of the Buddha's listeners. Thus we can say that each school has its own tradition or figure of speech bearing its own stamp to which each adheres faithfully throughout their respective Tripiṭaka.

7. — *Formulae of address :*

Each school adopted a set of formulae of address to be used by the monks when they spoke to the Buddha or when they addressed one another In the Pāli version, the monks addressed Lord Buddha with the term *Bhante*, while the Chinese uses the expression *Shih-tsun* (世 尊) : *The World Honoured One.* When the monks addressed among themselves, if the monk addressed to was an elder one, they used the term *Bhante* according to the Pāli version, and the term *Tsun-che* (尊 者) : The Respected One, according to the Chinese version. If the monk addressed to happened to be a younger one, the Pāli

(1) Chapter viii.

uses the term *Āvuso* and the Chinese, the term *Hsien-che* (賢者) : The Good One. Thus the Ther. by using the term *Bhante* to be a form of address to the Buddha and to elder monks as well seems to be faithful to its own tradition of putting almost on the same footing the Buddha and the monks, the attainments of both are almost the same, except that the Buddha was a discoverer, a shower of the Path, while the Arahants are not. But the Sarv. used the term *The World Honoured One* and thus put the Buddha in a very high level above the monks. This might account for the later deification of the Buddha by the Mahāyānists who developed a kind of *Bhakti* cult towards the Buddha, while the Ther. always considered the monks eligible for arahanthood and thus deserved to be placed in the same rank with the Buddha.

8. — *The term Theravādin :*

In *C.S. N°* 22, the Pāli sutta N° 26, *Ariyapariyesana* contains the following passage in which the term *Theravāda* is referred to : « So kho ahaṃ bhikkhave tāvataken'eva oṭṭhapahatamattena lapitalāpanamattena ñāṇavādañ ca vadāmi theravādañ ca, jānāmi passāmīti ca paṭijānāmi ahañ c'eva aññe ca » (I, oh monks, as far as mere lip service and mere talk are concerned, spoke the doctrine of knowledge, the doctrine of the elders and I proclaim along with other people that I know, that I see) (i, 164, 3-6). But the Chinese corresponding sūtra N° 204 omits the whole passage. In this context, some comments by Dr Anesaki deserve attention : « We see in the Pāli Nikāyas pretty often mention of Theras. In the Chinese the title occurs as far as I know only thrice ; title *āyushman* being used other-wise in such cases. Can we conclude either that the Chinese version is derived from traditions dating from an age in the history of Buddhism when the authority of the Theras was not solidified, or it descended from a school antagonistic to the authority of the orthodox theras? » (1).

9. — *The term Bodhisatta :*

Another term which finds its way into the Pāli version but not into the Chinese version is the term *Bodhisatta*. Thus in *C S. N°* 16, the Pāli passage *N°* 19 : (i, 114. 25) mentions the term *Bodhisatta* designating the Buddha before his enlightenment ; but this term is not found in the Chinese corresponding passage and in any sūtras among the 98 Chinese sūtras taken up for comparative study. Again in *C S. N°* 78, while relating the former life of the Buddha in Tāvatiṃsa and the present life in the royal palace, the Pāli always refers to the term *Bodhisatta* for the Buddha before his enlightenment as found in *P N°* 123, *iii,* 119, lines 20, 21, 25, 26, 27, 30, 31, 32, 35 ; p. 120, lines 1, 5, 21, 23, 28, 29 etc... while its Chinese counterpart uses the term *Shih-tsun* (The World Honoured One) throughout (*C N°* 32, *v,* 44*a, lines* 2, 4, 11 *etc...*).

---

(1) *JRAS* 1901, p. 897f.

This anomaly might be explained by admitting that in the earliest version of the Sacred Canon, the term *Bodhisatta did not occur at all*, as testified to by the omission of the term in the Chinese version. But later on, when the doctrine of Bodhisatta found currency among some Mahāyānic schools and threatened to supersede the supremacy of arahantship, the Ther. compilers introduced the term *Bodhisatta* into their piṭakas and gave it the special meaning of the Buddha before his enlightenment and thus discarded any other meaning attributed to it by the Mahāyānists (1).

10. — *Kamma or action :*

In *C.S. N*° 40, the interpretation of the definition of actions is not the same in both the versions, and this difference is very important as it shows the different attitudes of the two schools which the 2 versions represent.

In the Chinese version N° 14 : (*v*, 17*a*, 5-20 ; 17*b*, 1-2), it is clearly mentioned that if the bodily deed (or vocal, mental) is *permissible* (*literally pure*), but if it leads to oneself's harm, to others'harm or to the harm of both, so it is an evil deed and the monk has to abstain from it. By the term *permissible*, the Chinese means that it is approved by the Scriptures or it does not infringe the monastic rules. But the Pāli definition is that if the bodily deed (or vocal, mental) he is about to perform will lead to oneself's harm, to others'harm, to the harm of both, then it is an evil deed leading to suffering, resulting in suffering, then he should surely not perform this deed... (*P* N° 61, i, 415, 25-36 ; 416, 417 ; 418 ; 419). Thus the Pāli by omiting the term *permissible* does not allow any infringment of the established monastic rules, while in the Sarv. definition, there is wide scope for a liberal attitude towards the interpretation of the monastic regulations. We night find out in this difference, an explanation of the rigid orthodoxy of the Ther. monks who up to now-a-days would frown on any attempt to relax or to interpret differently the established rules while the Sarv. and its offshot schools adopted a more or less liberal attitude towards the observance of monastic rules (2).

11. — *Some fundamental dharmas :*

Both versions enumerate a set of fundamental dharmas not exactly the same, and this shows the different traditions represented by each version. Thus in *C. S. N*° 1, the Chinese sūtra N° 100 (*vi*, 29b, 20 ; 30a, 1-4) enumerates 29 fundamental dharmas in the following order : 1) Earth, 2) water, 3) fire, 4) wind, 5) spirits, 6) deities, 7) Lord of beings, 8) Brahmā, 9) no-worry-plane, 10) no-distress-plane, 11) purity, 12) plane of infinite

---

(1) Dr. Bapat mentions another possibility that the C version deliberately omitted it, because the editor wanted to show greater respect to the Buddha by applying that term even to the period of his life before his enlightenment.

(2) See infra, para C Panna, g) kamma and kammavipaka.

space, 13) plane of infinite consciousness, 14) plane of nothingness, 15) plane of neither-perception nor non-perception, 16) oneness, 17) diversity, 18) plurality, 19) the seen, 20) the heard, 21) the sensed, 22) the cognised, 23) the obtained, 24) the contemplated, 25) mindfulness, 26) the thought by the mind, 27) from this world to that world, 28) from that world to this world, 29) all.

The Pāli, (P N° 1, i, 1-2) refers to only 24 dhammas in the following order : 1) Earth, 2) water, 3) fire, 4) wind, 5) beings, 6) deities, 7) Pajāpati, 8) Brahmā, 9) Ābhassara, 10) Subhakiṇṇa, 11) Vehapphala, 12) Abhibhū, 13) plane of infinite space, 14) plane of infinite consciousness, 15) plane of nothingness, 16) plane of neither perception nor non-perception, 17) the seen, 18) the heard, 19) the sensed, 20) the cognised, 21) oneness, 22) diversity, 23) all, 24) Nibbāna.

Thus the following dharmas are not found in Pāli : 1) Spirits, 2) no-worry-plane, 3) no-distress plane, 4) purity, 5) plurality, 6) the obtained, 7) the contemplated, 8) mindfulness, 9) the thought by the mind, 10) from this world to that world, 11) from that world to this world. 6 dhammas are not found in Chinese : 1) Beings, 2) Ābhassara, 3) Subhakiṇṇa, 4) Vehapphala, 5) Abhibhū, 6) Nibbāna. This difference in the fundamental dharmas shows the different tradition followed by each version, with the Pāli representing the Ther. tradition and with the CMA representing the Sarv. tradition.

12. — *Programme of training :*

In *C. S. N°* 98, the Chinese version *N°* 86 : (*vi*, 2*a*-5*a*) presents a programme to train new young monks, advocated by the W. H. One to Ven. A-nan, when the latter came to see him along with many young monks and ask him the way how to educate, admonish, preach the dharma to these young monks. The Buddha enumerated a list of 30 dharmas to be taught, which bears a distinctive feature of the Sarv., widely different from the Ther.. The 30 dharmas are as follows : 1) 5 aggregates, 2) 6 inner sense-spheres, 3) 6 external sense-spheres, 4) 6 consciousnesses, from eye-consciousness to mind-consciousness, 5) 6 contacts, 6) 6 kinds of feeling, from eye-feeling to mind-feeling, 7) 6 kinds of perceptions, from eye-perception, to mind-perception, 8) 6 kinds of thought, from eye-thought to mind-thought, 9) 6 classes of craving, from eye-craving to mind-craving, 10) 6 elements, 11) the dependent origination, 12) 4 applications of mindfulness, 13) 5 right eradications, 14) 4 psychic powers, 15) 4 dhyānas of the rūpa-plane, 16) 4 noble truths, 17) 4 perceptions, small, big, infinite and perception of nothingness, 18) 4 Illimitables, 19) 4 dhyānas of the arūpa-plane, 20) 4 noble things, use of robes, food, lodging (one thing is missing here), 21) 4 fruits of recluseship, stream-attainer, once-returner, no-returner, arahantship, 22) 5 ripe perceptions of emancipation, perception of impermanence, perception of suffering, of no-self, perception of impurity, of evil showing, perception of all unpleasant perceptions in the world, 23) 5 places of emancipation, preaching of dharma, recitation of what has been recited, heard before, extensive explanation of what has been recited, heard before, pondering over, analysis of what has been recited, heard, well grasping and bearing the characteristic of meditation, 24) 5 faculties, 25) 5 powers, 26) 5 realms of freedom, contemplation on desire, malevolence, harming, material forms, on one's own body, 27) 7 properties of faith, moral precepts, conscientionness, scrupulousness, hearing, charity and of wisdom, 28) 7 powers of faith, exertion, conscientionness, scrupulousness, mindfulness, concentration and of wisdom, 29) 7 factors of wisdom, 30) the Noble Eightfold Path.

This division of the programme of training into 30 dharmas is very far from the usual division into 37 Bodhipakkhiyas as seen in the Pāli version and testifies to a rather later stage of development, far from early Buddhism. Again in the last C sūtras *N*° 222. *Li-ching*, besides the usual 37 Bodhipakkhiyas, the Chinese version adds 2 more dharmas, the 10 pervading sense-spheres (Kṛtsnāyatanāni) and the 10 Dharmas of the Asekha, that is the usual noble eightfold Path plus right emancipation and right wisdom. If we compare with the usual Pāli list, the P mentions the 8 Abhibhāyatanāni, but not the 10 Kṛtsnāyatanāni. As for the 10 Dharmas of the Asekha, the Pāli mentions them also but interchanges the place of the last 2 dhammas, sammāvimutti and sammāpaññā. All these differences show that even in the Suttapiṭaka, traditions are not the same in the Sarv. School and the Ther. School and these dissimilarities pave the way to their fundamental differences in their respective abhidharma works.

13. — *Miraculous powers :*

The Chinese version seems prone to show the miraculous powers of the Buddha and of his disciples, while the Pāli version prefers to ignore them. Thus in *C.S. N*° 54, the Chinese text relates that after Lai-cha-ho-lo's visit to his parents, he flew back through the air and sat down in the forest (*C N*° 132 *vi*, 53*b*, 8) ; while its Pāli counterpart mentions simply that elder Raṭṭhapāla, having uttered the gāthā came to the deerpark of king Koravya and sat down for a day-rest under the root of a certain tree (*P N*° 82, *vi*, 65, 7-9). Again in *C.S. N*° 83, the Chinese version relates that after reciting a gāthā, the W.H. One used psychic power to fly through the air and came to P'o-lo-lou-lo village (*C N*° 72, *v*, 97*a*, 18), while its Pāli corresponding passage omits it.

This fondness for display of miraculous power of the Sarv. might account for the later exuberance of miraculous powers attributed to the Buddha and his disciples in the Mahāyānic texts.

14. — *Akin to Mahāyānic ideas :*

Along with this fondness of miraculous powers, the Chinese version abounds in passages which are reminiscent of Mahāyānic ideas foreign to early Buddhism.

Thus in *C.S.* *N*° 36, while relating the story of former Buddha Chio-liang-chü-hsün-ta (P : Kakusandha), the Chinese version describes him as surrounded by countless hundred thousand followers (*C N*° 131, *vi*, 50*b*, 8), while its Pāli counterpart ignores this detail. Again in *C.S.* N° 63, when the Buddha ended his discourse, the Chinese version *N*° 27 (*v*, 34*b*, 11) related that Ven. Shê-li-tzu (P : Sāriputta) along with countless hundred thousand monks were delighted at the Buddha's speech, while the Pāli corresponding passage omits even its usual conclusion. Thus these figures far outnumber the usual 1,250 monks who followed the Buddha in his peregrinations. Again these descriptions of the Buddha, sitting, beautiful like the moon among the stars, shining, reverberating with light like a golden mountain etc... as found in *C.S.* *N*° 48 (*C* N° 153, *vi*, 90*a*, 1) in *C.S.* *N*° 53 (*C N*° 63, *v*, 69*a*, 15-16), and also in *C. S.* *N*° 64 (*C N*° 152, *vi*, 87*a*, 11) strike a rather exaggerated note, unknown to the moderate attitude of early Buddhism. All these details are missing in the Pāli version.

Another instance of this exaggeration is another Chinese passage in *C.S.* *N*° 91, hailing the Tathāgata as the best debater, living up to 100 years and preaching the dharma to his disciples for the whole 100 years except when eating, when obeying the calls of nature, when sleeping and taking rest, and when attending meeting (*C N*° 163, *vii*, 7*b*, 16-17).

All the above considerations testify to a later stage of Buddhism, into which some Mahāyānic ideas were already slowly creeping in, and which served as a spring-board for later blossoming of the Mahāyānic literature.

The differences between the 2 Chinese and Pāli versions do not stop here. A detailed study of the Buddha's 32 auspicious marks (1), of his marvellous qualities (2), of the various kinds of tortures and punishments (3), of various kinds of hells (4), of different parts of the body (5), of the story of Raṭṭhapāla (6) etc. shows that both versions inherit a different and independent tradition.

Thus the characteristics collected above show clearly that each version represents a different school, the Pāli the Ther. school, the Chinese the Sarv. school. These characteristics serve also to testify that even in the Sūtrapiṭaka, separative forces were already at work which eventually crystallised into pronounced dissimilarities in their respective Abhidharma texts and led to a division between the two schools. They also help us to find out the cause of some differences in practice actually followed by the Buddhists of some countries even in modern time.

---

(1) Chapter V, 4, 32 Auspicious marks.
(2) Chapter V, 2, Marvellous qualities.
(3) Chapter IV, C Panna, g) Kammavipaka, ii, 2nd kind of suffering.
(4) Chapter IV, C Panna, g) Kammavipaka, iii, Suffering in the Hell.
(5) Chapter IV, B Samadhi, a) 4 Satipatthana, i) Contemplation of body.
(6) Chapter III, m) To Lai-cha-ho Lo.

IV. — MUTUAL RELATIONS BETWEEN THE CMA AND THE PMN WITH OTHER NIKĀYAS AND OTHER ĀGAMAS

Prof. CHIZEN AKANUMA in his « THE COMPARATIVE CATALOGUE OF CHINESE ĀGAMAS AND PĀLI NIKĀYAS» had given a catalogue of corresponding sūtras between Dīghanikāya and Dīrghāgama, Majjhimanikāya and Madhyamāgama, Samyuttanikāya and Samyuktāgama and between Aṅguttaranikāya and Ekottarāgama.

His study on the relations between the CMA with PMN and other Nikāyas (1) reveals that among the 222 Chinese sūtras, 99 find their 98 Pāli corresponding suttas in the Majjhima Nikāya, 78 in the Aṅguttara Nikāya, 10 in the Samyutta Nikāya, 9 in the Dīgha Nikāya, 6 in the Khuddaka Nikāya, one in the Mahāvagga and 18 sūtras cannot be traced. Two Chinese sūtras, N° 107, and N° 108, Lin-ching correspond to the Pāli N° 17, Vanapattha-sutta.

His study on the relations between the PMN with the CMA and other Āgamas (2) shows that among the 152 suttas of the Majjhima Nikāya, 98 suttas find their 99 corresponding sūtras in the CMA, 40 suttas in the Ekottarāgama, 28 in the Samyuktāgama and 22 suttas cannot be traced.

---

(1) C. A. P. M. p. 7 to p. 25.
(2) C. A. P. M. p. 163 to p. 171.

V. — LIST OF 98 PĀLI AND CHINESE CORRESPONDING SŪTRAS SELECTED FOR COMPARATIVE STUDY

C.S. N° 1 : P N° 1, Mūlapariyāya = C N° 106, Hsiang-ching.
C.S. N° 2 : P N° 2, Sabbāsava = C N° 10, Lou-chin-ching.
C.S. N° 3 : P N° 3, Dhammadāyāda = C N° 88, Ch'iu-fa-ching.
C.S. N° 4 : P N° 5, Anaṅgaṇa = C N° 87, Wei-p'in-ching.
C.S. N° 5 : P N° 6, Ākaṅkheyya = C N° 105, Yüan-ching.
C.S. N° 6 : P N° 7, Vatthūpama = C N° 93, Shui-ching-fan-chih-ching.
C.S. N° 7 : P N° 8, Sallekha = C N° 91, Chou-na-wên-chien-ching.
C.S. N° 8 : P N° 10, Satipaṭṭhāna = C N° 98, Nien-ch'u-ching.
C.S. N° 9 : P N° 11, Cūḷasīhanāda = C N° 103, Shih-tzu-hou-ching.
C.S. N° 10 : P N° 13, Mahādukkhakkhandha = C N° 99, K'u-yin-ching.
C.S. N° 11 : P N° 14, Cūḷadukkhakkhandha = C N° 100, K'u-yin-ching.
C.S. N° 12 : P N° 15, Anumāna = C N° 89, Pi-ch'iu-ch'ing-ching.
C.S. N° 13 : P N° 16, Cetokhila = C N° 206, Hsin-wei-ching.
C.S. N° 14 : P N° 17, Vanapaṭṭha = C N° 107, Lin-ching.
= C N° 108, Lin-ching.
C.S. N° 15 : P N° 18, Madhupiṇḍika = C N° 115, Mi-wan-yü-ching.
C.S. N° 16 : P N° 19, Dvedhāvitakka = C N° 102, Nien-ching.
C.S. N° 17 : P N° 20, Vitakkasanthāna = C N° 101, Tsêng-shang-hsin-ching.
C.S. N° 18 : P N° 21, Kakacūpama = C N° 193, Mou-li-p'o-ch'ün-na-ching.
C.S. N° 19 : P N° 22, Alagaddūpama = C N° 200, A-li-cha-ching.
C.S. N° 20 : P N° 24, Rathavinīta = C N° 9, Ch'i-ch'ê-ching.
C.S. N° 21 : P N° 25, Nivāpa = C N° 178, Lieh-shih-ching.
C.S. N° 22 : P N° 26, Ariyapariyesana = C N° 204, Lo-mo-ching.
C.S. N° 23 : P N° 27, Cūḷahatthipadopama = C N° 146, Hsiang-chi-yü-ching.
C.S. N° 24 : P N° 28, Mahāhatthipadopama = C N° 30, Hsiang-chi-yü-ching.
C.S. N° 25 : P N° 31, Cūḷagosiṅga = C N° 185, Niu-chiao-so-lo-lin-ching.
C.S. N° 26 : P N° 32, Mahāgosiṅga = C N° 184, Niu-chiao-so-lo-lin-ching.

C.S. *N*° 27 : P N° 38, Mahātaṇhāsaṅkhaya = C N° 201, Ch'a-ti-ching.
C.S. *N*° 28 : P N° 39, Mahāassapura = C N° 182, Ma-i-ching.
C.S. *N*° 29 : P N° 40, Cūḷaassapura = C N° 183, Ma-i-ching.
C.S. *N*° 30 : P N° 43, Mahāvedalla = C N° 211, Ta-chü-hsi-lo-ching
C.S. *N*° 31 : P N° 44, Cūḷavedalla = C N° 210, Fa-lo-pi-ch'iu-ni-ching.
C.S. *N*° 32 : P N° 45, Cūḷadhammasamādāna = C N° 174, Shou-fa-ching.
C.S. *N*° 33 : P N° 46, Mahādhammasamādāna = C N° 175, Shou-fa-ching.
C.S. *N*° 34 : P N° 47, Vīmaṃsaka = C N° 186, Ch'iu-chieh-ching.
C.S. *N*° 35 : P N° 49, Brahmanimantaṇika = C N° 78, Fan-t'ien-ch'ing-*fu-ching*.
C.S. *N*° 36 : P N° 50, Māratajjaniya = C N° 131, Hsiang-mo-ching.
C.S. *N*° 37 : P N° 52, Aṭṭhakanāgara = C N° 217, Pa-ch'êng-ching.
C.S. *N*° 38 : P N° 54, Potaliya = C N° 203, Pu-li-to-ching.
C.S. *N*° 39 : P N° 56, Upāli = C N° 133, Yu-p'o-li-ching.
C.S. *N*° 40 : P N° 61, Ambalaṭṭhikārāhulovāda = C N° 14, Lo-yün-ching.
C.S. *N*° 41 : P N° 63, Cūḷamāluṅkya = C N° 221, Chien-yü-ching.
C.S. *N*° 42 : P N° 64, Mahāmāluṅkya = C N° 205, Wu-hsia-fên-chieh-ching.
C.S. *N*° 43 : P N° 65, Bhaddāli = C N° 194, Po-t'o-ho-li-ching.
C.S. *N*° 44 : P N° 66, Laṭukīkopama = C N° 192, Chia-lou-wu-t'o-i-ching.
C.S. *N*° 45 : P N° 68, Naḷakapāna = C N° 77, So-chi-ti-san-tsu-hsing-tzu-ching.
C.S. *N*° 46 : P N° 69, Gulissāni = C N° 26, Ch'u-ni-shih-ching.
C.S. *N*° 47 : P N° 70, Kīṭāgiri = C N° 195, A-shih-pei-ching.
C.S. *N*° 48 : P N° 75, Māgandiya = C N° 153, Hsü-hsien-t'i-ching.
C.S. *N*° 49 : P N° 77, Mahāsakulūdāyi = C N° 207, Chien-mao-ching.
C.S. *N*° 50 : P N° 78, Samaṇamaṇḍika = C N° 179, Wu-chih-wu-chu-ching.
C.S. *N*° 51 : P N° 79, Cūḷasakulūdāyi = C N° 208, Chien-mao-ching.
C.S. *N*° 52 : P N° 80, Vekhanassa = C N° 209, Pei-mo-na-hsiu-ching.
C.S. *N*° 53 : P N° 81, Ghaṭīkāra = C N° 63, Pei-p'o-ling-ch'i-ching.
C.S. *N*° 54 : P N° 82, Raṭṭhapāla = C N° 132, Lai-cha-ho-lo-ching.
C.S. *N*° 55 : P N° 83, Makhādeva = C N° 67, Ta-thien-na-lin-ching.
C.S. *N*° 56 : P N° 87, Piyajātika = C N° 216, Ai-shêng-ching.
C.S. *N*° 57 : P N° 88, Bāhitika = C N° 214, Pei-ho-t'i-ching.
C.S. *N*° 58 : P N° 89, Dhammacetiya = C N° 213, Fa-chuang-yen-ching.
C.S. *N*° 59 : P N° 90, Kaṇṇakatthala = C N° 212, I-ch'ieh-chih-ching.
C.S. *N*° 60 : P N° 91, Brahmāyu = C N° 161, Fan-mo-ching.

C.S. *N*° 61 : P N° 93, Assalāyana = C N° 151, A-shê-ho-ching.

C.S. *N*° 62 : P N° 96, Esukārī = C N° 150, Yü-shou-ko-lo-ching.

C.S. *N*° 63 : P N° 97, Dhānañjāni = C N° 27, Fan-chih-t'o-jan-ching.

C.S. *N*° 64 : P N° 99, Subha = C N° 152, Ying-wu-ching.

C.S. *N*° 65 : P N° 101, Devadaha = C N° 19, Ni-kan-ching.

C.S. *N*° 66 : P N° 104, Sāmagāma = C N° 196, Chou-na-ching.

C.S. *N*° 67 : P N° 106, Āṇañjasappāya = C N° 75, Ching-pu-tung-tao-ching.

C.S. *N*° 68 : P N° 107, Gaṇakamoggallāna = C N° 144, Suan-shu-mu-chien-lien-ching.

C.S. *N*° 69 : P N° 108, Gopakamoggallāna = C N° 145, Ch'ü-mê-mu-chien-lien-ching.

C.S. *N*° 70 : P N° 112, Chabbisodhana = C N° 187, Shuo-chih-ching.

C.S. *N*° 71 : P N° 113, Sappurisa = C N° 85, Chên-jên-ching.

C.S. *N*° 72 : P N° 115, Bahudhātuka = C N° 181, To-chieh-ching.

C.S. *N*° 73 : P N° 117, Mahācattārīsaka = C N° 189, Shêng-tao-ching.

C.S. *N*° 74 : P N° 119, Kāyagatāsati = C N° 81, Nien-shên-ching.

C.S. *N*° 75 : P N° 120, Saṅkhāruppati = C N° 168, I-hsing-ching.

C.S. *N*° 76 : P N° 121, Cūḷasuññatā = C N° 190, Hsiao-k'ung-ching.

C.S. *N*° 77 : P N° 122, Mahāsuññatā = C N° 191, Ta-k'ung-ching.

C.S. *N*° 78 : P N° 123, Acchariyabbhutadhamma = C N° 32, Wei-ts'êng-yu-fa-ching.

C.S. *N*° 79 : P N° 124, Bakkula = C N° 34, Po-chü-lo-ching.

C.S. *N*° 80 : P N° 125, Dantabhūmi = C N° 198, T'iao-yü-ti-ching.

C.S. *N*° 81 : P N° 126, Bhūmija = C N° 173, Fou-mi-ching.

C.S. *N*° 82 : P N° 127, Anuruddha = C N° 79, Yu-shêng-t'ien-ching.

C.S. *N*° 83 : P N° 128, Upakkilesa = C N° 72, Ch'ang-shou-wang-pên-ch'i-ching.

C.S. *N*° 84 : P N° 129, Bālapaṇḍita = C N° 199, Ch'ih-hui-ti-ching.

C.S. *N*° 85 : P N° 130, Devadūta = C N° 64, T'ien-shih-ching.

C.S. *N*° 86 : P N° 132, Ānandabhaddekaratta = C N° 167, A-nan-shuo-ching.

C.S. *N*° 87 : P N° 133, Mahākaccānabhaddekaratta = C N° 165, Wên-ch'üan-lin-t'ien-ching.

C.S. *N*° 88 : P N° 134, Lomasakaṅgiyabhaddekaratta = C N° 166, Shih-chung-ch'an-shih-tsun-ching.

C.S. *N*° 89 : P N° 135, Cūḷakammavibhaṅga = C N° 170, Ying-wu-ching.

C.S. *N*° 90 : P N° 136, Mahākammavibhaṅga = C N° 171, Fên-pieh-ta-yeh-ching.

C.S. N° 91 : P N° 137, Saḷāyatanavibhaṅga = C N° 163, Fên-pieh-liu-ch'u-ching.

C.S. N° 92 : P N° 138, Uddesavibhaṅga = C N° 164, Fên-pieh-kuan-fa-ching.

C.S. N° 93 : P N° 139, Araṇavibhaṅga = C N° 169, Chü-lou-shou-wu-chêng-ching.

C.S. N° 94 : P N° 140, Dhātuvibhaṅga = C N° 162, Fên-pieh-liu-chieh-ching.

C.S. N° 95 : P N° 141, Saccavibhaṅga = C N° 31, Fên-pieh-shêng-ti-ching.

C.S. N° 96 : P N° 142, Dakkhiṇāvibhaṅga = C N° 180, Ch'ü-t'an-mi-ching.

C.S. N° 97 : P N° 143, Anāthapiṇḍikovāda = C N° 28, Chiao-hua-ping-ching.

C.S. N° 98 : P N° 148, Chachakka = C N° 86, Shuo-ch'u-ching.

PART TWO

SIMILARITIES AND DIFFERENCES BETWEEN THE CHINESE AND THE PĀLI VERSIONS.

Chapter I. — ARRANGEMENT OF VARGAS AND SŪTRAS (1)

A. — Chinese version

1. — *According to vargas or chapters :*

The 222 Chinese sūtras of the CMA are classified into 18 vargas as follows :

1)	*Ch'i-fa-p'in* (Sattadhammavagga) containing	10 Sūtras
2)	*Yeh-hsiang-ying-p'in* (Kammasamyuttavagga)	10 —
3)	*Shê-li-tzu-hsiang-ying-p'in* (Sāriputtasamyuttav.)	11 —
4)	*Wei-ts'êng-yu-fa-p'in* (Abbhutadhammavagga)	10 —
5)	*Hsi-hsiang-ying-p'in* (Samudayasamyuttavagga)	16 —
6)	*Wang-hsiang-ying-p'in* (Rājasamyuttavagga)	14 —
7)	*Ch'ang-shou-wang-p'in* (Dīghāyurājavagga)	15 —
8)	*Wei-p'in* (Aṅgaṇavagga)	10 —
9)	*Yin-p'in* (Nidānavagga)	10 —
10)	*Lin-p'in* (Vanavagga)	10 —
11)	*Ta-p'in* (Mahāvagga)	25 —
12)	*Fan-chih-p'in* (Brāhmaṇavagga)	20 —
13)	*Kên-pên-fên-pieh-p'in* (Mūlavibhaṅgavagga)	10 —
14)	*Hsin-p'in* (Cittavagga)	10 —
15)	*Shuang-p'in* (Yamakavagga)	10 —
16)	*Ta-p'in* (Mahāvagga)	10 —
17)	*Pu-li-to-p'in* (Potaliyavagga)	10 —
18)	*Li-p'in* (Saṃvidahanavagga)	11 —
	Total :	222 sūtras

The 1st chapter, *Ch'i-fa-p'in*, on 7 dharmas, is so named because its 10 sūtras deal with 7 kinds of dharmas. Thus in C N° 1, *Shan-fa-ching*, discourse on meritorious dharmas, the Buddha said that a monk who was endowed with 7 meritorious dharmas would put an end to the cankers and he explained these 7 dharmas. In C. N° 9, *Ch'i-ch'ê-ching*, discourse on 7 chariots, the simile of a relay of 7 chariots to illustrate the 7 stages of training of a monk is stated.

The 2nd chapter, *Yeh-hsiang-yin-p'in*, chapter on sūtras connected with karma, is so named because its sūtras treat the question of karma and its results. Thus in C N° 11, *Yen-yü-ching*, discourse on simile of salt, the

(1) See infra, Appendixes 4 for details.

Buddha explained that people would reap results according to their deeds. In C N° 12, *Ho-p'o-ching*, discourse on Ho-p'o, a discussion took place between Ven. Ta-mu-chien-lien and a Ni-chien called Ho-p'o on actions leading to a future life in an unhappy place.

The 3rd chapter, *Shê-li-tzu-hsiang-ying-p'in*, on sūtras connected with Shê-li-tzu is so named because in its sūtras, Ven. Shê-li-tzu played the main role. Thus in C N° 27, *Fan-chih t'o-jan-ching*, discourse on brāhmaṇa T'o-jan, Ven. Shê-li-tzu preached to this brāhmaṇa the dangers of committing demeritorious actions. In C N° 26, *Ch'ü-ni-shih-ching*, discourse on Ch'ü-ni-shih, Ven. Shê-li-tzu enumerated 13 rules of conduct of a monk.

The 4th chapter, *Wei-ts'êng-yu-fa-p'in*, on wonderful dharmas, owes its name to its sūtras dealing with wonderful dharmas. Thus in C N° 32, *Wei-ts'êng-yu-fa-ching*, discourse on wonderful dharmas, Ven. A-nan enumerated 24 marvellous qualities of the Buddha, C N° 33, *Shih-che-ching*, discourse on attendant, refers to the selection of Ven. A-nan as attendant of the Buddha and the Buddha's praise of Ven. A-nan's distinguished qualities.

The 5th chapter, *Hsi-hsiang-p'in* « On origination », gets its name on account of the reference to origination contained in its sūtras. Thus in C N° 42, *Ho-i-ching* « Discourse On what is the meaning », the Buddha explained to Ven. A-nan the dependent origination of successive dharmas, from observance of precepts to knowledge of emancipation. In C N° 44, *Nien-ching*, discourse on mindfulness, the Buddha dealt also with the origination of successive dharmas, starting first with forgetfulness of a monk leading to non-attainment of right knowledge and consequently leading to non-attainment of Nirvāṇa.

The 6th chapter, *Wang-hsiang-ying-p'in* « On connection with kings », owes its name to its sūtras referring to kings. Thus in C N° 64, *T'ien-shih-ching*, « Discourse On heaven-messenger », king Ya-mo (P : Yama) told about the 5 heaven-messengers who warned people of the coming old age and death and urged them to engage in religious duties. C N° 62, *P'in-pi-so-lo-wang-ying-fo-ching*, « discourse on king P'in-pi-so-lo welcoming the Buddha » relates the reception of the Buddha by the king when the former visited him.

The 7th chapter, *Ch'ang-shou-wang-p'in*, « On King of Long life », owes its name to its first sūtra C N° 72, *Ch'ang-shou-wang-pên-chi-ching*, « Discourse on the former life of king Ch'ang-chou ». In C N° 75, *Ching-pu-tung-tao-ching*, « Discourse on the ways of pure immovability », the Buddha explained to Ven. A-nan the pure immovability of state obtained by a monk who engaged himself energetically in spiritual training.

The 8th chapter, *Wei-p'in*, « On blemishes », is so named on account of ifs sūtras dealing with blemishes which defile the mind. Thus in C N° 87, *Wei-p'in-ching* « Discourse on blemishes », Ven. Shê-li-tzu described four kinds of people with blemishes and without blemishes. In C N° 88, *Ch'iu-fa-ching*. « Discourse on seeking the dharma », the Buddha advised the monks to be heirs of dharma but not heirs of food and drink.

The 9th chapter, *Yin-p'in* « On causes », deals principally with cause. Thus in C N° 97, *Ta-yin-ching,* « discourse on great cause », the Buddha explained to Ven. A-nan the dependent origination. In C N° 106, *Hsiang-ching,* « Discourse on perception », the Buddha explained to the monks, different attitudes of different people towards various dharmas, the cause which determined these attitudes and their degree of emancipation due to these attitudes.

The 10th chapter, *Lin-p'in,* « On forest », groups mostly sūtras dealing with the life in the forest. Thus in C N° 107, *Lin-ching-ti-i,* « Discourse on the forest », 1st sūtra, the Buddha exhorted the monks to dwell in the forest so as to obtain right mindfulness, concentration, emancipation, extinction of cankers and Nirvāṇa. In the 2nd sūtra, C N° 108, *Lin-ching-ti-êrh,* the Buddha exhorted the monks to dwell in forest so as to achieve the goal of recluseship and to obtain easily requisites for life.

The 11th chapter, *Ta-p'in,* « On greatness » which covers as many as 25 sūtras, the largest of all, derives its name perhaps from the large number of sūtras grouped in this chapter. In C N° 117, *Jou-juan-ching,* « Discourse on softness, » the Buddha recalled his former luxurious life in the palace, his sitting under the Jambu-tree, his entering into the 1st dhyāna and his meditation on the dharmas of the ignorant ones, and the dharmas of his own in the light of this meditation. In C N° 131, *Hsiang-mo-ching,* Ven. Ta-mu-chien-lien challenged Māra who came to disturb him and succeeded in driving him away.

The 12th chapter, *Fan-chih-p'in,* « On Brāhmaṇas » takes its name from its sūtras dealing with the brāhmaṇas. Thus in C N° 144, *Suan-shu-mu-chien-lien-ching,* « Discourse about brāhmaṇa Suan-shu-mu-chien-lien », who asked the Buddha about his gradual teaching in his Dharma-vinaya. In C N° 145, *Ch'ü-mê-mu-chien-lien-ching,* Ven. A-nan talked with the brāhmaṇa on what had governed the Order of monks after the Buddha's demise, which enabled the Order to preserve its unity.

The 13th chapter, *Kên-pên-fên-pieh-p'in,* « On analysis of the fundamentals, deals mostly with analysis of various dharmas. Thus in C N° 162, *Fên-pieh-liu-chieh-ching,* the Buddha spoke about the analysis of 6 elements. In C N° 163, *Fên-pieh-liu-ch'u-ching,* the Buddha spoke about the analysis of 6 sense-fields.

The 14th chapter, *Hsin-p'in,* « On mind » derives its name, from its 1st sūtra, C N° 172, *Hsin-ching,* « Discourse on mind », in which the Buddha explained the sway of the mind over the learned and the unlearned. In the same chapter, C N° 173, *Fou-mi-ching,* « Discourse on Fou-mi », deals with the doctrine saying that if one fares the brahma-life with determination or without determination, with both or without both, one surely obtains results.

The 15th chapter, *Shuang-p'in,* chapter « On pairs », derives its name from the grouping of sūtras by pairs of sūtras of the same titles, such as C N° 182, 183, *Ma-i-ching,* C N° 184, 185, *Niu-chiao-so-lo-lin-ching.*

The 16th chapter, *Ta-p'in*, « On greatness » possesses the same title as the 11th chapter. Here it contains only 10 sūtras. In C N° 193, *Mou-li-p'o-ch'ün-na-ching*, discourse on the monk Mou-li-p'o-ch'ün-na, the Buddha reproached this monk for having close association with the nuns and asked him to dwell in compassion and friendliness. In C N° 194, *P'o-t'o-ho-li-ching*, the Buddha showed to Ven. P'o-t'o-ho-li the dangers of breaking the rules of taking meals at one-session, the way to treat the guilty monks and the advantages of respecting this rule.

The 17th chapter, *Pu-li-to-p'in*, « On Pu-li-to » derives its name from its first sūtra, C N° 203, *Pu-li-to-ching*, in which the Buddha told the householder Pu-li-to that, by merely giving up worldly things, one cannot be called a true recluse in the Dharma-vinaya of the Noble Ones. In C N° 204, *Lo-mo-ching*, « Discourse about Lo-mo », the Buddha preached two kinds of quest, the ariyan one and the unariyan one.

The 18th chapter, the last one, *Li-p'in*, « On arrangement », takes the name of its last sūtra C N° 222, *Li-ching*, discourse on arrangement, in which the Buddha explains that in order to eradicate and to know ignorance, old age and death, to put an end to suffering, one should practise 4 applications of mindfulness, 4 right eradications (1), 4 psychic powers, 4 dhyānas, 5 faculties, 5 powers, 7 factors of wisdom, eightfold Path, 10 pervading sense-spheres, 10 dharmas of one who is beyond instruction.

In front of each chapter, there is a verse of four or more lines, which enumerates in an abridged form the names of sūtras contained in this chapter. For instance, in the 1st chapter, the verse is as follows :

« Shan-fa chou-tu-shu, Ch'êng, shui, mu-chi-yü »

« Shan-jên-wang, shih-fu, Jih, ch'ê, lou-chin ch'i »

Shan-fa : shan-fa-ching. *Chou-tu-shu :* chou-tu-shu-ching. *Ch'êng :* ch'êng-yü-ching. *Shui :* shui-yü-ching. *Mu-chi-yü :* mu-chi-yü-ching. *Shan-jên-wang :* shan-jên-wang-ching. *Shih-fu :* shih-chien-fu-ching. *Jih :* ch'i-jih-ching. *Ch'ê :* ch'i-ch'ê-ching. *Lou-chin :* lou-chin-ching.

II. — *According to fasciculi :*

Again these 222 sūtras are classified according to fasciculi or volumes which number 60 in all. Thus *fasc.* 1 *&* 2 contain chapter 1, with 10 sūtras ; *fasc.* 3 *&* 4, chapter 2 with 10 sūtras ; *fasc.* 5 *to* 7, chapter 3 with 11 sūtras ; *fasc.* 8 *&* 9, chapter 4 with 10 sūtras ; *fasc.* 10, chapter 5 with 16 sūtras ; *fasc.* 11 *to* 16, chapter 6 with 14 sūtras ; *fasc.* 17 *to* 21, chapter 7 with 15 sūtras ; *fasc.* 22 *&* 23, chapter 8 with 10 sūtras ; *fasc.* 24 *to* 26, chapter 9 with 10 sūtras ; *fasc.* 27 *&* 28, chapter 10 with

(1) It is a misunderstanding of the C translator of the original word pahana, which means pradhana, effort, exertion and not eradication. See Abhidharmakosa, karika.

10 sūtras ; *fasc.* 29 *to* 34, chapter 11 with 25 sūtras ; *fasc.* 35 *to* 41, chapter 12 with 20 sūtras ; *fasc.* 42 *to* 44, chapter 13 with 10 sūtras ; *fasc.* 45 *to* 47, chapter 14 with 10 sūtras ; *fasc.* 48 *&* 49, chapter 15 with 10 sūtras ; *fasc.* 50 *to* 54, chapter 16 with 10 sūtras ; *fasc.* 55 *to* 58, chapter 17 with 10 sūtras ; *fasc.* 59 *&* 60, chapter 18 with 11 sūtras.

III. — *According to days of recital :*

Again these 222 sūtras are classified according to 5 days of recital. *1st day* covers from chapter 1 to the first half of chapter 6, containing 64 sūtras ; *2nd day* covers from the 2nd half of chapter 6 to chapter 10, containing 52 sūtras ; *3rd day* covers from chapter 11 to the first half of chapter 12, containing 35 sūtras ; *4th day* covers from the second half of chapter 12 to the first half of chapter 15, containing 35 sūtras ; and *5th day* covers from the second half of chapter 15 to chapter 18, containing 36 sūtras. This classification shows that in former times, this Āgama occupied also a place in the daily prayer of the monks who completed the whole Āgama in 5 days of recital.

In order to prevent any addition or omission, the compiler added at the end of each sūtra, the number of words contained in that sūtra. For instance, in *Shan-fa-ching,* the 1st sūtra, it is mentioned at the end of the sūtra that it contains 1,423 words. *Li-ching,* the last sūtra contains 4,873 words.

At the end of each fascicule also, the number of words is mentioned. Thus fascicule 1st contains in all 8,109 words ; fascicule 60th, the last one, contains 11,377 words.

At the end of each chapter also, the number of words is mentioned. Thus we come to know that chapter 1 contains 16,043 words, chapter 18 contains 22,149 words. (1)

It is stated that the CMA was translated by *Chi-pin-san-ts'ang-ch'ü-t'an-sêng-chia-t'i-p'o* (Kashmiri Traipiṭaka Gautama Sanghadeva) and written down by *Tao-tsu,* in Eastern Tsin dynasty, under the reign of king *Hsiao-wu* and king *An-ti,* of *Lung-an* reign, at *Tung-t'ing* monastery. King Hsiao-wu's accession to the throne corresponds to 373 A.D. and king An-ti's accession to the throne, to 397 A.D.

B. — PĀLI VERSION

The 152 Pāli suttas are classified into 3 big divisions, *Mūlapaṇṇāsa* which includes the first 50 discourses, *Majjhimapaṇṇāsa* which includes the middle 50 discourses and the *Uparipaṇṇāsa* which includes the final 52 discourses. They are classified into 15 vaggas as follows :

(1) For details, see Appendix N° 4.

1) *Mūlapariyāyavagga*, chapter on Fundamentals,	10	suttas
2) *Sīhanādavagga*, chapter on Lion's roar,	10	—
3) *Tatiyavagga*, the Third chapter	10	—
4) *Mahāyamakavagga*, Great chapter on the Pairs	10	—
5) *Cūḷayamakavagga*, Lesser chapter on the Pairs	10	—
6) *Gahapativagga*, chapter on householders	10	—
7) *Bhikkhuvagga*, chapter on Monks,	10	—
8) *Paribbājakavagga*, chapter on wanderers,	10	—
9) *Rājavagga*, chapter on kings,	10	—
10) *Brāhmaṇavagga*, chapter on brāhmaṇas,	10	—
11) *Devadahavagga*, chapter on Devadaha,	10	—
12) *Anupadavagga*, chapter on the Non-interruption	10	—
13) *Suññatavagga*, chapter on emptiness	10	—
14) *Vibhaṅgavagga*, chapter on analysis,	10	—
15) *Saḷāyatanavagga*, chapter on 6 sense-spheres	12	—

Thus the 152 Pāli suttas are classified into 15 chapters of 10 suttas each, except the last one which contains 12 suttas, while the 222 Chinese sūtras are classified into 18 chapters. But the number of sūtras contained in the chapters is not homogeneous. 4 chapters in the Chinese version bear almost the same name with 5 chapters in the Pāli version. *C* 6 = *P* 9 ; *C* 12 = *P* 10 ; *C* 13 = *P* 14 ; *C* 15 = *P* 4 & *P* 5 ; The remaining chapters of the 2 versions have nothing in common and we can safely say that the compilers of the 2 versions had a free hand in classifying the sūtras or suttas as they thought fit, without following any previous classification done by their predecessors. We notice also that the Pāli ignores the classification according to fasciculi and according to days of recital. Probably the classification into fasciculi is a distinctive feature of Chinese books, and the Chinese compilers or editors introduced it for convenience's sake. As to the division according to days of recital, it appears to be an old classification for helping the monks in their daily recital, as the whole volume could not be recited in one day. Such a classification which is ignored in the PMN, is found also in Mahāvagga, with its Bhāṇavāra division.

Chapter II. — NIDĀNA

A. — TITLES : (1)

A comparative study of the titles of the 98 Pāli and its Chinese corresponding sūtras shows that there are 45 sūtras which have similar titles, 15 sūtras which have almost similar titles and 38 sūtras, the titles of which are totally different.

1. — 45 *sūtras of similar titles :*

C.S. N° 5, N° 8, N° 9, N° 10, N° 11, N° 13, N° 14, N° 19, N° 23, N° 24, N° 28, N° 29, N° 32, N° 33, N° 35, N° 36, N° 37, N° 38, N° 39, N° 43, N° 46, N° 49, N° 51, N° 52, N° 54, N° 56, N° 57, N° 58, N° 60, N° 62, N° 68, N° 69, N° 71, N° 72, N° 74, N° 76, N° 77, N° 78, N° 79, N° 80, N° 81, N° 84, N° 85, N° 90, N° 91.

2. — 15 *sūtras of nearly similar titles :*

C.S. N° 2, N° 3, N° 4, N° 15, N° 20, N° 25, N° 26, N° 40, N° 55, N° 61, N° 63, N° 67, N° 86, N° 94, N° 95.

3. — 38 *sūtras of totally different titles but of almost the same contents :*

38 sūtras have titles which are totally different in the 2 Chinese and Pāli versions. Sometimes, the Chinese selects the name of the principal personage in the sūtra for ther title, while the Pāli prefers the name of the doctrine expounded. Ex. in *C. S. N°* 7 : C N° 91, Chou-na-wên-chien-ching = P N° 8, Sallekhasutta. In *C.S. N°* 22 : C N° 204, Lo-mo-ching = P N° 26, Ariyapariyesanasutta. Sometimes the Pāli opts for the simile while the Chinese maintains its preference for the name of personage. Ex. in *C.S. N°* 6 : C. N° 93, Shui-ching-fan-chih-ching = P N° 7, Vatthūpamasutta. In *C. S. N°* 18, C N° 193, Mou-li-p'o-chün-na-ching = P N° 21, Kakacūpamasutta. Sometimes we witness the reverse phenomenon with the Pāli choice for the personage and the Chinese choice for the simile or for the doctrine. Ex. in *C. S. N°* 41 : C N° 221, Chien-yü-ching = P N° 63, Cūḷamāluṅkyasutta. In *C. S. N°* 42 : C N° 205, Wu-hsia-fên-

(1) Appendix N° 5.

chieh-ching = P N° 64, Mahāmāluṅkyasutta. In *C.S. N°* 82 : C N° 79, Yu-shêng-t'ien-ching = P N° 127, Anuruddhasutta. But the preference of the personage as the title for the sūtras is found by far much stronger in the Sanskrit compilation than in the Pāli. Thus in *C.S. N°* 6, N° 7, N° 12, N° 18, N° 21, N° 22, N° 27, N° 30, N° 31, N° 44, N° 45, N° 52, N° 65, N° 66, N° 83, and N° 96, sixteen sūtras in all, the Chinese opts for the personage while the Pāli prefers the simile or the doctrine for titles. But the reverse phenomenon is seen only in 7 cases, *C.S. N°* 41, N° 42, N° 64, N° 82, N° 87, N° 88 and N° 97.

We observe that in the Pāli version, when 2 suttas of varying length bear the same title, the term *Cūḷa* and *Mahā* are appended to the titles to distinguish the 2 suttas, but the Chinese omits this distinction and uses the same title for both the sutras. Ex. in *C.S. N°* 10 & N° 11 : C N° 99 & 100, K'u-yin-ching = P N° 13, Mahādukkhakkhandhasutta and P N° 14, Cūḷadukkhakkhandhasutta. In *C.S. N°* 25 & 26 : C N° 185 & N° 184, Niu-chioh-so-lo-lin-ching = P N° 31, Cūlagosiṅgasutta and P N° 32, Mahāgosiṅgasutta. The same can be said of *C.S.* N° 28 & N° 29, of N° 31 & N° 32, of N° 49 & N° 51 except the *C.S. N°* 76 *and* N° 77, in which the Chinese has made a distinction between the 2 sūtras by adding the term *Hsiao* meaning lesser and *Ta* meaning greater. There exists a case in which the Chinese has the same title for 2 sūtras while the Pāli possesses two different titles. Thus in *C. S. N°* 64 : C N° 152, Ying-wu-ching = P N° 99, Subhasutta ; in *C. S. N°* 89 : C N° 170, Ying-wu-ching = P N° 135, Cūḷakammavibhaṅgasutta.

This general review shows that there are 45 sūtras with similar titles and 15 sūtras of nearly similar titles out of 98 sūtras. This explains that at least these 45 sūtras were very well known at the time of their compilation, either owing to the importance of these sūtras or to the interest and vivid memory of the compilers. This general stock of sūtras offered a common source from which the compilers drew their materials and this explains the high percentage of similarities between the two versions, as far as the titles are concerned.

B. — LOCATION OF SŪTRAS :

Among the 98 sūtras which are taken up for comparative study, there are 62 Chinese and Pāli sūtras, the locations of which are the same, 15 sūtras, the locations of which are almost the same, and 21 sūtras which have different locations altogether.

1. — *Sūtras with same location :*

a) At *Shê-wei* (Sāvatthi), *Shêng-lin* (Jetavana), *Kei-ku-tu's park* (Anāthapiṇḍikārāma) : 37 sūtras : *C. S. N°* 5, N° 10, N° 13, N° 14, N° 16, N° 17, N° 18, N° 19, N° 23, N° 24, N° 27, N° 32, N° 33, N° 35,

N° 41, N° 42, N° 43, N° 50, N° 52, N° 56, N° 57, N° 61, N° 70, N° 71, N° 72, N° 75, N° 78, N° 82, N° 84, N° 85, N° 86, N° 88, N° 89, N° 91, N° 92, N° 97, N° 98.

b) At *Wang-shê town* (Rājagaha), *Bamboo-grove* (Veluvana), *Chia-lan-to park* (Kalandakanivāpa) : 7 sūtras : *C. S.* N° 46, N° 51, N° 63, N° 79, N° 80, N° 81, N° 90.

c) Among the *Chü-lou-shou* (Kurus), at *Chien-mô-sê-t'an* (Kammāsadamma) : 3 sūtras : *C. S.* N° 8, N° 48, N° 67.

d) Among the *Shih-chi-shou* (Sakkas), at *Chia-wei-lo-wei* (Kapilavatthu), in *Ni-chü-lei grove* (Nigrodha) : 3 sūtras : *C. S.* N° 11, N° 77, N° 96.

e) At *Shê-wei* (Sāvatthi) *Lu-tzu-mu's palace* (Migāramātu's palace), : 2 sūtras : *C. S.* N° 68, N° 76.

f) In *Mo-chieh-t'o* (Magadha), at *Wang-shê town* (Rājagaha), one sūtra : *C. S.* N° 94.

g) At *Shê-wei* (Sāvatthi), *An-t'o-lin* (Andhavana) : one sūtra : *C.S.* N° 20.

h) Among the *P'o-ch'i-shou* (Bhagga), at *T'o mountain* (Suṃsumāragiri), in *Fearful forest* (Bhesakalāvana), *Deer-park* : one sūtra : *C. S.* N° 36.

i) At *Na-nan-t'o* (Nālandā), in *P'o-p o-li-nai forest* (Pāvārikambavana) : one sūtra : *C. S.* N° 39.

j) At *Chü-shê-mi* (Kosambī), in *Ch'ü-shih-lo park* (Ghositārāma) : one sūtra : *C. S.* N° 83.

k) Among the *Shih-chi-shou* (Sakkas), at *T'ien-i* (Devadaha), one sūtra : *C. S.* N° 65.

l) Among the *Shih-chi-shou* (Sakkas), at *Mi-lou-li* (Medaḷumpa) : one sūtra : *C. S.* N° 58.

m) *Among the Chü-so-lo* (Kosala) : one sūtra : C.S. N° 53.

n) At *Na-mo-t'i-shou* (Nādikā), in *Chien-ch'i monastery* (Giñjakāvasatha) : one sūtra : C.S. N° 25.

o) In *Pei-t'o-t'i* (Videha) : one sūtra : C.S. N° 60.

2. — *Sūtras with almost similar locations :*

The 2 versions are almost the same, simply, there is an addition or omission or alteration of a particular place. 15 such sūtras are found :

a) *C.S. N°* 15 : C : Among the Shih-chi-shou, at Chia-wei-lo-wei ; after his begging alms and his meal, the Buddha came to a Bamboo-grove, in a Sakyan monastery, entered a Great forest, and sat down at the root of a tree. P : the Pāli adds Nigrodha, omits Bamboo grove, in a Sakyan monastery.

b) *C.S.* *N*° 22 : C : At Shê-wei, at Lu-tzu-mu's palace. P : First the Buddha was staying at Sāvatthi, Jetavana, Anāthapiṇḍikārāma. Then he went to Pubbārāma, Migāramātu's palace for a day's rest.

c) *C.S.* *N*° 54 : C : Among the Chü-lou-shou, at Yü-lu-cha village, in North village of T'i-shê-ho = P : Among the Kurus, at Thullakoṭṭhita.

d) *C.S.* *N*° 37 : C : At Pei-shê-li (Vesāli), on the bank of the Monkey-river, at the upper terrace of a mansion = P : At Vesāli, in Beluvagāmaka.

e) *C.S.* *N*° 55 : C : The Buddha was travelling in Pei-t'o-ti, came to Mi-sa-lo and stayed in Ta-t'ien forest = P : At Mithilā, in Makhādevambavana.

f) *C.S.* *N*° 26 : C : Among the P'o-ch'i-shou, at Niu-chioh-so-lo forest. = P : At Gosiṅgasālavanadāya.

g) *C.S.* *N*° 28 *and* N° 29 : C : Among the Ying-ch'i, at Ma-i market-town, in Ma-lin monastery = P : Among the Aṅgas at Assapura.

h) *C.S.* *N*° 40 : C : The Buddha was staying at Wang-shê, in the Bamboo-grove, at Chia-lan-to park. He came to see Ven. Lo-yün who was staying at Wang-shê, in the Hot-spring forest. P : Almost the same. But it mentions that elder Rāhula was staying not in the Hot-spring forest, but at Ambalaṭṭhikā.

i) *C.S.* *N*° 49 : C : The Buddha was staying at Wang-shê town, in the Bamboo grove, at Chia-lan-to park. Then he came to the Peacock forest. P : The same. It adds : At Paribbājakārāma.

j) *C.S.* *N*° 69 : C : After the Buddha's Parinibbāna, Ven. A-nan was staying at Wang-shê town = P : The same. It adds : Veluvana, Kalandakanivāpa.

k) *C.S.* *N*° 44 : C : Among the Ying-chia, at A-ho-na, in Chien-jo monastery = P : Almost the same. It omits Chien-jo.

l) *C.S.* *N*° 47 : C : At Chia-shih, Chia-lo-lai, the North village in T'i-shê-ho forest = P : Kāsi, Kīṭāgiri and Kāsi market-town.

m) *C.S.* *N*° 59 : C : At Yü-t'ou-sui-jo, in the forest of P'u-chi-tz'u = P : Ujuññā, Kaṇṇakatthala, in the Deer-park.

n) *C.S.* *N*° 66 : C : Among the P'o-ch'i, at Shê-mi village = P : Among the Sakkas, at Sāmagāma.

3. — 21 *sūtras with different locations :*

21 sūtras are with different locations. They are : C.S. N° 1, N° 2, N° 3, N° 4, N° 6, N° 7, N° 9, N° 12, N° 21, N° 30, N° 31, N° 34, N° 38, N° 45, N° 62, N° 64, N° 73, N° 74, N° 87, N° 93, N° 95.

Among these 21 sūtras which have different locations, we observe that the Pāli has a strong preference for Sāvatthi, Jetavana, Anāthapiṇḍikārāma. Out of 21 sūtras, 14 Pāli suttas opt for this place such as Pāli suttas N° 2, N° 3, N° 5, N° 7, N° 8, N° 11, N° 25, N° 43, N° 47, N° 96, N° 99, N° 117, N° 119, N° 139, while the Chinese mentions only 3 sūtras C N° 106, N° 210 and N° 141. On the contrary, we notice that the Chinese has a preference for Wang-shê town, Bamboo-grove, Chia-lan-to park. Thus 6 Chinese sūtras mention these places : C N° 89, N° 178, N° 211, N° 150, N° 152, N° 165, while only one Pāli sutta refers to these places P N° 44. The Chinese has also a preference for Chu-lou-shou, Chien-mo-se-t'an as found in C N° 10, N° 103, N° 186, N° 189.

Thus among the 98 sūtras which are taken up for comparative study, there are only 21 sūtras which are with different locations, while there are as many as 62 sūtras with the same locations, and 15 sūtras with almost similar locations. This shows that there is nearly 80 % agreement between the 2 versions and this proves that both versions drew their contents from almost the same source, perhaps the old lost Canon, and that at the time of compilation of these sūtras, Sanskrit and Pāli, the oral traditions handed down were still fresh in the memory of the compilers. But we should also attempt to explain the divergences of the 21 sūtras with different locations. First there is the possibility that the same discourse was delivered by the Buddha in different places. During the 45 years of the Buddha's preaching the dharma, there was absolute certainty that the same discourse was repeated in many places. And this explains the divergence in the location of certain sūtras. Thus in *C. S.* N° 95, the Chinese sūtra N° 31 refers to Chü-lou-shou, Chien-mo-sê-t'an as location of the sūtra, while the Pāli sutta N° 141 refers to Dārāṇasī, Isipatana, Migadāya as place of location. Again we observe that the Pāli compilers had a preference for Sāvatthi, Jetavana, Anāthapiṇḍikārāma, while those of the Chinese version seemed to favour Wang-shê town and Chü-lou-shou, at Chien-mo-sê-t'an. So for these sūtras, the recollection of which was rather dimmed in the mind of the compilers, they would prefer the places which were either the stronghold of their own sect, or their own native places. Another reason to explain the difference in the locations of certain sūtras may be attributed to the compilers' mistakes. Thus we find in *C. S. N°* 37, the Chinese refers to North of T'i-shê-ho as belonging to Chü-so-lo, but in C. S. N° 54, North of T'i-shê-ho was referred to as belonging to the Chü-lou-shou. In many sūtras, *C. S. N°* 2, *N°* 9, N° 34, etc., Chien-mo-sê-t'an was mentioned as belonging to the Chü-lou-shou, but in C. S. N° 93, this place is referred to as belonging to P'o-ch'i-shou. In *C. S. N°* 40, the Chinese mentions that Ven. Lo-yun was staying in the Hot-spring forest, but the Pāli mentions Ambalaṭṭhikā instead. So one of the compilers must have been at fault. In *C. S. N°* 66, the Chinese refers to Shê-mi as belonging to the P'o-chi, but the Pāli refers to this Sāmagāma as belonging to the Kurus. Among the sūtras of different locations, 2 sūtras deserve attention. In *C. S. N°* 6, the Chinese version mentions that the discourse took place, when the Buddha obtained enlightenment recently and the place mentioned is Yü-pei-lo, on the bank of Ni-lien-jan, under A-yeh-ho-lo-ni-chü-lei tree. According to the traditions, the Buddha went to Bārāṇasī to set in motion the dharma and to convert the 5 monks as his first disciples. Then he returned to Uruvelā to convert the 3 Kassapa brothers. So if this discourse took place prior to the Buddha's departure for Bārāṇasī, it would be difficult to explain the presence of the monks in the sūtra. So this anomaly may be due either to the compiler's mistake or to the differences among various schools of Buddhism as to the whereabouts of the Buddha immediately after his enlightenment. In *C.S. N*° 95, the Pāli refers to Bārāṇasī, Isipatana, Migadāya as the place where the discourse P N° 141, Saccavibhaṅgasutta took place. In this discourse, Ven. Sāriputta explained the 4 noble Truths in a way similar to the Dhammacakkapavattanasutta; so the Pāli compilers put it in the same place, that is at Bārāṇasī, Isipatana, Migadāya. The Chinese preference for Chien-mo-sê-t'an, among the Chü-lou-shou is significant here. One curious feature is to be noted in *C.S. N*° 31. The Chinese sūtra refers to Pi-shê-ch'ü, the famous lady-devotee as asking dharma-question of bhikṣuṇī Fa-lo, so the location of the sūtra is at Shê-wei, the place of residence of Pi-shê-ch'ü. But the Pāli speaks of Visākha as former husband of Dhammadinnā who had gone forth and was residing at Rājagaha. So the Pāli localises the sutta at Rājagaha. But the purport of the sūtra is almost the same in both versions. This anomaly shows us that the location of the sūtras is much left to the discretion of the compilers.

Chapter III. — ROLES PLAYED BY DIVERSE PERSONAGES IN THE SŪTRAS. WAYS OF PREACHING THE DHARMA

Now we shall study the 98 sūtras taken up for comparative study, with reference to the roles played by diverse personages in these discourses, and also to the ways of preaching the Dharma. Here we confine our study only to the difference in attitude, in deportment of diverse personages in the sūtras, leaving the doctrine itself which is dealt with extensively in the next chapters.

The discourses can be classified into 8 ways of preaching the dharma : 1) The Buddha preached the dharma without any apparent reason ; 2) The Buddha preached the dharma to correct some wrong views entertained by his disciples or by others ; 3) The Buddha preached the dharma in brief and one of his disciples elaborated it ; 4) The Buddha preached the dharma to meet the challenge of non-buddhist sects ; 5) The Buddha preached the dharma to his monk-disciples ; 6) The Buddha preached the dharma to his lay-disciples or other people ; 7) The Buddha's disciples met together and discussed about the dharma ; 8) One of the Buddha's disciples preached the entire sermon.

1. — *The Buddha preached the dharma without any apparent reason :*

Sometimes the Buddha just called the monks and preached the dharma without giving any apparent reason and without any special occasion. The listeners here are the monks in general, without their names mentioned. Among the 98 sūtras taken up for comparative study, the following 22 can be classified under this category : *C.S. N°* 1, N° 2, N° 8, N° 9, N° 13, N° 14, N° 16, N° 17, N° 21, N° 28, N° 29, N° 32, N° 33, N° 34, N° 70, N° 71, N° 73, N° 75, N° 84, N° 85, N° 91, N° 93.

2. — *The Buddha preached the dharma to correct some wrong views held by some of his disciples or by others :*

Sometimes some of the Buddha's disciples held a wrong view. Their fellow-monks tried to correct them but without success. Then the matter was brought before the Buddha who summoned the culprits, admonished them and pointed out their error. The C.S. N° 19, N° 27, N° 35 and N° 47 fall under this category.

In *C.S. N°* 27, the Chinese text mentions the Buddha's asking the other monks' opinion first, then scolded the monk Ch'a-ti and the latter became repentant. In the Pāli, the monk Sāti's repentance was placed first, then came the answer of other monks to the Buddha's questions. The Chinese adds at the end, the shaking of 30,000 worlds, 3 times, when the Buddha finished his sermon.

In *C.S. N*° 35, a certain brahmā of the brahma-world held the wrong view that the brahma-world was permanent. The Pāli adds the name of this brahmā as Baka. In the Chinese, the Buddha vanished from Shê-wei, Shêng-lin, Kei-ku-tu's park and came to the brahma-world ; in the Pāli, the Blessed One vanished from Subhagavana at Ukkaṭṭhā and appeared in the Brahma-world. The Chinese mentions that when the Buddha recognised Māra, the Evil One, the latter became dejected and vanished from that place, but the Pāli records that the Buddha pointed out to Māra that Brahmā and his followers might be within the grasp of Māra, but not the Buddha. The challenge in psychic powers between the Buddha and Brahmā is not the same. In the Chinese, Brahmā with all his psychic powers tried to hide himself here and there, but the W.H. One saw him through, so he could not hide himself and came back to the Brahma-world again. In the Pāli, Baka the Brahmā could not vanish away in the Buddha's presence. In the Chinese, the Buddha emitted rays of extremely wonderful radiance shining all the Brahma-worlds and hid himself in it, so that the Brahmas and their followers could only hear his voice but could not see his form. In the Pāli, when the Buddha vanished away, he did so in such a way that Brahmā, Brahmaparisā, Brahmapārisajja could not see him but only heard his voice reciting the gāthā :

« Subject to becoming, I seek the non-becoming »

« Having seen the danger of becoming ».

« I do not enjoy becoming and do not grasp delight ».

and Brahmā, Brahmaparisā and Brahmapārisajja stood in awe and wonder.

3. — *The Buddha preached the dharma in brief and one of his disciples elaborated it :*

Elder Shê-li-tzu (Sāriputta) elaborated the Buddha's speech in C.S. N° 3, N° 95 ; and elder Chia-chan-yen (Mahākaccāna) in C.S. N° 15, N° 87 and N° 92.

a) *Elaborated by Elder Shê-li-tzu :*

In *C.S. N*° 3, the Chinese mentions the presence of many respected and great disciples living near the Buddha's thatched hut, such as Ven. Shê-li-tzu, Ta-mu-chien-lien, Ta-chia-yeh, Ta-chia-chan-yen, A-na-lü-t'o, Li-yüeh, A-nan etc..., but the Pāli omits it. In the Chinese version, the W.H. One asked Ven. Shê-li-tzu to elaborate his speech as the Buddha had a backache and wanted a little rest. Then he folded up into four his Yu-to-lo-sêng (Uttarāsaṅga), spread over the bed, rolled his Sêng-chia-li (Saṅghāṭi), to make it a pillow and lay down on his right side, with one leg resting upon the other, meditating on the light-sign, with right mindfulness, right understanding and constantly thinking of wanting to get up. (1) But the Pāli simply says that the Well-Farer (Sugata) got up from his seat and entered the monastery. In the Chinese, elder Shê-li-tzu asked the monks to interpret the Buddha's brief speech and 2 monks attempted a reply which was not satisfactory. In the Pāli, there is omission of the Buddha's brief speech and the monks' attempt to reply, although elder Sāriputta did ask the same question. At the end of Elder Shê-li-tzu's explanation, the W.H. One, his ache being abated and feeling at ease, rose from his sleeping position, sat cross-legged and praised elder Shê-li-tzu. (1) These details are missing in the Pāli.

In *C.S. N°* 95, the Chinese mentions elder Shê-li-tzu reciting a verse to sum up his explanation, while the Pāli omits the stanza but repeats again the proclamation of the Dhammacakkapavattana at Bārāṇasī, Isipatana, Migadāya at the beginning of the sutta.

b) *Elaborated by elder Ta-chia-chan-yen :*

In *C.S. N°* 15, the Buddha met a stick-in-hand Sakya who asked him about the aim of his teachings. The Buddha's answer did not satisfy him and the Sakyan, according to the Chinese, did not approve, did not reject, raised his head and went away. In the Pāli, it omits : « dit not approve, did not reject», but adds : « lolling his tongue, with his brow lined up with 3 wrinkles and leaning on the stick. » In the Chinese, the Buddha quoted the simile of the honey-ball, while the Pāli mentions elder Ānanda instead. The Pāli omits the attitude of elder A-nan, standing behind the Buddha with a whisk of hair. It omits also a short exhortation to the monks by the Buddha at the end of the discourse.

In *C.S. N°* 87, Ven. San-mi-t'i (P : Samiddhi) came to the Hot-Spring to take bath. When the bath was over, he was approached by a deity of radiant beauty, of wonderful feature, who paid homage to him and asked the monk if he knew the gāthā of Pa-ti-lo-ti (P : Bhaddekaratta). To the monk's negative reply, the deity said that the W.H. One knew the Gāthā and he advised the monk to approach the W.H. One and have the gāthā explained. Then he paid homage to the monk, went round him 3 times and disappeared. The Pāli adds that the deity illuminated the whole of the Tapodā with his radiant beauty. It omits the monk's enquiry as to who knew the gāthā and the deity's advice to approach the Blessed One. The Pāli mentions simply that the deity advised the monk to learn that gāthā, to master it and to bear it in mind. Then he disappeared without paying homage to the monk and going round him 3 times. The Chinese gives the name of the deity as Chêng-tien, an army-officer of the heaven of Thirty-three, while the Pāli omits it.

---

(1) This pattern is found in P N° 53, Sekhasutta, where Ananda gave the exposition.

4. — *The Buddha preached the dharma to meet the challenge of non-buddhist sects :*

In *C. S. N° 39 and N°* 65, the Buddha refuted the Jainas' views ; in *C.S.* N° 6, N° 61, N° 62 and N° 64, the brāhmaṇas' doctrine and practice and in *C. S.* N° 10, N° 48, N° 50, N° 51 and N° 52, he met the challenge of the paribbājakas.

a) *Against the Jainas :*

In *C. S. N°* 39, Ch'ang-k'u-hsing (Dīghatapassī) had a conversation with the Buddha, in which he expounded Ch'in-tzu's doctrine on punishment and the predominant part played by bodily punishment in any wrong action. But the Buddha expounded his doctrine of karma and the predominant part played by mental action in any wrong doing. Ch'ang-k'u-hsing reported this conversation to Ch'in-tzu in Yu-p'o-li's presence. While in the Pāli, Upāli repeated Nātaputta's praise to extol Dīghatapassī and expressed his readiness to go and challenge the Buddha, the Chinese version adds that Yu-p'o-li was along with 500 householders in the assembly. He joined his hands towards Ch'in-tzu and asked Ch'ang-k'u-hsing if really he had thrice pinned down recluse Ch'ü-t'an in such a matter and to Ch'ang-k'u-hsing's positive reply, he said that he also could pin down recluse Ch'ü-t'an in such a matter and drag him down. Then Yu-p'o-li, with Ch'in-tzu's approval but with Ch'ang-k'u-hsing's fear and disapproval came to challenge the Buddha who with 4 parables succeeded in converting Yu-p'o-li to his own view. In the 4th parable, when the Buddha asked who had made these troublefree places become troublefree places, Yu-p'o-li, according to the Chinese, kept silent for a while and being urged by the Buddha, he replied that it was not that he wanted to keep silent, but he was thinking of something, he was thinking that Ni-chien was foolish and ignorant and had cheated him for a long time. In the Pāli version, Upāli replied at once that these forests Kaṇḍaka, Kāliṅga, Mejjha and Mātaṅga became forests, due to the angry thoughts of the seers of those forests. At the end of the discourse, the Chinese adds that Yu-p'o-li attained the stainless and dustless dharma-eye and Ch'in-tzu vomitted hot blood, came to Po-ho (Pāvā) and died there due to sickness. The Pāli omits Nātaputta's death and mentions only that he vomitted hot blood.

b) *Against the Brāhmaṇas' practices and views :*

In *C. S. N°* 6, the Buddha spoke against the brāhmaṇas' practice of taking bath in the supposed holy water to wash away sins. The Chinese mentions brāhmaṇa Shui-ching at the very beginning of the sūtra, while the Pāli speaks of the presence of brāhmaṇa Sundarikabhāradvāja only at the end of the discourse. In the Chinese, the brāhmaṇa declared his taking refuge in the Triple Gem and his asking the Buddha to accept him as a disciple.

But in the Pāli version, Sundarika Bhāradvāja asked the Buddha to allow him to adopt the monk's life and receive high ordination. When all his requests were granted, he exerted himself strenuously in the spiritual training and at the end attained arahantship.

In *C. S. N°* 61, the Chinese mentions that a great number of brāhmaṇas at Chü-sa-lo (Kosala) assembled in a school-hall and were discussing recluse Ch'ü-t'an's proclamation of the purity of the 4 castes whereas they claimed that the brāhmaṇa caste was the highest, the purest. They opted for young A-shê-ho-lo-yen-to to go and challenge the Buddha. But the Pāli mentions that 500 brāhmaṇas of various districts came to Sāvatthi for some business and they referred only to recluse Gotama's proclamation about the purity of the 4 castes. It adds that Assalāyana was 16 years old and with head shaven. In the Chinese, A-shê-ho accepted by remaining silent, while in the Pāli, Assalāyana said that truly recluse Gotama spoke in accordance with dhamma and it was difficult to argue with those who spoke in accordance with dhamma and that he was unable to argue with recluse Gotama. But all the same, he would go as requested. After the Buddha's arguments, according to the Chinese, A-shê-ho wanted to worship the Buddha but the assembly shouted loudly their marvel and wonder. The Buddha knew their mind and asked A-shê-ho to resume his seat, saying that A-shê-ho's heart being pleased was enough. Then the Buddha preached the dharma to gladden, arouse and please him. The Pāli is not the same. It mentions simply that Assalāyana exclaimed that it was marvellous, it was wonderful, then he asked the Buddha to accept him as a disciple from now on as long as life lasted.

In *C. S. N°* 64, the Pāli adds a meeting between Subha and brāhmaṇa Jāṇussoṇī who enquired of Subha where he came from and about the wisdom of recluse Gotama. Subha's reply and praises made him get down from the chariot drawn by all white mares, wear his robe showing one shoulder, join his hands towards the Blessed One and say that it was a great gain, it was well-gotten to king Pasenadi of Kosala to have the Tathāgata living in his kingdom. The Chinese omits this meeting.

c) *Against the members of different sect :*

In *C. S. N.* 10, according to the Chinese, the monks having finished their midday-meal assembled and sat in the preaching-hall for some work. And there, a great number of followers of different sects came to challenge them. In the Pāli version, the monks, having entered Sāvatthi for alms, found the time early and came to the abode of the paribbājakas and the conversation took place.

In *C. S. N°* 48, Hsü-hsien-t'i (Paribbājaka Māgandiya) saw the grass-seat serving as couch to the Buddha in brāhmaṇa P'o-lo-p'o's house (Bhāradvājagotta), was greatly displeased and accused the Buddha as being a destroyer of good things (Huai-pai-ti 壞敗地) (1). P'o-lo-p'o warned Hsü-hsien-t'o not to abuse the Buddha, but Hsü-hsien-ti said that he would say the same in front of recluse Ch'ü-t'an. In the Chinese, the Buddha was at that time, sitting in meditation in a certain forest ; with his divine ear, he heard what had taken place, came back to P'o-lo-p'o's house, spread his sitting mat and sat cross-legged. When P'o-lo-p'o came to greet him, the Buddha asked if really the brāhmaṇa had a conversation with Hsü-hsien-t'i about his grass-seat. P'o-lo-po said that he wanted to inform him but the Buddha knew it beforehand. At that moment, Hsü-hsien-t'i came and the conversation took place. The Pāli omits all the details about the Buddha carrying and spreading the sitting mat and sitting beautiful and shining like the moon and the stars. It adds that Bhāradvājagotta became agitated with hair raising on his head when he heard the Buddha anticipate his thoughts. In the Chinese version, after the Buddha's explanation, Hsü-hsien-t'i attained the spotless and stainless dharma-eye. Then he asked the Buddha to allow him to go forth to learn the dharma and to ordain him as a monk. Then the Buddha ordained him saying : « Well come, be a monk and live the brahma-life ». Having gone forth and become a monk, Hsü-hsien-t'i attained arahantship. The Pāli omits Māgandiya obtaining the dhamma-eye. It adds Māgandiya's exclamation of wonder in the usual way and his declaring to take refuge in the Triple Gem. Here also Māgandiya asked the Buddha to ordain him as a monk. The Buddha said that the members of different sect would need 4 months' probation but the Buddha knew differences between individuals and he ordained Māgandiya. The Pāli mentions also that Māgandiya attained arahantship but with more details and concluded that elder Māgandiya became one of the arahants.

In *C. S. N°* 52, Pei-mo-na-hsiu (Vekhanassa) spoke to the Buddha about the most beautiful colour « vaṇṇa ». (The Pāli vord (vaṇṇa) is used here in a double sense : 1) colour and 2) social class. This double sense obviously is not given by the Chinese word) and the Buddha pointed out the hollowness of such an assertion. The Chinese adds a passage in which Pei-mo-na-hsiu adopted a repenting attitude, bending his head in shame and keeping silent. When Pei-mo-na-hsiu praised the Buddha's explanations as being marvellous, the Buddha stopped him saying that Pei-mo-na-hsiu being of different views was unable to understand his preaching. This made Pei-mo-na-hsiu angry and he abused the Buddha. The Pāli is almost the same, but it omits the Buddha asking him to stop. Then the Buddha with the help of 3 parables (only one in Pāli) illustrated his teachings and succeeded in converting Pei-mo-na-hsiu. Here the Chinese mentions that Pei-mo-na-hsiu obtained the stainless dharma-eye and begged the Buddha to ordain him. And after his ordination, he strove hard and attained arahantship. In the Pāli version, Vekhanassa declared the Buddha's speech as being marvellous in the usual way, took refuge in the Triple Gem and begged the Buddha to accept him as a lay-disciple.

---

(1) This interpretation exactly follow that of the Pali commentators. But the original Pali word Bhunahu corresponds to the Sanskrit word Bhruna-ha, the foetus-killer which is the correct interpretation of this term.

5. — *The Buddha preached the dharma to his disciples :*

28 C. S. fall into this category : a) to a certain monk, C. S. N° 5 ; b) to a number of monks, N° 22, N° 74 ; c) to Ven. Lo yun (Rāhula), N° 40 ; d) to Man-tung-tzu (Māluṅkyaputta), N° 41 ; N° 42 ; e) to A-na-lü-t'o, Nan-t'i, Chin-p'i-lo (Anuruddha, Nandiya, Kimbila), N° 25, N° 45, N° 83 ; f) to Ma-ha-nan (Mahānāma), N° 11 ; g) to Mou-li-p'o-ch'ün-na (Moliyaphagguṇa), N° 18 ; h) to P'o-t'o-ho-li (Bhaddāli), N° 43 ; i) to Wu-t'o-i Udāyī), N° 44 : j) to A-nan, N° 53, N° 55, N° 67, N° 72, N° 76, N° 78, N° 98 ; k) to A-nan and novice Chou-na (Cunda), N° 66; l) to A-nan and many monks, N° 77 ; m) to Lai-cha-ho-lo (Raṭṭhapāla), N° 54 ; n) to Fou-mi (Bhūmija), N° 81 ; o) to Lü-i-ch'iang-ch'i (Lomasakaṅgiya), N° 88 ; p) to San-mi-t'i (Samiddhi), N° 90 ; q) to Fu-chia-lo-so-li (Pukkusāti), N° 94 ; r) to Ta-chou-na (Mahācunda), N° 7 ; s) to novice A-i-na-ho-t'i (Aciravata), N° 80.

a) *To a certain monk :*

In *C. S. N°* 5, a certain monk, while sitting in a secluded place thought of the Buddha's great benefit to him, got up from his meditation-seat and went to the Buddha's place. The W.H. One, having seen that monk, on account of him, preached the dharma to the monks. The Pāli omits this particular circumstance. He preached the dhamma without any preamble.

b) *To a certain number of monks :*

In *C. S. N°* 22, the Buddha was staying at Lu-tzu-mu's palace. Towards evening, he rose from his meditation-seat, came down from the upper palace and asked elder A-nan to go to take bath at A-i-lo-p'o-t'i river. Then elder A-nan took a key, went to see the monks in their huts and asked them to go to brāhmaṇa Lo-mo's house. Then the Buddha and Elder A-nan went to the river to take bath. Having finished bathing, the Buddha came out of the river, wiped dry the body and donned his robe. The Pāli starts with the Buddha staying at Sāvatthi, Jetavana, at Anāthapiṇḍikārāma. Then the Buddha entered Sāvatthi for alms. Many monks came to elder Ānanda telling him that they wanted to hear a discourse from the Buddha face to face, as for a long time, they had no such occasion. Elder Ānanda then asked them to go to brāhmṇa Rammaka's house. When the Buddha came back from his begging round and finished his meal, he with elder Ānanda went to Pubbārāma at Migāramātu's palace for the day-rest. In the evening, the Buddha rose from his seclusion and with elder Ānanda went to Pubbakoṭṭhaka to bathe his limbs. After the bath, the Buddha came out of the water, stood with a single cīvara, drying his limbs. Then at Ven. A-nan's request, the Buddha went to Lo-mo's house where the discourse took place.

c) *To Ven. Lo-yün* (Rāhula) :

In *C. S. N*° 40, according to the Chinese, the Buddha, when night was over, early in the morning, entered Wang-shê town for alms. When he finished his meal, he came to the Hot-spring forest where elder Lo-yün was. Elder Lo-yün saw the Buddha coming from afar, went out to welcome him, took his robe and bowl, spread the seat and fetched water to wash feet. The Buddha having washed his feet, sat on Lo-yün's seat. According to the Pāli, the Buddha in the evening, rose from his seclusion, came to Ambalaṭṭhikā where elder Rāhula was. Elder Rāhula seeing the Buddha coming from afar, prepared seat and water for washing feet, but did not come out to meet him and take his robe and begging bowl. The Buddha sat on the prepared seat and washed his feet. To admonish elder Lo-yün, the Buddha showed the little quantity of water in the basin, then he threw it away, overturned the basin and upturned it and each time, he admonished the elder. The Pāli adds a 5th gesture of the Buddha who pointing out the emptiness of the upturned basin declared that void and empty was the recluseship of one who knowingly told a lie without shame.

d) *To Ven. Man-tung-tzu (Māluṅkyaputta) : C. S. N° 41, N° 42 :*

In *C. S. N°* 42, the Buddha upbraided Ven. Man-tung-tzu for his wrong understanding of the 5 fetters binding one to a lower existence and Man-tung-tzu adopted a repentant attitude. Then elder A-nan who was standing behind the Buddha and fanning him with a fan, requested the Buddha to explain the 5 fetters and the Buddha acquiesced to elder A-nan's request. In the Pāli, the Buddha did not openly upbraid elder Māluṅkyaputta. It omits also Māluṅkyaputta's repentant attitude, Ven. A-nan standing behind the Buddha and fanning him with a fan.

e) *To Ven. A-na-lü-t'o, Nan-t'i and Chin-p'i-lo : (Anuruddha, Nandiya, Kimbila) : C. S. N° 25, N° 45 and N° 83 :*

There is not much difference between the two versions in C. S. N° 25 and N° 45.

In *C. S. N°* 83, according to the Chinese version, the Buddha in order to pacify the monks of Chü-shê-mi (Kosambī) related the long story of king Fan-mo-ta-to's forgiveness to king Ch'ang-shou (Brahmadatta and Dīghīti), but this story failed to influence the monks of Chü-shê-mi. Then the W.H. One recited a gāthā to show the hopelessness and foolishness of quarrelling and abusing. The Pāli is not the same. It refers also to the monks of Kosambī, who quarrelled with each other, wounding each other with the weapons of the tongue. The Pāli adds that one monk came to report the matter to the Blessed One who came and advised the monks not to quarrel. 3 times the Buddha advised, 3 times a certain monk requested him not to interfere as they were responsible for these quarrels. Here the Pāli omits the story of Brahmadatta. According to the Chinese version, the W.H. One after reciting the gāthā, used psychic power to fly through the air and came to P'o-lo-lou-lo village. There a monk called P'o-chiu (Bhagu) engaged himself day and night in meditation and the Buddha preached the dharma to him. Then he entered Hu-szu forest, sat down cross-legged under a tree and there he met an elephant king who also sought solitude to escape disturbances from the elephant herd. The Pāli mentions the meeting with the monk Bhagu but omits the Buddha's meeting with the elephant. It omits also the Buddha flying through the air. The rest is almost the same in both versions.

f) *To Ven. Mo-ho-nan (Mahānāma) : C. S. N*° 11 :

Both versions are almost the same.

g) *To Mou-li-p'o-ch'ün-na (Moliyaphagguna) C. S. N*° 18 :

Both versions are almost the same.

h) *To Ven. P'o-t'o-ho-li (Bhaddāli) : C. S. N*° 43 :

Almost the same in both versions.

i) *To Wu-t'o-i (Udāyī) : C. S. N*° 44 :

There is not much difference between the 2 versions. While the Chinese mentions a certain monk who went begging at night, the Pāli states clearly that it was Udāyī himself.

j) *To Ven. A-nan, C. S. N*° 53, 55, 67, 72, 76, 78, 98 :

In *C. S. N*° 53, *N*° 67, both versions are almost the same. In *C. S. N*° 55, the Chinese interprets Makhādeva as Ta-t'ien, meaning Mahādeva.

In *C. S. N*° 72, Ven. A-nan, while sitting in meditation came upon the knowledge that all fears, troubles, calamities and grief were due to ignorance, but not due to wisdom. He reported his thoughts to the Buddha who approved of it and gave a definition of an ignorant monk and of a wise monk. The Pāli omits elder Ānanda sitting in meditation and his report of his thoughts to the Buddha and the Buddha's approval of it. Here the Buddha called the monks and stated that all fears, troubles, misfortunes came to the ignorant men but not to the wise men. Then he advised the monks to train themselves to be wise through investigation. Here only, the Pāli mentions about elder Ānanda who asked the Buddha how far it sufficed to say that a monk was wise while investigating.

In *C. S. N*° 78, Ven. A-nan, having emerged from his meditation in the evening, came to the Buddha, paid respect to him, sat at one side and enumerated the various marvellous qualities of the Buddha. In the Pāli, a number of monks, having returned from their begging round and finished their meals, assembled in the assembly-hall and praised the Tathāgata as being marvellous and wonderful, endowed with psychic powers, knower of previous Buddhas. Then elder Ānanda approved the monks saying that the Tathāgata was endowed with marvellous qualities. This conversation was interrupted by the Buddha who just got up from his seclusion. He asked the monks of the nature of their conversation which was reported to the Buddha, who then asked elder Ānanda to relate the marvellous qualities of the Blessed One.

In *C. S. N*° 98, Ven. A-nan in the evening got up from his meditation and taking along with him the young monks, came to pay homage to the Buddha and asked the W. H. One how he should instruct, admonish and preach the dharma to the young monks. Then the Buddha explained the various dharmas to be taught to the young monks. The Pāli omits totally Ven. A-nan and the young monks and mentions simply that the Blessed One called the monks and preached the Dhamma to them.

k) *To Ven. A-nan and novice Chou-na (Cunda), C. S. N*° 66.

l) *To Ven. A-nan and many monks, C. S. N*° 77 *:*

Both versions are almost the same in C. S. N° 66, N° 77.

m) *To Lai-cha-ho-lo (Raṭṭhapāla), C. S. N*° 54 *:*

The story of Raṭṭhapāla is not the same in both versions. Raṭṭhapāla's listening to the Buddha's discourse, his asking the Buddha to allow him to be ordained, the Buddha's refusal as Raṭṭhapāla's parents'consent was not yet obtained, Raṭṭhapāla's parents' refusal to give their consent, Raṭṭhapāla's fast to bring pressure upon his parents, Raṭṭhapāla's parents'yield, Raṭṭhapāla's ordination and attainment of arahantship, all these facts are almost the same in both versions. Then Lai-cha-ho-lo early in the morning took his bowl and entered Yü-lu-cha for alms. He thought that the W. H. One had praised the gradual begging round so he went begging from house to house and came to his father's. At that time his father was trimming his beard and hair. When he saw Lai-cha-ho-lo, he said : « These bald-headed recluses were given to black (actions), having no offspring, no lineage the destructors of my family. I had a dearly loved son, but they took him away and ordained him. Do not give him anything to eat. Thus Lai-cha-ho-lo did not receive any alms from his own father's house except abuse. At that time, a maid-servant filled a basket of rotten and ill-smelling food and threw them away on a refuse-heap. Lai-cha-ho-lo saw her and asked her to put this rotten food into his alms-bowl. While the maid-servant was putting the food into the begging bowl, she recognised him by his voice, his hands and feet. She came to inform Lai-cha-ho-lo's father who was overjoyed at the news. Then with his left hand holding the robe, with his right hand stroking beard and hair, he came hastily to Lai-cha-ho-lo's place, where Lai-cha-ho-lo was eating his rotten food leaning against the wall. Lai-cha-ho-lo's father asked his son how he could eat this rotten food, as he was of soft body and got used to dainty and delicious food. He asked his son also why he did not come to his parents'house. Lai-cha-ho-lo replied that he did come to his parents'house, but he received nothing there except abuse. Then the father begged pardon of his son, respectfully guided him into the house, spread the seat and invited him to sit down. After that, he informed Lai-cha-ho-lo's mother of the coming of their son and asked her to prepare food for him. She gladly had the food prepared. Then she had a big heap of coins collected in the middle of the yard, so big that one man standing at one side and another man sitting at the other side could not see each other. Then she came to Lai-cha-ho-lo and said that this heap of coins was his mother's share, and his father's share was countless and could not be counted by hundreds, by thousands. All this money would be given to him, if he would renounce the religious life. Then Lai-cha-ho-lo advised his mother to dump this money into the water as it was due to this money that people experienced grief, suffering, despair. The mother knew that this method could not induce him to give up the religious life. Then she asked Lai-cha-ho-lo's former wives to bedeck themselves with necklaces and various garments, come to him, embrace one of his feet and say : « Oh indiscriminate husband, who are the nymphs whose beauty beat mine and for whose sake did you embrace the religious life ? » Lai-cha-ho-lo's former wives followed their mother-in-law's instructions. But Lai-cha-ho-lo called them as sisters and said that it was not for any nymph's sake that he embraced the religious life, but only for the sake of obtaining the Buddha dharma and now his purpose had been fulfilled. The former wives stood up, wept, saying that they were not Lai-cha-ho-lo's sisters but he called them so. Then Lai-cha-ho-lo asked his parents to offer him food as it was time already, and not harass him any more. Then his parents got up, offered water for washing, and with their own hands served him dainty and delicious food. After his meal, Ven. Lai-cha-ho-lo preached the dharma to his parents in various ways, gladdened, excited and pleased them. Then he got up and recited a stanza. The Pāli account is rather different. When Raṭṭhapāla reached Thullakoṭṭhita, the Pāli adds that he stayed in the deer park of the Kuru king. While going for alms, Raṭṭhapāla went from house to house, but the Pāli omits Raṭṭhapāla thinking of the Buddha's praise of this way of going for alms. When Raṭṭhapāla came to his own house, his father was having his hair combed in the middle of a hall with a door. While in the Chinese, Lai-cha-ho-lo's father abused the monks as being given to black (actions), having no offspring, no lineage-the destructor of his family, the Pāli mentions simply that he said that his only and dearly loved son went forth on account of these bald-headed monks, and thus elder Raṭṭhapāla in the house of his father did not receive alms, did not receive a refusal but abuse. Here the food thrown away by the woman-slave was junket of the previous day. While the Chinese mentions that the maid-servant directly came to inform the father, the Pāli mentions that she informed first the mother who reported this to her husband. The Pāli adds that when Raṭṭhapāla's mother was informed of Raṭṭhapāla's presence, she told the woman-slave that if this were true, she would no longer be a slave. The Pāli omits the father's attitude when he became overjoyed at the news. When Raṭṭhapāla's father saw his son sitting against the wall and eating the previous day's junket, he asked: « Is it really that you are eating the previous day's junket ? you should go to your own house ». And Raṭṭhapāla replied that there was no home for him, he who had gone forth from home to a homeless life. He had no home and he had gone to the householder but he did not receive either alms or refusal but abuse. Then the father invited him to enter the house, but Raṭṭhapāla declined saying that he had already taken his meal. Then the father invited him to come for next day's meal and he accepted by remaining silent. While in the Chinese, it was the mother who had the money heaped and the former wives adorned, in the Pāli, it was the father who did all this. In the Chinese, the mother attempted first with money then with the wives ; but in the Pāli, the father resorted to both methods at one time. He first had a big heap of gold coins and gold to be collected and hidden behind a screen. Then he asked Raṭṭhapāla's former wives to bedeck themselves. When food was ready, he sent word to invite the Elder and when Raṭṭhapāla was seated, he uncovered the heap of coins and gold and said to Raṭṭhapāla that one heap belonged to his mother, one heap to his father, another heap to his grand-father. There was possibility for him to enjoy riches and perform meritorious deeds. So he asked his son to give up the religious life, revert to the lower life, enjoying riches and performing meritorious deeds. Raṭṭhapāla's reply, the former wives'role are almost the same as in the Chinese, except that in the Pāli, the wives fell to the ground and fainted when Raṭṭhapāla called them sisters. The Pāli omits Raṭṭhapāla preaching the dharma to his parents. Then according to the Chinese version, Lai-cha-ho-lo flew back to Yü-lu-cha through the air, entered that forest and sat down on his sitting mat. At that time king Chü-lao-p'o was sitting with his ministers in his palace, speaking about and praising Lai-cha-ho-lo and expressing his desire to meet him. Then the king ordered his game-hunter to prepare Yü-lu-cha forest for hunting. When the game-hunter came to Yü-lu-cha forest, he saw elder Lai-cha-ho-lo and informed the king, who at once set out to meet the Elder. When the Elder saw the king coming, he asked the king if he wanted to sit down. The king replied that although this place belonged to him, he would like to be invited by the Elder and Ven. Lai-cha-ho-lo invited the king to sit down. The king asked if really the Elder went forth because of shortage of money. If so, he was ready to offer all necessary money so that Lai-cha-ho-lo could disrobe, enjoy sense-pleasure, give charity and perform meritorious deeds. Then the Elder said that the king had offered him impure things, but not pure things. Being asked by the king how to offer pure things, the

Elder said that the king would say that his country and people were secure and happy, without any fear, any disturbances, without any trouble, without being a slave. Then the king said that he wanted to offer the Elder pure things and not impure things. The Pāli is not exactly the same. It does not state Raṭṭhapāla flying back through the air. He just went back to the Deer-park of king Kuru, sat down under a certain tree for a day-rest. The Pāli does not mention king Chü-lao-p'o sitting with his ministers in the palace, praising elder Raṭṭhapāla and expressing the desire to meet him. It mentions simply that the king ordered his deer-trapper to clear the garden ground of the deer-park so that he might go to see the lovely ground. The deer-trapper went there, saw elder Raṭṭhapāla sitting under a tree, came to inform the king who ordered vehicles to be ready and he went there to meet Raṭṭhapāla. When he met the Elder, he greeted him and invited the elder to sit on the elephant-rug, but elder Raṭṭhapāla refused and invited the king to sit instead, as he had already his own seat. Here the Pāli omits the attempt of the king to induce elder Raṭṭhapāla to give up the religious life, as found in the Chinese. Then the king enquired as to what reasons had induced Lai-cha-ho-lo to embrace the religious life and the Elder explained to the king the reasons which induced him to become a monk.

n) *To Ven. Fou-mi (Bhumija), C. S. N° 81* :

Elder Fou-mi was staying in a troublefree meditation-hut. One morning, he was ready to enter Wang-shê town for alms. Then he postponed it and went to Prince Ch'i-p'o-hsien-na instead. There he was welcomed and greeted respectfully by the Prince who paid homage to him, offered him seat and asked permission to question him. Permission being granted, the Prince asked questions and the Elder replied. Then the Prince invited the Elder to take lunch ; he himself brought water, served him with most excellent food. When the meal was over, he sat down on a low seat and listened to a sermon. The Elder gladdened, satisfied, aroused the Prince with a dharma talk, using various ways to preach the Dharma. When the sermon was over, the Elder went to the W. H. One's place, paid homage to him and reported his conversation with the Prince to him. The Pāli is not exactly the same. It omits the Elder getting ready for alms, his postponement, his respectful welcome and greetings by the Prince, the latter's permission to ask questions. The Pāli mentions simply that elder Bhūmija dressed himself in the morning, and taking his robe and begging bowl came to the abode of Prince Jayasena and sat on the prepared seat. Then the Prince came to greet him and asked him questions. While the Chinese mentions at length the Prince's invitation to the Elder to take lunch, his serving the elder with the most excellent food, the Ven. preaching the Dharma to him, the Pāli mentions simply that the Prince offered elder Bhūmija his own rice cooked in milk. After reporting this conversation to the Buddha, the Elder in the Pāli asked the Lord if when questioned and answered like this, he interpreted correctly what the Lord had said and that he did not misrepresent the Lord. And the Buddha asked the Elder for what reason he did not tell the Prince about the four similes.

o) *To Ven. Lü-i-ch'iang-ch'i (Lomasakaṅgiya), C. S. N° 88 :*

One big difference is to be noted between the 2 versions. In the Chinese, the Buddha was reported to have preached the stanza of Pa-ti-lo-ti (Bhaddekaratta) at Wang-shê town, in the Bamboo-grove, at Chia-lan-to park. But the Pāli mentions that the Buddha explained this verse at Tāvatiṃsa, among the deities, at the root of Pāricchattaka, on the Paṇḍukambalasilā.

p) *To Ven. San-mi-t'i (Samiddhi), C. S. N° 90 :*
In the Chinese, it was elder A-nan who took up San-mi-t'i's view and was scolded by the Buddha, but in the Pāli, it was elder Udāyī who shared Samiddhi's view and took the blame from the Buddha.

q) *To Ven. Fu-chia-lo-so-li (Pukkusāti), C. S. N° 94 :*

According to the Chinese, after the Buddha's discourse, Ven. Fu-chia-lo-so-li attained the dharma-eye. Then he confessed his offence of addressing the Buddha as a friend and the Buddha accepted his confession. Here the Pāli is totally different. Elder Pukkusāti confessed in almost the same way. But after his confession, he asked the Buddha to ordain him as a monk ; but the Buddha refused as the Elder had no robe and begging bowl with him. While going in search of robes and bowl, the Elder was gored to death by a cow. The news was reported to the Buddha by the monks who asked about the future state of Pukkusāti. The Buddha replied that with the complete destruction of the 5 fetters, Pukkusāti was of spontaneous birth and would attain Nibbāna from there, not liable to return to this world. All these details are missing in the Chinese.

r) *To Ven. Ta-chou-na (Mahācunda), C. S. N° 7 :*

Almost the same in both versions.

s) *To novice A-i-na-ho-t'i (Aciravata), C. S. N° 80 :*

Both versions present no notable differences.

6. — *The Buddha preached the Dharma to his lay-disciples and to other peoples :*

There are 10 C. S. which fall under this category : *a*) to Ch'ü-t'an-mi, N° 96 ; *b*) to brāhmaṇa Shêng-wên, N° 23 ; *c*) to Po-li-to, N° 38 ; *d*) to Chien-mao, N° 49 ; *e*) to king Po-ssu-ni, N° 56, 58, 59 ; *f*) to brāhmaṇa Fan-mo, N° 60 ; *g*) to brāhmaṇa Suan-shu-mu-chien-lien, N° 68 ; *h*) to Ying-wu-mɔ-na-tu-t'i-tzu, N° 89.

a) *To Ch'ü-t'an-mi (Gotamī), C. S. N° 96 :*

Almost the same in both versions.

b) *To brāhmaṇa Shêng-wên (Jāṇussoṇī), C. S. N° 23 :*

Pei-lü, a follower of different sect came from listening to a dharma-talk by the W. H. One. He met brāhmaṇa Shêng-wên who drove in an all white chariot together with 500 disciples, all coming out of Shê-wei to reach a trouble-free place with the intention of reading sacred books. The Pāli omits the passage of Pei-lü's approaching the Buddha and being preached the dharma by him. It refers directly to brāhmaṇa Jāṇussoṇī driving in an all white chariot drawn by mares early in the morning and he met paribbājaka Pilotika coming from afar and he talked to him. The rest is almost the same in both versions.

c) *To Pu-li-to (Potaliya), C. S. N° 38 :*

According to the Chinese, householder Pu-li-to wore clean white clothes, with white napkin wrapped round his head, leaned on stick, holding umbrella and wearing worldly shoes. With such a dressing up, he was roaming about. When he met the Buddha, at first he discarded his stick, his umbrella, his shoes, then he took off his white napkin. In the Pāli, Potaliya is depicted as all dressed up, with umbrella and shoes, but not with other details. He did not resort to outward demonstrations of respect as seen in Chinese. After the Buddha's discourse, Pu-li-to obtained the Dharma-eye, asked to be given the three Refuges 3 times and to be accepted as a lay-disciple. In the Pāli, there is no mention of Potaliya obtaining the Dharma-eye. He proclaimed his wonder in the usual way and took refuge in the Triple Gem and asked to be accepted as disciple of the Buddha.

d) *To Chien-mao (Sakuludāyī) C. S. N° 49 :*

While the Chinese mentions that the Buddha after finishing his meal came to the Peacock garden, the Pāli states that the Buddha entered Rājagaha for alms but found the time early so he came to the Peacock-feeding ground. The Pāli omits Chien-mao rising from his seat, wearing his robe showing one shoulder, joining his hands towards the Buddha, but it adds that Sakuludāyī took a low seat and sat at one side. After the Buddha's discourse, Chien-mao praised the Buddha, saying that his preaching was marvellous, wonderful, drenching him like nectar, just like rain water falling from above and drenching all lands high and low. Then he declared his taking refuge in the Triple Gem and asked the Buddha to accept him as a lay-disciple. This passage is missing in the Pāli.

e) *To king Po-ssu-ni (Pasenadi), C. S. N° 56*, N° 58, *N°* 59 :

Both versions are almost the same, with some minor details more or less. In *C. S. N°* 56, according to the Chinese, king Po-ssu-ni sent brāhmaṇa Na-li-yang-chia to go to the Buddha, first to enquire after the Buddha's health then asked him about his view. In the Pāli, it was queen Mallikā who sent brāhmaṇa Nālijaṅgha to go to the Buddha, first to worship him and enquire after his health, then to ask him to explain his view.

f) *To brāhmaṇa Fan-mo (Brahmāyu), C. S. N°* 60 *:*

Both versions are almost the same. The following differences are to be noted : As to the long and large tongue, which is said in the Chinese to cover the whole face of the Buddha, in the Pāli, the Buddha put out his tongue, stroke it forward and backward over his two ears and his two nostrils and covered the whole surface of his forehead with his tongue. In the Chinese, Yü-to-lo asked permission from brāhmaṇa Fan-mo to go forth under recluse Ch'ü-t'an, and the brāhmaṇa agreed. And Yü-to-lo received high ordination from the Buddha. These details are missing in the Pāli. In the Chinese, brāhmaṇa Fan-mo wanted to worship the Buddha, but the big assembly of householders and brāhmaṇas shouted loudly their applause and admiration. The Buddha knew the assembly's mind and asked Fan-mo to resume his seat. Then he preached the dharma to him, gladdened, aroused and pleased him. At the end of the Buddha's discourse, Fan-mo obtained the dharma-eye. Then he got up from his seat, bowed down his head at the Buddha's feet, declared his taking refuge in the Triple Gem and asked the Buddha to accept him as a lay-disciple. In the Pāli, the brāhmaṇa did actually worship the Buddha, arranged his upper robe showing one shoulder, kissed round the Buddha's feet, stroke them on all sides with his two hands and made known his name, without being prevented by the assembly.

g) *To brāhmaṇa Suan-shu-mu-chien-lien (Gaṇakamoggallāna), C. S. N°* 68 :

Both versions are almost the same.

h) *To Ying-wu-mo-na-tu-t'i-tzu (Subha māṇava Todeyyaputta) C. S. N°* 89 :

The Chinese starts with the incident of the dog, who was the former father of Ying-wu-mo-na-tu-t'i-tzu (Subha māṇava Todeyyaputta), while the Pāli omits completely this incident.

7. — *Discussion among the monks :*

3 C. S. fall under this category. C. S. N° 20 relates a discussion between Ven. Shê-li-tzu and Man-tz'u-tzu ; C. S. N° 26 refers to a discussion among the Ven. Shê-li-tzu, Ta-mu-chien-lien, Ta-chia-yeh, Ta-chia-chan-yen, A-na-lü-t'o, Li-yüeh-to, and A-nan. In C. S. N° 30, there is a dharma discussion between Ven. Shê-li-tzu and Ta-chü-ch'ih-lo.

a) *Between Shê-li-tzu and Man-tz'u-tzu, C. S. N° 20 :*

Both versions are almost the same.

b) *Discussion among Shê-li-tzu, Ta-mu-chien-lien, Ta-chia-yeh, Ta-chia-chan-yen, A-na-lü-t'o, Li-yüeh-to and A-nan, C. S. N° 26 :*

The Chinese mentions 7 elders, but the Pāli mentions only 6 and omits Ta-chia-chan-yen (Mahākaccāna). In the Chinese, Ven. Ta-chia-chan-yen referred to the monk who was clever in dharma-discussion about Abhidharma, such a monk would illuminate the forest called Cow-horn. But in the Pāli version, this reply was put in Mahāmoggallāna's mouth. In the Chinese version, Ta-mu-chien-lien's reply referred to the monks who were proficient in psychic powers.

c) *Discussion between Shê-li-tzu and Ta-chü-ch'ih-lo, C. S. N° 30 :*

In the Chinese, Elder Shê-li-tzu asked questions to elder Ta-chü-ch'ih-lo and the latter answered these questions. In the Pāli, elder Mahākoṭṭhita asked questions to elder Sāriputta and the latter replied to these questions.

8. — *Sermons preached by the Buddha's disciples :*

14 C. S. fall under this category. Ven. Shê-li-tzu preached the dharma in C. S. N° 4, N° 24, N° 46, N° 63, N° 97. Ven. Ta-mu-chien-lien preached in C. S. N° 12, N° 36. Ven. A-nan delivered 4 sermons in C. S. N° 37, N° 57, N° 69 and N° 86. Ven. A-na-lü-t'o preached in one sermon in C. S. N° 82, nun Fa-lo in one sermon in C. S. N° 31 and Ven. Po-chü-lo in one sermon, C. S. N° 79.

a) *By Ven. Shê-li-tzu, C. S. N° 4, N° 24, N° 46, N° 63, N° 97 :*

There is not much divergence between the Chinese and the Pāli versions in *C. S.* N° 4, N° 24 & N° 46. But much difference is seen in *C. S.* N° 63, relating to the meeting between Elder Shê-li-tzu and brāhmaṇa T'o-jan. Early in the morning, Ven. Shê-li-tzu wearing his robe and taking his bowl entered Wang-she town for alms. Having begged alms, he came to brāhmaṇa T'o-jan's house. At that time, T'o-jan came out of the house and proceeded to the river bank to exploit the people. Having seen Ven. Shê-li-tzu from afar, he got up from his seat (?), wore his robe showing one shoulder, joined his hands to welcome the Elder, led him into the house, had good couch prepared and invited him to sit down. Then he offered food in a golden vessel to the Elder who refused. The brāhmaṇa insisted 3 times, and 3 times the Elder refused. The Pāli is not exactly the same. Here brāhmaṇa Dhānañjāni was referred to be outside the town and had cows milked in a cowpen. It omits : the brāhmaṇa getting up from his seat, wearing his robe uncovering one shoulder, his leading the Elder into the house, his ordering good bed to be prepared, his presenting food in a gold vessel. The Pāli mentions simply that when he saw elder Sāriputta from afar, brāhmaṇa Dhānañjāni came to him and said to the Elder to drink milk till the time for food and elder Sāriputta refused, saying that he had eaten and asked the brāhmaṇa to join him under a certain tree. The rest is almost the same in both versions. In *C. S. N*° 97, both texts refer to Kei-ku-tu's sickness, his request to elder Shê-li-tzu to come and preach the dharma to him, the coming of the Elder and his preaching the dharma to Kei-ku-tu. But in the Chinese, Ven. Shê-li-tzu asked Kei-ku-tu not to be afraid as he was endowed with great faith, meritorious moral precepts, much learning, wise charity, wise wisdom, right view, right purpose, and due to that, suffering and pain would cease, extreme happiness would arise, due to that one could obtain either once-returner or non-returner and Kei-ku-tu obtained already the state of stream-attainer. In the Pāli, elder Sāriputta advised Anāthapiṇḍika not to have any grasping. And after Elder Sāriputta's speech, Anāthapiṇḍika wept. After the Elder's departure, Anāthapiṇḍika passed away and was born as a deity in Tusita heaven. Here both versions diverge considerably. Then according to the Chinese version, Kei-ku-tu got cured of his sickness, related to the Elder his first meeting with the Buddha, his listening to the Buddha's sermon, his realization of the 4 Noble Truths, his purchase of Shêng-lin (Jetavana) andhis offering it to the Buddha. But the Pāli mentioned that after Anāthapiṇḍika's death and being reborn as a deity in Tusita heaven, the young Deva Anāthapiṇḍika illuminated the whole Jetavana with his radiance, approached the Buddha, greeted him and recited a gāthā where he praised the Buddha, the Dhamma and elder Sāriputta. Then the young deva Anāthapiṇḍika departed.

b) *Sermons preached by Ta-mu-chien-lien, C. S. N*° 12, *N*° 36 :

Both versions are almost the same.

c) *By A-nan, C. S. N*° 37, *N*° 57, *N*° 69, *N*° 86 :

There is not much difference between the 2 versions in *C. S. N*° 37, *N*° 57, *and N*° 86. But in *C. S. N*° 69, the Chinese mentions that at that time the great minister Yü-shih (Vassakāra) of Mo-chieh-t'o (Magadha) was fortifying Wang-shê town against the P'o-ch'i. But in the Pāli, it was king Ajātasattu of Magadha who fortified Rājagaha against king Pajjota. The rest is almost the same.

d) *By A-na-lü-t'o* (*Anuruddha*), *C. S. N°* 82 :

Both versions are almost the same.

e) *By nun Fa-lo* (*Dhammadinnā*) *C. S. N°* 31 :

Here the Chinese refers to P'i-shê-ch'ü (Vīsakhā) as the famous lady-devotee of Sāvatthi, this lady-devotee came to nun Fa-lo and asked questions about the Dharma. In the Pāli, Visākha is referred to as the former husband of Dhammadinnā. According to the Chinese text, nun Fa-lo came to the Buddha and reported her speech to him ; while the Pāli mentions that it was Visākha who came to the Buddha and reported the conversation to him.

f) *By Po-chü-lo* (*Bakkula*), *C. S. N°* 79 :

Here the Pāli adds the name of the questioner to Ven. Po-chü-lo as Acela Kassapa but omits to mention that he was a member of other sect. At the end of elder Bakkula's speecch, the Pāli adds a long passage in which Acela Kassapa asked elder Bakkula to ordain him and give him high ordination. Not long after his receiving ordination, Acela Kassapa attained arahantship. Then after a time, elder Bakkula took his key and informed the other monks that he would attain Nibbāna that day. And elder Bakkula as he was sitting in the middle of the Sangha entered into Nibbāna. These details are missing in the Chinese.

GENERAL REMARKS

A general survey of the roles played by diverse personages in the 98 sūtras taken up for comparative study reveals the unmistakenly common source of the Chinese and the Pāli versions, from which the compilers selected their documents and data. But differences in the details are not lacking, and this is due either to the compilers' choice or to the characteristics of the schools they represented.

Thus as far as personages are concerned, in *C. S. N°* 15, the Chinese sūtra N° 115 mentions that it was the Buddha who quoted the simile of the honey-ball, while the Pāli sūtta N° 18 says that it was elder Ānanda. In *C. S. N°* 10, the Chinese sūtra N° 99 relates that a great number of followers of different sects came to meet the monks in the preaching-hall where the latter assembled after their midday-meal. But in the Pāli sutta N° 13, the monks, having entered Sāvatthi for alms, found the time early and came to the abode of the paribbājakas and the conversation took place. In *C. S.* N° 26, Ta-chia-chan-yen's reply in the Chinese sūtra N° 184, which refers to the monks who were clever in dharma-discussion about the Abhidharma was put in the place of Mahāmoggallāna's reply in the Pāli sutta N° 32 ; while in the Chinese, Ta-mu-chien-lien's reply referred to the monks who were proficient in psychic powers. Thus the Chinese version here is more faithful and more reliable as Mahākaccāna is well known as being expert in Dharma discussion and Moggallāna is well known as being expert in supernatural powers. We quote here a remark by Dr. ANESAKI (1) : « In the Pāli Gosiṅga (2), we see the mention of 6 disciples of Buddha. In the Chinese version of the same text, one more Katyāyana is added. In the conversations among them, Moggallāna plays, in the Pāli, the part of a disciple who is well versed in the principles of the dhamma and their analysis. In the Chinese version, that role is played by Katyāyana, and Maudgalyāyana is the one who is famous in his exertions and in the practice of iddhi. When we compare this with the talents of the disciples as mentioned in Pāli Aṅguttara i, 14, we may see that the Chinese version is in accordance with the general tradition. For as set forth in the Aṅguttara, i, 14, Moggallāna is the best of the iddhimantānaṃ, and Kaccāna of « saṅkhittena bhāsitassa vitthārena atthaṃ vibhajantānaṃ. » The same is mentioned in the Chinese Ekottara. May this deviation show that the Pāli version is not always more original or purer than the Chinese. »

One more discrepancy is observed in *C. S. N°* 31. Here the Chinese sūtra 210 refers to lady-devotee P'i-shê-ch'ü (Visākhā) of Shê-wei (Sāvatthi) who came to ask question of nun Fa-lo. But the Pāli sutta N° 44 refers to Visākha as a layman, who was the former husband of Dhammadinnā. In *D.P.P.N.* (3) Visākha is referred to as the husband of Dhammadinnā. He was a rich merchant of Rājagaha. He became an Anāgāmī and his behaviour towards his wife changed completely. When he offered her all the wealth and her freedom, she asked leave to join the Order. When she had attained arahantship, she returned to Rājagaha. Visākha visited her and asked her various questions regarding the Buddh's teachings all of which she answered (4). Their conversation is recorded in the Cullavedallasutta. Visākha then visited the Buddha and reported their conversation to him, winning the Buddh'as praise for Dhammadinnā. » Thus it is plausible that the Chinese compilers confused the name of Visākha.

In *C. S. N°* 30, the Chinese sūtra N° 211 mentions that it was Ven. Shê-li-tzu who put questions to Ven. Ta-chü-ch'ih-lo and the latter answered ; while in the Pāli sutta N° 43, it was elder Mahākoṭṭhita who asked question to elder Sāriputta who replied. Again in *C. S. N°* 56, the Chinese sūtra N° 216 mentions that king Po-ssu-ni sent a brāhmaṇa to enquire of the Buddha the meaning of his Teachings, while the Pāli sutta N° 87 refers

(1) *JRAS*, 1901, p. 899.
(2) Treckner 212 f.
(3) ii, p. 898.
(4) *MA*, i, 514 f ; Thig A. 15, 19.

to queen Mallikā who sent the messenger. We notice also that in *C.S. N°* 53 according to the Chinese sūtra N° 63, king Chia-pei ordered 500 cart-loads of white non-glutinous rice and various kinds of food used by the king to be sent to Nan-t'i-po-lo as a gift from the king. But Nan-t'i-po-lo refused to accept saying that king Chia-pei had great state-duties and the king's expenditure was heavy and enormous, so he could not accept. But the Pāli sutta N° 81 mentions that king Kikī had 500 cart-loads of husked rice, of yellow rice and suitable curries to be sent to Ghaṭīkāra the potter, but here the potter accepted the gift saying that the king had much work and this would be enough for him from the king. Thus these conflicting accounts show us that either the compilers'memory failed them or that the story was so dimmed in the past that only confused and faint recollections reached the compilers.

As to the conversion of the members of other sects, after they had listened to the Buddha's sermon, similar details are observed in *C.S. N°* 64, N° 23, N° 60, N° 68, N° 89. But in *C.S. N°* 6, N° 61, N° 62, N° 48, N° 52, N° 38, N° 49, N° 56, N° 63, they are not the same. Thus in *C.S. N°* 6, brāhmaṇa Shui-Ching in the Chinese sūtra N° 93 declared his taking refuge in the Triple Gem and his asking the Buddha to accept him as a lay-disciple. But in the Pāli sutta N° 7, it adds that brāhmaṇa Sundarika Bhāradvāja asked the Buddha to allow him to adopt the monk's life and receive high ordination. When all his requests were granted, he exerted himself strenuously in the spiritual training and at the end attained arahantship. In *C.S. N°* 48, according to the Chinese sūtra N° 153, after the Buddha's discourse, Hsü-hsien-t'i attained the spotless and stainless dharma-eye. He was ordained by the Buddha and attained arahantship. But the Pāli sutta N° 75 does not mention Māgandiya obtaining the Dharma-eye on this very seat. It adds Māgandiya's exclamation of wonder in the usual way, his declaring to take refuge in the Triple Gem, his asking the Buddha to ordain him. Here the Buddha said that Māgandiya as a member of a different sect should need 4 months'probation ; but as the Buddha knew differences among individuals, he ordained Māgandiya. Here the Pāli mentions also that Māgandiya attained arahantship but with more details.

We observe that the Chinese version likes to display the Buddha's psychic powers while the Pāli does not mention them. Thus in *C.S. N°* 27, at the end of the Buddha's discourse, the Chinese sūtra N° 201 adds that 3 times 30,000 worlds shook. In *C.S. N°* 83, the Chinese sūtra N° 72 reports that the W.H. One after reciting the gāthā, used psychic powers to fly through the air and came to P'o-lo-lou-lo village, while the Pāli sutta N° 128 ignores it. The same is observed in *C.S. N°* 54, where elder Lai-cha-ho-lo was mentioned to fly back to Yü-lu-cha through the air in the Chinese sūtra N° 132, while the Pāli sutta N° 82 forgets this detail. The Chinese has also a preference to mentioning Ven. A-nan standing behind the Buddha and fanning him with a fan or attending him with a whisk of hair, while the Pāli totally ignores these details, as seen in *C.S. N°* 15, *N°* 42, *N°* 67, *N°* 96, *N°* 22. Sometimes one version adds one more detail. Thus in *C. S. N*° 35, the Pāli sutta N° 49 adds the name of the brāhmaṇa as Baka, in *C. S. N*° 44, (P sutta N° 66) the name of the monk as Udāyī, in *C. S. N*° 39 (P sutta N° 56) the name of the dyer as Rattapāṇi. These names are omitted in the Chinese version. Sometimes the Pāli adds one more detail. Thus in *C. S. N*° 64, the Pāli sutta N° 99 adds a meeting between Subha and brāhmaṇa Jāṇussoṇī ; in *C. S. N*° 94, the Pāli sutta N° 140 adds that elder Pukkusāti asked the Buddha to ordain him, but the Buddha refused as the Elder had no robe and begging bowl. While going in search of robes and bowl, he was gored to death by a cow. But sometimes the reverse is noticed with the Chinese giving more details. Thus in *C. S. N*° 3 (C sūtra N° 88), the W.H. One as he had a backache and wanted a little rest, folded up into four his yu–to–lo–sêng, spread over the bed, rolled his sêng–chia–li to make a pillow and lay down on his right side, with 2 legs resting along side one upon the other. But the Pāli simply says that the Well–Farer got up from his sea tand entered the monastery. In *C. S. N*° 89, the Chinese sūtra N° 170 adds the story of the dog of Ying–wu–mo–na–tu–t'i–tzu, in *C. S. N*° 83 (C sūtra N° 72) the story of Fan–mo–ta–to (Brahmadatta), of the Buddha keeping company with the elephant.

Thus the similarities observed here show the common source of information followed by both Chinese and Pāli versions and the discrepancies rather reveal the characteristics of each school or the faults of the compilers. They serve also to prove that at the time of compilation, some facts were so dim and so confused that they led to contradictory accounts in both the Chinese and the Pāli versions.

PART TWO

SIMILARITIES AND DIFFERENCES BETWEEN THE CHINESE AND THE PĀLI VERSIONS

Chapter IV. — DOCTRINE.

A. — SĪLA OR MORAL PRECEPTS :

Chapter IV. — DOCTRINE

Now we go into a detailed study of the similarities and differences between the 2 versions, as far as the doctrine is concerned. We opt for the Visuddhi Magga's classification into Sīla, Samādhi and Paññā, although some dharmas cover the whole classification, such as the Aṭṭhaṅgika magga.

A. — SĪLA OR MORAL PRECEPTS :

First we deal with the training of a monk which covers the *Pātimokkhasaṃvara* (Observance of the moral code), the *Indriyasaṃvara* (Control of faculties), the *Ājīvaparisuddhi* (Purity of livelihood), the *Paccayasannissita* which refers to the use of requisites.

In *C.S.* *N°* 68, the Buddha explained that there was a gradual training for a young monk who newly entered into this dharma-vinaya. First was the observance of moral practices which covered 5 stages, then the meditation-practices which covered 2 stages and the wisdom-training, which is dealt with in brief in the Chinese and which covers 2 stages in the Pāli version. Now we confine our study only to the observance of moral practices.

1. — *Pāṭimokkhasaṃvara or observance of the moral code :*

C N° 144 : (*vii*, 39*b*, 14–20 ; 40*a*, 1–10) : Here the monk said that after his going forth, he observed the moral-code of a monk and lived in accordance with the Prāṭimokṣa. He controlled his deportment and his behaviour, saw danger even in small offences and observed the principal code of training. Then he enumerated 20 rules to be observed.

P. N° 107 : (*iii*, 32, 5–9 ; 33, 18–33 ; 34, 1–22) : The monk is taught to be of moral habit, controlled by the direction of the Pātimokkha, of (right) behaviour and right sphere of movement and to be fearful of small faults. And he observed 26 rules of conduct, 6 more than the Chinese version.

These rules are as follows :

C 1 = P 1 : to abstain from killing. C 2 = P 2 : to abstain from taking what is not given. C 3 = P 3 : to abstain from unchastity. C 4 = P 4 : to abstain from telling lies. C 5 = P 5 : to abstain from double tongue (P : slander). C 6 = P 6 : to abstain from harsh words. C 7 = P 7 : to abstain from frivolous speech. C 8 = P 8 : to abstain from living by planting (C : chih-shêng = P : bījagāmabhūtagāma, seed-growth, vegetable-growth). C 9 = P 16 : not to accept (as gifts) widows and girls (P : women, girls).

C 10 = P 17 : not to receive servants and women-servants. C 11 = P 20 & P 18 : not to receive elephants, horses, cows, sheep (P : goats, sheep, elephants, cows, horses, mares). C 12 = P 19 : not to receive fowls and swines. C 13 = P 21 : not to receive fields, shops (P : khettavatthu, fields, sites). C 14 = P 14 : not to receive raw paddy, wheat, beans (P : raw crops). C 15 = P no : not to drink wine. C 16 = P 12 : not to use high and large beds. C 17 = P 11 : not to use flower-garlands, necklaces, scents, unguents, powder (P : garlands, scents, unguents, ornaments, finery). C 18 = P 10 : to abstain from singing, dancing, acting and from seeing and hearing songs, dances, theatrical shows (P : dancing, singing, music, seeing shows). C 19 = P 13 : not to accept shêng sê (P : jātarūpa, gold), hsiang pao (P : rajata, silver). C 20 = P 9 : to abstain from eating past-midday, to eat one meal a day, to train to eat at right time (P : a one-meal eater, to refrain from eating at night). The Pāli adds : P 15 : not to accept raw meat ; P 22 : to abstain from sending, going on messages ; P 23 : to abstain from buying, from selling ; P 24 : to abstain from cheating with weights, bronzes, measures ; P 25 : to abstain from crooked ways of bribery, fraud and deceit (ukkoṭanavañcananikatisāciyogā) ; P 26 : to abstain from maiming, murdering, confining, highway robbery (chedanavadhabandhanaviparāmosa).

Remarks : The Pāli adds : not to accept raw meat, implying thereby that cooked meat is allowed. But the Chinese drops this rule, implying that all kinds of meat are prohibited.

2. — *Santuṭṭhi or contentment :*

C : (*vii*, 40*a*, 10–11) : Having accomplished this aryan moral precept, the monk practised contentment, wearing robe for covering the body, eating food for sustaining the body ; wherever he went, he took along with him his robe and his bowl, without any attachment, just like the wild goose flying into the sky with its wings.

P : (*iii*, 34, 22–32) : Almost the same. C : sustaining the body = P : sustaining the stomach. C : like the wild goose = P : like a bird.

3. — *Indriyasaṃvara or control of faculties :*

C : (*viii*, 40*a*, 11–14) : Then the monk should control his faculties, keep them shut, well control his mind and thoughts, always be endowed with right knowledge. When the eye sees material forms, he should not grasp the general appearance, not to take delight in material forms. For the sake of (calming down) hatred and quarrel, for the sake of preventing the emergence of covetousness, sorrow, grief, evil and demeritorious dharmas, that the faculties should be controlled. In the same way with ears, nose, tongue, body and mind.

P : (35, 11–17) : Almost the same. C : the monk should control his faculties... endowed with right knowledge = P : indriyesu guttadvāra (the door of his faculties should be guarded). C : not to take delight in material forms = P : not to grasp the details of material forms. It cmits : for the sake of (calming down) hatred and quarrels.

4. — *Jāgariyaṃ anuyutta or awareness of deportment :*

C : (40*a*, 11–14) : Then the monk should be rightly aware when going out and entering, well reflect and well aware in bending, stretching (the arms), lower down or raise up (the head), with dignified and quiet behaviour and (facial) expression, carry properly the outer cloak, the robe and the begging bowl. While going, standing, lying down, sleeping, being awake, speaking or keeping silent, he should be well conscious (of these attitudes).

P : (35, 11–17) : Almost the same. About the monk's deportment, the Pāli adds : approaching, going away, looking up, looking down, eating, drinking, mumching, savouring, passing water, passing motion. It omits : going out, entering, lower down, raise up (the head), with dignified and quiet behaviour and (facial) expressions.

But at *C N*° 144 : (*vi*, 75*a*, 11–13), the Chinese adds two more stages, contemplation of mindfulness and avoidance of thoughts connected with desire as follows : « When the monk has completed the first stage, he should be taught to contemplate the inner body as the body up to contemplation of feelings, of mind and dharmas as dharmas, he should not think of thoughts connected with desires ». *Pāli :* not available.

But the Pāli (*iii*, 2, 26–33 ; 3, 1–18) adds two stages more after the state of awareness of deportment, a) to be moderate in eating, well mindful in eating, not for fun, not for intoxication, not for making oneself charming and beautiful but only for the sake of maintaining the body, keeping it living and out of harm, for observing the brahma-life, for eradicating old feelings and preventing new feelings to arise, so that the monk may live in comfort and without blame ; b) then the monk should be vigilant ; while pacing up and down, during day time and in the first watch of the night, he should cleanse his mind of obstructive dhammes ; in the 2nd watch of the night, while lying down in the lion-posture, on the right side, with foot resting on foot, he should be mindful, conscious and thinking of getting up ; in the last watch, having got up, and while pacing up and down, he should get his mind rid of obstructive dhammas.

5. — *Paccayasannissita or use of requisites :*

C N° 10 : (*v*. 13*b*, 5–9) : « If a monk uses robe, it is not for the sake of gain, not for the sake of pride, not for adornment, but only for protection against mosquitoes, gad-flies, wind, rain, cold, heat, for the sake of shame. If he uses food and drink, it is not for the sake of gain, not for pride, not for joy of becoming fat, but only for the sake of maintaining the body for a long time, of eliminating distress, vexation, grief, sorrow, for the sake of carrying the brahma-life, of getting rid of old disease and preventing new disease to arise, for the sake of living long, secure, without diseases. If he uses residential quarters, rooms, houses, beds, mattresses, beddings, it is not for the sake of gain, not for pride, not for adornment, but only for the sake of stopping weariness, of sitting in meditation. If he uses lotion, medicine, it is not for the sake of gain, not for pride, not for joy of becoming fat, but only for the sake of eliminating distress (generated by) disease, for the sake of preserving life, for living secure, without sickness».

P : N° 2 : (i, 10, 4-23) : Not exactly the same. For the use of robe, the Pāli adds yoniso paṭisankhā, wise reflection, to the attitude of the monk and siriṃsapa to the list of mosquitoes and flies. It omits : not for the sake of gain, not for pride, not for adornment. For the use of food and drink, C : food and drink = P; alms-food. Here the Pāli mentions that the monk uses alms-food not for the sake of sport (davā), not for indulging (madāya), not for decorating, not for personal beauty, but for the sake of maintaining life, of keeping it from harm, for carrying on the brahma-life, for destroying old feelings, for preventing new feelings to arise, for living without fault, with ease and comfort. For the use of dwelling places, the Pāli uses the term *senāsana* only. It omits : « not for the sake of... not for adornment » and mentions for the sake of protection against cold, heat, for warding off mosquitoes, flies, wind, sun, creeping creatures, for removing hardship of the season, for enjoying seclusion. For the use of medicine, the Pāli uses the term *gilānapaccayabhesajjaparikkhāra*. It omits : not for the sake of... but mentions for the sake of eradicating the arising feelings which are causing pain, for the sake of the utmost well-being.

Remarks : For *siriṃsapa*, its place is rather queer as it should be placed near ḍaṃsa, makasa. In the Pāli tradition, only positive necessities of cīvara are stated, but no occasions of misuse are enumerated. In the Chinese version, the term *pride* is used to translate the term *mādāya*, which means both pride and intoxication, and here intoxication suits better. As to the use of alms-food, the Pāli mentions : « Not for the sake of adornment (vibhūsana), not for the sake of decoration, » it looks rather forced here. The Chinese version seems more plausible.

General Remarks :

Thus as far as the Sīla is concerned, there is not much divergence as to the moral practices adopted. And the dissimilarities here and there show only minor differences between the 2 schools, which the respective version represents. Thus the dropping of the precept : « Not to accept raw meat » from the Chinese version is significant, as it shows the pro-vegetarianism attitude of the Sarvāstivādins already at so early a time.

Chapter IV. — DOCTRINE

B. — SAMĀDHI OR CONCENTRATION :

Chapter IV. — DOCTRINE

B. — SAMĀDHI

In the Samādhi paragraph, we deal first with the 37 Bodhipakkhiyā dhammas, then the elimination of 5 hindrances, the 4 jhānas of the rūpabhūmi, the 4 brahmavihārā, the 4 jhānas of the arūpabhūmi, the saññā-vedayitanirodha and the asaññī, and last of all the 5 abhiññā.

1. — *The* 37 *Bodhipakkhiyā dhammas :*

In *C. S. N°* 66, the Chinese sūtra *N°* 196 : (*vii,* 56*a,* 13) refers to these dharmas as the 4 applications of mindfulness, the 4 right eradications, the 4 constituents of psychic power, the 5 faculties, the 5 powers, the 7 factors of wisdom and the noble eightfold Path. To compare them with their Pāli correspondences, we say that there are no differences between the 2 versions, except that for the Pāli cattāro sammappadhānā, the Chinese prefers the four right eradications.

a) *Cattāro satipaṭṭhānā or the* 4 *applications of mindfulness :*

The parallelism between the Chinese and the Pāli versions is seen clearly in *C. S. N°* 8, where the 4 applications of mindfulness are described at length as under :

C N° 98 *:* (*vi,* 18*a,* 13-14)*:* « What are the four ? Application of mindfulness of contemplating the body as body. In the same way application of mindfulness of contemplating feelings, mind, dharmas as dharmas.

P N° 10 *:* (*i,* 56, 4-11) *:* Almost the same. The Pāli does not use the abridged form as in the Chinese.

i) *Contemplation of body :*

The Chinese enumerates up to 18 ways of contemplation of the body, while the Pāli mentions only 9 ways. The corresponding ways are as follows : C 1 = P 2 ; C 2 = P 3 ; C 5 = P1 ; C 12 = P 4 ; C 13 = P 5 ; C 14 = P 7 ; The Chinese 3, 4, 6, 7, 8, 9, 10, 11, 15 are missing in the Pāli.

C 1 : (18*b,* 14-15) : « The monk, when walking knows that he is walking, when sitting knows that he is sitting, when lying down knows that he is lying down, when sleeping knows that he is sleeping, when awake knows that he is awake, when sleeping and awake, knows that he is sleeping and awake. Thus he contemplates inner body as body, contemplates external body as body, establishes his mind upon the body, obtaining knowledge, obtaining vision, obtaining light, obtaining attainment. This is called the monk contemplating the body as the body.

P 2 : (56, 11–14 ; 27–38 ; 57, 1–4) : Almost the same. It adds the case of a monk who goes to a forest, or under a tree, or to an empty place and there he sits cross-legged, the body erect and establishes himself in mindfulness. As to the contemplation, it is almost the same. The Pāli omits cases of a monk sleeping, awake, sleeping and awake but adds a general sentence saying that whatever the position of his body, he is clearly conscious of it. As to the refrain at the end of each paragraph, the Pāli offers more details. It adds : « The contemplation of the body now internally, now externally, the contemplation of the origination of dharmas, of the dissolution of dharmas, of the origination and dissolution of dhammas in the body. While the Pāli is silent about obtaining knowledge, obtaining vision, obtaining light, obtaining attainment, it states instead : « He establishes his mindfulness upon the body as far as knowledge and remembrance can be obtained, detached not grasping anything in the world ».

C 2 : (18*b*, 15–17) : « Again he rightly knows when he is going out, when he is going in, he contemplates well, distinguishes well ; when he doubles up, stretches out (his arms), bends down, looks up, with deportment mannerly and orderly, when he wears properly the outer cloak and robes and holds alms-bowl, when he walks, stands, sits, lies down, sleeps, is awake, speaks, keeps silent, he all knows rightly ».

P 3 : (57, 6–13) : The P omits : « when he is going out, when he is going in, with deportment mannerly and orderly », but adds : « when he is going forward, coming back, looking ahead, looking round, when eating, drinking, mumching, savouring, obeying calls of nature ». C : contemplates well, distinguishes well, he all knows rightly = P : to be clearly aware of.

C 3 : (18*b*, 17–19) : « When evil, demeritorious thoughts arise, the monk uses meritorious dharmas to rectify, to cut off, to extinguish, to stop them. It is like a carpenter, a carpenter's apprentice who takes an ink-string and draws lines on the wood. Then with a sharp axe, he chops off and makes it straight ».

P : no.

C 4 : (18*b*, 19–20 ; 19*a*, 1–2) : « The monk with teeth setting upon teeth, with tongue applied to upper palate, uses his mind to rectify his mind, to cut off, to extinguish, to stop. It is like two wrestlers grasping a weak man, grabbing, twisting him this place, that place and beat him as they like ».

P : no.

C 5 : (19*a*, 2–4) : When the monk thinks of inhaling, he knows that he is thinking of inhaling ; when he thinks of exhaling, he knows that he is thinking of exhaling ; when inhaling with a long breath, he knows that he is inhaling with a long breath ; when exhaling with a long breath, he knows that he is exhaling with a long breath ; when inhaling with a short breath, he knows that he is inhaling with a short breath ; when exhaling with a short breath, he knows that he is exhaling with a short breath ; he trains himself, having inhaled experiencing the whole body ; he trains himself, having exhaled experiencing the whole body ; he trains himself, having inhaled stilling the body-activities ; he trains himself, having exhaled stilling the activities of speech.

P 1 : (56, 14-32) : Almost the same. One difference : C : he trains himself, having exhaled stilling the activities of speech. The P replaces by activities of body and thus offers more correct reading. In order to illustrate this passage, the P adds the simile of a turner who is well aware of, when he gives a short or a long turn to the lathe.

Remarks : In the passage : « He trains himself, having inhaled experiencing the whole body », the C editor in a foot-note expressed his doubt of mixing the two terms *hsüeh* (學), to train, to study, and *chüeh* (覺), to feel, to experience, and hesitated as to which term to be used here. Really the C translator used the term *hsüeh* to translate the term *sikkhati* and the term *chüeh* to translate the term *vedanā*. The later translators preferred the term *shou* (受), to translate the term *vedanā*. If we compare the Pāli passage : « sabbakāyapaṭisaṃvedī assissāmīti sikkhati, we find that both terms should be used here, *hsüeh* for *sikkhati* and *chüeh* for *paṭisaṃvedī*.

C 6 : (19*a*, 4-7) : With that joy and happiness from aloofness, the monk pervades the body, imbibes, moistens all over and fully. In this body, that joy and happiness from aloofness, pervades all over, without a single place left unpervaded. Il is like a bath-attendant who cleanses the basin, fills it with washing beans, churns the water, making it into a lump. The water pervades, imbibes, moistens all over and fully, without a single place left unpervaded.

P : no. (1)

C 7 : (19*a*, 7-10) : With that joy and happiness from meditation, the monk pervades the body, imbibes, moistens all over and fully. In this body, that joy and happiness from meditation pervades all over without a single place left unpervaded. It is like a mountain-spring, which is pure, clear, not dirty, flowing abundant and full. Water from four directions cannot run in, but the water wells up from the bottom of that spring, overflows and spreads outside, pervading, imbibing, enriching, filling the lake, without a single place left unpervaded.

P : no. (1)

C 8 : (19*a*, 10-13) : With that happiness from absence of joy, the monk pervades the body, imbibes, moistens all over, fully. In that body,

(1) Not available here, but available in other passages.

that happiness from absence of joy pervades all over, without a single place left unpervaded. It is like blue lotuses, rosy, red, white lotuses born in the water, grown up in the water and remained at the bottom of the water ; its roots, stems, flowers, leaves are all pervaded, imbibed, moistened all over and fully, without a single place left unpervaded.

P : no. (1)

C 9 : (19*a*, 13–15) : With a pure mind and comprehensing consciousness, the monk pervades all over this body and dwells in it ; in this body, not a single place is left unpervaded by the pure mind and comprehensing consciousness. It is like a man who covers himself with a robe of 7 armlengths or of 8 armlengths. From his head down to his feet, not a single place over his body is not covered up.

P : no. (1)

C 10 : (19*a*, 16–18) : The monk contemplates the brilliant perception, well receives, well holds, well keeps in mind what the mind thinks of. Like the beginning, the end is the same ; like the end, the beginning is the same ; like the day, the night is the same ; like the night, the day is the same ; like the below, the above is the same ; like the above, the below is the same. Thus with a mind not confused, without entanglement, (he) develops his mind endowed with a brilliant perception, his mind never being enveloped in darkness.

P : no.

C 11 : (19*a*, 18–20) : The monk well receives the contemplating image, well remembers what the mind perceives. It is like a sitting man who is looking at a man lying down or a man lying down who is looking at a sitting man.

P : no.

C 12 : (19*a*, 20 ; 19*b*, 1–4) : This body, which is now living, following its likes and dislikes, from the head down to the feet, the monk contemplates and sees it as full of various impure parts : « This body of mine has hairs of the head, hairs of the body, nails, teeth, rough, fine, thin epidermic and derm, flesh, sinews, bones, heart, kidneys, liver, lungs, big intestines, small intestines, spleen, stomach, lumps of excrements, brains and brains-base (?), tears, sweat, nasal mucus, phlegm, pus, blood, fat, marrow, saliva, bile, urine. It is like a vessel holding various kinds of seeds. A man with eyes would clearly distinguish them such as paddy, millet, rape turnips, mustard seeds. »

P 4 : (57, 13–34) : In the P, the impurities of the body amount to 31, one more than the number in the C version. The order of the impurities is not the same, although many impurities occupy the same position in the

(1) Not available here, but available in other passages.

enumeration. The P omits : brains, brains-base. The C omits : kilomakaṃ (diaphragm), vasā (skin grease) and lasikā (oil of the joints). C : rough, fine, thin, epidermic and derm = P : taco. Here is the P order : kesā, lomā, nakhā, dantā, taco, maṃsaṃ, nahāru, aṭṭhī, aṭṭhimiñjā, vakkaṃ, hadayaṃ, yakanaṃ, kilomakaṃ, pihakaṃ papphāsaṃ, antaṃ, antaguṇaṃ, udariyaṃ, karīsaṃ, pittaṃ, semhaṃ, pubbo, lohitaṃ, sedo, medo, assu, vasā, kheḷo, siṅghāṇikā, lasikā, muttaṃ. In the simile, the C mentions a vessel while the P uses the term ubhatomukhā mutolī, a kind of double-mouthed bag. It enumerates 6 kinds of grains : sālī, vīhī, muggā, māsā, tilā and taṇḍulā (good kinds of rice, paddy, green peas, beans, sesamum and husked rice).

C 13 : (19*b*, 4-6) : Again the monk contemplates upon the body as the body. The monk contemplates upon the body with its elements : « This body of mine has earth-element, water-element, fire-element, wind-element, space-element, consciousness-element. It is like a butcher who kills a cow, removes its hide, lays it on the ground and divides it into 6 portions ».

P 5 : (57, 35-37 ; 58, 1-8) : The P mentions only the first 4 elements and omits space element and consciousness element. In the P simile, it mentions a clever butcher or his apprentice who sits on the cross-road and exhibits the portions of the cow killed by him.

Contemplation of the decaying phases of the body :

Here both versions describe the monk contemplating upon the decaying phases of a dead body, thrown in a charnel-field (P), up to 7 days (C), or up to 3 days (P).

C 1 : (19*b*, 6-8) : Again the monk contemplates upon the body as the body. The monk contemplates that dead body which has been dead for 1, 2 days up to 6, 7 days, pecked by crows and vultures, eaten by wolves and jackals, burnt by fire, buried in the ground and subject to decay, festering and decaying.

P 1 : (58, 9-11) : The P mentions a body thrown in a charnel field for one day or 2 days, or 3 days, which is swollen, of blue colour and festering.

C 2 : (19*b*, 8-10) : . . . a skeleton of bluish colour, fettered, rotten and eaten more than half with bones connected together on the ground.

P 2 : (58, 15-19) : This body thrown in a charnel-field and eaten by crows, by hawks, by vultures, by dogs, by jackals, by various kinds of worms.

C 3 and *C* 4 : (19*b*, 10-14) : . . . without skin, with flesh and blood removed, only connected by sinews . . . (the skeleton) with bones, joints dislocated, scattered in every direction, a foot-bone, a shin-bone, a thigh-bone, a hip-bone, a back-bone, a shoulder blade bone, a neck-bone, a skull-bone are scattered in different places.

P 3 : (58, 23-31) : A skeleton with flesh and blood connected by sinews, a skeleton with bones disconnected, scattered in every direction, here and there lies a hand-bone, a foot-bone, a leg-bone, a thigh-bone, a hip-bone, a back-bone, a head-bone.

C 5 : (19*b*, 14-17) :. . . The bones are white like shell, blue like pigeon colour, red as though besmeared with blood, decayed, rotten, broken and reduced to powder.

P 4 : (58, 34-37 : 59, 1) : The bones are white like colour of the conch shells, heaped up together and more than one year old (terovassikāni), bones which are putrid, crumbling away to dirt, and reduced to powder.

Reflection of the monk over these places :

C : (19*b*, 7-8) : Having seen this, he compares it with his own body : « Now, my body will be like this, subject to that law, ultimately cannot escape (from it) ». Thus the monk contemplates the inner body as the body, the external body as the body, establishes his mind over the body, connected with knowledge, connected with vision. . . as the body.

P : (59, 1-10) : The monk contemplates this body of his as being evaṃ dhamme (subject to the same nature), evambhāvī (is to come to be like that), evaṃ anatīto (not going beyond that) the rest is as above.

Remarks : Here the P omits the C phase 6th up to phase 9th. But in *C. S. N°* 74, these four phases related to the attainment of 4 jhānas are available also in the P version. The comparative study of these phases in both versions shows the following similarities and differences.

C 6=*P* 10 : (*P N°* 119. *iii*, 92, 23-33 ; 93, 1-3): Almost the same. The P adds the attainment of the 1st jhāna with its five concomitants. The simile is almost the same. C : washing beans = P : nahāniyacuṇṇāni (bath-powder), The P adds : na ca paggharinī (without oozing out). The rest is the same.

C 7=*P* 11 : (*P* : 93, 4-23) : Almost the same. Here the P adds the attainment of the 2nd jhāna with its concomitants. The simile is almost the same. C : a stream of the mountain, pure, clear, flowing abundant and full = P : a lake of water welling up from within. While the C mentions that the water wells up from the bottom and spreads outside, pervading the mountain, the P says that although the god does not send down rain from time to time, yet the cool water welling up from within will pervade the lake with its cool water.

C 8=*P* 12 : (*P* : 93, 24-33 ; 94, 1-8) : Almost the same. Here the P adds the attainment of the 3rd jhāna in its usual form. The simile is almost the same. The P adds : « in a pool of blue lotuses, of red lotuses, of white lotuses ». It omits : rosy lotuses. C : its roots, stems, flowers, leaves = P : from its tips up to its roots.

C 9 = *P* 13 : (*P* : 94, 9–21) : Almost the same. Here the P adds the attainment of the 4th jhāna in its usual form. The simile is almost the same. The P mentions the man as sitting. C : a robe of 7 arm-lengths or of 8 arm-lengths = P : white cloth.

ii) *Contemplation of feelings :*

C : (19*b*, 17–20) : How is the contemplation of feelings as feelings? The monk when experiencing a pleasant feeling knows that he is experiencing a pleasant ; feeling when experiencing an unpleasant feeling knows that he is experiencing an unpleasant feeling ; when experiencing a neither pleasant nor unpleasant feeling knows that he is experiencing a neither pleasant nor unpleasant feeling when ; experiencing a pleasant bodily feeling, an unpleasant bodily feeling, a neither pleasant nor unpleasant bodily feeling, a pleasant mental feeling, an unpleasant mental feeling, a neither pleasant nor unpleasant mental feeling, a pleasant feeling connected with food, an unpleasant feeling connected with food, a neither pleasant nor unpleasant feeling connected with food, a pleasant feeling unconnected with food, an unpleasant feeling unconnected with food, a neither pleasant nor unpleasant feeling unconnected with food, a pleasant feeling of desire, an unpleasant feeling of desire, a neither pleasant nor unpleasant feeling of desire, a pleasant feeling of no-desire, an unpleasant feeling of no-desire, a neither pleasant nor unpleasant feeling of no-desire, then he knows that he is experiencing a neither pleasant nor unpleasant feeling of no-desire. (The rest is the same as in the case of contemplation of the body).

P : (*i*, 59, 11–28) : Almost the same. The P omits : pleasant bodily feeling, unpleasant bodily feeling, neither pleasant nor unpleasant bodily feeling, pleasant mental feeling, unpleasant mental feeling, neither pleasant nor unpleasant mental feeling, pleasant feeling of desire, unpleasant feeling of desire, neither pleasant nor unpleasant feeling of desire, pleasant feeling of no-desire, unpleasant feeling of no-desire, neither pleasant nor unpleasant feeling of no-desire. C : pleasant feeling connected with food = P : pleasant feeling connected with material gains. Same remarks with the other two feelings and the 3 feelings unconnected with food.

iii) *Contemplation of the mind :*

C : (20*a*, 1–4) : The monk when his mind is with desire, knows that his mind is with desire as it really is; when his mind is without desire, he knows that his mind is without desire as it really is. Similarly with hatred, without hatred, with delusion, without delusion, with blemishes, without blemishes, with fixed mind, with dissipated mind, with low mind, with lofty mind, with small mind, with big mind, with cultivated mind, with non-cultivated mind, with concentrated mind, with unconcentrated mind, with unemancipated mind, he knows that he is with unemancipated mind as it really is ; with emancipated mind he knows that he is with emancipated mind as it really is. (The rest is the same as in previous chapters.)

P : (59, 29–37 ; 60, 1–6) : Almost the same. The P omits : mind with blemishes, mind without blemishes, with cultivated mind, with uncultivated mind. It omits also : as it really is.

iv) *Contemplation of the dharmas :*

C : (20*a*, 4–15) : The eye due to material forms gives rise to inner fetters. The monk, when inwardly really has fetters knows that he has fetters as it really is ; when inwardly really has no fetters, knows that he has no fetters as it really is ; when the not yet arisen internal fetters arise, he knows them as it really is ; when the already arisen internal fetters are extinguished and do not come up again, he knows them as it really is. In the same way with ear, nose, tongue, body and mind This is called the monk contemplating the dharmas as the dharmas according to 6 sense-spheres (āyatana). Then the C proceeds with the same method and way of explanation for the 5 hindrances, the 7 factors of wisdom.

P : (60, 6–37 ; 61, 1–17) : Almost the same, with the following differences : a) the dhammas taken up for contemplation in the P are 5 nīvaraṇāni, 5 upādānakkhandhā, 6 ajjhattikabāhirāni āyatanāni, 7 bojjhaṅgāni, cattāri saccāni ; thus the C omits 5 upādānakkhandhā and the 4 saccāni ; b) the C mentions only 6 ajjhatika-āyatanāni but not together with bāhirāni āyatanāni ; c) the C starts first with the 6 ajjhatikāni āyatanāni, then the 5 hindrances, the P starts first with the 5 hindrances, then the 5 upādānakkhandhā then the 6 ajjhatikabāhirāni āyatanāni.

v) 2 *fruits to be obtained from the practice of mindfulness :*

C : (20*a*, 15–19) = *P* : (62, 34–37 ; 63, 1–19)

Both versions agree in describing the 2 fruits to be obtained from the pratice of mindfulness, either the supreme knowledge here-now (C), the diṭṭhadhammā aññā (P), or if there is any residual, the state of non-returning (C) and sati vā upādisese anāgāmita (P).

As to the duration of the practice required to attain the 2 above fruits, the C starts with 7 years, and gradually comes down to 6, 5, 4, 3, 2, 1 years, then 7 months, 6, 5, 4, 3, 2, 1 months, then 7 days, 6, 5, 4, 3, 2, 1 days and one night. It further states : « In the morning he (or she) practises like that, in the evening he (or she) will obtain high attainment ; if in the evening he or she practises like that, in the morning he (or she) will obtain high attainment ». The P starts with 7 years, then gradually comes down to 6, 5, 4, 3, 2, 1 years, 7 months, then 6, 5, 4, 3, 2, 1 months, half month and 7 days not less than that, which is considered as the time limit to obtain the high knowledge or the non-returner's state.

Remarks : Of this application on mindfulness, both versions offer almost the same materials, as the basic approach to the contemplation is identical.

But the compilers of both versions seem to have a free hand in collecting materials and this explains the difference in details we witness here. We can safely conclude that both versions were derived from the same source but the selection of details was left to the compilers more or less freely.

b) *Cattāro sammappadhānā* : C : *the* 4 *right eradications* :

Here the C uses the term 4 right eradications (Sk. Samyakprahāna). They are as follows :

C N° 222 : (*vii*, 98*a*, 6–9) : «... Towards evil demeritorious dharmas which have already arisen, he exerts his mind to eradicate them so that they are eradicated. Towards evil demeritorious dharmas which have not yet arisen, he exerts his mind to eradicate them so that they cannot arise. Towards good meritorious dharmas which have not yet arisen he exerts his mind so that they can arise. Towards good meritorious dharmas which have already arisen, he exerts his mind so that they persist for a long time, they do not vanish, but increase.

P N° 77 : (*ii*, 11, 10–22) : The P renders as follows: « anuppannānaṃ pāpakānaṃ akusalānaṃ dhammānaṃ anuppādāya ; uppannānaṃ pahānāya ; anuppannānaṃ kusalānaṃ dhammānaṃ uppādāya ; uppannānaṃ thītiyā.

c) 4 *iddhipādās or constituents of psychic power* :

C N° 206 : (*vii*, 78*a*, 13–15) : The monk is said to cultivate the eradicating basis of psychic power, accomplished in meditation based on wish, which depends on aloofness, on no desire, on cessation, on giving up, which leads towards fei–p'in (perhaps nirvāṇa). In the same way the eradicating basic of psychic power, accomplished in meditation based on exertion, on mind, on discrimination which depends on aloofness... towards fei–p'in.

P N° 16 : (*i*, 103, 32–37) : Almost the same. The 4 kinds of samādhi referred to here are chanda, viriya, citta, vīmaṃsā. The epithet qualifying iddhipādaṃ is chandāsamādhipadhānasaṅkhārasamannāgataṃ (with chanda replaced by the other 3 in subsequent cases), which means endowed with meditation based on chanda, with activities of striving, while the C replaces the term padhānasaṅkhāra by tuan meaning eradication.

d) *Pañcindriyāni or the five faculties* :

These dharmas are referred to in *C. S. N°* 98, *C N°* 86: (*vi*, 4*a*, 2–3) as faculty of faith, faculty of exertion, faculty of mindfulness, faculty of concentration and faculty of wisdom. They are the same as in the Pāli list, saddhindriyaṃ, viriyindriyaṃ, satindriyaṃ, samādhindriyaṃ, paññindriyaṃ.

e) *Pañcabalāni or the five powers :*

These dharmas are referred to in *C N°* 86 : (*vi*, 4*a*, 3–5) and in *P N°* 77 : (*ii*, 12, 7–13). They are enumerated as powers of faith, of exertion, of mindfulness, of concentration and of wisdom, just the same as in Pāli saddhābalam, viriyabalaṃ, satibalaṃ, samādhibalaṃ, and paññābalaṃ.

f) *Sattabojjhaṅgāni or 7 factors of wisdom :*

They are referred to in C.S. N° 2, N° 49, N° 66, N° 72 and N° 98.

C N° 86 : (*vi*, 4*b*, 15–17) : They are enumerated as follows : factors of wisdom, of mindfulness, of analysing the dharma, of exertion, of delight, of calmness, of concentration and of equanimity.

P N° 77 : (*ii*, 12, 14–23) : The same : satisambojjhaṅgaṃ, dhammavicayasambojjhaṅgaṃ, viriyasambojjhaṅgaṃ, pītisambojjhaṅgaṃ, passaddhisambojjhaṅgaṃ, samādhisambojjhaṅgam and upekhāsambojjhaṅgaṃ.

g) *Aṭṭhaṅgikamagga or the Eightfold Path :*

The Noble Eightfold Path is mentioned in C.S. N° 31, N° 48, N° 65, N° 73, N° 93, N° 95 and N° 98.

C N° 31 : (43*a*, 9–11) : « What is right view ? When the noble disciple thinks of suffering as suffering, of origination as origination, of cessation as cessation, of path as path, or when he considers his previous actions, or when he trains in and thinks of various courses, or he sees the dangers in various courses, or when he sees the tranquillity of nirvāṇa or when without grasping he thinks, he considers good emancipation of mind. In these moments, he analyses, broadly analyses, deeply analyses, considers, broadly considers, clearly distinguishes and observes, clearly attains, this is called right view. »

P N° 141 : (*iii*, 251, 12–15) : Very simple. Whatever is knowledge of suffering, knowledge of the origin of suffering, knowledge of the cessation of suffering, knowledge of the path leading to the cessation of suffering, this is called right view.

C : (43*a*, 11–13) : What is right aspiration ? When the noble disciple thinks of suffering as suffering... good emancipation of mind. In these moments, he considers, broadly considers, appropriately considers. He thinks of what should be thought of, he aspires to what should be aspired to, this is called right aspiration.

P : (251, 16–18) : Not exactly the same. Here is the aspiration of getting rid of desires (nekkhammasaṅkappa), aspiration of non-malevolence (abyāpādasaṅkappa), aspiration of harmlessness (avihiṃsasaṅkappa).

C : (43*a*, 13–15) : When the noble disciple thinks of suffering as suffering... good emancipation of mind, in these moments, except for 4 meritorious speeches, he abstains from other demeritorious speeches, discards them, eradicates, removes them, does not practise, does not perform, has no connection with them, this is called right speech.

P : (251, 19–22) : Almost the same, but the wording is different. Here it mentions the abstention from speaking lies, back biting, harsh words, frivolous talk, this is called right speech.

C : (43*a*, 15–17) : When the noble disciple thinks of suffering... emancipation of mind, in these moments, except for 3 meritorious bodily actions, he abstains from other demeritorious actions, discards them, eradicates them, removes them, does not practise, does not perform them, has no connection with them, this is called right action.

P : (251, 23–25) : Same remark as in right speech.

C : (43*a*, 17–19) : When the noble disciple... emancipation of mind, in these moments, he does not go in search in a wrong way, he is not with much desire, without contentment, he does not perform various tricks, reciting mantras, he does not indulge in wrong livelihood. He only seeks robes in accordance with the dharma, not against the dharma, only seeks food, beds, seats in accordance with the dharma, not against the dharma. This is called right livelihood.

P : (251, 26–28) : Very simple. The noble disciple having given up wrong livelihood makes his living with right livelihood.

C : (43*a*, 19–20 ; 43*b*, 1) : When the noble disciple... good emancipation of mind, in these moments, he displays exertion and means, absolutely striving for, with strength, pushing forwards with zeal and steadiness, not giving up, not retreating backwards and rightly mastering his mind, this is called right means.

P : (251, 29–34 ; 252, 1–4) : Not exactly the same. Here the term used is sammāvāyāma (right exertion), while the C uses right means. Here the monk brings forth desire, strives for, displays his exertion, exerts his mind and strives for the non-arising of evil demeritorious dhammas, for the arising of good, meritorious dhammas and for the maintenance, the preservation, the increase, the growth, the development, the fulfilment of meritorious dhammas already arisen.

C : (43*b*, 1–3) : The noble disciple... good emancipation of mind, in these moments, when there is mindfulness for, mindfulness against or having no mindfulness towards (anything), he is mindful, widely mindful, keeping in mind, not forgetful, this is called right mindfulness.

P : (252, 5–9) : Not exactly the same. Here the monk dwells contemplating the body in the body, contemplating feelings in the feelings, the mind in the mind, the mental states in the mental states, ardent, clearly conscious, mindful for the control of attachment and dejection in the world.

C : (43*b*, 3–5) : When the noble disciple... good emancipation of mind, in these moments, he dwells in dhyānic states, firm, steady, not wavering, not scattering away, one-pointed, firm, rightly concentrated, this is called right concentration.

P : (252, 10–17) : Not the same. Here it refers to the attainment of 4 jhānic states, from the 1st jhāna up to the 4th jhāna.

In *C. S. N°* 31, there are questions and answers about the noble eightfold path as under :

C N° 210 : (*vii*, 84*a*, 4–5) : Q : What is the noble eightfold path? A : The noble eightfold path is right view up to right concentration, this is called the noble eightfold path.

P N° 44 : (*i*, 300, 31–34) : Almost the same. The Pāli enumerates the whole 8 constituents.

C : (84*a*, 6–7) : Q : Is the noble eightfold a conditioned dharma? A : The noble eightfold path is a conditioned dharma.

P : (300, 35–36 ; 301, 1) : The same.

C : (84*a*, 7–8) : Q : How many groups are there? A : There are three groups : moral precept group, concentration group and wisdom group.

P : Not available.

C : (84*a*, 8–11) : Q : Does the noble eightfold path include the 3 groups, or the 3 groups include the noble eightfold path? A : The noble eightfold path does not include the 3 groups, but the 3 groups include the noble eightfold path. Right speech, right action, right livelihood, these 3 constituents are included in the noble moral precept group ; right mindfulness, right concentration, these two constituents are included in the noble concentration group ; right view, right aspiration, right means, these 3 constituents are included in the noble wisdom-group. This is why the noble eightfold path does not include the 3 groups but the 3 groups include the eightfold path.

P : (301, 1–11) : One difference. The P includes sammāvāyāmo (right exertion) in the samādhi-group, while the C includes right means in the wisdom-group. The rest is almost the same.

Thus as far as the Noble Eightfold Path is concerned, there is only one main difference in the C and the P versions, that is the classification of the C right means into wisdom-group, while the P puts sammāvāyāma in the samādhi-group. As to the C translation right means, it is rather an old translation, the later translators preferred Chêng-ching-chin, right exertion and this term renders the exact meaning of sammāvāyāma.

2. — *Elimination of hindrances:*

C. S. N° 23, N° 28, N° 68 refer to the elimination of the 5 hindrances, in more or less the same way.

Thus in *C. S. N°* 23, it is referred to as under :

C N° 146 *:* (*vi*, 79*b*, 6-9) : Having fulfilled these noble moral practices, having practised utter contentment, having controlled his faculties, being well aware of in going out and going in, the monk again dwells alone, aloof, in a troublefree place, or at the root of a tree, or in an open and quiet place, at a mountain cliff or in a rock cave, in the open air or on a heap of straw; or he comes to a forest or to a cemetery. He, having come to a forest (1), or to the root of a tree, an empty and quiet place, spreads his sitting mat, sits crosslegged with body erect, with right vow, with thoughts well controlled not going astray, he gets rid of covetousness, with mind free from quarrel, he sees others' properties and requisites for life, without coveting them for himself, he cleanses his mind od covetousness. In the same way with hatred, with sloth and torpor, with worry and restlessness, he has destroyed doubts, overcome uncertainty, towards meritorious dharmas he harbours no doubts, he cleanses his mind of doubts.

P N° 27*:* (*i*, 181, 9-24) : Simpler. It omits : « in going out and going in, in an open and quiet place, spreads his sitting mat, with right vow, with thoughts well controlled, not going astray, he gets rid of covetousness, with mind free from quarrel, he sees others' « properties and requisites for life, without coveting them for himself ». The P adds : « when he has returned from his begging round and finished his meal ; he keeps his mindfulness present in front of him. » The 5 hindrances are the same in both versions; but while the C deals very briefly with the remaining four hindrances, the P gives more details.

3. — *The four dhyānas of the material world:*

The four dhyānas of the material world are treated in *C. S.* N° 5, N° 7, N° 21, N° 23, N° 25, N° 28, N° 30, N° 31, N° 37, N° 32, N° 42, N° 43, N° 44, N° 64, N° 65, either in an abridged form or at length.

Thus in *C. S. N°* 23, the treatment of these dharmas is referred to as under :

a) *The* 1*st dhyāna :*

C N° 146 : (*vi*, 79*b*, 9-10) : He (the monk) having got rid of these 5 hindrances, of blemished mind and of weak knowledges, aloof from desire, aloof from evil, demeritorious dharmas, he attains and dwells in the 1st

(1) Wu-shih-ch'u (P : Aranna), place where there is not much to do.

dhyāna, which is endowed with initial thoughts, with applied thoughts, endowed with joy and happiness born out of aloofness.

P N° 27 : (*i*, 181, 25–28) : Almost the same. C : of weak knowledge = P : paññāya dubbalīkaraṇe. P : savitakkaṃ = C : yu–chüeh (有覺 : along with perception, with conscience of) ; later translators preferred yu-hsin (有尋, with investigation, with searching thoughts). P : Savicāraṃ = C : yu-kuan (有觀, with contemplating thoughts) ; later translators preferred yu–t'zu or szu (有伺, with investigating thoughts).

b) *2nd dhyāna* :

C : (79*b*, 10–12) : He, by stopping the initial and applied thoughts, his inner mind tranquilized and onepointed, he attains and dwells in the 2nd dhyāna, which is free from initial and applied thoughts, which is endowed with joy and happiness born out of concentration.

P (181, 32–35) : The same.

c) *3rd dhyāna* :

C : (79*b*, 13–14) : He gives up joy and desires, dwells in equanimity, without longing for, with right mindfulness, with right knowledge, he bodily experiences that happiness that the Noble Ones call : Dwelling in equanimity and mindful in the abode of happiness, he attains and dwells in the 3rd dhyāna.

P (182, 2–6) : Almost the same. 2 minor differences : the P omits without longing for ; C : the abode of happiness = P : sukhavihārī, which means the same.

d) *4th dhyāna.*

C : (79*b*, 14–15) : He, having got rid of happiness and suffering, with joy and sorrow already destroyed, he attains and dwells in the 4th dhyāna, which is without suffering and happiness, which is pure, endowed with equanimity and mindfulness.

P : (182, 10–14) : The same.

In *C. S. N°* 30, there is a series of 3 questions and answers available only in P, which deals with the 1st jhāna of the material world. The first two questions and answers are also available in the C version, but in *C. S. N°* 31 :

P N° 44 : (*i*, 294, 24–28) : Q : What is the 1st jhāna stage of concentration ? A : When a monk is aloof from sense–desires, aloof from evil, demeritorious dhammas, he enters and abides in the 1st jhāna, which is with initial thoughts, with applied thoughts, which is endowed with joy and happiness born out of seclusion.

P : (*i*, 294, 28–32) : Q : How many factors are there in the first jhāna ? A : There are five factors in the 1st jhāna. When a monk obtains the 1st jhāna, there are initial thoughts, applied thoughts, joy, happiness and one-pointedness of mind.

P : (*i*, 294, 32–37 ; 295, 1–4) : Q : How many factors are got rid of and how many factors are obtained in the 1st jhāna ? A : In the 1st jhāna, 5 factors are eradicated and five factors are obtained. To the monk who enters the 1st jhāna, sense-desire, ill-will, sloth and torpor, restlessness and worry, doubts are eradicated, initial thoughts, applied thoughts, joy, happiness and one-pointedness of mind arise.

In *C. S. N°* 37, the jhānas of the rūpāvacara are mentioned as follows :

C N° 217 : (*vii*, 95*a*, 6–8) : It refers to the attainment of the 4 dhyānas of the rūpāvacara plane by a learned noble disciple who dwelling in these dhyānas contemplates the dharma in accordance with the dharma. Having dwelt in these 4 dhyānas and contemplated the dharma in accordance with the dharma, he either obtains the complete extinction of the cankers, or if the extinction of the cankers is not complete due to his desire for, his delight in and his like for this dharma, he will destroy the 5 lower fetters, will be born by spontaneous birth in (this) plane and from there he will attain the parinirvāṇa ; he obtains the non-returner's state.

P N° 52 : (*i*, 349, 29–30 ; 350 ; 351, 1–17) : Almost the same. The 4 jhānas are described at length as usual, not in an abridged form as seen in the C. After the attainment of each jhāna, the monk thinks that such a jhāna is created and mind-made and whatever is created and mind-made is impermanent and subject to cessation. Having dwelt firm in this, he obtains the extinction of the cankers, and if not, due to his love for, his delight in that dhamma, he will obtain the destruction of the 5 lower fetters, be of spontaneous birth and will attain nibbāna there, not liable to return to this world.

All these passages show us that there is not much difference between the two versions as far as the dhyānic stages are concerned.

4. — *Cattāro brahmavihārā or the four Illimitables :*

These dharmas are taken up in C S. N° 6, N° 18, N° 21, N° 24, N° 25, N° 29, N° 36, N° 37, N° 63, N° 64, N° 82, N° 98.

We select the *C.S. N°* 6 for a close study of these dharmas :

C N° 93 : (*vi*, 13*a*, 15–17) : The monk dwells, suffusing one direction with a mind endowed with benevolence, in the same way the 2nd direction, the 3rd direction, the 4th direction, the 4 intermediate directions, the above, the below, suffusing all over, everywhere with a mind endowed with benevolence, which is without bondage, without enmity, without hatred, without quarrel, extremely extensive, extremely big, immeasurable, suffusing it all over the world, he well develops and abides by it. In the same way with compassion, sympathetic joy and a mind endowed with equanimity, without bondage, without enmity, without hatred... and abides by.

P N° 7 : (*i*, 38, 20–30) : Almost the same. C : 4 intermediate directions = P tiriyaṃ. C : without bondage, without enmity, without hatred, without quarrel = P : avereṇa abyābajjhena (without enmity, without ill-will). C : extremely extensive, extremely big, immeasurable = P : vipulena, mahaggatena appamāṇena (almost the same with the term « extremely » omitted). C : he well develops it = P no.

Both versions C and P agree that the practice of the four Illimitables would lead people to be born in the brahma-world as seen in *C. S. N*° 63 :

C N° 27 : (*v*, 34*b*, 1–5) : Ven. Shê-li-tzu preached the 4 brahma-abodes to brāhmaṇa T'o-jan ; the practice of these dharmas would lead to the eradication of sense-desire and after death, would lead to a rebirth in the brahmadeva sphere.

P N° 97 : (*ii*, 195, 1–17) : Almost the same. Here elder Sāriputta preached to brāhmaṇa Dhānañjāni the four brahmavihārā which were termed as the way to companionship with Brahmā.

The practice of the 4 Illimitables is usually placed in between the practice of the 4 dhyānas of the rūpa-world and that of the 4 dhyānas of the arūpa-world, as seen in *C. S. N*° 37, *C N*° 217 : (*vii*, 95*a*, 8–13) and *P N*° 52 : (*i*, 351, 18–36 ; 352, 1–2). But in *C. S. N*° 25, *N*° 21, *N*° 64, while the C follows this tradition faithfully by inserting the practice of the 4 Illimitables in between the practices of the dhyānas of the rūpa and the arūpa-worlds, the Pāli omits it.

Sometimes the practice of the 4 Illimitables is placed immediately before the attainment of arahantship, implying thereby that this practice can lead to the realization of arahantship, as seen under :

C N° 183 : (*vii*, 33*b*, 17–20 ; 34*a*, 1–2) : He thinks : Whatever thoughts gross or subtle, come up and go away, he knows as it really is. Having known thus, his mind is free from cankers of desires, from cankers of becoming, from cankers of ignorance. Being free, he knows that he is free. Birth is destroyed ; the holy life has been fulfilled ; what should be done is done ; there will be no more becoming. True is the knowledge.

P N° 7 : (*i*, 38, 31–36 ; 39, 1–2) : The P version, after dealing with the four Brahmavihāras refers also to the attainment of arahantship, with the knowledge of *idaṃ* (arahantship), of *hīnaṃ* (defilement, literally inferior) and *paṇītaṃ* (means of rejecting defilement, literally superior). Such a knowledge leads to the eradication of the 3 cankers, the destruction of birth, the establishment of holy life, the accomplishment of his duty and the elimination of rebirth.

Thus the comparative study of the practice of the 4 Brahmavihāras of the 2 versions shows a more or less identity in between the 2 traditions represented by its respective texts. But the tradition represented by the C texts seems to be more fond of this practice than the tradition represented by the Pāli Canon. This tendency already latent in the early texts of Sanskrit Buddhism might account for the stress on Maitrī or compassion taken by the Mahāyānists which put Maitrī almost on the same footing with Prajñā or wisdom and which insisted on the observance of the vegetarian diet.

5. — *The 4 dhyānas of the arūpa-world :*

The practice of the 4 dhyānas of the arūpa-world is dealt with in C.S. N° 21, N° 25, N° 30, N° 37, N° 42, N° 67 and N° 75.

In *C. S. N°* 42, this practice is referred to as follows :

C N° 205 : (*vii*, 77*a*, 12–18) : Then by transcending all perceptions of material forms, by eradicating all obstructive perceptions, by not thinking of various perceptions, he attains and dwells in the infinite space... Having transcended the infinite space, he attains and dwells in the infinite consciousness... Having transcended all infinite consciousness, he attains and dwells in the plane of nothingness. If he has any feeling whether pleasant or unpleasant or neither pleasant nor unpleasant, he contemplates on this feeling as impermanent, he contemplates on the rise and the fall, he contemplates on no-desire, on cessation, on eradication, on giving up. Having contemplated on these feelings as impermanent, their rise and their fall, having contemplated on absence of desire, on cessation, on eradication, on giving up, he is not to be reborn in this world. Having not to be reborn into this world, he will have no fear; having no fear, he enters into parinirvāṇa. Birth is extinguished, the brahma-life has been fulfilled, what should be done has been done; there will be no more rebirth ; he knows it as it really is.

P N° 64 : (*i*, 436, 18–26 ; 437, 1–6): Almost the same. C : Then by transcending all perceptions of material forms, by eradicating all obstrusive perceptions, by not thinking of various perceptions, he attains and dwells in the infinite space = P bhikkhu sabbaso rūpasaññānaṃ samatikkamā paṭigha-saññānaṃ atthagamā nānattasaññānaṃ amanasikārā ananto ākāso ti ākāsanañ-cāyatanam upasampajja viharati. Thus it is the same as with the Chinese. Here the contemplation is rather different. He contemplates on whatever material forms, feelings, perceptions, mental tendencies, consciousness as impermanent, painful, as a disease, a boil, a dart, an evil thing, an affliction, as alien, corruptible, void, without self, he turns his mind away from these dhammas, concentrates his mind on the deathless elements, thinking : « This is good, this is excellent, the calming down of all activities, the eradication of all clingings, the extinction of craving, dispassion, cessation, nibbāna ». If he is steadfast in this, he will attain the extinction of all cankers. If he fails to attain the extinction of all cankers, through attachment to that dharma, through delight in that dhamma, by the complete eradication of 5 fetters binding to a lower world, he will be of spontaneous birth, and from there he will attain parinibbāna, without returning to this world.

Here we observe that the P and the C omit the 4th stage that is the neither perception nor non-perception stage, which is considered more or less as a hindrance to the final stage of emancipation and because the subject of the sutta is restricted to the abandonment of the five lower fetters only.

Usually the C prefers an abridged form to describe the practice of the 4 dhyānas, while the P gives all stages in full, as seen in *C. S. N°* 25 :

C N° 185 : (*vii*, 37*b*, 2–5) : We have crossed over the perceptions of all material shapes up to the attainment of the state of neither perception nor non-perception and abided in it.

P N° 31 : (*i*, 208, 31–37 ; 209, 1–16) : Almost the same. Here the P explains the 4 stages of jhānas of the arūpa world in full.

Remarks : Thus as far as the 4 dhyānic stages of the arūpaloka are concerned, there is not much divergence between the two versions.

6. — *Concentration of complete cessation and concentration of no-perception : Saññāvedayitanirodha and asaññī :*

After the practice of the 4 dhyānas of the arūpa world, the P usually refers to another concentration called saññāvedayitanirodha, cessation of perceptions and feelings, which is frequently omitted in the C, as seen in *P N°* 66 : (*i*, 456, 3–6) and in *P N°* 113 : (*iii*, 45, 1–5).

In *C. S. N°* 30 *and N°* 31, there is a series of questions and answers dealing with the concentration of complete cessation and the concentration of no-perception, which are equivalent to the P saññāvedayitanirodha and asaññī.

C N° 211 : (*vii*, 86*b*, 4–6) : Q : What is the difference between death and entering in the concentration of complete cessation ? A : In death, life has been extinguished, heat has gone away, and the faculties are broken up. But of the monk who enters the concentration of complete cessation, life is not extinguished, heat has not gone away and the faculties are not broken up.

P N° 43 : (*i*, 296, 11–23) : Q : What is the difference between a dead thing which has passed away and the monk who has attained this cessation of perception and feeling ? A : In one who dies, who has passed away, his bodily activities have ceased, are subsided, his mental activities have ceased, are subsided, the vitality is extinguished, the heat has cooled down, the faculties are broken. Of the monk who has attained the cessation of perception and of feeling, the bodily activities have ceased, his vocal activities have ceased, are subsided, his mental activities have ceased, are subsided, the vitality is not extinguished, the heat is not cooled down, the faculties are clear.

C : (vii, 86b, 6–8) : Q : What is the difference between entering into the meditation of complete cessation and entering into meditation of no-perception ? A : When the monk enters into the meditation of complete cessation, perception and knowledge are extinguished. When the monk enters into the meditation of no-perception, perception and knowledge are not extinguished.

P : not available.

C : (vii, 86b, 8–11) : Q : What is the difference when one arises from the meditation of complete cessation and from the meditation of no-perception ? A : When a monk arises from the meditation of complete cessation, he does not think thus : « I arise from the meditation of complete cessation ». When a monk arises from the meditation of no-perception, he thinks thus : « I have perception (or) I have no perception ».

P : no.

C : (vii, 86b, 11–12) : Q : When a monk enters into the meditation of complete cessation, what dharmas does he eradicate first, bodily activities, vocal activities or mental activities ? A : When a monk enters into the meditation of complete cessation, he eradicates first bodily activities, then vocal activities, and finally mental activities.

P : not available here but available in *P : N°* 44 : (*i*, 301, 36 ; 362, 1–5) : The P mentions that vocal activities cease first, then bodily activities, then mental activities.

C : (vii, 86b, 12–14) : Q : When a monk emerges from the meditation of complete cessation, what dharmas arise first, bodily activities, vocal activities or mental activities ? A : When a monk emerges from the meditation of complete cessation, mental activities arise first, then vocal activities and finally bodily activities.

P : not available here but available in *P N°* 44 : (*i*, 302, 13–18) : Here the P mentions that mental activities appear first, then bodily activities, then vocal activities.

C : (vii, 86b, 14–16) : Q : When a monk emerges from the meditation of complete cessation, how many kinds of touch does he come into contact with first ? A : When a monk emerges from the meditation of complete cessation, he comes into contact with 3 kinds of touch : no-hankering (without craving) touch, substanceless touch and signless touch.

P : not available here, but available in *P N°* 44 : (*i*, 302, 18–22) : Here the P mentions first substanceless touch (suññata), then signless touch (animitta) then desireless touch (appaṇihita).

In *C. S. N°* 31, there is again a series of questions and answers related to these 2 kinds of concentration :

C N° 210 : (*vii*, 84*b*, 5–7) : Q : When a monk enters into the concentration of complete cessation, does he think : « I am entering into the concentration of complete cessation ? A : When a monk... cessation, he does not think : « Now I enter into the concentration of complete cessation». Due to his former practice and training of the mind, it leads him to such an attainment.

P N° 44 : (*i*, 301, 30–36) : Almost the same. Q : How is the attainment of the cessation of perception and of feeling ? A : The monk who is attaining the cessation of perception and feeling does not think : « I shall attain the cessation of perception and feeling », or « I am attaining the cessation of perception and feeling » or « I have attained the cessation of perception and feeling ». As he formerly has trained his mind in such way that this leads him to such an attainment.

C : (84*b*, 7–9) : When a monk arises from the concentration of complete cessation, does he think : « I arise from the concentration of complete cessation » ? A : When a monk arises from the concentration of complete cessation, he does not think : « I arise from the concentration of complete cessation. » But it is due to this body and the 6 sense-organs associating with vitality that he arises from the concentration.

P : (302, 6–13) : Same difference as seen in the preceding question. Another difference : C : But due to this body... from concentration = P : As formerly he has trained his mind in such way, this leads him to such a state.

C : (84*b*, 9–10) : Q : When a monk arises from the concentration of complete cessation, what does his mind enjoy, where does his mind bend to, what does his mind incline to ? A : When a monk arises from the cessation of complete cessation, his mind enjoys aloofness, bends on aloofness, inclines towards aloofness.

P : (302, 22–27) : Almost the same. C : Aloofness = P : viveka.

Remarks : Thus as far as concentration of complete cessation and concentration of no-perception are concerned, there is not much difference between the C and the P versions. Although the C uses the term *concentration of complete cessation* and the P the term *saññāvedayitanirodha*, their definition is the same. As to the difference of what activities arise or cease first, it is rather difficult to distinguish between bodily activities and vocal activities as if the mouth moves to utter a sound, it includes both vocal and bodily activities as well. So the difference as to which activities arise or cease first between the C and the P versions is not an important one.

7. — *The 5 Abhiññā or super-knowledges :*

The 5 super-knowledges are dealt with in *C. S.* N° 5, N° 25, N° 74. Thus in *C.S. N°* 74, the dharmas are referred to as follows.

C N° 81 : (*v*, 114*b*, 15–17) : The monk can obtain the *ju-i-chu* (如意足 : power to do what one wishes to do), the *t'ien-êrh* (天耳 : divine ear), the *t'a-hsin-chih* (他心智 : knowledge of others' mind), the *su-ming-chih* (宿命智 knowledge of former births), and the *shêng-ssu-chih* (生死智 : knowledge of birth and death) ; then with the eradication of cankers, he knows and realizes by himself here-now and dwells in mind-emancipation, wisdom-emancipation which is cankerless, he attains arahantship.

P N° 119 : (*iii*, 98, 2–28 ; 99, 1–7) : Almost the same. C: power to do what one wishes to do = P: anekavihitaṃ iddhividhaṃ. C : divine ear = P: dibbasotaṃ. C: knowledge of others' mind = P: parasattānaṃ parapuggalānaṃ cetasā ceto paricca pajānāti. C: knowledge of former births = P: anekavihitaṃ pubbenivāsaṃ anussarati. C : knowledge of birth and death = P : dibbaṃ cakkhuṃ (other places: cutūpapātañāṇaṃ). But here the P deals at length as usual with all the five super-knowledges.

In *C. S. N*° 5, the monk formulates the wishes of attaining the 5 super-knowledges as seen under :

C N° 105 : (*vi*, 29*b*, 12–13) : « May I be able to obtain the psychic powers, the divine ear, the knowledge of others' mind, the knowledge of previous births, the knowledge about birth and death . . . »

P N° 6 : (*i*, 34, 10–37 ; 35 ; 36, 1–3) : Here the P treats the same subject, but divides it into 6 wishes, 12th for iddhividhaṃ, 13th for dibbasotañāṇaṃ, 14th for cetopariyañāṇaṃ, 15th tor pubbenivāsānussati, 16th for dibbacakkhuñāṇaṃ and 17th for the destruction of all cankers.

a) *Iddhividhañāṇaṃ* : Power to do what one wishes to do :

In *C. S. N*° 26, this super-knowledge is treated as follows :

C N° 184 : (*vii*, 35*a*, 14–19) : There is a monk who possesses great psychic power, great merit, great blessedness, great supernatural power, who masters innumerable psychic powers, who performs innumerable psychic powers, being one he becomes many, being many he becomes one ; being one he becomes one endowed with knowledge, with vision ; he goes through stone, through walls without hindrance as through empty space ; he comes out, he enters the earth as through water ; he walks on the water without sinking as on the earth ; he flies up the sky and sits cross-legged there like the birds. Now these sun and moon possess great psychic powers, great merit, great blessedness, great supernatural powers, he with his hand touches, rubs the body of the sun and of the moon, up to the Brahma-world.

P N° 32 : (*i*, 214, 18–28) : Here the P is totally different, as it refers to elder Kaccāna's reply about knowledge of the Abhidhamma. But in *P N*° 108 : (*iii*, 11, 28–33 ; 12, 1–4), it is almost the same with the C text. It omits : who possesses great psychic power, great merit, great blessedness, great supernatural power, who masters innumerable psychic powers and performs innumerable psychic powers ; being one he becomes one endowed with knowledge, with vision. C: he goes through stone, through walls without hindrance like through empty space = P: Āvibhāvaṃ tirobhāvaṃ tirokuḍḍaṃ tiropākāraṃ tiropabbataṃ asajjamāno gacchati seyyathāpi ākāse (manifest or invisible, he goes through the wall, through the rampart, through the mountain as if through the air). C : great psychic power, great merit, great blessedness, great supernatural powers = P evaṃ mahiddhike evaṃ mahānubhāve (such supernatural power, such strength). The P adds : he yields power with his body (kāyena vasaṃ vatteti).

b) *Dibbasotam or Divine ear :*

In *C. S. N*° 74, the *C N*° 81 : (*v*, 114*b*, 15–17) mentions simply divine ear, while the *P N*° 119 : (*iii*, 98, 10–12) writes : « With the pure divine ear, which surpasses that of human beings, he hears the deity-sounds and the human sounds both far and near ».

c) *Cetopariyañāṇaṃ : Knowledge of others' mind :*

Again in *C. S.* 74, the *C N*° 81 : (*v*, 114*b*, 15–17) mentions simply the knowledge of others' mind, while the *P N*° 119 : (*iii*, 98, 12–27) deals at length as follows : « He knows the mind of other beings, of other people with the mind. If the mind is with lust, he knows that the mind is with lust ; if the mind is without lust, he knows that the mind is without lust ; in the same way with malevolence, without malevolence, with delusion, without delusion, which is contracted (saṃkhittaṃ), which is distracted (vikkhittaṃ), which is big, which is not big, which has some mind superior to it, which has no other mind superior to it, which is concentrated, which is not concentrated, which is emancipated, which is not emancipated.

d) *Pubbenivāsānussatiñāṇaṃ or knowledge of former births :*

In *C. S. N*° 43, the knowledge of former births is referred to in the following terms :

C N° 194 : (*vii*, 51*b*, 14–17) : He, with his mind thus concentrated, pure, without blemishes, without worry, soft, well fixed, with mind not shaking, he remembers previous births, having realized it with wisdom, he has such a life, such a feature, remembers countless previous lives, one birth, two births, hundred births, thousand births, ascending aeon, descending aeon, countless ascending and descending aeons, those beings have such a name, they previously have passed (through those lives) : « I was born there, with such a surname, with such a name, with such a clan, eating such a food and drink, experiencing such unpleasant and pleasant feelings, with such a length of life, living such a long time, passing away in such a way ; having passed away there, I was born here. Being born here, I have such a surname, such a name, such a clan, eating such a food and drink, experiencing such a pleasant and unpleasant feelings, with such a length of life, living such a long time, passing away in such a way.

This C passage can be compared with the P one in *C. S. N°* 28 :

P N° 39 : (*i*, 278, 6–20) : Almost the same. As to the epithets qualifying the mind, the P adds pariyodāte (clean), kammaniye (workable). C : without worry = P : vigatūpakkilese (without defilement). C : with mind not shaking = P āneñjjappatte. It omits : having realized with wisdom, he has such a life, such a feature. C : he remembers countless previous lives = P : remembers a variety of former lives. C : 1 birth, 2 births, 100 births, 1,000 births = P : 1 birth, 2 births, 3, 4, 5, 10, 20, 30, 40, 50, 100, 1,000, 100,000 births. The P omits : living such a long time, passing away in such a way. It adds: iti sākāraṃ sauddesaṃ (in all their modes and details).

e. — *Dibbacakkhu or cutūpapātañāṇaṃ : The divine eye or knowledge of birth and death :*

This knowledge is dealt with in C. S. N° 26, N° 28, N° 38 and also in N° 43. Thus in *C. S. N°* 43, it is referred to as follows :

C N° 194 : (*vii*, 51*b*, 18–20 ; 52*a*, 1–2) : He, with his mind thus concentrated, pure, without blemishes, without worry, soft, well fixed, with mind not shaking, he trains himself in the knowledge of birth and death, attained and realized through knowledge. He with a pure heavenly eye, surpassing that of human beings, sees these living beings dying and being born, handsome, ugly, subtle, rough, passing through happy states and unhappy states, in accordance with the actions of these living beings. He sees them in accordance with truth. If these living beings perform evil bodily, vocal and mental deeds, abuse holy people, are endowed with wrong view, with wrong actions. Due to these, after death they will be born in woeful places, in the Hell. If these living beings perform meritorious bodily, vocal and mental deeds, do not abuse holy people, are endowed with right view, with right action ; due to these actions after death they will be born in happy places, in the heaven.

This C passage can be compared with the P passage in *C. S. N°* 28 :

P N° 39 : (*i*, 278, 32–37 ; 279, 1–18) : Almost the same. It omits : « he trains himself, attained and realized through knowledge » but adds : « he bends his mind on ». C : handsome, ugly, subtle, rough, passing through happy states and unhappy states, in accordance with the actions of these living beings = P : hīne paṇīte suvaṇṇe dubbaṇṇe sugate duggate yathākammūpage. The P omits : he sees them in accordance with truth. C : endowed with wrong actions = P micchādiṭṭhikammasamādānā (performing wrong actions according to wrong view). C : in woeful places, in the Hell = P : apāyaṃ duggatiṃ vinipātaṃ nirayaṃ (in woeful place, in bad state, in bad fall, in the Hell). C : endowed with right actions = P : sammādiṭṭhikammasamādānā.

Remarks : Thus the comparative study of the 5 superknowledges of the C and P versions shows us that there is not much difference between the two traditons, except for some epithets more or less or slightly different.

We can say safely that as far as the meditation-group is concerned, there is almost identical view between the Chinese and the Pāli versions. Barring some differences in the exposition of the four applications of mindfulness, both versions seem to draw their respective materials from the same source and this explains the similarities between the C and the P versions as far as the meditation-group is concerned.

Chapter IV. — DOCTRINE

C. — PAÑÑĀ OR WISDOM

C. — PAÑÑĀ OR WISDOM

Dealing with the wisdom-group, we start first with Paññābhūmi or foundation of wisdom, then with the 7 visuddhis or purities, then with the 2 vimuttis or emancipations and finally with the 4 maggas and phalas, including the āsavakhayañāṇaṃ.

1. — PAÑÑĀBHŪMI

a) *Khandhā or aggregates :*

These dharmas are treated in C. S. N° 19, N° 24, N° 31, N° 70, N° 77, N° 95 and N° 98.

In *C. S. N°* 31, the 5 aggregates are referred to as follows :

C N° 210 : (*vii*, 83*b*, 11–13) : The W.H. One spoke of the 5 growing aggregates of one's own body, the growing aggregate of material forms, of feelings, of perceptions, of activities and of consciousness.

P N° 44 : (*i*, 299, 7–15) : Almost the same. C : 5 growing aggregates = P : pañcupādānakkhandhā. Here the C uses the term *Shêng* (盛) meaning growing for the P term *upādāna*. The later translators preferred the term *Ch'u* (取) meaning grasping, and thus rendered the exact meaning of the term *upādāna*.

In *C. S. N°* 24, the inter dependent nature of the 5 aggregates is treated in details :

C N° 30 : (*v*, 41*a*, 20 ; 41*b*, 1–9) : « Rev. fr., just as due to wood and beams, due to mud and earth, due to water and grass which surround and cover that, in the empty space there comes to be known as a dwelling. Rev. fr. should know, this body is also the same. Due to sinews and bones, due to skin, due to flesh, blood which surround and cover that, in the empty space there comes to be known as a body. Rev. fr., if internal eyes are broken, if external material forms are not reflected by light, and there is no thought (then), eye-consciousness does not arise. Rev. fr., if internal eyes are not broken, if external material forms are reflected by light and there is thought (then), eye-consciousness arises. Rev. fr., internal eyes, material forms, all these belong to the aggregate of material forms. If there are feelings, they belong to the aggregate of feelings ; if there are perceptions, they belong to the aggregate of perceptions ; if there are reflections (or volitions), they belong to the aggregate of reflections (or volitions) ; if there are consciousnesses, they belong to the aggregate of consciousness. Thus you should reflect on the collecting, the coming together of the aggregates. Rev. fr., the W. H. One had said the same thing. When (you) see the dependent origination, you see the dharma, when you see the dharma, you see the dependent origination. Why is it so? Rev. fr., the W. H. One has said that the 5 growing (1) aggregates are generated by conditions, the growing (1) aggregate of material forms, of feelings, of perceptions, of (mental) activities, of consciousness (In the same way with the other sense-organs).

P N° 28 : (*i*, 190, 15-37 ; 191, 1-34) : Almost the same, with more details. C : due to wood and beams, due to mud and earth, due to water and grass = P : due to timbers, creeper, grass and clay. With reference to the body, the P omits : due to blood. While the C enumerates only 2 cases, one in which the eye-consciousness cannot arise due to lack of some appropriate conditions, and one in which eye-consciousness arises due to the presence of some appropriate conditions, the P enumerates up to 3 cases. The following case is missing in the C: « If internal eyes are not broken, if external material forms enter into focus (but), there is no appropriate coming together, then there is no appropriate consciousness ». C : If internal eyes are broken, if external material forms are not reflected by light, and there is no thought (then), eye-consciousness does not arise = P : If internal eyes are broken, if external material forms do not enter into focus, there is no appropriate coming together, then there is no appearance of the appropriate consciousness. Here the P treats all the 5 aggregates with the same length while the C skips over the 3 middle aggregates. The C uses the term *ssu* (思 : thought, volition) for the term *saṅkhāra*.

In *C. S. N*° 19, the 5 aggregates are the subjects for meditation.

C N° 200: (*vii*, 65*b*, 13-19) : Again there are 6 basic views. What are the six?: 1) whatever is material form, past, future, present, internal or external, subtle or coarse, refined or unrefined, near or far, they all should be considered by wisdom as it really is : « This is not mine ; I am not this; this is not the soul»; 2) whatever feeling ; 3) whatever perception; 4) whatever view that « They do not belong to me, I have them not, they shall not exist and I shall not not to exist», they all should be considered by wisdom as it really is: « This is not mine ; I am not this ; this is not the soul» ; 5) whatever is seen, heard, perceived, cognised and known, whatever is obtained, whatever is reflected, whatever is thought of by the mind, from this world to that world, from that world to this world, they all should be considered by wisdom as it really is: « They are not mine, I am not theirs, they are not the soul » ; 6) whatever is this view : « This is the soul, this is the world, this is the self, I shall become in the next life, eternal, not liable to change, lasting, not subject to destruction, they all should be considered by wisdom as it really is : « They are not mine, I am not theirs, they are not the soul. »

(1) See ante, p. 113.

P N° 22 : (*i*, 138, 36–37 ; 139, 1–10) : Not exactly the same. It does not refer to the 6 views but only to 5 aggregates : rūpa, vedanā, saññā, saṅkhārā and viññāṇa. All these dhammas should be considered as : « They are not mine, I am not theirs, these are not myself. » Here we note that the C translates the term *Ātman* as soul, while the P refers to the term atta, self.

b) 12 *āyatanāni or sense–spheres :*

The 12 sense–spheres are treated in C. S. N° 72, N° 87, N° 91 and N° 98.

Thus in *C. S. N°* 72, they are referred to as follows :

C N° 181 : (*vii*, 32*a*, 5–7) : « If there is a monk who sees the 12 spheres as they really are, eye–sphere, material form–sphere, ear–sphere, sound–sphere, nose–sphere, smell–sphere, tongue–sphere, taste–sphere, body–sphere, contact-sphere, mind–sphere, dharma–sphere. A–nan, seeing these 12 spheres as they really are, A–nan, such a monk knows the 12 spheres. »

P N° 115 : (*iii*, 63, 18–23) : Almost the same. The 12 spheres are the same. C: Who knows as they really are = P: When he knows and sees these 12 spheres. C: Such a monk knows the 12 spheres = P: Then it suffices to say that he is expert in the spheres.

c) *Dhātu or elements :*

The elements are treated at length in the *C. S. N°* 72, in which various elements are analysed and explained.

In this C. S., the C mentions up to 13 divisions of elements, one division of 18, 3 divisions of 6, one division of 4, 6 divisions of 3 and 2 divisions of 2. The P mentions only 6 divisions of elements, one division of 18, 3 divisions of 6, one division of 3 and one division of 2. Thus the C mentions up to a total of 62 elements, while the P mentions only 41.

i) 18 *elements* : C 1 = P 1.

C N° 181 : (*vii*, 31*b*, 15–17) : There is a monk who sees the 18 elements according to the truth. The 18 elements are : eyes, material forms, eye–consciousness, ears, sounds, ear–consciousness, nose, smell, nose–consciousness, tongue, taste, tongue–consciousness, body, touch, body–consciousness, mind, mental states, mind–consciousness.

P N° 115 : (*iii*, 62, 10–18) : Almost the same. The 18 elements are the same. C : Who knows according to the truth = P : When he knows and sees these 18 elements, then it suffices to say that he is expert in the elements. The same difference is observed in the other divisions of elements.

ii) 6 *elements : C* 2 = *P* 2 :

C : (31*b*, 17) *:* The 6 elements are : earth, water, fire, wind, space, consciousness.

P : (62, 21–25) *:* The same.

iii) 6 *elements : C* 3 = *P* 4 :

C : (31*b*, 17–18) *:* The elements are : sense-desire, malevolence, harming, no sense-desire, no malevolence and no harming.

P : (62, 35–36 ; 63, 1–3) *:* The same, although the order is slightly different. P : kāmadhātu, nekkhamadhātu, vyāpādadhātu, avyāpādadhātu, vihesādhātu, avihesādhātu.

iv) 6 *elements : C* 4 = *P* 3 :

C : (31*b*, 18–19) *:* The 6 elements are : happiness, suffering, gladness, sorrow, equanimity and ignorance.

P : (62, 28–32) *:* The same.

v) 4 *elements :* C 5 = P no.

C : (31*b*, 19) *:* The four elements are : feelings, perceptions, mental activities and consciousness.

P : Not available.

vi) 3 *elements : C* 6 = *P* 5 :

C : (31*b*, 19–20) *:* The 3 elements are : sense-desire, material forms and immaterial forms.

P : (63, 6–9) *:* The same.

vii) 3 *elements :* C 7 = P no.

C : (31*b*, 20 : 32*a*, 1) *:* The 3 elements are : material forms, immaterial forms and cessation.

viii, ix, x, xi) 3 *elements : C* 8, *C* 9, *C* 10, *C* 11 *: P : no.*

C : (32*a*, 1–3) *:* The 3 elements are respectively : 8th, past, future and present ; 9th, excellence, no-excellence and middle ; 10th, meritorious elements, demeritorious elements, neutral elements, 11th, of learner, of no-learner, of neither learner nor no-learner.

xii) 2 *elements : C* 12 = *P no.*

C : (32*a*, 3-4) *:* Element of cankers and element of no-cankers.

xiii) 2 *elements : C* 13 = *P* 6 *:*

C : (32*a*, 4) *:* The conditioned element and the unconditioned element.

P: (63, 12-15) The same.

In *C. S. N*° 94, there is a long passage dealing with the meditation of the 6 elements as under :

i) *About earth-element :*

C N° 162 : (*vii*, 5*b*, 7-10) : There is a monk who analyses the body-element, saying that this body has the internal earth-element, receiving life. This internal earth-element is as follows : hair, hair of the body, nail, teeth, rough outer skin, thin inner skin, flesh, bone, sinews, kidneys, heart, liver, lungs, spleen, big intestines, stomach, excrements and other internal matters similar to them, which are hard, internal and receiving life. This is called the internal earth-element. Whatever internal element and whatever external element are called earth-element. He considers the earth-element : « This is not mine, I am not this, this also is not the soul ». He considers the earth-element with wisdom and knows it as it really is and thus his mind is not blemished by the earth-element, does not grasp the earth-element.

P N° 140 : (*iii*, 240, 14-33) : Almost the same. As to the earth-element, it is almost the same, although its definition is slightly different. It reads : « What is the earth element ? the earth-element may be internal and may be external. What is the internal earth-element ? Whatever is hard (kakkhaḷaṃ), rough (kharigataṃ), internal, related to the individual (paccattaṃ), and derived therefrom (upādiṇṇa). As to the enumeration of internal elements, it is almost the same. The P adds : marrow of the bone, pleura (kilomakaṃ) mesentery (antagunaṃ). For the C rough outer skin, thin inner skin, the P mentions simply taco. C : Thus his mind is not blemished by earth-element, his mind does not grasp it = P : Thus he is disgusted with earth-element and his mind is cleansed of earth-element. The C classifies marrow of bone under water-element.

ii) *About water-element :*

C : (5*b*, 10-13) : It is treated in the same way as with earth-element with the term « Whatever is hard » replaced by « Whatever is fluid ». As to matters classified as water-elements, they are : marrow of the brains, tear of the eye, sweat, mucus, phlegm, pus, blood, fat, marrow of the bone, saliva, bile, urine.

P : (240, 34 ; 241, 1-11) : Same remarks as above. Here the term āpogataṃ replaces the terme kakkhaḷaṃ kharigataṃ. As to the enumeration of water-elements, the P omits : marrow of the brains, marrow of the bone (which is placed in the earth-element). It adds : serum (vasā), synovial fluid (lasikā).

iii) *About fire-element :*

C : (5*b*, 13-16) : It is treated in the same way as with earth-element with « whatever is hard » replaced by « whatewer is hot and warm ». As to matters classified as fire-elements, they are : heat of body, warmth of body, burning sensation of body, what is nourishing to the body, that is digestion of food and drink.

P : (241, 12-22) : Same remarks as before. Here the term tejogataṃ replaces the term kakkhaḷaṃ kharigataṃ. As to matters classified as fire elements, they are : yena ca satappati (that by which one is consumed), yena ca jarīyati (1) (that by which one is worn out), yena ca pariḍayhati (that by which one is burnt up), yena ca asitapītakhāyitasāyitaṃ sammāpariṇāmaṃ gacchati (that by which one has mumched, drunk, eaten, and tasted which is properly digested).

iv) *About wind-element :*

C : (5*b*, 16-19) : It is treated in the same way as with earth-element, with « whatever is hard » replaced by « whatever is moving ». As to matters classified as wind-elements, they are : up-wind, down-wind, flank-wind, tearing wind, kicking wind, (tsuan-fêng : 蹴 風), no-path-wind (wu-tao-fêng 無 道 風 ?), limb by limb-wind, inhaling, exhaling...

P : (241, 23-32) : Same remarks as above. Here vāyogataṃ replaces kakkhaḷaṃ kharigataṃ. As to the enumeration of matters classified as wind-element, the P omits : flank-wind, tearing-wind, kicking-wind, no-path-wind ; but adds : abdomen-wind, belly-wind. C : limb by limb-wind = P : aṅgamaṅgānusārino vātā (wind shooting through various limbs).

v) *About space-element :*

C : (5*b*, 19-20 ; 6*a*, 1-3) : Here « whatever is hard, solid » is replaced by « whatever space inside the body, not obstructed by flesh, skin, bones, sinews ». As to matters classified as space-elements, they are : eye-orifice, ear-orifice, nose-orifice, mouth-orifice, throat-orifice, through which food is swallowed and digested and where it remains and where it passes out down below.

---

(1) Not Jariyati of the text (P.T.S.).

P : (241, 33–34 ; 242, 1–9) : Same remarks as above. Here the term ākāsagataṃ replaces the term kakkhaḷaṃ kharigataṃ. As to the matters classified as space-elements, the P omits : eye-orifice, throat-orifice. It mentions not only food, but what is mumched, drunk, eaten and tasted.

vi) *About consciousness-element :*

Knowledge of feelings :

C: (6*a*, 3–13) : When the monk knows the 5 elements as they really are, he is not sullied by them, but what is emancipated is consciousness. And what does he cognise ? he cognises pleasant feeling, unpleasant feeling, happy feeling, unhappy feeling and equanimity. Due to pleasant strong enjoyment he experiences pleasant feeling; experiencing pleasant feeling he knows that he is experiencing a pleasant feeling. Then the monk destroys that pleasant strong enjoyment ; that pleasant strong enjoyment being destroyed, the pleasant feeling which arises from that pleasant strong enjoyment is also destroyed, stopped ; then he knows that he is cool. In the same way for the other four feelings. Whatever strong enjoyment he experiences, he receives the corresponding feeling. With the destruction of strong enjoyment, the corresponding feeling also is destroyed. He knows that this feeling depends on strong enjoyment, having strong enjoyment as root, having strong enjoyment as origin, comes from strong enjoyment and having strong enjoyment as head, depends on strong enjoyment to fare about. Just like due to friction of two sticks that fire comes out, and from the fire, one experiences heat ; but when the sticks are separated, the fire dies out, and with the dying out of the fire, heat also dies out and the wood remains cold.

P : (242, 10–34 ; 243, 1–10) : Almost the same. Here the P says that the consciousness that remains is pure and clean and he knows something due to this consciousness. The P refers only to 3 feelings, pleasant, unpleasant, and neither pleasant nor unpleasant feeling. The treatment of the feelings is the same in both versions, but the P omits the last expression : « Then he knows that he is cool ». The P also omits : Whatever strong enjoyment he experiences... to fare about ». As to the simile, it refers simply to heat and light obtained due to contact and friction of the 2 sticks : with the 2 sticks separated, then heat is stopped, allayed.

About equanimity :

C : (6*a*, 13–20 ; 6*b*, 1–6) : When the monk is not sullied by the 3 feelings, then he is emancipated and he possesses only equanimity which is very pure. Then that monk thinks to take this totally pure equanimity and focus it on the plane of infinite space and thus he develops such a mind, depending on it, dwelling on it, standing on this, binding to it, he thinks to take this totally pure equanimity and focus it on the plane of infinite consciousness, on the plane of nothingness and the plane of neither perception nor non-perception, and thus he develops such a mind depending on it, dwelling on it, standing on it, binding to it. Just like a very skillful goldsmith, using fire to burn gold and refine it, making it very thin, burning it in a melting furnace, rendering it pure, very malleable and shining. Then with such a pure, very malleable and shining gold, the goldsmith can make into whatever ornament he likes, either golden silky ribbon to ornate new garment, or finger-ring, arm-bracelet, necklace, jewel-garland. Then the monk thinks that this pure equanimity being dependent on the plane of infinite space is a conditioned dharma. Being a conditioned dharma, it is subject to impermanence and thereby to suffering. With this, he knows suffering. Having known suffering, he does not focus this equanimity into the plane of infinite space. In the same way with the other 3 planes. Having known these 4 planes with wisdom as they really are, having not focussed on them, the monk then knows that equanimity is no longer a conditioned dharma, he does not think either for becoming or for non-becoming. Experiencing a feeling limited by the body, he knows that he is experiencing a feeling limited by the body, experiencing a feeling limited by life-principle, he knows that he is experiencing a feeling limited by life-principle. He knows that at the breaking up of the body, when he dies, all his feelings come to extinction, to cessation. He knows that they become very cool. Just as a lamp burns depending on wick, depending on oil, if no one brings fresh supply of oil, no one renews the wick, then with the burning up of old supply of oil and old wick, the lamp extinguishes itself.

P: (243, 11-32 ; 244-245, 1-13) : Here the P places the simile of the goldsmith first with more details, depicting the goldsmith or his apprentice preparing the furnace, lighting the melting pot, from time to time blowing on it, sprinkling water on it, examining it carefully and thus the gold becomes purified, malleable, free from dross, shining, ready for making ring, earring, necklace or golden garland. Thus this equanimity is compared to such a gold. Here also the monk thinks to focus this equanimity upon the 4 planes of the arūpāvācāra, considering if this equanimity supported, nourished by this focussing upon these 4 planes would stand by him for a long time. He comprehends that in so doing, this equanimity would be a conditioned dharma. Therefore he does not build up for, does not think out for becoming or no-becoming, he does not grasp anything in the world. Having no grasping, he is not disturbed ; being undisturbed, he realizes tranquillity by himself ; he knows that birth is destroyed, the brahma-life is fulfilled, what should be done has been done ; there will be no more becoming. When he experiences a pleasant feeling or an unpleasant feeling or a neither pleasant nor upleasant feeling, he knows that it is impermanent, not to be attached to, not an object of enjoyment ; thus he experiences these kinds of feeling with detachment. When he is experiencing a feeling limited by the body, he knows that he is experiencing a feeling limited by the body ; when he is experiencing a feeling limited by life, he knows that he is experiencing a feeling limited by life. He knows that after the breaking up of the body, when life comes to an and, all the enjoyable feelings will become cool. The simile of the lamp is almost the same. Here the C version places the attainment of arahantship in the next paragraph.

d) *Cattāri ariyasaccāni or the four noble truths :*

The four noble Truths are treated in C. S. N° 16, N° 22, N° 24, N° 28, N° 30, N° 38, N° 95, N° 98.

Thus in *C. S. N°* 48, they are defined as under :

C N° 153 : (*vi,* 91*b,* 16–19) : What is knowledge of suffering as it really is? Birth is suffering, old age is suffering, sickness is suffering, death is suffering, association with people we hate is suffering, dissociation with people we love is suffering, not to get what we desire is suffering, in short the five growing (1) aggregates are suffering. This is called knowledge of suffering as it really is. What is the knowledge of the practice (2), the habit of suffering ? This craving which leads to a future becoming, which is associated with pleasure and desire, which aspires to obtain this, to obtain that becoming, this is called knowledge of the practice (2), of the habit of suffering as it really is. What is the knowledge of the cessation of suffering as it really is ? the cessation without remainder of this craving which leads to a future becoming, which is associated with pleasure and desire, which aspires to obtain this, to obtain that becoming, the eradication, the complete forsaking, the non-attachment, the ceasing, the stopping; this is called knowledge of the cessation of suffering as it really is. What is the knowledge of the path (leading) to the cessation of suffering? This is the noble eightfold path from right view up to right concentration. This is called the path (leading) to the cessation of suffering.

Here the P corresponding passage does not refer to the four noble truths, but we can compare the C passage with the P passage in other sutta.

P N° 141 : (*iii,* 249, 9–13) : Almost the same. It omits : sickness is suffering, association with people one dislikes is suffering, dissociation with people we love is suffering. It adds : soko, paridevo, dukkhaṃ, domanassaṃ, upāyāso are suffering. C : the five growing aggregates = P : pañcupādānakkhandhā.

P : (250, 32–34 : 251, 1–2) : As to the cause of suffering, it is almost the same. C: the practice, the habit of suffering = P : dukkhassa samudayo. Here the C uses the term *Hsi* (習) (2) meaning practice, habit to translate the term *samudayo*; but later translators opted for the term *Chi* (集), meaning assembling, heaping to translate this term samudayo. C : which aspires to obtain this, to obtain that becoming = P : tatratatrābhinandinī, seyyathīdaṃ kāmataṇhā, bhavataṇhā, vibhavataṇhā.

P : (251, 3–6) : As to the cessation of suffering, it is almost the same. C : The cessation without remainder of this craving, which leads to a future becoming, which is associated with pleasure and desire, which aspires to obtain this, to obtain that becoming = P : Yo tassā yeva taṇhāya asesavirāga-

(1) See ante, p. 113.

(2) In Yüan and Ming editions, *Chi* (集) meaning origin used instead of *Hsi* (習).

nirodho, which is almost the same, with the omission of the various qualitative adjectives of taṇhā. C: the eradication, the complete forsaking, the non-attachment, the ceasing, the stopping = P: paṭinissaggo mutti anālayo.

P : (251, 7-11) : As to the path leading to the cessation of suffering, the C omits : « leading to » and put in an abridged form the 8 constituents of the Path while the P enumerates the whole eight.

In *C. S. N°* 95, there is a detailed study of the 4 noble truths which deserves to be analysed in details.

The noble truth of suffering :

i) *Birth is suffering :*

C N° 31 : (*v*, 41*b*, 20 ; 42*a*, 1-6) : The noble truth of suffering is defined as : birth is suffering, old age is suffering, sickness is suffering, association with what one dislikes is suffering, separation with what one likes is suffering, not getting what one desires is suffering, and in brief the 5 growing (1) aggregates are suffering. With reference to what is it said that birth is suffering ? those living beings of various classes of beings are born, come out, being formed, being endowed with the 5 aggregates, with life-principle, this is called birth. How is birth suffering ? When living beings are born, the body, the heart, the body and the heart receive heat, receive wide-spread heat, receive feeling, receive wide-spread feeling ; the body, the heart, the body and the heart receive growth, heat, disturbance, grief, sorrow, receive wide-spread growth, heat, disturbance, grief, sorrow, receive feeling, wide-spread feeling.

P N° 141 : (*iii*, 249, 9-17) : Almost the same, but far more simple. It omits : sickness is suffering, association with what one dislikes is suffering, separation with what one likes is suffering. It adds : soko, paridevo, dukkhaṃ, domanassaṃ, upāyāso. As to the definition of birth, it is almost the same. It refers to jāti (conception), sañjāti (production), okkanti (descend into the womb), nibbati (rebirth), abhinibbati (coming forth), appearance of the aggregates, and acquisition of sense-spheres. The P omits the definition of « how is birth suffering ».

ii) *Old age is suffering :*

C : (42*b*, 6-10) : Those living beings of various classes of beings are old, with white head, teeth broken, with strength daily weakened, with bent body, with twisted legs (Chiao-li 脚戾), with heavy body, with breath taken up, with going leaning on a stick, with wrinkling skin like a sesame seed, with faculties collapsing and out of use, with complexion and

(1) See ante, p. 113.

feature ugly and bad. This is old age. How is old age suffering ? (Same defition as in birth is suffering, here it refers to old age).

P : (249, 18-21) : Almost the same, but simpler. It refers to jarā (old age), jīraṇatā (decrepitude), khaṇḍiccaṃ (broken teeth), pāliccaṃ (greyness of hair), valittacatā (wrinkling skin), āyuno saṃhānī (with reducing of life-span), indriyānaṃ paripāko (with faculties broken, out of use). Here also it omits the definition of suffering of old age.

iii) *Sickness is suffering :* P not available.

C : (42*a*, 10-14) : Various kinds of sickness are enumerated here : headache, eye-sore, ear-sore, nose-sore, facial-sore, lip-sore, toothache, tongue-sore, palate-sore, throat-sore, hiccough (feng-ch'uan 風喘), cough, vomiting, diphtheria (hou-pi 喉啤), epilepsy (tien-hsien 癲癇), cancer (yung 癰), goitre (ying 癭), ching-i (經溢 ?), red gall (ch'ih-tan 赤膽), excess of heat, withering away, piles (chih 痔), tumour (lü 瘻), dysentery. As to sickness is suffering, it is the same as in the previous paragraph.

iv) *Death is suffering :*

C : (42*a*, 14-18) : Death is the end of life-principle, the impermanence, the death, the scattering away, the cessation, the extinction, the destruction of life-span, the shutting up of the life-root of these living beings of various classes of beings, this is called death. As to death is suffering, it is the same as in the previous paragraph.

P : (249, 22-26) : Almost the same. It is the passing away (cuti), the falling away (cavanatā), the breaking up (bhedo), the disappearance (antaradhānaṃ), the death (maccu), the decease (maraṇaṃ) the work of time (kālakiriyā), the breaking up of the aggregates, the throwing away of the body (kaḷebarassa nikkhepo). Here the P omits the definition of suffering of death.

v) *To associate with what one dislikes is suffering :* P no. (1)

C : (42*a*, 18-20 : 42*b*, 1) : This is the association, the coming together with the 6 internal sense-fields which one dislikes such as eyes, ears, nose, tongue, body, mind. In the same way with the 6 external sense-fields which one dislikes but one has to be in touch with, to feel, to think of, to perceive ; in the same way with the 6 elements which one dislikes, such as earth-element, water-element, fire-element, wind-element, space-element, consciousness-element. As to association with what one dislikes is suffering, it is the same as in the previous paragraphs, but here it refers to suffering when one is in association with what one dislikes.

---

(1) Not available here but available in PMN N° 9, p. 65, line 8 Nalanda edition.

vi) *Dissociation with what one likes is suffering:* P: no.

C: (42*b*, 1–5) : It is treated in the same way as with the preceding case, but here what one likes are the 6 internal, the 6 external sense-spheres and the 6 elements, but one has to part from them, cannot associate with them, cannot come together with them.

vii) *Not getting what one desires is suffering :*

C: (42*b*, 5–11) : Beings are liable to birth, cannot escape from it and one wishes not to be liable to birth and such a desire cannot be obtained. In the same way when one wishes not to be liable to old age, to death, to sorrow, to grief, to lamentation, when one encounters suffering but wishes to convert it into happiness but of no avail; when one encounters happiness and wishes it to last for ever but of no avail ; in the same way, when one encounters unhappy thoughts and wishes to convert them into happy thoughts; when one encounters happy thoughts and wishes them to last for ever but of no avail. All these cannot be got for the wishing.

P: (250, 13–25) : Almost the same. Wishes not to be liable to birth, to old age, to death, to sorrow, to grief, to suffering, to dejection, to despair are also formulated here. The remaining wishes are omitted.

viii) *In brief, the* 5 *growing* (1) *aggregates are suffering :*

C: (42*b*, 11–13) : There are the growing (1) aggregate of material forms, the growing (1) aggregate of feelings, the growing (1) aggregate of perceptions, the growing (1) aggregate of (mental) activities, the growing (1) aggregate of conscioueness ; in brief, these 5 growing (1) aggregates are suffering. Thus this noble truth of suffering has existed in the past, is existing in the present and will be existing in the future ; this is real truth, not false truth, not moving away from reality, obtained by the Noble Ones, known, seen, understood, attained and fully and rightly realised by the Noble Ones, that is why this is called the noble truth of suffering.

P: (250, 26–31) : Almost the same. It omits the last portion: « Thus this noble truth of suffering has existed in the past... that is why this is called the noble truth of suffering.

Remarks : This stress on the existence of the noble truth of suffering in the past, in the present and in the future in the C version is very important. It serves to explain the doctrine « Sarvaṃ asti » of the Sarv. who maintain the existence of 5 dharmas in their subtlest form at all times, whether in the past, present or future. The omission of this passage in the P is significant as it shows that the Ther. deny any such existence.

(1) See ante p. 113.

ix) *Grief, sorrow, suffering, dejection and despair are suffering :* (Chinese not available).

P : (249, 27-30) : *Soko* : When one encounters some kinds of calamity or other, some kinds of suffering or other, one grieves, is in a state of grief, subject to inner grief, inwardly subject to strong grief (soko, socanā, socitattaṃ antosoko antoparisoko).

P : (249, 31-33 ; 250, 1-2) : *Paridevo* when one encounters some kinds of calamity or other, s me kinds of suffering or other, one wails, laments, is in a state of wailing, of lamenting, is subject to wailing, to lamenting (ādevo paridevo, ādevanā paridevanā ādevitattaṃ paridevitattaṃ).

P : (250, 3-5) : *Dukkhaṃ* : This is physical suffering, physical pain, physical suffering and physical pain due to bodily touch.

P : (250, 6-8) : *Domanassaṃ* : The same as above, but here is mental suffering, mental pain but not physical suffering, physical pain.

P : (250, 9-12) : *Upāyāso* : When one encounters some kinds of calamity or other, some kinds of suffering or other, one despairs, become despondent, is in a state of despair, in a state of despondency (āyāso upāyāso, āyāsitattaṃ upāyāsitattaṃ).

The Noble Truth of the origin of suffering :

C : (42*b*, 13-20 ; 43*a*, 1) : What is the noble truth of the practice of suffering. Living beings really have craving for the internal sense-spheres, crave for them get attached to them, are defiled by them and grasp them, this is called the pratice of suffering. The learned disciple knows of such a knowledge, realizes such a view, understands and realises such a dharma, that is the noble truth of the practice of suffering. What does he know of ? he knows that if there is craving for wife and children, servants, slaves, relatives, fields, lands, houses, shops, selling and buying properties, transacting in business. If he has craving, has attachment for them, is defiled by them, grasps them, this is called the practice and he knows the noble truth of craving, the practice of suffering. In the same way with the external sense-spheres which one comes in touch with, feels, perceives, thinks, craves for ; in the same way with the 6 elements of earth, water, fire, wind, space and consciousness. As to the definition of truth and noble, it is the same as in the first case.

P : (250, 32-34 ; 251, 1-2) : Not exactly the same. It refers to the same definition as seen above : « Whatever craving which leads to new becoming, which is connected with delight and attachment, taking delight in this and that namely craving for sense-desires, craving for becoming, craving for non-becoming ». Here also it omits the definition of truth and of noble.

The noble truth of the cessation of suffering :

C : (43*a*, 19) : What is the noble truth of the cessation of suffering? Living beings really have craving for the 6 internal sense-spheres, eyes, ears, nose, tongue, body and mind. If they are free from them, are not defiled by them, do not grasp them, if they eradicate them, give them up, throw them away, without desire, cease, stop, are without them, this is said to be the cessation of suffering. The learned noble disciple knows of such a knowledge, realizes such a view, understands and realises such a dharma, that is the noble truth of the cessation of craving, the cessation of suffering. What does he know of? he knows that if there is no craving for wife and children, servants, slaves, relatives, fields, lands, houses, shops, selling and buying properties, for transacting in business, if he is free from them, is not defiled by them, does not grasp them, eradicates them, gives them up, throws them away, without desire, ceases, stops, is without them, this is called the cessation of suffering and he knows the noble truth of the cessation of craving, the cessation of suffering. In the same way with the external sense-spheres, which one comes in touch with, feels, perceives, thinks of and craves for, and with the 6 elements of earth, water, fire, wind, space and consciousness. Here the C repeats the same definition of truth and of noble.

P : (251, 3-6) : Not exactly the same. The definition is as follows : Whatever is the cessation of any remaining attachment for craving, the relinquishment of it, the getting rid of it, the release from it, the independence of it, this is called the cessation of suffering.

The noble truth of the path leading to the cessation of suffering :

Here it refers to the noble eightfold Path as already described page 96.

e) *Paṭiccasamuppāda or the dependent origination :*

This dharma is treated in C.S. N° 9, N° 24, N° 27, N° 72 and N° 98. Thus in *C.S. N°* 98, this dharma is referred to as follows :

C N° 86 : (*vi*, 2*b*, 17-20 ; 3*a*, 1-2) : « A-nan, formerly I spoke to you about the dependent origination and the dharmas arisen out of the dependent origination. If this exists, then that exists ; if this does not exist then that does not exist ; if this arises then that arises ; if this does not arise, then that does not arise. If this ceases then that ceases ; dependent on ignorance are the activities ; dependent on activities is consciousness ; dependent on consciousness is name-and-form ; dependent on name-and-form are the 6 spheres ; dependent on 6 spheres are the 6 strong enjoyments ; dependent on 6 strong enjoyments are feelings ; dependent on feelings is craving ; dependent on craving is receiving; dependent on receiving is becoming ; dependent on becoming is birth ; dependent on birth are old age and death. If ignorance ceases then activities cease; if activities cease then consciousness ceases; if consciousness ceases then name-and-form ceases; if name-and-form ceases then the 6 spheres cease; if the 6 spheres cease, then feelings cease; if feelings cease then craving ceases; if craving ceases then receiving ceases; if receiving ceases then becoming ceases; if becoming ceases then birth ceases; if birth ceases then old age and death cease.

P N° 115 : (*iii*, 63, 24-32 ; 64, 1-13) : Almost the same. C: if this exists... then that ceases = P: Imasmiṃ sati, idaṃ hoti ; imass'uppādā idaṃuppajjati; imasmiṃ asati, idaṃ na hoti; imassa nirodhā idaṃ nirujjhati. It is almost the same with the C, although the order is slightly different and that the P omits : if this does not arise, then that does not arise. C. strong enjoyment = P: phasso ; śparśa means enjoyment and touch and the C prefers strong enjoyment here. C : receiving (受) = P: upādāna ; later translators preferred Ch'ü (取) meaning holding, grasping. C : dependent on birth are old age and death = P: jātipaccayā jarāmaraṇaṃ sokaparidevadukkhadomanassupāyāsā sambhavanti. The P adds : evaṃ etassa kevalassa dukkhakkhandhassa samudayo hoti. C: If ignorance ceases then activities ceases = P : avijjāya tveva asesavirāganirodhā sankhāranirodho. The P adds : evaṃ etassa kevalassa dukkhakkhandhassa nirodho hoti.

In *C. S. N*° 27, the dependent origination is dealt with, but it starts first with four kinds of food, which have craving as cause, then subsequently feelings, strong enjoyment, 6 spheres, name-and-form, consciousness, (mental) activities, ignorance. Then it refers to : dependent on ignorance are the activities... up to... dependent on birth are old age, death, grief, sorrow, lamentation, suffering, dejection. Thus this is the arising of the great aggregate of suffering. Here we remark that the C version *N*° 201 : (*vii*, 67*b*, 2-9) does not omit to mention grief, sorrow, lamentation, suffering, dejection as seen in previous paragraph.

As to the inter-dependent nature of the 5 aggregates dealt with in *C. S. N*° 24, it is already referred to in the paragraph of the 5 aggregates page 113.

Thus we can say that there is no important difference between the C and the P versions as far as the dependent origination is concerned.

f) *Cattāro āhārā or four kinds of food* :

Four kinds of food are mentioned in *C. S. N*° 27 and *N*° 70. Thus in *C. S. N*° 27, they are referred to as follows :

C N° 201 : (*vii*, 67*b*, 2) : One is t'uan-shih (摶食), meaning morsel food, gross and subtle, then kêng-lo (更樂), meaning strong enjoyment food, I-nien-shih (意念食), meaning volition food and shih-shih (識食), meaning consciousness-food.

P N° 38 : (*i*, 261, 5–8) : Almost the same. C : morsel food, gross and subtle = P : kabaḷiṅkāro āhāro oḷāriko, vā sukhumo vā. C : strong enjoyment food = P : phasso āhāro. C : volition food = P : manosañcetanā āhāra. C : consciousness-food = P : viññāṇaṃ āhāro.

g) *Kamma and kammavipāka or actions and results of actions :*

These dharmas are dealt with in C. S. N° 39, N° 40, N° 65, N° 84, N° 85, N° 89 and N° 90.

Thus in *C. S. N°* 89, they are referred to as follows :

C N° 170 : (*vii*, 16*b*, 12–18) : At that time Ying-wu-ma-na came to the Buddha, greeted him and asked permission to question him. Permission being granted, he asked the W. H. One that for what reason, for what cause, among the living beings, although they assumed the human form, but some were low, some were high, some were mean, some were noble. He said that he saw some were of short life, some of long life, some of many diseases, some of few diseases, some ugly, some handsome, some had no authority, no influence, some had authority and influence, some were of low families, some of noble families, some poor, some rich, some of evil wisdom, some of good wisdom. Then the W. H. One replied that living beings performed their own actions, they received results of their own actions. They depended on their actions, they relied upon their actions, their actions were their arbiters. This brief explanation did not satisfy Ying-wu who requested the W.H. One to explain it in details and the W.H. One acquiesced in Ying-wu's request.

P N° 135 : (*iii*, 202, 12–24 ; 203, 1–15) : Almost the same. C : Ying-wu-ma-na-tu-t'i-tzu = P : Subha māṇava Todeyyaputta. Subha's question is the same, but it places questions about poor people and rich people before questions about people of low families, of noble families. The Buddha's reply is slightly different as follows : « Kammassakā sattā, kammadāyādā kammayonī kammabandhū kammapaṭisaraṇā (Living beings are masters of their own actions, they are heirs of their actions, matrix of their actions, kin to their actions, having their actions as place of refuge). The rest is the same.

i) *Why people are of short life and of long life :*

C : (16*b*, 18–20 ; 17*a*, 1–3) : There are people who kill living beings, cruel, extremely wicked, blood-thirsty, with harmful thoughts, without mercy to living beings up to insects. Having received these actions fully, when they die, they will be born in the hell ; when they are reborn as human beings, they will be of short life, because that way is conducive to short life and these actions yield that result. There are people who abstain from killing, who give up killing, who lay aside knifes and sticks, who have shame and remorse, with mercy towards all living beings up to insects. Having received these actions fully, when they die, they will be born in happy states, in the heaven. When they are reborn as human beings, they will be of long life, because that way is conducive to long life and those actions yield that result.

P : (203, 16–34 ; 204, 1–2) : Almost the same with some slight differences as to expressions used. C : extremely wicked, with harmful thoughts = P : hatapahate niviṭṭho (intent on injuring and killing). C : having received these actions fully = P : so tena kammena evaṃ samattena evaṃ samādiṇṇena (because of that action done and firmly accomplished). C : they will be born in the Hell — P : they will be born in unhappy places, in the miserable realms of existence, in the down-fall, in the Hell.

ii) *Why people are of many diseases and of few diseases :*

C : (17*a*, 3–7) : The way of explanation is the same as in the 1st case, only actions are different. Here people are doing harm to living beings, either with hand, with log of wood, with stone, with knife or with stick. These actions will lead to many diseases. The case of few diseases is just the reverse.

P : (204, 3–17) : Almost the same, with the same differences as in previous case. C : with knife = P : with sword. C : with stone = P : with clod of earth.

iii) *Why people are ugly and handsome :*

C : (17*a*, 7–12) : These people are turbulent, quick to be worried, are greatly offended on being spoken to even a little, evince anger and hatred, easy to be sorrowful, ever ready to enlarge quarrels and disputes. These actions will lead people to be born as ugly person. The other case is just the reserve

P : (204, 18–31) : Almost the same. It omits : ever ready to enlarge quarrels and disputes. It adds : kuppati byāpajjati patitthīyati (gets angry, disagrees, resists).

iv) *Why people have no authority, no influence and some have authority and influence :*

C : (17*a*, 12–16) : There are people who harbour jealousy and envy when they see people getting offerings, respects. They want to obtain what other people have obtained. These actions will lead them to be born as human beings without authority, without power. The other case is just the reverse.

P : (204, 32–37 ; 205, 1–5) : Almost the same. C: without authority, without influence = P: appesakkho (of little influence). It omits : They want to obtain what others have obtained. C : other people getting offerings, respect = P : paralābhasakkāragarukāra-mānanavandanapūjā (others' gains, honour, respect, marks of reverence). The rest is almost the same.

v) *Why some people are born in low families, some in noble families :*

C : (17*a*, 16–20; 17*b*, 1–2): There are people who are vain and proud. They do not respect one who deserves to be respected, do not revere one who deserves to be revered, do not honour one who deserves to be honoured, do not offer gifts to one who deserves to be offered gifts, do not give the path to one who deserves to be given the path, do not give seat to one who deserves to be given the seat, do not join hands, greet and pay homage to one who deserves to be greeted and paid homage with joint hands. These actions will lead them to be born in low families. The other case is just the reverse.

P : (205, 16–26): Almost the same, with some slight differences in some expressions.

vi) *Why some people are born poor, some are born rich :*

C: (17*b*, 2–8): There are people who are not a giver, do not give charity, towards recluses, brāhmaṇas, poor people, orphans and beggers coming from afar, they do not give food and drink, robes, blankets, garlands of flowers, smearing scents, houses, beds, couches and lights. These actions will lead them to be born poor. The other case is just the reverse.

P : (205, 6–15) : Almost the same. It mentions charity to be given only to recluses and brāhmaṇas and omits poor people, orphans and beggers coming from afar. Among the gifts to be given, it omits robes, blankets but adds clothes, vehicles.

vii) *Why some people are born with evil wisdom, some with good wisdom :*

C : (17*b*, 8–15): There are people who do not frequently come to ask famous recluses and brāhmaṇas about what is meritorious, what is demeritorious, what is an offence, what is not an offence, what is excellent, what is not excellent, what is white, what is black, where white and black come from ? what is the here-now result, what is the here-after result ? These actions lead them to be born with evil wisdom. The other case is just the reverse.

P : (205, 27–34 ; 206, 1–5): Almost the same. It omits these questions: What is excellent, what is not excellent, what is white, what is black, where white and black come from, what is the here-now result, what is the here-after result ? It adds : what should be practised, what should not be practised, what being performed by me is for my unhappiness and suffering for a long time, what being performed by me, is for my happiness and joy for a long time ?

In *C. S. N*° 90, the W.H. One gave the reasons of the apparent discrepancies between causes and results :

C N° 171 : (*vii*, 19*b*, 7-20) : In the case of people who did not abstain from bad actions but were born in a happy state, in the heaven, this was due to : a) they had already and completely suffered the results of their bad actions here-now, in this world, so they were reborn there in the happy state, in the heaven ; b) or they had to suffer the results of their bad actions not now, not in the next life, but in the life after next; c) or they had done good actions formerly and its good results were not exhausted so they were born in a happy state, in the heaven, after their death ; d) or at the moment of dying, they harboured meritorious mind or consciousness and psychic factors connected with right riew. The other remaining causes, case of people who abstained from bad actions but were born in an unhappy state, in the hell, case of people who did not abstain from bad actions and who were born after their death in an unhappy state, in the hell, then case of people who abstained from bad actions and were born after their death in a happy state, in the heaven, these 3 cases are of the same interpretation as in the first case, but with appropriate changes in some words and expressions.

P : N° 136 : (*iii*, 214, 6-34 ; 215, 1-14) : Not exactly the same. Here the P enumerates 4 reasons : a) he might have performed earlier good actions resulting in happiness ; b) he might have performed later good actions resulting in happiness ; c) at the time of dying, he might hold firmly to a right view ; d) as to his present bad actions, he might receive its bad results here-now or in another life. The other 3 cases are also of the same interpretation, with appropriate changes.

Thus we notice that there is not much difference as to the interpretation of karma and its results as seen above. But in *C. S. N*° 40, in which the W. H. One advised Ven. Lo-yün how to perform actions, there are some conspicuous differences.

C N° 14 : (*v*, 17*a*, 5-13) : The W. H. One advised Lo-yün that before performing a bodily deed, if he reflected and saw that this bodily deed was permissable (lit. pure : P. kappiya), but for oneself or for others, it would bring evil fruit and suffering, then he should give up this bodily deed. If before performing a bodily deed, he reflected and saw that this bodily deed was not permissable, but for oneself and for others it would bring meritorious fruit and happiness, then he should perform such a bodily deed. In the same way while performing the bodily deed. For the bodily deed already performed, he should also reflect. If he saw that the bodily deed, he had already performed was permissable, but for oneself or for others, it would bring evil fruit and suffering, then he should approach well learned fellow-monks, confess to them and be repentant, not to conceal and be well restrained in the future. If after reflection, he saw that the bodily deed he had already performed *was not permissable* but for oneself or for others, it brought meritorious fruit and happiness, then day and night he should rejoice and abide in right mindfulness and right wisdom.

P N° 61 : (*i*, 415, 25-36 ; 416 ; 417, 1-7) : The reflection here is not the same. Elder Rāhula is advised to reflect if the bodily deed he is about to perform will lead to oneself's harm, to others' harm, to the harm of both, it is an evil deed leading to suffering, resulting in suffering, then he should surely not perform this deed. If he sees that the bodily deed he is about to perform will not lead to oneself's harm, to others' harm, to the harm of both, it is a meritorious deed leading to happiness, resulting in happiness, then he should perform such a deed. (In the same way, while the bodily deed is being performed). For the bodily deed already performed, if after reflection, he sees that it leads to oneself's harm... then he should approach the Master or learned fellow-monks, disclose, confess and open to them and in the future restrain from performing such a deed. If after reflection, he sees that this bodily deed already performed does not lead to oneself's harm... then he dwells rejoicing over, day and night training himself in such a deed.

The vocal and mental actions are treated in the same way in the C and the P versions.

Remarks: The C interpretation gives rather a wide latitude to the monks as to the definition of a meritorious deed and of a monastic rule. But the P omits the term permissable and does not allow any wide interpretation as to the definition of a meritorious action and of a monastic rule.

In *C. S. N°* 84, the actions and their results are dealt with very intensively :

3 *kinds of dejection and suffering here-now for a fool :*

i) 1*st kind of dejection and suffering :*

C N° 199 : (*vii*, 60*b*, 10-14) : The fool is subject here-now to 3 kinds of bodily and mental suffering. Any of the fool's behaviour will be spoken of appropriately, either he is sitting in the assembly or on the road, or in the market, or at the cross-road. If a fool kills living beings, takes what is not given, indulges in wrong sense-pleasures, tells lies up to having wrong view, and is endowed with innumerable evil, demeritorious dharmas, people will comment upon his wickedness accordingly. The fool becomes worried and uneasy, when he thinks that he has committed also such a wrong behaviour and people will comment upon his wickedness in the same way. This is the 1st kind of dejection and suffering he is subjected herenow.

P N° 129 : (*iii*, 163, 14–25) : Almost the same. It omits : in the market and also up to having wrong view, and is endowed with innumerable evil, demeritorious dharmas. It adds : drinking liquor. Here the C refers to the 10 fold akusalakammapathā. The rest is the same.

ii) 2*nd kind of dejection and suffering :*

C : (60*b*, 14–19) : That foolish man sees a criminal caught by the king's men and subject to various tortures, such as 1) hands cut off, 2) legs cut off, 3) hands and legs cut off, 4) ears cut off, 5) nose cut off, 6) ears and nose cut off, 7) flesh cut slice by slice, 8) beards plucked off, 9) hairs plucked off, 10) beard and hairs plucked off, 11) put into bars, 12) wrapped in cloth and burnt, 13) apertures blocked by sand, 14) twisted by grass, 15) baked by fire, 16) put into the belly of an iron donkey and heated with fire, 17) put into the mouth of an iron pig and heated with fire, 18) put into the mouth of an iron tiger and heated with fire, 19) put into a bronze cauldron and boiled, 20) put into an iron cauldron and boiled, 21) body cut into pieces, 22) pierced by a sharp fork, 23) hooked by iron hook, 24) laid down on an iron bed and sprinkled with boiling oil, 25) seated in an iron mortar and pounded by an iron pestle, 26) bitten by dragons, 27) bitten by snakes, 28) lashed by whip, 29) beaten by sticks, 30) hit by staff, 31) hung alive from a high pole, 32) head decapited (and publicly exposed). The fool seeing this thinks that he has committed the same crime, and if the king comes to know about this, he will be caught and subjected to the same tortures. Thus is his 2nd kind of dejection and suffering.

P : (163, 26–27 ; 164, 1–23) : Almost the same, with the same differences as above. While the C speaks of a criminal, the P speaks of a thief. As to the various punishments inflicted by the king, they are in the following order : 1) Flogged by whip, 2) flogged by canes, 3) lashed by rod (addhadaṇḍaka), 4) hands cut off, 5) feet cut off, 6) hands and feet cut off, 7) ears cut off, 8) nose cut off, 9) ears and nose cut off, 10) gruel-pot torture (bilaṅgathālikaṃ), 11) shell-tonsure (saṅkhamuṇḍikaṃ), 12) Rāhu's mouth torture (Rāhumukhaṃ), 13) fire-garland torture (jotimālikaṃ), 14) hand-burning-torch torture (hatthapajjotikaṃ), 15) grass-twisted torture (erakavattikaṃ), 16) bark-dress torture (cīrakavāsikaṃ), 17) antelope torture (eṇeyyakaṃ), 18) flesh-hooking torture (baḷisamaṃsikaṃ), 19) coin-sliced torture (kahāpaṇakaṃ), 20) pickling process (khārāpatacchikaṃ), 21) bar-turn torture (palighaparivattikaṃ), 22) straw-foot-stool or straw-mattress torture (palālapiṭhakaṃ), 23) with boiled oil poured over body, 24) torn to pieces by dogs, 25) impaled alive on stakes (jīvantaṃ pi sūle uttāsenti), 26) head cut off by swords.

Remarks : The C enumerates 32 kinds of torture and punishment while the P enumerates only 26. The following 14 tortures are found in both versions : C 1 = P 4 ; C 2 = P 5 ; C 3 = P 6 ; C 4 = P 7 ; C 5 = P 8 ; C 6 = P 9 ; C 7 P 19 ; C 8 & C 9 & C 10 = P 20 ; C 14 = P 15 ; C 23 = P 18 ; C 24 =

P 23 ; C 28 = P 1 ; C 29 = P 3 ; C 30 = P 1 ; Here P 20 Khārāpatacchikaṃ equals to C 8, C 9, C 10: beard plucked off, hair plucked off and beard and hair plucked off.

16 tortures in the C version are wanting in the P version : C 11 : put into bars ; C 12 : to be wrapped into cloth and burnt ; C 13 : apertures blocked by sand ; C 15 : baked by fire ; C 16 : put into the belly of an iron donkey and heated with fire ; C 17 : put into the mouth of an iron pig and heated with fire ; C 18 : put into the mouth of an iron tiger and heated with fire ; C 19 : put into a bronze cauldron and boiled ; C 20 : put into an iron cauldron and boiled ; C 21 : body cut into pieces ; C 22 : pierced by sharp fork ; C 25 : seated in an iron mortar and pounded by an iron pestle ; C 26 : bitten by dragon ; C 27 : bitten by snakes ; C 31 : hung alive from a high pole ; C 32 : hanged with head downwards.

12 tortures in the P are not found in the C version : P 10 : gruel pot torture ; P 11 : shell tonsure torture ; P 12 : Rāhu's mouth torture ; P 13 : fire garland torture ; P 14 : hand burning torch torture ; P 21 : bark turn torture ; P 22 : straw mattress torture ; P 24 : to be torn into pieces by dogs ; P 25 : to be impaled alive on stakes ; P 26 : head cut off by sword.

iii) *3rd kind of dejection and suffering :*

C: (60*b*, 19 ; 61*a*, 1–4) : If a fool performs evil bodily deeds, evil vocal deeds and evil mental deeds, when he becomes sick and suffers pains, either he is sitting or lying down on a bed, on a couch, or on the ground, he suffers acute pains up to near dying and all his evil actions, bodily, vocal and mental ones hover upon him, settle upon him, just like at sunset the shadow of a big mountain hovers upon the earth, settles upon the earth. He thinks that formerly he has done no meritorious acts but many demeritorious actions. In so far as there is a place for the evil doers, for those who commit violence and foolish things, who do not perform merit and meritorious acts, who do not make a refuge against fearful consequences, then he himself hereafter will have to go to that place. So he regrets his former actions and due to that he dies not as a noble man and not in a meritorious way.

P : (164, 24–32 ; 165, 1–11) : Almost the same. It omits : he becomes sick and suffers acute pains up to near dying. But it mentions ; he is lying on a chair, or a bed or on the ground. It omits : So he regrets his former actions and due to that he dies not as a noble man and not in a meritorious way. It adds instead : He mourns, wails, beats his breast and becomes deluded.

After his death, he will be reborn in the Hell :

i) *Reborn in the Hell :*

C : (61*a*, 4–6) : Then that foolish man, due to his bodily vocal and menlat evil actions, after his death will be born in the evil states, in the Hell.

There he suffers evil result, totally unpleasant, totally disagreeable, totally undesirable as a Hell is a place of total unpleasantness, of total disagreeableness, of total undesirableness.

P: (165, 12-20): Almost the same. It adds: It is difficult to give a simile of hell-suffering.

ii) *Simile to depict suffering in the Hell:*

C: (61*a*, 6-20) : Then a monk asked about suffering in the Hell, which the W.H. One described as unspeakable and he gave a simile to illustrate suffering in the Hell. Suppose a robber who is condemned by the king to be pierced in the morning by 100 spears. The punishment is repeated at noon and in the afternoon as the criminal is still living ; but his body is pierced totally by the spear like the hole of a coin. One piercing of the spear results already in acute suffering not to speak of 300 piercings in one day. Then the Buddha picked up a small stone of the size of a small bean or pea, and asked the monk to compare it with the Himālayan mountain. The monk had to recognise that the Himālayan mountain was 100 times, 1,000 times, 100,000 times, 1,000,000 times bigger than the small stone. Then the Buddha said that suffering in the Hell was 100 times, 1,000 times, 100,000 times and 1,000,000 times more acute than the suffering undergone by the criminal in one day when he was pierced by 300 spears.

P : (165, 21-36 ; 166, 1-18) : Almost the same. The P omits : like the hole of a coin. C : a small stone of the size of a small bean = P: a stone, the size of his hand.

iii) *Suffering in the Hell* :

C : (61*b*, 20 ; 62*a*, 1-8) : Here the C enumerates up to 11 kinds of suffering or tortures in the Hell : 1) When one is born in the Hell, its guardians catch hold of him and use a blazing axe to chop off his body, making it octogonal or hexagonal or square, or a circle, or long, or short, or beautiful, or ugly. Thus he is subjected to painful tortures, to acute suffering up to 100 and 1,000 years of suffering, not ending in death which occurs only up to the exhaustion of his evil, demeritorious actions; 2) the same as above, with the blazing axe replaced by blazing iron *chin* (釿): 3) the hell-guardians take a blazing iron spear and compel him to sit on it ; they use iron pincers to squeeze open his mouth and pour blazing ironball into it, thus burning his lips, his tongue, his palate, his throat, his heart, his stomach, the iron-ball coming out under the body ; the rest is the same as in the previous case ; 4) the same as in the 3rd case with blazing iron spear replaced by a blazing iron ch'iang (鏘 bell ?) and with blazing iron ball replaced by blazing melted copper ; 5) the Hell-guardians compel him to lie down on a heated iron floor, bound him with arms and legs extended and subject him to fivefold pinion, driving iron nail through each hand, each foot and in his stomach ; 6) the Hell-guardians make him prostrate on the ground, pull out his tongue and drive 100 nails into it to make it extend but not shrink in, just like an oxen hide extended by 100 nails but not shrunk in ; 7) the Hell-guardians pell off his skin from head to feet and from feet to head then tie him to a blazing chariot and drag him forth and back and across a blazing iron ground ; 8) the Hell-guardians boil copper up to melting and compel the criminal to pour the melting copper over his own body ; 9) the Hell-guardians build up a mountain-fire and lower the criminal down and pull him up. When he is lowered down, his skin, flesh and blood are burnt out, when he is pulled up. his skin, flesh and blood become sound as before ; 10) the Hell-guardians lower him head downwards feet upwards in a cauldron full of boiling water and boil him inside, his body is tossed upwards, downwards, in four directions, in four intermediate directions, the scum or froth coming out from his own body again boils his own body ; just like small beans, big beans, white beans (wên-tou : 穩豆), black beans, brown beans (k'u-tou : 苦豆) and mustard seed, all put into a cauldron full of boiled water and are boiled. These beans inside are tossed up and down, in four directions, in four intermediate directions and its own scum or froth boil their own body ; 11) that Hell has one Hell called, 6 strong enjoyment-Hell (kêng-lo) ; living beings are born in it ; when their eyes see material forms, they are not pleased, but they cannot not to be pleased ; their mind does not crave for but it cannot not to crave for ; their mind is not well satisfied but it cannot not to be well satisfied ; in the same way with ear hearing sounds, with nose smelling scents, with tongue feeling tastes, with body perceiving touch, with mind thinking things. Thus the W. H. One used various ways to speak about that Hell, but the suffering in that Hell cannot fully be described, that Hell has only suffering.

P : (166, 18-32 ; 167, 1-20) : Here the P enumerates only 7 kinds of suffering in the Hell. The corresponding sufferings in both versions are as follows : C 5=P 1 ; C 7=P 4 ; C 9=P 5 ; C 10=P 6 ; C 11=P 7 ; The P omits : C 1, C 2, C 3, C 4, C 6 and C 8. The C omits : P 2, P 3.

C 5=*P* 1 : The P omits : compelling him to lie down on a heated iron floor. C : driving an iron nail in the stomach=P : driving an iron stake in the middle of his breast.

C 7=*P* 4 : The P omits the guardians peeling off his skin from head to feet and from feet to head. It mentions simply chariot, not blazing chariot, simply blazing ground, not blazing iron ground.

C 9=*P* 5 : The P omits : when he is lowered down, his skin, flesh and blood are burnt up and when he is pulled up, his skin flesh and blood are sound as before.

C 10=*P* 6 : The P mentions simply that he is boiled and comes up to the surface with the scum, unlike the C which mentions that the scum coming out from his own body again boils his own body. It omits the simile of small and big beans boiling.

C 11 = *P* 7: Completely different. Here the P says that he is tossed by the guardians of Niraya into the Great Niraya, which is described as having 4 corners, 4 gates, divided into equal portions, encircled by an iron wall, with an iron roof; its floor is incandescent and all around, it stands 100 yojanas square.

P 2 & P 3 are not available in the C:

P 2: The Hell-guardians lay him down and cut him with a hatchet; P 3: The Hell-guardians place him feet up and head down and cut him with razors.

iv) *Suffering in the animal kingdom:*

C: (62*a*, 8-20; 62*b*, 1): « The foolish man from the Hell can be born in the animal kingdom and there he suffers also acute pain. 5 kinds of suffering are found in the animal kingdom: 1) He may be born in the animal kingdom, born, grown up and died in darkness, that is as insects in the earth. Because the foolish man formerly was greedy of eating and performed evil bodily, vocal and mental deeds, so now he is born as insects, in the earth; 2) He may be born in the animal kingdom, born in the body, grown up in the body and died in the body as ulcer worms. The rest is the same; 3) Animals which are born, grown up and died in the water, such as fish, mo-chieh-yü (摩竭魚) (1), turtle, crocodile, p'o-liu-ni (婆留尼), t'i-pi (提鼻 = P = Timi, it should he t'i-pi-t'i-pi-chia-lo = P = Timi timingala) (2) T'i-mi-chia-lo (提鼻伽羅 = P = Timingalo); t'i-pi-chia-lo (提鼻伽羅); 4) Born as chewing animals, eating grass, plants and trees, as elephants, horses, camels, cows, donkeys, deer, water-buffaloes, pigs; 5) Born as animals who, smelling dung and urine scent at once run up to eat them; just like young boys and girls, when they scent food. These animals are hens, pigs, dogs, jackals, crows, chü-lou-lo (拘樓羅?), chü-lêng-chia (拘棱伽?). Thus the W.H. One uses various means to speak about these animals as suffering in the animal kingdom cannot be spoken fully. In the animal kingdom, there is nothing except suffering ».

P: (167, 21-34; 168, 1-34; 169, 1-8): Almost the same. It refers also to 5 kinds of animals, but not in the same order. The corresponding passages are as follows: C 1 = P 3; C 2 = P no; C 3 = P 4; C 4 = P 1; C 5 = P 2; P 5 = C no.

---

(1) Perhaps magadha fish.

(2) It refers to 3 kinds of fish, Timi, Timingala, Timitimingala, all fabulous fish of monstruous size. Cullavagga, vol. II, Nalanda edition, p. 355 refers to Timi, Timingalo, Timitimingalo. Milinda, Bombay university edition of, p. 256 speaks of Timi, Timingala, timirapingala. Divyavadanam, Mithila edition p. 438 refers to Timibhayam, Timingilabhayam and timitimingilabhayam.

C 1 = *P* 3 : Almost the same. C: insect of the earth = P: kītā pulave gaṇḍuppādā (beetles, maggots, earth-worms) and whatever animals which arā born, lived and died in the dark. C: due to their greed for food = P: due to their enjoying tastes here.

C 3 = *P* 4 : Almost the same. The P enumerates only 3 kinds of animals: fishes, turtles and crocodiles and whatever animals which are born, live and die in the water.

C 4 = *P* 1 : Almost the same. The P mentions them as eating moist and dry grass and chewing them with their teeth. It mentions horses, cattle, donkeys, sheep and deer and whatever animals which are eating grass.

C 5 = P 2 : Almost the same. It refers only to dung but not to urine. While the C quotes the simile of young boys and young girls running up at the smell of food, the P refers to the brāhmaṇas running up at the smell of oblations thrown into fire. The P omits : crow, chü-lou-lo, chü-lêng-chia.

P 5 = *C no*. There are animals born, grown and died in the filth, such as beings born, grown and died in rotten fish, rotten carcass, rotten rice or in the pool at the entrance of or near a village.

v) *Difficulty in getting back human forms :*

C : (62*b*, 1–8) : It is very difficult for the foolish man to assume human form again, once being born in the animal kingdom, as in the animal kingdom, there are no meritorious actions, no respectful manner, no excellent goodness. The animals eat each other, the strong devour the weak, the big devour the small. It is extremely difficult for a blind (1) turtle of 100, 1,000 years old to put his head into a hole of a light wooden stick. Every 100 years, he emerges his head once ; if he emerges from the East, an eastern wind tosses the stick towards South ; if he emerges from the South, a southern wind tosses the stick towards West; if he emerges from the West, a western wind tosses the stick towards the North ; if he emerges from the North, a northern wind tosses the stick towards another direction. There is still possibility for this turtle to put his head into the hole, although it takes exceedingly long and long time. The foolish man will face the same difficulty and the same length of time to be born from the animal kingdom into the human world again.

P : (169, 9–25) : Almost the same. C : blind turtle = P : turtle blind of one eye (1). The P refers simply to the Eastern wind tossing the stick towards West, the western wind tossing the stick towards East, the northern wind tossing the stick towards the South and the southern wind tossing the stick towards the North. C : the foolish man faces the same difficulty, the same length of time to be born from the animal kingdom into the human world again = P : it is more difficult for the fool...

---

(1) Kana means sprint-eyed.

vi) *Born in low families :*

C : (62*b*, 8-15) : The foolish man from the animal kingdom is born into low and small families which are poor and lacking of food, families of guardians of prison, of workers, of handicraftmen, of potters. There he is born as a blind man, a cripple, of short arms, as a hunchback, using left hand, of bad complexion, of sheep face, ugly, of short span of life, being a slave to others. There he performs evil bodily, vocal and mental acts and due to that, when he dies he will be born in evil states again. It is as though there are 2 gamblers playing together. One of them, due to his playing loses servants, wife, and sons even up to being hanged downwards in the dark house, this loss of his in gambling cannot be compared with the loss he undergoes when he performs evil bodily, vocal and mental acts.

P : (169, 25-32 ; 170, 1-17) : Almost the same. Here the families enumerated are totally different. They are hunters, bamboo-plaiters, cartwrights, refuse-scavengers. He would be ugly, dwarf, sickly, blind of one eye, deformed, paralysed. C : not enough food to eat = P : unable to get food, drink, clothes, conveyances, garlands, scents, perfumes, beds, dwellings, lights. The simile is almost the same. The P adds his losing his properties but omits servants. C : to be hanged downwards in the dark house = P : to be put into prison.

In *C. S. N°* 85, there is a more detailed description of Hells. There are 6 kinds of Hell, of which the corresponding ones are as follows : C 1 = P 1 ; C 2 = P no. C 3 = P 2 ; C 4 = P 5 ; C 5 = P 4 ; C 6 = P 6 ; P 3 = C no.

i) *The great Hell of four gates : C 1 = P 1.*

C N° 64 : (72*a*, 18-20 ; 72*b*, 1-7) : Having well questioned, well censured, well instructed, well blamed him about the 5th heaven messenger, the king Yen-wang handed him over to the Hell-guardians who put him into the great Hell of four gates. This Hell is described in a gāthā :

a) Four pillars have 4 gates, the wall is square with 12 corners ; the walls are made up of iron, above is covered by an iron roof ;

b) The iron floor in the Hell is blazing and incandescent, deep up to innumerable leagues ; he is put at the bottom of the floor.

c) It is so horrible that it is unbearable and the colour of the fire is very difficult to look at ; when one sees it, the hair of the body stands up, and fear (overcomes) and acute suffering assails him.

d) When he falls into the Hell, his legs come upwards and his head downwards. Abusing the Noble Ones, the tamer, the good purely good. (Here the verses stop short).

After a very, very long time, because of these living beings, the Eastern gate of this Hell opens and those living beings rush in, seeking comfort, seeking refuge. When they are assembled up to the number of many hundred thousands, that Eastern gate shuts in and those people inside suffer acute pains, wailing, shouting, lamenting, with mind dejected and lying on the ground. They cannot die before the exhaustion of their previous evil demeritorious actions. The same thing happens at the other 3 gates. After a very, very long time, they come out of the great Hell of four gates.

P : N° 130: (182, 31–34; 183; 184, 1–30): Not exactly the same. Here king Yama, having questioned him about the 5th messenger kept silent. The P adds a passage in which the Hell-guardians subject him to fivefold pinion and to a series of tortures as seen ante pages 135–6. The description of the Great Hell of 4 gates is not the same. In a gāthā of only 4 lines, it mentions simply that this Hell has 4 corners and 4 gates divided equally, encircled by an iron-wall with an iron-roof above, its iron floor is blazing and burning and all round, it stands one hundred yojanas square. Here the P adds another detail in the description of the Great Hell, that flames coming from the Eastern Wall are hurled against the Western Wall ; the flames from the Western Wall are hurled against the Eastern-Wall. In the same way with the other 2 directions and the above, the below. It mentions also the opening of the 4 gates with the criminals rushing in (but not living beings assembling up to 100, 1,000 seeking comfort, seeking refuge). C: those people inside suffer acute pain, wailing, shouting, lamenting, with mind dejected and lying on the ground = P : his skin, his hide, his flesh, his tendons are burnt and his bones are smouldering. Although he reaches much (near the door, or he suffers like that for a long time), the door remains closed.

ii) *The great Hell of high peak : C 2 = P no.*

C : (72b, 7–8) : Then he is born in the Great Hell of high peak in which fire is constantly burning without smoke without flame and he is compelled to walk on and round it. When he puts his feet down, his skin, flesh and blood are burnt out, when he raises his feet up, his skin, flesh and blood become sound as before. Thus he is suffering acute pains up to innumerable 100 thousand years. The rest is the same.

iii) *The Great Hell of filth : C 3 = P 2.*

C : 72b, 8–12) : After a very, very long time, he comes out of the Great Hell of high peak and is born in the Great Hell of filth, where excrements and urine are accumulated of innumerable changs (a chinese measure of 10 feet) deep. In that hell, there are creatures like worms called Lêng-ch'ü (淩瞿) of white body, of black head with its mouth like needle. These creatures gnaw away these living beings' feet, then their rectum bones (Po ch'ang 膞腸), then buttock bones, then k'uan-ku bones (髖骨), then spine-bones, then shoulder-bones, then neck-bones, then head-bones. Having destroyed the head-bones, these worms eat all the marrow inside. The rest is the same.

P: (184, 31 ; 185, 1-8) : Not exactly the same. It mentions that adjacent to the Great Hell of the 4 gates, there is a great Hell of filth (gūtha-niraya) and that man falls into it. It omits to mention about what kind of filth. It mentions also the needle-mouthed creatures which cut away his skin, his flesh, his tendons, his bones, then they devour the marrow of the bones.

iv) *The Great Hell of iron-leafed forest: C 4 = P 5 :*

C : (72*b*, 12-18) : After a very, very long time, those people come out of the Great Hell of filth and are born in the Great Hell of iron-leafed forest. When they see this Hell they think it to be cool and rush in seeking comfort, seeking refuge. They assemble up to innumerable 100 thousands and enter this Hell. There a scorching wind from four directions blow strongly and the iron-leaves fall down and cut their hands, their feet, their hands and feet, their ears, their nose, their ears and nose, and other limbs of their body and shedding blood up to innumerable 100 thousands of years; in this Hell, there are extremely big dogs with very long teeth. These creatures tear to pieces these living beings, tear away the skin from feet to head and eat them, from head to feet and eat them. In this Hell, there are big crows of 2 heads with an iron beak. They stand on the forehead of these people, pluck out their eyes and eat them, split their skull and eat the marrow inside.

P: (185, 20-26): Not exactly the same. Here the Hell is called asipattavanaṃ (sword-leafed forest). It mentions simply that its leaves stirred by the wind cut off his hand, his feet, his hand and feet, his ears, his nose, his ears and his nose.

v) *The Great Hell of the forest iron-sword-trees: C 5 = P 4 :*

C: (72*b*, 19-20 ; 73*a*, 1) : After a very, very long time, these living beings come out of the Great Hell of iron-leafed forest and are born in the Great Hell of iron-sword-forest and these big sword-trees are of one league high and with prickles 6 meters long. They are ordered to climb up and down these trees. When they climb up, all the prickles are pointed downwards, when they climb down, all the prickles are pointed upwards. These prickles pierce through these people, pierce hands, feet, pierce hands and feet, pierce ears, nose, pierce ears and nose, pierce other limbs of the body, shedding blood.

P : (185, 14-19): Not exactly the same. Here the Great Hell is called simbalivana, forest of silk-cotton trees. C : one league high with prickles of 6 meters long = P : one yojana high with prickles of 16 fingers long. It mentions simply that these prickles are burning ablaze and he is made to climb up and down.

vi) *The Great Hell of caustic river : C 6 = P 6 :*

C : (73*a*, 1–14) : After a very, very long time, these living beings come out of the Great Hell of the forest of iron-sword trees and are born in the Great Hell of caustic river. Both banks are very high, surrounded by spears ; caustic water is boiling and it is very dark inside. These living beings when they see it, think to be cold water and rush in to take bath and to drink to satisfaction its cold water. When they assemble together up to innumerable 100 thousands, they fall into that river and there they are carried up-stream, down-stream, up and down stream, their skin and flesh are burnt and peeled off with only skeleton remained. On the 2 banks, the guardians of the Hell armed with knives, swords, big staff, iron pronged stick, push them to the middle of the stream if they try to climb the banks. Again on the 2 banks of the river, there are Hell-guardians armed with hooks and nets. They haul these beings up and put them on the blazing iron-ground, throw them down on the ground, make them sprawl here and there and ask them where do they come from. They reply that they do not know from where they come, but now they suffer very much from hunger. Then these guardians put them on a blazing iron bed, burn them, compel them to sit on it. They then take a blazing iron pincers, squeeze open their mounth and throw blazing iron ball into it. This blazing iron ball burns their lips, then their tongue, their palate, their throat, their heart, their big intestines, their small intestines, their stomach and comes out the other side of the body. Then these guardians ask them where they would like to go ? They reply that they do not know where to go but now they are suffering from great thirst. The same punishment is meted out to them but now the Hell-guardians pour melted copper into their mouth. Then these living beings fall down again in the Great Hell of caustic river, again in the Great Hell of the forest of iron sword-trees, again in the Great Hell of the iron-leafed forest, again in the Great Hell of filth, again in the Great Hell of high peak, again in the Great Hell of four gates.

P : (185, 27–33 ; 186, 1–22) : Not exactly the same. C : caustic river = P : khārodakā. There is no description of this river, the P simply says that he falls into this caustic water, is carried up-stream, or down-stream or up and down-stream and he suffers untold, acute suffering. All other details are missing. The P mentions also 2 cases of the Hell guardians hauling him out with hook and ask him what he wants. As he replies in the first case that he is hungry, and in the 2nd case that he is thirsty, they open his mouth with a burning iron spike (ayosaṅku) and push into his mouth in the first case a blazing iron ball and in the 2nd case they pour into his mouth blazing melted copper. The blazing iron ball and the blazing melted copper burn his lips, his mouth, his throat, his chest, and come down below carrying with them his bowels and intestines. Then the Niraya guardians push him back again into the Great Hell.

P 3 : The P adds another Hell called Kukkuḷaniraya, Ember Hell. And he falls into it and suffers acute pains.

In *C. S. N*° 75, the Buddha explained that places of birth depended upon one's own aspiration of mind. But this paragraph is so differently treated in both versions that it is impossible to make a comparative study portion by portion. So here both versions are treated separately.

i) *Ist dhyāna of the rūpa-world :*

C N° 168 : (13*a*, 19–20 ; 13*b*, 1–2) : There is a monk who, aloof from desire, from evil, demeritorious dharmas, obtains the 1st dhyāna which is with initial thoughts and discursive thoughts, with joy and happiness born out of aloofness. Then he likes to enjoy and dwell in this dhyāna state. With such a liking, he enjoys and dwells in that dhyāna state. When he dies, he will be born in the Brahma-heaven. The Brahma-heaven deities who are born and dwell in that brahma-heaven, experience joy and happiness born out of aloofness ; that joy and happiness is similar to that enjoyed by the monk when he enters the 1st dhyāna, because due to the practice of that dhyāna that he later on is born in the Brahma-heaven.

ii) *2nd dhyāna up to 4th dhyāna :*

C : (13*b*, 2–11) : With the practice of the 2nd dhyāna, he will be born in Huang-yü-t'ien (晃昱天 : dazzling heaven) ; with the practice of the 3rd dhyāna, he will be born in P'ien-ching-t'ien (遍淨天 : all pure heaven) ; with the practice of the 4th dhyāna, he will born in Kuo-shih-t'ien (果實天 : Fruit-heaven).

iii) 4 *dhyānas of the arūpa-world :*

C : (13*b*, 11–20 ; 14*a*, 1–4): With the practice of the 1st dhyāna, he will be born in the heaven of infinite space ; with the practice of the 2nd dhyāna, he will be born in the heaven of infinite consciousness ; with the practice of the 3rd dhyāna, he will be born in the heaven of nothingness ; with the practice of the 4th dhyāna, he will be born in the heaven of neither perception nor non-perception.

iv) *The highest dhyāna :*

C : (14*a*, 4–6) : Then the monk transcends the dhyāna of neither perception nor non-perception, he knows the cessation of bodily touch. With wisdom he knows the eradication of all cankers. Thus that dhyāna is the highest of all dhyānas, the most excellent, the most wonderful. Thus dwelling in that dhyāna, the monk will not be born again and put an end to suffering of birth, old age, sickness and of death, that is the end of suffering.

The Pāli enumerates up to 34 cases to illustrate the Buddha's explanation :

i) *1st case:*

P N° 120 : (99, 22-27 ; 100, 1-3): A monk is endowed with faith, with moral precepts, with learning, with inclination to giving charity, with wisdom. He wishes that after his death, he might arise in the company of nobles and rich people (khattiyamahāsālā). He fixes his mind on this, develops his mind on this. These aspirations (saṅkhārā) and abidings (vihārā) thus developed and enlarged will lead him to be born there.

ii) *2nd case up to 33rd case:*

P: (100, 4-33 ; 101 ; 102 ; 103, 1-14) : These cases are the same as with the 1st case, with the only difference in the people in whose company the monk wishes to be born. They are as follows : rich brāhmaṇas, rich householders, cātummahārājikā devā, Tāvatiṃsā devā, Yāmādevā, Tusitā devā, Nimmānaratī devā, Paranimmitavasavattino devā, Sahasso Brahmā, Dvisahasso Brahmā, Tisahasso Brahmā, Catusahasso Brahmā, Pañcasahasso Brahmā, Dasasahasso Brahmā, Satasahasso Brahmā, Abhā devā, Parittabhā devā, Appamāṇābhā devā, Ābhassarā devā, Subhā devā, Parittasubhādevā, Appamāṇasubhā devā, Subhakiṇṇādevā, Vehapphalā devā, Avihā devā, Ātappā devā, Sudassī devā, Akaniṭṭhā devā, Ākāsānañcāyatanūpagā devā, Viññāṇañcāyatanūpagā devā, Ākiñcaññāyatanūpagā devā, Nevasaññānāsaññāyatanūpagā devā.

iii) *The 34th case:*

P: (103, 15-22) : Here the monk wishes, by the eradication of the cankers, having realized here-now by his own superknowledge, emancipation of mind and emancipation by wisdom that are cankerless, to abide therein. Thus the monk will not be born anywhere.

2. — *The seven Purities or Visuddhi:*

The 7 purities are treated in *C. S. N°* 20 as follows :

C N° 9 : (12*a*, 3-8) : Ven. Shê-li-tzu in the evening, got up from his meditation seat, came to the place where Ven. Man-tz'u-tzu was, exchanged greetings with him, sat on one side and asked Ven. Man-tz'u-tzu : « Rev. fr., are you leading the holy life under recluse Ch'ü-t'an ? » — « Yes » — « Rev. fr., are you leading the holy life under recluse Ch'u-t'an for the sake of purity of moral practices ? » — « No » — « Is it for the sake of purity of mind, purity of views, purity of doubt-hindrance, purity of knowledge and vision into the right path and the wrong path, purity of knowledge and vision into the mode of progress, purity arising out from the eradicating wisdom into the mode of progress (I-tao-hsi-tuan-chih-ching : 以道跡斷智淨) that you are leading the holy life under recluse Ch'ü-t'an ? » —

« No » — « I have asked your reverence, are you leading the holy life under recluse Ch'ü-t'an ? Then you said : « Yes ». Now I asked : « Are you leading... into the mode of progress, that you are leading the holy life under recluse Ch'ü-t'an ? and you replied : « No ». Then for what meaning (purpose) did you live the holy life under recluse Ch'ü-tan ? » — « Rev. fr., for the sake of Nirvāṇa without remainder ».

P N° 24 : (147, 11-37 ; 148, 1-3 : Almost the same with some slight differences. C : for the sake of purity of doubt-hindrance = P : kaṅkhāvitaraṇavisuddhatthaṃ (for the sake of purity with the removal of doubts). C : for the sake of purity arising out from the eradicating wisdom into the mode of progress = P : ñāṇadassanavisuddhatthaṃ (for the sake of purity of knowledge and of vision). C : for the sake of nirvāṇa without a remainder = P anupādā parinibbānatthaṃ (for the sake of nibbāna without grasping).

Thus the 7 purities are almost the same in both versions with some slight differences as to their wording.

3. — *Cetovimutti, Paññāvimutti : Freedom of mind and freedom by wisdom :*

These two dharmas are treated in C. S. N° 25, N° 30, N° 47, N° 69, N° 74, N° 75 and N° 82 :

Thus in *C. S. N*° 74, these two dharmas are referred to as follows :

C N° 81 : (*v*, 114*b*, 15-17) : Then the monk can obtain the psychic powers, the divine ear, the knowledge of others' mind, the knowledge of former births, the knowledge of births and deaths. Then with the eradication of cankers, he knows and realizes by himself here-now and dwells in mind-emancipation, wisdom-emancipation, which is cankerless, he attains arahantship.

P N° 119 : (*iii*, 98, 2-28 ; 99, 1-7) : Almost the same. Here the P deals at length as usual with the psychic powers, the divine ear... up to knowledge of births and deaths. The 2 emancipations are the same. C : mind-emancipation = P : cetovimutti. C : wisdom-emancipation = P : paññāvimutti. Here the P omits to mention clearly the attainment of arahantship.

The *C. S. N*° 30 shows how to obtain mind-freedom and wisdom-freedom.

C N° 211 : (*vii*, 85*b*, 19-20 ; 86*a*, 1-3) : Q : With how many factors does right view associate to obtain fruit of mind-freedom, fruit of wisdom-freedom, to obtain merits of mind-freedom, merits of wisdom-freedom ? A : There are 5 factors to associate with right view to obtain fruit of mind-freedom, fruit of wisdom-freedom, merits of mind-freedom, merits of wisdom-freedom. What are the five ? a) to associate with truth, b) to associate with moral conduct, c) to associate with extensive hearing, d) to associate with quietude, e) to associate with insight.

P N° 43 *:* (*i*, 294, 4–15) : The question is the same, the answer is slightly different. C : fruit and merits = P : fruit and advantages. In the P, the 5 are : moral conduct, learning, discussion, quietude, insight.

The *C. S. N*° 82 deals solely with mind-freedom :

C N° 79 *:* (*v*, 108*b*, 13–20 ; 109*a*, 1–2) : Ven. A-na-lu-t'o explained first great mind-freedom. There is a recluse or a brāmaṇa who comes to a forest or under a tree or a calm and quiet place. There he takes a single tree as a limit and suffuses his great mind-freedom up to this extent and dwells in it, not going beyond this limit. Then he gives up a single tree as a limit but takes 2, 3 trees as a limit, gradually one forest, 2, 3 forests, one village, 2, 3 villages, one country, 2, 3 countries, this great earth up to the great ocean. This is called great mind-freedom. As to boundless mind-freedom, a monk abides, having suffused the 1st direction with a mind endowed with friendliness, likewise the 2nd, the 3rd, the 4th directions, the intermediate directions, the above, the below, spreading everywhere the mind of friendliness, without enmity, without malevolence, without anger, without quarrel, extremely large, exceedingly big, far reaching all over the world and abides in. In the same way with a mind endowed with compassion, with sympathetic joy and with equanimity. This is called boundless mind-freedom.

P N° 127 *:* (*iii*, 146, 8–30 ; 147, 1–13) : Almost the same. The P explains boundless mind-freedom first then great mind-freedom. As to the great mind-freedom, it is almost the same, but the limits set are rather different. First root of a single tree, then roots of 2, 3 trees, the one-village-field, 2, 3 village-fields, one kingdom, 2, 3 kingdoms, and the earth surrounding the ocean. As to boundless mind-freedom, it is almost the same.

But in *C. S. N*° 30, there is a series of questions and answers concerning mind-freedom, which is not available in the C version.

P. N° 43 *:* (296, 24–31 : Q : How many conditions are there to attain mind-freedom which is neither pleasant nor unpleasant ? A : there are 4 conditions to attain mind-freedom which is neither pleasant nor unpleasant. A monk, having given up pleasant feeling, unpleasant feeling, having reduced former pleasures and sorrows, enters and abides into the 4th jhāna which is pure and endowed with equanimity and mindfulness.

P : (296, 31–35) : Q : How many conditions are there to attain mind-freedom which is signless ? A : There are 2 conditions to attain mind-freedom which is signless, not to think of all signs and to think of the plane of the signless.

P : (296, 36-37 ; 297, 1-3) : Q : How many conditions are there to dwell into mind-freedom which is signless ? A : There are 3 conditions to dwell into mind-freedom which is signless, not to think of all signs, to think of the plane of the signless and a previous preparation.

P : (297, 4-8) : Q : What are the conditions to emerge from mind-freedom which is signless ? A : There are 2 conditions to emerge from mind-freedom which is signless, to reflect on all signs and not to reflect over the plane of the signless.

P : (297, 9-37 ; 298, 1-27) : The P proceeds to explain that by adopting the practice of the 4 Brahmavihārā, the monk obtains mind-freedom which is immeasurable, by adopting the practice of going beyond all viññā-ṇañcāyatanaṃ and of entering into the plane of infinite nothingness, he obtains mind-freedom which is nothingness, by going to an empty place and pondering over voidness of self and of what belongs to the self, the monk obtains mind-freedom which is substanceless, and by not thinking over all signs, by entering into the concentration of mind on signless, he obtains freedom of mind which is signless. Thus this is the method according to which these states are different in meaning and also in letter. Further the P explains that by eradicating rāga, dosa and moha, which are productive of something measurable, something obstructive, something productive of the sign, the monk obtains that mind-freedom which is immeasurable, which is nothingness, which is substanceless, which is signless. Thus by this method, these 4 states are of the same meaning but different in the letters.

In *C. S. N*° 69, there is reference to 3 kinds of freedom, but only in the C version.

C N° 145: (*vi*, 78*a*, 5-10): Ch'ü-mê-mu-chien-lien asked if there was any difference among the emancipation of the Tathāgata, having no attachment, completely and rightly enlightened, the wisdom-freedom and the freedom of the Arahant, and which was higher. Ven. A-nan replied that there was no difference among these three freedoms, no one was higher than any other one.

4. — *Magga, phala, āsavakhayañāṇaṃ : Path, fruit and knowledge of the extinction of the cankers :*

In *C. S. N*° 19, the first three Paths and Fruits are dealt with.

a) *Sotāpanna or stream-attainer :*

C N° 200 : (*vii*, 66*a*, 18-20) : If the 3 fetters are eradicated, he obtains the Hsü-t'o-yüan (Sotāpanna) not to fall again into evil dharmas and surely to obtain complete enlightenment ; at the utmost he will be born again in the world of Devas and men ; after being born 7 times, he will put an end to suffering.

P N° 22: (*i*, 141, 35–47; 142, 1–2): Almost the same. C: 3 fetters are eradicated = P: tīṇi saṃyojanāni pahīnāni. C: not to fall again into evil dharmas = P: avinipātadhammā (not liable to be born into purgatory). C: Surely to obtain complete enlightenment = P: niyatā sambodhiparāyanā. It omits: at the utmost, he will be born again in the world of the devas and men; after being born 7 times, he will put an end to suffering.

b) *Sakadāgāmī or Once-returner:*

C: (66*a*, 17–18): If the 3 fetters are eradicated and lust, aversion and delusion are thinned out, he obtains the once-returner stage, returns to the world of Devas and men once again and then puts an end to suffering.

P: (141, 31–35): Almost the same. It omits: Devas and men.

c) *Anāgāmī or non-returner:*

C: (66*a*, 15–17): If the 5 fetters binding to a lower world are destroyed, when he dies, he will be born in that place and from there, he realizes Nirvāṇa, obtaining the state of non-returner, not to return to this world.

P: (141, 26–30): Almost the same. C: if the 5 fetters binding to a lower world are destroyed = P: pañc'orambhāgiyāni saṃyojanāni pahīnāni. The P adds: opapātikā (to be of spontaneous birth).

d) *Arahan, āsavakhayañāṇaṃ: Arahantship and knowledge of the extinction of cankers:*

In *C. S. N*° 16, the attainment of arahantship and the knowledge of the extinction of cankers are treated at length:

C N° 102: (*vi*, 24*b*, 6–9): With such concentrated mind, purified, without blemishes, without defilements, soft and malleable, with mind well fixed and immovable, he bends his mind towards the extinction of the cankers, towards knowledge of attainment, towards realization. Then he knows suffering as it really is, the origination of suffering as it really is, the cessation of suffering as it really is, the path leading to the cessation of suffering as it really is. He also knows these cankers as they really are, the origination of these cankers, the cessation of these cankers, the path leading to the cessation of these cankers as it really is. He has obtained such a knowledge, such a vision, with his mind free from cankers of sense-desires cankers of becoming, cankers of ignorance. When he is emancipated, he know, that he is emancipated; birth is destroyed, the holy life is fulfilled, what should be done has been done; there will be no more becoming. True is his knowledge.

P. N° 19 : (*i*, 23, 11–26) : Almost the same. C : with such concentrated mind, purified, without blemishes, without defilements, soft and malleable, with mind well fixed and immovable = P: evaṃ samāhite citte parisuddhe pariyodāte anaṅgaṇe vigatūpakkilese mudubhūte kammaniye ṭhite anejjappatte (almost the same). C: True is his knowledge = P : Abhhaññāsiṃ (I knew thus).

In *C. S. N*° 67, Arahantship is treated in a different way :

C N° 75 *:* (*v*, 103*a*, 17–20 ; 103*b*, 1–3) : Ven. A-nan said that the W.H. One had already spoken the way of pure immovability, the way of the pure plane of nothingness, the way of the pure no-perception, the Nirvāṇa without a remainder. Then he requested the Buddha to explain what was the ariyan emancipation. The Buddha explained that the learned ariyan disciple reflected thus : « If there are here-now and here-after sense-desires, here-now and here-after material forms, here-now and here-after perceptions of sense-desires, here-now and here-after perceptions of material forms and perceptions of immovability, the plane of nothingness, the perceptions of perceptions and no-perceptions, all these perceptions are impermanent, suffering and subject to destruction. This is called pertaining to oneself. If (he considers that as) there is pertaining to oneself, then there is birth, there is old age, sickness, death. If there is such dharma, in which all these are destroyed completely, without a remainder, without another becoming, then there is no-rebirth, old age, sickness and death. If the ariyan reflects like that, if there is (remainder) then it is emancipated dharma ; if there is nirvāṇa without a remainder, then it is called the deathless (ambrosia). If he reflects like that, sees like that, his mind is emancipated from cankers of sense-desire, of becoming and of ignorance. Being emancipated, he knows that he is emancipated. Birth is destroyed, the brahma-life is established, what should be done has been done, there will be no more becoming. True is his knowledge.

P N° 106 : (*ii*, 265, 21–31) : Here elder Ānanda exclaimed as marvellous and wonderful and said that by means of this or that the Buddha preached the crossing over of the flood. Then he asked about the noble emancipation. The P mentions the same dhammas to be reflected upon, with the difference in their order. In the P, the monk's reflection is very simple: « Esa sakkāyo yāvatā sakkāyo etaṃ amataṃ yadidaṃ anupādā cittassa vimokho » (Whatever is one's own body is one's own body. But further, it is this deathless that is the emancipation of the mind without grasping).

We have already seen above the attainment of arahantship with reflection upon the nature of the aggregates, p. 113, upon the nature of equanimity, p. 119-20, upon the practice of the 4 Brahmavihārā or Illimitables p. 101.

Remarks: Thus on a whole as far as the wisdom-paragraph is concerned, we can say that there is not much difference between the C and the P versions. Three important points however should be noticed : the division of the C version into 62 dhātus and that of the P into 41 elements, the stress on the existence of suffering in the Past, in the Present and in the Future in the C version and the definition of actions which are permissable. Again the description of different kinds of tortures or punishments, that of various kinds of Hells are not the same in both versions. All these above mentioned differences show that both versions are more or less independent in the selection of documents and each reflects the tenets of the school it represents.

PART TWO

SIMILARITIFS AND DIFFERENCES BETWEEN THE CHINESE AND THE PĀLI VERSIONS

Chapter V. — LORD BUDDHA

1. — ACCOUNTS OF THE BUDDHA'S LIFE :

In *C.S. N°* 22, there is an account of the life of the Buddha, narrated by himself to Ven. A-nan :

a) *Going forth :*

C N° 204 : (*vii,* 74*a,* 12–13) : « Myself, when I did not yet obtain the supreme, fully complete enlightenment, the same thought occurred to me : « I am liable to disease, why should I foolishly seek what is liable to disease ; I am liable to old age, death, sorrow, grief, despair, blemishes, why should I foolishly seek what is liable to old age... blemishes ? What if now I seek the diseaseless, the supreme peacefulness, Nirvāṇa, seek the ageless, deathless, sorrowless, griefless, despairless, blemishless, the supreme peacefulness, Nirvāṇa ».

P N° 26 : (*i,* 163, 9–26) : Almost the same. C : Myself, when I did not yet obtain the supreme, fully complete enlightenment = P : Myself, before my enlightenment, not yet a perfect Buddha, a Bodhisatta. Here the C omits the term Bodhisatta. C : liable to old age, death, sorrow, grief, despair, blemishes = P : liable to birth, old age, disease, death, sorrow, blemishes.

C : (74*a,* 13–15) : « I, at that time, in the prime of life, being a lad, in the purity of youth, of blue hair, of youthful vigour, 29 years of age, enjoying pleasures, living in opulence, although at that time my parents were weeping, wailing and my relatives not at all happy and pleased, I shaved my beard and hair, put on the yellow robe, out of faith forsook the home-life and adopted the homeless life to learn the Dharma ».

P : (163, 27–31) : Almost the same. The P omits : In the purity of youth, of 29 years of age, enjoying pleasures, living in opulence, my relatives not at all happy and pleased, out of faith, to learn the Dharma. It adds : Against the wishes of father and mother.

b) *Spiritual training under the 2 sages :*

i) *Under A-lo-lo-chia-lo-mo = P: Āḷāra Kālāma.*

C: (74*a,* 15–20; 74*b,* 1–5): « I observed the purity of my body, my speech and my thoughts. Having mastered the purity of the body, I wanted to seek the diseaseless... the supreme peacefulness, Nirvāṇa. Then I approached A-lo-lo-chia-lo-mo and asked : « A-lo-lo, I wish to live the brahma-life under your doctrine, can it be done or not? » A-lo-lo replied: « Your reverence, for me, there is nothing impossible. If you want to practise yourself, please do so ». Again I asked : « A-lo-lo, how is the dharma that you know, perceive and realize by yourself? » A-lo-lo replied to me : « Your reverence, I have passed beyond all planes of consciousness, attained and abided in the plane of nothingness. That is what I have known, perceived and realized that dharma » Again I thought: « Not A-lo-lo alone has such a faith, I too have that faith. Not A-lo-lo alone has such an endeavour, I too have that endeavour. Not A-lo-lo alone has such a wisdom, I too have that wisdom. A-lo-lo has known, perceived, realized that dharma by himself ». As I wanted to realize that dharma, I dwelt alone in a far off, secluded and calm place, my mind not negligent, mindful, exerting myself in meditation. Thus dwelling in a far-off, secluded and calm place, my mind not negligent, mindful, exerting myself in meditation, before long I realized that dharma. Having realized that dharma, I approached A-lo-lo and asked : « A-lo-lo, is such a dharma that you have known, perceived and realized, that is to pass beyond all planes of consciousness, attain the plane of nothingness and abide in it » ? A-lo-lo replied to me: « W. H. One, it is that dharma that I have known, perceived, realized, that is to pass... and abide in it ». A-lo-lo again said to me: « W. H. One, the dharma that I have realized, that dharma you have also realized. The dharma that you have realized, that dharma I also have realized. W. H. One, come and together (with me), let us lead this group ». This is A-lo-lo's position as a teacher, I am also equal to him, the highest respect, the best offering, the supreme happiness». Again I thought : « This dharma is not conducive to wisdom, to enlightenment, to Nirvāṇa. Now I should give up that dharma and seek the diseaseless... the supreme peacefulness, Nirvāṇa ». Then I gave up that dharma and sought the diseaseless... the supreme peacefulness, Nirvāṇa.

P: (163, 31-37; 164; 165, 1-14): Almost the same. C: I observed the purity of my body... Nirvāṇa = P: Thus, having gone forth, a seeker after what is meritorious, in search of the supreme peaceful path. C: Nothing is impossible to me ; if you want to train yourself, please do so = P : May your reverence abide in it ; this dhamma is such that an intelligent person before long, under his own teacher having known by himself, having realized it, will attain and abide in it ». The P adds a passage in which the Buddha related how he had mastered that dhamma as revealed by Āḷāra Kālāma as far as mere lip service, recitation and explanation were concerned, he had hnown as well as others the doctrine of wisdom, the doctrine of the Elders. C: Again I thought: « This dhamma is not conducive to disgust, to dispassion, to cessation, to calmness, to high knowledge, to enlightenment, to Nibbāna, but only up to the extent of the attainment of the plane of nothingness. The rest is more or less the same.

c) *Under Yü-t'o-lo-lo-mo-tzu : P : Uddaka Rāmaputta :*

C : (74*b*, 5-15) = *P :* (165, 15-37 ; 166, 1-34) : This paragraph is almost the same with the preceding passage in the C and in P versions, with A-lo-lo-chia-lo-mo replaced by Yü-t'o-lo-lo-mo-tzu and with the plane of nothingness replaced by the plane of neither perception nor non-perception.

d) *Enlightenment :*

C ; (74*b*, 15-20) : « Then I gave up that dharma and went in search of the diseaseless... Nirvāṇa. I came to the South of Hsiang-t'ing mountain, to the brāhmaṇa village Yü-pei-lo, called Ssu-na. In the middle of it, there was a delightful place, with luxuriant woodland and the Ni-lien-shan limpid, clear and full to the brim. When I saw this plot of land, I thought: « This land is extremely delightful and pleasant, the woodland is luxuriant, the Ni-lien-shan river is clear, limpid and full to the brim. If any young people of family wishes to learn the dharma, he should in this place learn the dharma. I also want to learn the dharma, I should now in this place learn the Dharma». Then I took some grass, came to the Bodhi tree. Having reached there. I scattered (the grass), spread my sitting mat, sat cross-legged, made a vow not to leave the seat till I attained the complete extinction of cankers. I did not leave this seat, I obtained the complete extinction of the cankers. I sought the diseaseless, the supreme peacefulness, Nirvāṇa... and I obtained the ageless, deathless, griefless, despairless, blemishless, the supreme peacefulness, Nirvāṇa. Knowledge arose, vision arose ; ting-tao-p'in-fa (定道品法) ; birth was destroyed ; the holy life was fulfilled ; what should be done was done, there was no more becoming. True was my knowledge. »

P : (166, 35-37 ; 167, 1-29) : Not exactly the same. The P omits South of Hsiang-ting mountain, but adds Magadha. Here the C mistook Gayāsīse for Gajasīse. C: Yü-pei-lo, a brāhmaṇa-village called Ssu-na = P : Uruvelā Senānigamo. Here the spot is described as : a lovely place, a pleasant forest grove, a river flowing transparent, easy of access, delightful, surrounded by villages suitable for alm-food. The P omits (1) : I took some grass, came to the Bodhi tree,... I obtained the complete extinction of cankers. C : Ting-tao-p'in-fa = P : Akuppā me vimutti. The rest is almost the same.

e) *Hesitation to preach the dharma :*

P : (167, 30-37; 168; 169, 1-30) : This long passage (in which the Buddha after his enlightenment hesitated to preach the dhamma, because living beings were steeped in sense-desire and ignorance ; and it was only after Brahmā Sahampati's request that the Buddha decided to turn the wheel of the dhamma), is missing in the C version.

(1) Found in the Nidanakatha of the jataka Atthakatha.

f) *Decision to preach the dharma :*

C : 74*b*, 20; 75*a*, 1-8) : When I first obtained the supreme, complete enilghtenment, this thought occurred to me : « To whom should I first preach the dharma ? » Then again I thought : « I would first preach the dharma to A-lo-lo-chia-lo-mo. » At that time a deity who stood in the air spoke to me : « Oh great deity, you should know that A-la-la-chia-lo-mo was dead 7 days ago ». I also knew that A-lo-lo-chia-lo-mo was dead 7 days ago. Again I thought : « It was a great loss to A-lo-lo-chia-lo-mo not to hear this dharma. If he had heard this dharma, he would have quickly understood it and penetrated it ». When I first obtained the supreme complete enlightenment, this thought occurred to me : « To whom should I first preach the dharma ? » Then again I thought : « I would first preach the dharma to Yü-t'o-lo-lo-mo-tzu. » Then again a deity who stood in the air spoke to me : « Oh great deity, you should know that Yü-t'o-lo-lo-mo-tzu was dead 2 seven days ago (14 days). » I also knew that Yü-t'o-lo-lo-mo-tzu was dead 2 seven days ago. Then I thought : « It was a great loss to Yü-to-lo-lo-mɔ-tzu not to hear this dharma. If he had heard it, he would have quickly understood it, penetrated it ». When I first obtained the complete enlightenment, this thought occurred to me : « To whom should I first preach the dharma ? » Then again I thought : « Formerly the 5 monks served me very well, were very helpful to me. When I practised austerities, these monks attended upon me. Now I should preach the dharma first to the 5 monks ». Then again I thought : « Where do these 5 former monks now live ? » Then with my pure divine eye surpassing all human beings, I saw the 5 monks now staying at Po-lo-nai, the Deities' » dwelling place, in the Deer-park. I stayed at the Bodhi tree, as long as I wished, then I arranged my robes, took up the bowl and went to Po-lo-nai, to the market town of Chia-shih.

P : (169, 31-35 ; 170, 1-32) : Almost the same. The P omits : When I first obtained the supreme complete enlightenment, to whom should I first preach the dharma ? The P adds : who w ll understand this dhamma quickly. It adds some epithets for Āḷāra Kālāma : « He is learned, experienced, wise, of few blemishes ». C : Oh great deity = P : Bhante. C : Yü-t'o-lo-lo-mɔ-tzu was dead 2 seven days ago = P : Uddaka Rāmaputta was dead last night (abhidosa).

g) *Encounter with Yu-t'o (P : Upako) :*

C : (75*a*, 8-16) = *P :* (170, 33-37 ; 171, 1-17)

At that time, a follower of different sect Yu-t'o saw me coming from afar and said to me : « Rev. fr. Ch'ü-t'an, your faculties are pure, your complexion is extremely brilliant, your face is radiant with light. Rev. fr. Ch'ü-t'an, who is your Teacher ? Under whom do you study the dharma ? What dharma do you believe in ? » Then I replied to Yu-t'o with these verses. (In the C, there are only 4 gāthās through which the Buddha replied to Yu-t'o. In the P version, there are up to 5 gāthās, which correspond with the C ones as follows : C 1 = P 1 ; C 2 = P 2 & P 3; C 3 = P 5; C 4 = P 4).

C 1 = P 1 :

C : I am supreme, victorious over all. Not attached to any dharma ; all cravings are destroyed, emancipated. I am self enlightened ; who then can be (my) Teacher ?

P : I am victorious over all, omniscient ; Among all dhammas, I remained unsullied. All given up, emancipated with the destruction of craving. I am self enlightened. Whom should I follow ?

C 2 = P 2 & P 3 :

C : I am peerless, no one excels me. I realized myself the supreme enlightenment. The Tathāgata is the Teacher of Gods and men. I know everything. (I am) powerful and mighty.

P : To me, there is no teacher ; an equal to me cannot be found. In this world with the deities, no one can match me. I am the perfect one in the world ; I am the supreme Teacher. Alone, I realized the perfect Enlightenment. I am cool and peaceful.

C 3 = P 5 :

C : I am a victor of all existences like this. This means that all my cankers are destroyed. I destroyed all demeritorious dharmas. Oh Yu-t'o, that is why I am a victor.

P : Those who are like me, they are victors, who have obtained the destruction of cankers. I have conquered all demeritorious dharmas. Therefore Upaka, I am a victor.

C 4 = P 4 :

C : I am going to the city of Po-lo-nai to beat the perfect ambrosial drum, to set in motion the supreme dharma, which is not yet set in motion in the world.

P : I am going to the city of Kāsī to set in motion the wheel of the law, beating the ambrosial drum in the world subject to blindness.

Then Yu-t'o said : « Rev. fr., it may be so ». Having said thus, he took a bye path and departed ».

h) *Conversion of the 5 monks :*

C : (75*a*, 14-20 ; 74*b*, 1-5) : Then I came myself to the deities' dwelling place in the Deer-park. At that time, the 5 monks, when they saw me coming from afar, they adopted the following resolution, saying : « Rev.

fr. should know, this recluse Ch'ü-t'an is coming, full of desires, full of longings, taking luxurious food and drink, fond of non-glutinous rice and fried rice, together with ghee, honey, using sesame oil to massage his body. Now he is coming again. You should keep your seat, neither get up to welcome him, nor pay respect to him. A seat is set apart for him, but do not to invite him to sit down. When he arrives, simply say : « If you want to sit down, do what you want to ». At that time, I reached the 5 monks' abode. The 5 monks could not bear the majestic power of my merits. They got up from their seat ; some took my bowl and robe, some spread the bed, some brought water to wash my feet. Then I thought : « Why are these ignorant people not firm in their resolutions and act contrary to what they formerly had decided ». At that time, the 5 monks addressed me by my family name and the term : « Your reverence ». I told them : « Oh 5 monks, I am the Tathāgata completely emancipated and fully enlightened. You should not address me by my family name and by the term : « Your reverence ». Why is it so ? (Because) I sought the diseaseless... true was my knowledge ». They addressed me thus : « Rev. fr. Ch'ü-t'an, formerly you led such a life, you practised such a religious mode of living, you underwent such an austerity, yet you were unable to obtain the worldly high dharma which was inferior to the ariyan knowledge and ariyan vision. So how is it possible now that you are full of desires, full of longing, taking luxurious food and drink, fond of non-glutinous rice and fried rice, together with ghee, honey, using sesame oil to massage the body. » Then I replied : « Oh 5 monks, formerly did you see me possess the purity of all my faculties, all shining and brilliant as I am now ». The 5 monks again replied to me : « Formerly we did not see your reverence with all the faculties pure, shining and brilliant. But rev. Ch'ü-t'an, now your faculties are pure, your complexion is brilliant and your face is radiant with light. »

P : (171, 18–34 ; 172 ; 173, 1–2) : Almost the same. C : full of desires, full of longings, taking... to massage the body = P : he lives in abundance, he has forsaken exertion, he has returned to a life of abundance. The P omits : « Then I thought : why are these ignorant people not firm in their resolution and acted contrary to what they formerly had decided. » The Buddha's reply was rather different : « Oh monks, do not call the Tathāgata by his name or by the appellation your reverence. Oh monks, the Tathāgata was the perfect one, fully, rightly enlightened. Listen attentively, the deathless is found. I admonish, I preach the Dhamma ; if you practise in accordance with what you are advised to do, not before long, you will perceive, realize, attain here-now and abide in that supreme goal of a holy life, for the sake of which sons of family rightly give up the home-life and adopt the homeless life. » C : So how is it possible now that you are full of desires... massage the body ? = P : Now that you live in abundance, you have forsaken exertion, you have returned to a life of abundance, how will you obtain the superhuman dhamma, the truly specific ariyan knowledge and vision ? » C : Then I replied : « Oh 5 monks, formerly did you see me possess the purity of my faculties... with light » = P: not the same. First the Buddha denied that he had led a life of abundance, had given up exertion as accused by the 5 monks. Then he stated that he was a Tathāgata, fully enlightened... for the sake of it, sons of family rightly gave up the family life and adopted the homeless life ». The 5 monks repeated their accusations 3 times, and the Buddha repeated the same statement 3 times. Then he asked the monks if they had heard him speak like that before. To the monks' negative reply, he repeated once more the previous statement and at the end succeeded in convincing the monks.

i) *The Buddha's preaching to the 5 monks :*

C: (75*b*, 5-10) : « Oh 5 monks, you should know : There are 2 extremes which religious people should not follow, the first is attachment to sensual pleasures, which is low, vulgar, practised by worldly people. The second is self austerity, self suffering, not adopted by the sages, not endowed with meaning (profit). Oh 5 monks, there is a middle path which avoids these 2 extremes, this path will bring about knowledge, wisdom, concentration, to complete mastery, which leads to wisdom, to enlightenment, to Nirvāṇa. This path is called the ariyan Path, from right understanding up to right concentration. This is called the noble 8 fold Path. (Now I) wanted to teach the 5 monks by turn. I taught 2 monks, the (other) 3 went begging for alms which were enough to be shared by 6. I taught 3 monks, the (other) 2 went begging for alms which were enough to be shared by 6. Thus I instructed them, thus I converted them, seeking the diseaseless... true was their knowledge ».

P: (173, 2-20): There is no beginning of the Dhammacakka-pavattana in the P version. The rest is almost the same.

2. — MARVELLOUS QUALITIES OF THE BUDDHA :

In *C. S. N°* 78, the C version enumerates 24 marvellous qualities of the Buddha, while the P mentions only 19. The corresponding qualities in the 2 versions are as follows :

C 2=P 1; C 3=P 3; C 4=P 4 & P 5; C 8=P 19; C 10=P 16; C 11=P 15; C 12=P 18; C 14=P 17. The P omits: C 1, C 5, C 6, C 7, C 9, C 13, C 15, C 16, C 17, C 18, C 19, C 20, C 21, C 22, C 23, C 24. The C omits: P 2, P 6, P 7, P 8, P 9, P 10, P 11, P 12, P 13, P 14.

C 1 = P no :

C N° 32: (*v.* 43*b*, 9): « I (elder A-nan) heard that at the time of the Buddha Chia-yeh (Kassapa), the W. H. One began to make the vow to become a Buddha and to practise the brahma-life. This I had accepted and recognised as one of the marvellous qualities of the W. H. One ».

C 2 = P 1 :

C; (43*b*, 9, 44*a*, 1–2): « I heard that at the time of Buddha Chia-yeh, the W. H. One after his vow to become the Buddha and to practise the brahma-life was born in the Tou-sêng-to heaven (Tusitā). This I had accepted... the W. H. One ».

P: N° 123: (*iii*, 119, 18–23) : Elder Ananda said that he had heard and learnt face to face with the Blessed One that the Bodhisatta was born in the Tusitā, mindful and clearly conscious. This he considered as one marvellous quality of the Blessed One.

Remarks : The P omits to mention Buddha Chia-yeh (Kassapa). Traditions usually mention that the Buddha made his vow under Buddha Dīpaṅkara. Here the C omits the term Bodhisatta.

C 3 = *P* 3 *:*

C: (44*a*, 2–6) : Elder A-nan's expressions are the same in all the marvellous qualities, only the subject-matter differs. Here it refers to the rejoicings of the deities of Tou-sêng-to, because after the Buddha's birth in Tou-sêng-to, 3 things became better than before his birth, the deities' age, the deities' beauty and the deities' fame.

P: (119, 29–33): Simply the Bodhisatta remained in the Tusitā as long as his life-span lasted.

C 4 = *P* 4 *&* *P* 5*:*

C: (44*a*, 6–11) : When the W. H. One from Tou-sêng-to heaven entered the mother's womb, the whole heaven and earth trembled and a glorious radiance shone over the whole world, including all dark and gloomy corners. Where sun and moon, although they possessed great psychic power, great strength, were unable to make their light prevail, this glorious radiance shed its light over these places. Living beings who dwelt there with the help of this glorious radiance came to know that there were wonderful beings being born there.

P; (119, 34–36; 120, 1–19): Almost the same. In P 4, the Bodhisatta mindful and conscious, descended from the Tusitā heaven and entered his mother's womb. In P 5, it mentions the appearance of this glorious radiance. Here the P adds that this glorious radiance surpassed even the majesty of the Devas. C: All over the world = P: Appeared in the world with its deitie , Māra, Brahmā, among recluses, brāhmaṇas, devas and men. The P adds that 10 thousand world-systems trembled and quaked.

C 5 = *P no :*

C : (44*a*, 11–12): The W.H. One in the mother's womb rested on the right side.

C 6 = *P no :*

C: (44*a*, 12) : In the mother's womb, the W.H. One had his body stretched.

C 7 = *P no :*

C : (44*a* 12–14): In the mother's womb, the W.H. One was not sullied by blood, mucus and dirty matters.

C 8 = *P* 19 *:*

C : (44*a*, 14–18): When the W.H. One came out of his mother's womb, there were tremor and glorious radiance (as in C 4).

P : (123, 26–33 ; 124, 1–8) : Same differences as in N° 4 above.

C 9 = *P no :*

C : (44*a*, 18–19) : The W.H. One came out of his mother's womb with his body stretched.

C 10 = *P* 16 *:*

C : (44*a*, 19–20) : When he came out of his mother's womb, he was not sullied by blood, mucus, by dirty matters.

P : (122, 31–34 : 123, 1–9) : Almost the same. The P adds a simile of a jewel placed on a Benares muslim, both things being pure do not stain each other.

C 11 = *P* 15 *:*

C : (44*a*, 20 ; 44*b*, 1–2) : When the W.H. One was born, there were 4 deities with soft cloths in their hands, standing in front of the mother and making her rejoice saying that that boy was very wonderful, having great psychic power, great strength, great merit.

P : (122, 24–30): Almost the same. It adds : The Bodhisatta did not touch the earth. It omits : With soft cloths in their hands. While the C says that the 4 deities stood in front of the mother, the P says that the 4 deities placed the Bodhisatta in front of the mother. C: A wonderful boy, with great psychic power... great merit = P: Mighty is the son born to you.

C 12 = *P* 18 *:*

C : (44*b*, 2–4) : When the W.H. One was just born, he paced 7 steps, fearless, dauntless and scanned the directions.

P : (123, 10–16) : With more details. While he paced 7 steps, a white umbrella was held over him and he proclaimed with the voice of a bull that he was the chief, the best, the highest in all quarters of the world. This was his last birth, there was no more becoming. The P adds : Standing on even feet and facing North.

C 13 = *P no:*

C : (44*b*, 4–5) : When the W.H. One was just born, a great lake appeared before the mother with its water full to the brim so that she could use it and clean herself.

C 14 = *P* 17:

C: (44*b*, 5–6) : When the W.H. One was just born, the sky rained down two streams of water, one cold and one warm to bathe the W.H. One's body.

P: (123, 10–16) : Almost the same. It adds that the water serves as a libation also to the mother.

C 15 = *P* *no*:

C: (44*b*, 6–9) : When the W.H. One was just born, the deities in the sky played heavenly music and scattered over the W.H. One heavenly blue lotuses, rosy, red, white lotuses, heavenly Wên-t'o-lo (mandāra) flowers (文陀羅), and fine scented sandal-powders.

C 16 = *P* *no*:

C: (44*b*, 9–14) : One day king Pai-ching (P : Suddhodhana) was watching ploughing and the W.H. One was placed under the shadow of a Yen-fu tree (Jambudīpa tree). The W.H. One entered the first dhyāna, aloof from sense-desires, aloof from demeritorious dharmas, with initial thoughts and discursive thoughts, with joy and happiness born out of seclusion and dwelt in it. In the afternoon, the shadow of the Yen-fu tree remained motionless on the W.H. One's body, protecting him from the sun. The king in search of his son witnessed this miracle of the tree and exclaimed his wonder and marvel.

C 17 = *P* *no*:

C: (44*b*, 14–19) : One day, at Pei-shê-li (P : Vesāli), the W.H. One, after his begging round and having finished his meal, put his sitting mat on his shoulder, entered a forest, came to a To-lo tree (Tāla : palm-tree), spread his sitting mat and sat in meditation. In the afternoon, the shadow of all the trees had moved but the shadow of the To-lo tree remained motionless on the W.H. One's body, protecting him from the sun. A Sakyan named Mo-ha-nan came to that forest, witnessed that miracle of the tree and exclaimed his wonder and marvel.

C 18 = *P* *no*:

C: (44*b*, 19–20 ; 45*a*, 1–4) : At one time, the W.H. One was staying at Pei-shê-li in the great forest. At that time, the monks put their begging bowls outside in the open air. A monkey came, took the W.H. One's begging bowl and went away. The monks wanted to prevent the monkey from taking the bowl for fear of its being broken. But the W.H. One asked them not to worry. The monkey took the bowl, climbed slowly a tree, fiilled the bowl with honey, climbed down slowly and offered the bowl to the W.H. One who refused. Then the monkey took a stick and removed the insects in the honey and offered to the W.H. One who again refused. Then the monkey poured water in the honey and offered it to the W.H. One, who now accepted the offering.

C 19 = *P no :*

C : (45*a*, 4-7) : At one time, at Pei-shê-li, on the bank of a big monkey river, the W.H. One was drying his sitting mat and beating it clean on a high terrace of a palace. At that time, an unusual cloud came, covered the whole sky and wanted to pour down heavy rain. But the cloud saw the W.H. One drying and beating clean his sitting mat. It stopped and waited till the W.H. One finished his work. Then the cloud poured down heavy rain and filled all lower spaces.

C 20 = *P no :*

C : (45*a*, 7-10) : At one time, the W. H. One was staying in Po-chi, in the Hot-spring forest, sitting at the foot of a king Sāla tree. At that time, in the afternoon, the shadow of all the trees had moved but the shadow of the king Sāla tree did not move from the W. H. One's body. The owner of Lo-mo park witnessed this miracle and exclaimed his wonder and marvel.

C 21 = *P no :*

C : (45*a*, 11-17) : At one time, the W. H. One was staying in the house of A-fu-shêng. After his begging round, having finished his meal and put back his begging bowl and robe, he spread his sitting mat and sat in meditation in the house of A-fu-shêng. At that time, there was loud thunder and heavy hail which killed 2 out of four farmers ploughing in the field. In the cremation ceremony, people cried and wailed loudly. The W. H. One, in the evening emerged from his meditation, came out of the house and paced up and down. A certain person seeing the W. H. One pace up and down, came to pay homage to him and followed him behind. The W. H. One enquired of him of the cause of the great noise and commotion. He reported the matter to the W. H. One, and marvelled at the deep meditation of the W. H. One, who did not hear and was not disturbed by all that noise and commotion.

C 22 = *P no :*

C : (45*a*, 17-19) : At one time, the W. H. One was staying in Yü-pei-lo (Uruvelā), near the bank of Ni-lien-jan river, at the foot of the tree A-shê-ho-lo-ni-chü-lei (Assattha Nigrodha), when he just got his enlightenment. At that time, there was a heavy rain lasting 7 days and submerging everything. But when the W. H. One came out in the open air to pace up and down, the earth emerged for him to pace up and down.

C 23 = *P no :*

C : (45*a*, 19-20 ; 45*b*, 1) : Māra had followed the W. H. One during 6 years waiting for an opportune moment to harm him but could not, and exhausted had gone away.

C 24 = *P no :*

C : (45*b*, 1) : The W. H. One for 7 years practised mindfulness on the body without interruption.

There are on the contrary up to 10 cases in Pāli not available in the C version :

P 2 *:* (119, 24–28) : The Bodhisatta remained in Tusitā heaven, mindful and clearly conscious.

P 6 *:* (120, 20–26) : When the Bodhisatta entered the mother's womb, 4 deities came and guarded the 4 directions preventing any human being or not human being from annoying the Bodhisatta and his mother.

P 7 *:* (120, 27–33) : When the Bodhisatta entered the mother's womb, his mother became virtuous by nature, not committing any infringement of the 5 moral precepts of killing up to drinking wine.

P 8 *:* (121, 1–7) : When the Bodhisatta entered the mother's womb, no thought connected with groups of sense-desire for men arose in the Bodhisatta's mother.

P 9 *:* (121, 8–14) : When the Bodhisatta was entering his mother's womb, his mother was enjoying the 5 groups of sensedesire ; she surrounded herself, with the 5 groups of sense-desire.

P 10 *:* (121, 15–32) : When the Bodhisatta was in his mother's womb, his mother did not suffer any illness, she lived at ease, without tiredness. She saw in her womb the Bodhisatta complete in his limbs and with his faculties perfect. Just like an emerald jewel lovely, well cut into 7 facets and a thread of blue colour or of yellow, red, white, orange colour runs through this jewel. A man with eye takes this jewel in his hand and examines it. He would see clearly the jewel with the thread in colour.

P 11*:* (122, 15): The Bodhisatta's mother soon died after 7 days of his birth and was reborn in the Tusitā heaven.

P 12*:* (122, 6–12): Other women carried their child for 9 or 10 months before giving birth ; but the Bodhisatta's mother carried her child up to 10 months only.

P 13*:* (122, 13–18): Other women gave birth sitting or lying down. The Bodhisatta's mother gave birth while standing.

P 14*:* (122, 19–23): When the Bodhisatta came out of his mother's womb, the deities received him first, then the men afterwards.

Another wonderful quality:

C: (45*b*, 1–3): Then the W. H. One told elder A-nan : «You should regard this too as another wonderful quality of the Tathāgata: The Tathāgata knows the feelings when they arise, (knows) when they persist, (knows the feelings) when they cease, he always knows them. In the same way with thoughts and perceptions. Then elder A-nan acknowledged this as another wonderful quality of the Tathāgata.

P: (124, 9-20): Almost the same. The P omits: « He always knows them. It puts saññā before vitakka.

Remarks: We remark that the expression Bodhisatta is not mentioned in the C version, while the P uses it to denote the Buddha when he was not yet enlightened. Thus we can surmise that the term Bodhisatta was later on introduced by the Ther. (1) to counteract the interpretation of this term by the Mahāyānists. We remark also that the traditions of the accounts of the Buddha's life and his marvellous qualities are not the same in both versions, each seems to derive from an independent source as far as the life and the marvellous qualities of the Buddha are concerned.

3. — THE TEN APPELLATIONS OF THE BUDDHA

In *C. S. N°* 27, the 10 appellations of the Buddha are referred to. A comparative study of both versions shows the following similarities and differences:

C N° 201: (*vii*, 69*a*, 1-2) = *P N°* 38: (*i*, 267, 13-16):

1) C: Ju-lai (如 來: The Tathāgata) = P: Tathāgata.
2) C: Wu-so-chu (無 所 著: Without attachment) = P: Arahaṃ.
3) C: Têng-chêng-chüeh (等 正 覺: Fully and rightly Enlightened) = P: Sammāsambuddho.
4) C: Ming-hsing-tsu (明 行 足: Endowed with wisdom and conduct) = P: Vijjācaraṇasampanno.
5) C: Shan-shih (善 逝: Well gone over) = P: Sugato.
6) C: Shih-chien-chieh (世 間 解: Knower of the world) — P: Lokavidū.
7) C: Wu-shang-shih (無 上 士: The Imcomparable One) = P: Anuttaro.
8) C: Tao-fa-yü (道 法 御: Tamer of Path and Dharma) — P: Purisadammasārathi.
9) C: T'ien-jên-shih: (天 人 師: Teacher of men and deities) = P: Satthā devamanussānaṃ.
10) C: Fu, Chung-yu (佛 衆 祐: Buddha, Protector of All) = P: Buddho, Bhagavā.

In Fo-hsüeh-ta-tzu-tien', (2), the 10 names of the Buddha are enumerated as follows: 1) Tathāgata, 2) Arhat, 3) Samyaksambuddha, 4) Vidyācaraṇasampanna, 5) Sugato, 6) Lokavid, 7) Anuttara, 8) Puruṣa damya Sārathi, 9) Śāstā-devamanusyānām, 10) Buddha-Lokanātha. If we compare this list

(1) See Ante p. 34. Note 1.
(2) Vol. iii, p. 251.

with that of the P version, we see that there is no difference, except for the last name. The Sanskrit writes Buddha lokanāth for the P Buddho Bhagavā. So we can say that in this passage, the C rendering Tamer of Path and of Dharma for the P Purisadammasārathi is not a happy one, with damya mistaken for Dhamma.

4. — THE 32 MARKS OF A GREAT MAN

In *C. S. N°* 60, the 32 marks of a great man are treated at length and we notice the following similarities and differences :

C N° 161 : (vii, 1b, 19–20 ; *2a,* 1–20 ; *2b,* 1–3) = *P N°* 91 : (*ii,* 135, 24–31 ; 136 ; 137, 1–12)*:*

The corresponding marks in both versions are as follows :

C 1 = P 2 ; C 2 = P 4 ; C 3 = P 8 ; C 4 = P 7 ; C 5 = P 3 ; C 6 = P 14 ; C 7 = P 6 ; C 8 = P 5 ; C 9 = P 12 ; C 10 = P 13 ; C 12 = P 10 ; C 13 = P 19 ; C 14 = P15 ; C 15 = P 9 ; C 16 = P 11 ; C 17 = P 16 ; C 18 = P 17 ; C 19 = P 22 ; C 20 = P 20 ; C 21 = P 18 ; C 22 = p 23 ; C 23 = P 25 ; C 24 = P 26 : C 25 = P 24 ; C 26 = P 21 ; C 27 = P 28 ; C 28 = P 27 ; C 29 = P 30 ; C 30 = P 29 : C 31 = P 32 ; C 32 = P 31 ; C 11 is not available in P and P 1 is not available in C.

C 1 = P 2 : C: On the sole appears a wheel with 1000 spokes complete in everything = P adds : with rim and hubs, in every way complete.

C 2 = P 4 : C: feet, fingers long and pointed at the end = P: long fingers.

C 3 = P 8 : C: feet round and straight = P: eṇijaṅgho (legs like antelope that is straight-limbed).

C 4 = P 7 : C: Heels and ankles, in the hind portion are full and even on both sides = P: ussaṅkhapādo (prominent ankles).

C 5 = P 3 : C: the 2 ankles of the feet are yung (傭) = P: āyatapaṇhi (with projecting heel).

C 6 = P 14 : C: Hairs of the body turn upwards = P adds: the upward hairs are blue colour of collyrium, curling in rings and towards the right (kuṇḍalāvaṭṭāni padakkhiṇāvaṭṭakajātāni).

C 7 = P 6 : C: With webbed fingers and toes like a goose king = P: Jālahatthapāda (with hands and feet endowed with net).

Remarks : Miss Horner preferred Buddhaghosa's interpretation that feet and hands were evenly spaced and apart. But the C meaning is clear.

C 8 = P 5 : C : Hands and feet are excellent, soft and tender like the tou-lo flower (Tūla : a kind of cotton flower very soft (1) = P : Soft and tender hands and feet.

(1) Fo-hsüeh-ta-tzu-tien, xi, p. 1943.

C 9=*P* 12: C: Skin is smooth, soft ; dirt and water cannot adhere to = P: Skin is shining and soft, so dust and water cannot adhere to the body.

C 10=*P* 13 : C : The hairs are separate. Each hair grows from one pore. Its colour is like blue and it turns to the right like a conch-shell = P : The hairs are separate. Each hair grows from one pore. (See P 14).

C 11=*P no* : C : His thigh is full like a deer-king.

C 12=*P* 10 : C : What is hidden is horse-like, just like a horse well-bred king = P : What is cloth-hid is sheath-cased.

C 13=*P* 19 : C : The body is well round, like a banyan tree, the up and down portions are symmetrically round = P : The body is like the round of a banyan tree, the height of the body is equal to the length of his arms.

C 14=*P* 15 : C : The body is not crooked = P : Brahmujjugatto (a divinely straight body).

C 15=*P* 9 : C : The body is not crooked. Standing erect, the hand can touch the knee = P : Standing erect and not bending, he can rub and stroke his knees with both palms of his hands.

C 16=*P* 11 : C : His body is of golden colour like colour of polished gold turning red = P : Of colour of gold.

C 17=*P* 16 : C : 7 places are full, 2 hands, 2 feet, 2 shoulders and neck = P : Sattussaddo (7 places have convex surfaces).

C 18=*P* 17 : C : Upper portion of the body is big like a lion = P: Sīhapubbaddhakāyo (the same).

C 19=*P* 22 : C : The jaw-bone is like the lion's one = P : Sīhahanu (the same).

C 20=*P* 20 : C : His back is even and straight = P : Samavattakkhandho (with shoulders round).

C 21=*P* 18 : C : The upper portion of the 2 shoulders is evenly connected with neck = P : Citantaraṃso (shoulder-hollow is heaped up).

C 22=*P* 23 : C : He had 40 teeth = P : The same.

C 23=*P* 25 : C : There is no space between the teeth = P: avivaradanto (the same).

C 24=*P* 26 : C : Of white teeth = P : susukkadāṭho (of shining teeth).

C 25=*P* 24 : C : The teeth are thorough = P : of even teeth (samadanto).

C 26=*P* 21 : C : Has a perfect taste = P: rasaggasaggī (the same).

C 27=*P* 28 *:* C : His brahma-voice is lovely, the sound is like the bird Chia-lo-p'i-chia (P : karavīka) = P : brahmassaro karavīkabhānī (the same).

C 28=*P* 27 *:* C : The tongue is large and long ; from the mouth, it can cover his face=P : pahūtajīvho (long tongue).

C 29=*P* 30 *:* C : The place to receive tears is full like a cow's king = P : gopakhumo (eye-lashes are like cow's ones).

C 30=*P* 29 *:* C : His eyes are of intense blue = P : abhinīlanetto (the same).

C 31=*P* 32 *:* C : There is a protuberance on the top of the head, symmetrically round. The hairs turn left like a conch-shell = P: uṇhīsasīso head shaped like a turban).

C 32=*P* 31 *:* C : between the eyebrows a clean and white hair grows turning right = P : uṇṇā bhamukantare jātā odātā mudutūlasannibhā (between the eyebrows a white hair grows soft like cotton).

P 1=*C : no :* He has feet with a level tread.

5. — THE BUDDHA'S DEPORTMENT

In *C. S. N*° 60, the Buddha's deportment is also reported. Thus the C describes the Buddha as wearing the robe, covering the robe, going out of the room, going out of the garden, going on the road up to the village, entering the village, on the lane of the village, entering the house, preparing to sit on the bed, sitting, washing his hands, receiving food, eating food, washing hands, giving blessings, getting up from the seat, going out of the house, on the lane and going out of the village, entering the garden and entering the house. The P starts first with going, entering the house, turning towards the seat, then sitting, taking water to wash the bowl, taking food, eating, taking water to wash bowl, giving admonition, departure, wearing robe, sitting in contemplation, preaching the dhamma.

C N° 161 : (*vii*, 2*b*, 3-20 ; 3*a*, 1-7) = *P N*° 91 : (*ii*, 137, 12-26 ; 138 ; 139 ; 140, 1-20) :

a) *Wearing robe :*

C : Recluse Ch'ü-t'an wears the robe properly, not high, not low, the robe not sticking near to the body, the wind cannot blow out the robe from the body.

P : Almost the same. After : the robe not sticking to the body, the P adds : the robe is not drawn away from his body. The P adds : dust and dirt do not cling to recluse Gotama's body. As to the sentence : The wind cannot blow out the robe from the body, Miss Horner (1) prefers to read *Kāyasmin* with the Siamese text instead of the text's *Kāyamhā*, but the C reading shows that *kāyamhā* is used here. (2)

b) *Covering robe :*

C : The same with wearing robe. It adds : recluse Ch'ü-t'an, when wearing new robe, followed the Nobles' way, to cut it with knife and to dye it with dark colour. He wears the robe not for the sake of money, or pride, not for the sake of self-ornamenting, or decoration ; but simply for the sake of protecting against the touch of mosquitoes, gad-flies, wind, sun and for the sake of shame that he covers the body.

P : no.

c) *Going out of the room :*

C : When he goes out of the room, his body does not bend upward or downward. When he wants to walk, he puts up first the right foot, puts it up rightly, puts it down rightly, without mixing up, without disorder. While walking, the 2 ankles do not strike each other. Dust and dirt do not affect him, as his former conduct was meritorious.

P : It omits : when he goes out of the room, his body does not bend upward or downward. C : puts it up rightly, puts it down rightly, without mixing up, without disorder = P : he does not put the foot too far, does not put the foot too near, walks neither quickly nor too slowly. It adds : while walking, he does not knock the knees together, does not put his thigh up, down, in and out ; he moves only the lower portion of the body, but not with the whole body's strength.

d) *Going out of the garden and up to the village, entering the village :*

C : While going out of the garden, he does not bend his body upward or downward. When he comes up to the village, he turns his body to the right and observes all round like a dragon (3) looking round, fearless, dauntless, as he is a Tathāgata, rightly and perfectly enlightened. While entering the village, he does not bend his body upward or downward. While in the village-lanes, he does not look down, he does not look up, but he looks straight, in the right way and thus there would be no hindrances to knowledge and vision. Recluse Ch'ü-t'an's faculties are always composed, due to former meritorious conduct.

---

(1) *M.L.S.* ii, p. 325, Note 6.

(2) Nalanda edition uses kayamha (ii, p. 388, l. 11).

(3) It should be translated as elephant.

P: It omits the Buddha's going out of the garden and up to the village. It mentions : when revered Gotama is looking around, he looks round with his whole body, does not look up and down, does not walk without observing, looking about one yoke (ahead), (but) further than that, his knowledge and vision is not unhindered.

e) *Entering the house and sitting on the seat :*

C : While entering the house, he does not bend his body upward or downward. He turns his body to the right side and sits on the right bed. He does not sit down with the whole body strength, he does not sit with his hands under his buttocks. While sitting, he does not look depressed, restless or happy.

P: On entering the house, (1) he does not bend his body upward, downward, in and out ; he turns round towards the seat, not too far, not too near. He sits down on the seat, not hanging (on the seat) with his hands. He does not fling his body on the seat. He does not sit with his hands and feet restless, he does not cross his knees, his ankles. He does not sit with his hand holding his jaw. While sitting in the house, he is fearless, unruffled and intent on aloofness.

f) *Receiving water for washing, food and taking food :*

C : While receiving washing water, he does not receive it high, low, too much or too little. While receiving food, he does not receive it high, low, too much or too little ; he receives food and rice in equal portion. He kneads into balls the food evenly, rightly and slowly puts it into his mouth. He does not open his mouth waiting for the food to come. He masticates the food 3 times before swallowing it. No rice and curry remains unbroken. When there is still food in the mouth, he swallows it before kneading another ball. Due to 3 things that recluse Ch'ü-t'an eats pure food, hoping to experience taste but not hoping to experience greed for taste, eating not for the sake of wealth and properties, not for pride, not for self-ornamentation, not for decoration ; but only for the sake of maintaining the body alive without sickness, for stopping old illness, for not arousing new illness, for having strength and happiness.

P : While receiving water for the bowl, he does not turn the bowl up, down, inwards, outwards ; he receives water not too little, not too much. He does not wash the bowl, making noise, turning it round. He does not put the bowl on the ground and wash his hand. Hands and bowl are washed at the same time. He throws the washing water not too far, not too near; he does not scatter it. While receiving boiled rice, he does not turn the bowl up, down, inwards, outwards ; he receives boiled rice, not too little, not

(1) *Antaraghara* here means house, not village, although in other passages, it can be interpreted as village.

too much. He eats curry with proportion. He does not forget (rice) with each mouthful of curry. He turns round 2,3 times the mouthful before swallowing it. Not a single grain of boiled rice remains unbroken when it is swallowed in the body. Not a single grain of boiled rice remains in the mouth before another mouthful is taken up. Experiencing the taste, he eats food, not for experiencing the greed for taste. Endowed with 8 qualities that recluse Gotama eats food, not for sport, not for intoxication, not for ornamentation, not for decoration, but just enough, for the maintenance of this body, keeping it going on, free from harm and for helping the brahma-life, thinking to kill old feelings, to prevent the rise of new feelings and thus living free from blame and abiding in comfort.

g) *Receiving washing water, washing bowl, preaching the dharma :*

C: While receiving water for washing hand and water for washing bowl, he does not receive it high, low, too much or too little. Hands and bowl are washed and wiped dry at the same time. Having washed and wiped dry the bowl, he puts it at one side, not too near, not too far, not looking at the bowl frequently, not overcaring for the bowl. He does not blame this food, he does not praise that food, but he remains silent. Then he preaches the dharma to the householders, gladdens, arouses, pleases them, using many ways to preach the dharma. Then he departs.

P : Almost the same with the preceding P paragraph. It adds: he puts the bowl, not too far, not too near, not without any concern for the bowl, but not overcare for the bowl. He sits silent for a while but not let the time pass without giving admonition. He admonishes, not blaming this food, not expecting another meal but he gladdens, arouses and pleases that assembly with a dharma talk. Then rising from his seat, he departs.

h) *Going out of the house, on the lanes, going out the village, entering the garden :*

C : When he comes out of the house, he does not bend upward or downward, does not look up but look straight, in the right way, thus there is no hindrance to knowledge and vision. The faculties of the revered Ch'ü-t'an are always composed due to former good conduct. When he comes out of the village, he does not bend his body upward or downward. When he enters the garden, he does not bend his body upward or downward.

P : It mentions simply that when recluse Gotama departs, he does not walk too quickly, too slowly, he does not walk as if he wants to be free (from the assembly).

i) *Sitting in meditation, preaching the dharma :*

C : After finishing his meal, having put back robe, begging bowl and having washed his hands and feet, he put the sitting mat over his shoulder and entered the room to sit for meditation. The revered recluse Ch'ü-t'an, for the welfare of the world enters the room for meditation. Then in the evening, he gets up from his meditation with his face radiant with light, because he is the Tathāgata, the perfectly and rightly Enlightened. 8 kinds of sound come out of the revered recluse Ch'ü-t'an : 1) Very deep, 2) P'i-mo-lou-po (毗摩樓簸), 3) entering the heart, 4) lovely, 5) very full, 6) lively, 7) clear, 8) endowed with wisdom. Many people love his voice, are pleased with it, remember it and become concentrated. The revered Ch'ü-t'an preaches the dharma to the assembly, his voice not going beyond the assembly but only inside the assembly. He preaches the dharma to the assembly, gladdens, arouses and pleases it, using numberless ways to explain the dharma. Having gladdened, aroused and pleased the assembly, he gets up from his seat and goes back to his place.

P : Having gone to the monastery, he sits on the appointed seat, washes his feet not for the sake of beauty. Having washed his feet, he sits cross-legged, with body erect and mindfulness established. He does not think harming oneself, harming others, harming both but thinks for the benefit of oneself, of others, of both. He preaches the dhamma to the assembly, not praising it, not blaming it, but gladdens, arouses and pleases it. His voice is endowed with 8 qualities : Vissaṭṭho (distinct), viññeyyo (comprehensive), mañju (sweet), savaniyo (audible), bindu (fully rounded voice), avisārī (clear), gambhīro (deep) and ninnādī (resonant). While instructing the assembly, his voice does not go beyond the assembly. Then people being gladdened, aroused and pleased by the dhamma talk of revered Gotama, get up from their seat and depart with reluctance keeping their eyes on him.

Remarks :

About the accounts of the Buddha's life, there is not much difference between the 2 versions, except that Rāmaputta was reported dead 2 weeks ago according to the C and on the previous night according to the P. About the marvellous qualities of the Buddha, many differences are observed, especially about his life in Tusitā heaven, in his mother's womb and some miraculous events of his life. These differences denote that the 2 versions follow different traditions. The same can be said of the 32 marks on the Buddha's body and his deportment. As to the 10 appellations, they are almost the same in both versions.

Chapter VI. — THE SANGHA OR ORDER OF THE MONKS

Now we take up the study of the similarities and the dissimilarities about the Sangha between the 2 versions. First we deal with the Pāti-mokkha which regulates the life of a monk and of the whole Sangha ; then the daily life of the monks, the ways to settle dispute, the annual retreat and finally the sitting mat.

1. — THE PĀTIMOKKHA

Although the Pātimokkha is mentioned in both the C and the P versions, it does not expressly mention the 250 rules of the C vinaya or the 227 rules of the P vinaya. But in *C. S. N°* 46, there is reference to some rules of conduct for a forest-dweller, which can be construed as a nucleous for the future codification of the complete Pātimokkha.

The C enumerates 13 rules of conduct, while the P counts up to 17. Some are the same, some are slightly different, some are not to be found in the other version. The corresponding rules are as follows : C 1 = P 1 ; C 2 = P 5 ; C 3 = P 6 ; C 5 = P 8 ; C 6 = P 9 ; C 7 = P 11 ; C 8 = P 12 & P 14 ; C 9 = P 3 ; C 10 = P 2 ; C 11 = P 15 ; C 12 = P 16 ; C 13 = P 17 ; C 4 is not available in the P. P 4, P 7, P 10 and P 13 are not available in the C.

C 1 : C N° 26 *:* (*v*, 31*b*, 17-19) : A monk who lives in a trouble-free place should learn to be respectful and to observe accordingly. If he is not respectful and does not observe accordingly, then (other) monks will scold him, saying : « What is the use for this monk who is a trouble-free place-dweller to live in a troublefree place ». That is why a monk who is a troublefree place-dweller, should be respectful and observe accordingly.

P 1 : P N° 69 *:* (*i*, 469, 7-15) : Almost the same. C : trouble-free place = P : araññā. It adds : when he comes in the middle of the Sangha. It omits : to observe accordingly and adds : to be deferential (sap-patissena). Other monks will upbraid him : What is the use of this forest dweller who lives in the forest of his own choice, but he is not respectful and deferential towards his fellow-monks.

C 2 : (32*a*, 1-3) : He should learn not to laugh inordinately, not to be agitated.

P 5 : (470, 9-16) : Not to be agitated (anuddhatena), not to be unstable of mind (acapalena).

C 3 : (32*a*, 3-5) : Not to engage in vulgar talk (Literally animal talk).

P 6 *:* (470, 17–23) : Not to be talkative, not to be of loose talk.

C 4 *:* (32*a*, 5–7) : He should learn not to be proud and be of few words.

P : no.

C 5 *:* (32*a*, 8–10) : He should learn to control his faculties.

P 8 *:* (470, 32–35 ; 471, 1–3) : He should learn to control the door of his faculties.

C 6 *:* (32*a*, 10–12) : He should learn to eat with moderation.

P 9 *:* (471, 4–9) : The same.

C 7 *:* (32*a*, 12–15) : He should learn to be energetic, not to be lazy.

P 11 *:* (471, 16–21) : He should learn to be energetic.

C 8 *:* (32*a*, 15–17) : He should learn to be with right mindfulness, with right wisdom.

P 12 *& P* 14 *:* (471, 22–27 ; 34–35 ; 472, 1–4) : He should be established in mindfulness and with wisdom.

C 9 *:* (32*a*, 17–19) : He should learn to know proper time, to be expert in time, not to enter the village too early for alms and not to come out of the village too late.

P 3 *:* (469, 26–33) : Not to enter the village too early, not to come out of the village late in the day.

Remarks : M.L.S. ii, p. 142, translates : during the day for diva. Here it rather means atidivā, late in the day.

C 10 *:* (32*a*, 20 ; 32*b*, 1–2) : He should learn to know how to sit, and to be expert in using seats.

P 2 *:* (469, 16–25) : To be expert in using seats.

C 11 *:* (32*b*, 2–5) : He should learn to discuss about the vinaya and the abhidharma.

P 15 *:* (472, 5–13) : He should engage himself in the study of abhivinaya and abhidhamma.

C 12 *:* (32*b*, 5–8) : He should learn how to discuss on tranquillity, on peaceful emancipated dhyāna states which transcend material forms and which are immaterial.

P 16 *:* (472, 14–24) : He should engage himself in these peaceful emancipated states which transcend material forms, which are immaterial.

C 13 *:* (32*b*, 8–11) : He should learn how to discuss about the extinction of cankers and the attainment of knowledge.

P 17 *:* (472, 25-33) : He should engage himself in the dhammas which are superhuman.

P 4 *:* (469, 34 ; 470, 1-8) : He should not call upon the family-houses before and after meals.

C : no.

P 7 *:* (470, 24-31) : He should be of pleasant speech and a good friend.

C : no.

P 10 *:* (471, 10-15) : He should be engaged in vigilance.

C : no.

P 13 *:* (471, 28-33) : He should have concentration.

C : no.

2. — DAILY LIFE OF THE MONKS

In *C. S. N*° 25, there is an account of the daily life of the monks who lived together ; this account shows how the monks should live together so as to ensure harmony and concord in the Sangha.

C N° 185 *:* (*vii*, 36*b*, 16-20 ; 37*a*, 1-3) : At that time, in the Niu-chieh-so-lo-forest, there lived together 3 sons of family, Ven. A-na-lü-t'o, Nan-t'i, Chin-p'i-lo. These elders lived together as follows : They go for alms. Who comes back first prepares the bed, fetches the water, puts out things to wash feet, sets a stool for washing feet, and a towel to rub the leg together with pot of drinking water and a basin for washing water. If he can finish all the alms he has begged, he may finish it. If there is some remainder, he puts it in a vessel and covers it. After eating, he puts back the bowl, washes hands and feet, takes the sitting mat, puts it over the shoulder, enters the house and sits for meditation. The monk who comes back later from his begging round, if he can finish all the food, he may finish it. If the food is not enough, he may take the remaining food left over and eats to his satisfaction. If there is something left, he throws it on pure ground or in the water where there is no insect. Then he washes clean the food vessel of that monk, wipes it (dry) and puts at one side, rolls back the bedding mat, puts away the stool for washing feet, the towel for wiping leg, the utensil for washing feet, the pot for drinking water and the basin for washing water. He sweeps the refectory, cleans away all rubbish, puts back (his own) robe and bowl, washes hands and feet, takes the sitting mat, puts it over the shoulder and enters the house for meditation. In the evening, the Elder who gets up from his meditation first, sees the pot for drinking water, the basin for washing water empty, takes them and fills them. If he can do it (by himself) he may do it and put them at one side.

If he cannot do it, he waves his hand to one monk and both carry them and put them at one side, without speaking, without asking. These elders, every five days assemble together to discuss about the dharma or to keep the ariyan silence.

P N° 31 : (i, 207, 6–26) : The P is very simple and lacks many details. The monk who comes back first, simply prepares the seat, sets out drinking water, washing water and a refuse-vessel. The monk who comes back late, if he wants to eat the remaining food, may eat it. If he does not want, he should throw it on a place where there is no green grass or in the water where there is no insect. Then he puts away the seat, the drinking water, the washing water, the refuse-vessel and sweeps the dining hall. While the C mentions the elders engaging in meditation, the P mentions simply that the monk who sees the drinking water pot, the washing water pot, the pot containing water to be used after evacuation empty, he fills them. The P mentions also the 3 elders meeting together every five days but omits : to keep the ariyan silence. The 3 monks here are Anuruddha, Nandiya and Kimbila.

3. — SEVEN WAYS TO SETTLE DISPUTES

In *C. S. N°* 66, 7 ways of settling disputes are dealt with.

1st way : C : By way of presence. = P : Sammukhāvinayo :

C N° 196 : (vii, 56b, 8–15) : There are 7 ways of settling disputes by way of presence, by way of remembrance, of no-insanity, of self-acknowledgement, with punishment given to you, by graduation, like sweeping dung. What is the rule to settle dispute by way of presence ? One person (commits an offence), one person reproves him, for the sake of protecting the dharma-vinaya and in accordance with the admonition of the teacher, reproving the offender in his presence and making him happy ; one person, two persons (reprovers) ; one person, many (reprovers) ; one person, the whole Order (reprover) ; two persons (commit offence), two persons reprovers ; two persons, many (reprovers) ; two persons, the whole Order (reprover) ; two persons, one (reprover) ; many persons (commit offence), many reprovers ; many persons, the whole Order (reprover) ; many persons, one (reprover) ; many persons, two (reprovers) ; the whole Order (commits offence), one reprover ; the whole Order, two (reprovers) ; the whole Order, many (reprovers) reprove it, for the sake of protecting the dharma-vinaya and in accordance with the admonition of the Teacher, reproving the offending Order in its presence, making it happy.

P N° 104 : (ii, 247, 7–19) : Not exactly the same. The P seven are as follows : 1) Sammukhāvinayo dātabbo, 2) Sativinayo dātabbo, 3) Amūḷhavinayo dātabbo, 4) Paṭiññāya kāretabbaṃ, 5) Yebhuyyassikā, 6) Tassapāpiyyasikā, 7) Tiṇavatthārako. Here the explantion of the verdict to be given in the presence of is not the same. The P explains that when there is dispute over : « It is dhamma, it is not dhamma, it is discipline, it is not discipline », all the monks should assemble in a complete order and what is the dhamma should be discussed and adopted, then the dispute should be settled accordingly.

2nd way : Verdict of remembrance = P : Sativinayo dātabbo :

C : (56*b*, 15–19) : If there is a man who commits an offence but does not remember it. Then the monks should tell him that he has committed an offence and does not remember it. He should request the Order to give the verdict of remembrance. And the Order should grant his request. If there is an Order who lives in harmony, that monk should wear his robe showing bare one shoulder, remove his slippers that have no heel-backs, pay respect to a venerable Elder, kneel straight, join his palms and say : « May the Venerables hear me. I have committed an offence but do not remember it. Now I request the Order to give me the verdict of remembrance ». The Order should in harmony give the verdict of remembrance to this monk, in accordance with the dharma and the discipline and the Master's teachings, making that monk happy in his presence.

P : (247, 28–33 ; 248, 1–4) : Although the purport is the same, but the explanation is quite different. Here the monks reprove a certain monk to have committed a pārājika offence or an offence bordering on the pārājika offence. But that monk replies that he does not remember to have fallen into such an offence. Then to that monk, a verdict of remembrance should be given by the Order.

3rd way : Giving no-insanity = P : Amūḷhavinayo dātabbo :

C : (56*b*, 19–20 : 57*a*, 1–5) : There is a man who becomes insane. Being insane, he says that he has committed many impure rules and offences, not worthy of a recluse, not in accordance with Doctrine and Discipline. Later on, he becomes normal. The (other) monks tell him what has happened and advise him to beg the Order to give him the verdict of no-insanity. And the Order together should give the rule of no-insanity. The rest is the same as in the preceding verdict.

P : (248, 5–20) : Here the explanation is different. The monks reprove a certain monk to have committed a pārājika offence or an offence bordering on the pārājika offence. But that monk replies that he does not remember to have fallen into such an offence. When pressed by the other monks again and again, he replies that he has become insane and lost his mental balance, and during that time, much is done and said unbecoming to a recluse and he does not remember all that. To that monk, a verdict of no-insanity should be given.

4th way : Giving self-acknowledgement = *P : Paṭiññāya kāretabbaṃ :*

C : (57*a*, 5–10) *:* If a man commits an offence, either he is told or not told, either there is someone to remind him or no one to remind him; if there is an Order who lives in harmony, that monk should wear his robe showing one shoulder, put off his slippers that have no heel-backs, enter the Order, bow down his head at the feet of an old and venerable monk, kneel straight, raise up his joint palms and say : « Ven. sirs, please hear me. I have committed such an offence. Now with a sincere heart, I confess before your reverence. I disclose it myself and dare not hide it. I shall well restrain myself and shall not commit it again. » Then the Order of monks should ask that monk : « Rev. fr., do you see the offence ? » That monk should reply : « Really I have seen the offence ». Then the Order of monks should tell him : « You should well restrain yourself, not to commit it again.»

P : (248, 21–31) *:* Almost the same, with the following differences : C : either he is told or not told ; either there is someone to remind him or none to remind him = P : whether a monk reproves or does not reprove, remembers and discloses an offence. The P omits : If there is an Order who lives in harmony, put off his slippers, enter the Order. C : kneel up = P : sitting on his haunches. It omits : please hear me, now with a sincere heart, before your venerable ; I disclose myself and dare not hide it ; I shall well restrain myself and shall not commit it again. » While the C mentions that the Order of monks should tell him, the P simply mentions that the Ven. elder monk should speak thus.

5th way : C : Punishment given to you (the offender) = *P : Tassapāpiyyasikā :*

C : (57*a*, 10–14) *:* If there is a man who does not know shame, who is reckless as to his seeing and hearing, thereby subject to be accused as of evil desires. Having committed an offence, he says he knows in one place, he says he sees in one place ; having said to have known in one place, he says he sees in one place ; having said to have seen in one place, he says he knows in one place. In the assembly he says he knows in one place ; in the assembly he says he sees in one place. Having said to have known in one place, he says he sees in one place ; having said to have seen in one place, he says he knows in one place. For that monk, the assembly should meet and perform punishment given to you, saying : « You have no morality, no knowledge. You are evil and demeritorious, because having committed an offence, you say you know in one place... (as above with *he* replaced by *you* up to...) ...you know in one place. »

P : (249, 1–31) : Not the same. Here the monks reprove a certain monk to have committed a pārājika offence or an offence bordering on the pārājika offence. But that monk replies that he does not remember to have fallen into such an offence. When pressed by other monks to remember it, he replies that he remembers to have committed only such and such slight offence but not the serious one. When pressed further, he replies that, although not asked he has confessed to have committed such a slight offence, so why can he, when asked, not acknowledge to have committed such a pārājika offence or an offence bordering on the pārājika offence. When pressed further, he confesses that he has committed a pārājika offence or an offence bordering on the pārājika offence. What he has spoken earlier is just speaking for fun, in jest. This is punishment given to him, the offender.

6th way of settling the dispute : C : By graduation ≙ P : Yebhuyyassikā (majority's decision) :

C : (57*a*, 14–20) : A number of quarrels arise between 2 monks : « This is the doctrine, this is not the doctrine ; this is the discipline, this is not the discipline ; this is an offence, this is not an offence ; this is slight, this is serious ; this should be spoken, this should not be spoken ; this should be restrained, this should not be restrained ; this has remainder, this has no remainder ; this should be confessed, this should not be confessed. » Then they should settle the dispute then and there. If the dispute is settled then and there, then this dispute can be said as settled. If not, this dispute should be reported to the Order. If it can be settled among the members of the Order, then this dispute can be said as settled. If not, when near by, there are monks who are expert in Sūtras, in Vinaya and in Mother, (This refers to Mātikā, meaning Abhidharma), this monk should come to them and report the dispute to them. If on the way, the dispute is settled, then this dispute can be said as settled. If not, this dispute should be reported to the Order. If it can be settled among the Order, then this dispute can be said as settled. If not, and when there are many friends and supporters who are expert in Sūtra, in Vinaya, in Mother (Mātikā), these monks should come to them and report the dispute to them to be settled. These monks should settle this dispute in accordance with the doctrine, with the discipline and with the Teachings of the Master, rendering them happy then and there.

P : (247, 19–27) : Here, this way is placed second and is a continuation of the first sammukhāvinayo. Is states that when the first way fails to settle the dispute in that place, then the monks should come to another place where there are more monks and there the monks should meet in a complete Order and have the matter thrashed out and settle the dispute according to the decision of the majority.

7th way : Like sweeping dung = P : Tiṇavatthārako :

C : (57*a*, 20 ; 57*b*, 1–9) : An Order of monks lives quarrelling and disputing. The monks are divided into 2 groups. In one group, an oldest venerable and one second to him, or a chief monk or one second to him, (this monk) should say to those monks as follows : « Rev. sirs, please hear me. We have no morality, no knowledge. We are evil, demeritorious. Because, in this good doctrine-discipline, we have gone forth out of faith to learn the dharma, but we live quarrelling and disputing. Due to this quarrel and dispute, we have committed offences except serious offence (T'ou-lo-che :

偸羅柘 = P : thullavajjaṃ), and except offence connected with laymen. For the sake of mine and also for the sake of your reverences, now I earnestly confess before your reverences, I disclose them and dare not hide them. I shall restrain myself well and not commit these offences again ». If in this group, there is no suitable monk, then that monk should come to the other group of monks, bow his head down at the feet of an older and venerable monk, kneel straight and with joined palms he says as follows : (the same as above). Then that monk should speak : « You should restrain yourself and do not commit it again ». Then the second group should do the same.

P : (250, 1-21) : Not exactly the same, although the idea is not different. Here it is simpler. It states that one experienced monk (byattatara) of one faction should get up, wear his robe covering one shoulder and with joined palms address the Order as follows : « Rev. Sirs, let the Order hear me. We live disputing and quarrelling and much was done and spoken unworthy of a recluse. If the Order thinks it right, I would confess whatsoever offence committed by me as well as by your reverences, for the sake of your reverences and for the sake of mine, except the serious offences and offences connected with laymen, covering up with grass. One experienced monk of the other faction does the same.

4. — THE ANNUAL RETREAT

The monks are prescribed to observe an annual-retreat of 3 months. But the Chinese version refers to summer-retreat, while the Pāli version speaks of rainy-season retreat.

Thus in *C. S. N°* 20, the retreat is referred to as under :

C N° 9 : (v, 11*b*, 4-6) : At one time, the Buddha was travelling in Wang-shê town, and staying at the Bamboo grove monastery and spent his *summer-retreat* there along with a great assembly of monks. Ven. Man-tz'u-tzu was spending his summer-retreat in his native place. At that time, the native local monks, having spent 3 months' summer-retreat there, after mending their robes, took their robes and proceeded towards Wang-shê town, reached the place and stayed at the monastery of the Bamboo-grove.

P N° 24 : (i, 145, 12-15) : The P at once referred to the Buddha as staying at Rājagaha, in Veluvana, in the squirrels' feeding ground. Then many local native monks, having spent their *rainy season retreat*, came to the Buddha, worshipped him and sat at one side ».

Again in *C. S. N°* 43, there is also reference to the annual retreat of the monks :

C N° 194 : (vii, 50*b*, 4-20 ; 51*a*, 1-2) : The Buddha was observing the summer-retreat along with a great number of monks. He advised them to observe the practice of taking food at one session, as he himself had practised it and found himself without desire, without hankering, without disease, of light body, strong, secure and happy... During the 3 months of summer-retreat, elder P'o-t'o-ho-li could not see the Buddha. At the end of the retreat, he came to the Buddha and confessed his guilt.

P N° 65 *:* (*i*, 437, 14-29; 438, 1-31)*:* Almost the same. But here it refers to rainy season retreat but not to summer-retreat.

This difference in the observance of the annual retreat is already pointed out in the paragraph on Some Sarv. and Ther characteristics p. 28-9.

5. — THE NISĪDANA OR SITTING MAT

One more difference, which we observe in both versions and which shows the different tradition of each school, is the observance of the sitting mat mentioned in the C version, but mostly ignored in the P texts.

Thus in *C. S. N°* 20, this observance is related as follows :

C N° 9*:* (*v*, 11*b*, 19-20; 12*a*, 1-3) : Ven. Man-tz'u-tzu, when night was over, in the morning, donned the robe, took his bowl and entered Shê-wei for alms. After his midday meal, having put back robe and bowl, having washed his hands and feet, he put his sitting mat over his shoulder, came to the walking place in An-t'o forest. Ven. Shê-li-tzu also, when night was over, in the morning, donned his robe, took his bowl and entered Shê-wei for alms. After his midday-meal, having put back robe and bowl, having washed his hands and feet, he put his sitting mat over his shoulder and came to the walking place in An-t'o forest. At that time, Ven. Man-tz'u tzu came to An-t'o forest, spread his sitting mat at the foot of the tree and was sitting cross-legged. Ven. Shê-li-tzu also came to An-t'o forest, and not so far from Ven. Man-tz'u-tzu, spread his sitting mat and sat cross-legged.

P N° 24*:* (146, 28-37 ; 147, 1-10) : Not exactly the same. The P omits all this passage of the 2 elders going for alms, entering the Andha forest and spreading their sitting mat. It mentions simply that elder Mantāniputta delighted with the Buddha's talk on Dhamma, worshipped him and keeping his right side towards the Buddha set out for Andhavana for the day-rest. Then a monk reported the matter to elder Sāriputta who hurriedly took his sitting mat and followed elder Mantāniputta.

Remarks : This is the only place when the P has mentioned the nisīdana.

This difference as to the observance of the nisīdana or sitting mat is already referred to in the chapter on Some Sarv. and Ther. characteristics p. 29-30.

General Remarks :

In this chapter, many dissimilarities are observed between the C and the P versions, and this shows the different traditions which the 2 versions represent. Thus some rules of conduct for a forest-dweller, the 7 ways to settle disputes are not exactly the same in both the C and the P texts.

Chapter VII. — GĀTHAS OR VERSES

Now we proceed to the comparative study of gāthas or verses in the 98 corresponding sūtras and find out the similarities and differences between the P and the C versions.

A first glance shows us that the C version is rather more profuse in verses than its P counterpart. Thus there are 3 C sūtras C. S. N° 40, N° 55 and N° 89 which contain verses, while the corresponding P suttas are without them.

In *C. S. N°* 40, two stanzas are added, both spoken by the Buddha, while admonishing Lo-yün (P : Rāhula).

1st stanza :

C N° 14 : (*v*, 17*a*, 2-3) :

« A man commits an offence, called telling lies ;
He does not fear the next world, there is no evil deed which he cannot do.
It is better to swallow an iron ball, which is hot like fire,
Than to infringe the rule and accept charity from the world.
If one is afraid of suffering, having no liking to think of (suffering),
He should not perform evil deeds, secretly or openly.
If demeritorious deeds have been performed, are being performed,
Ultimately, one cannot escape from them,
And also there is no shelter (from them) ».

2nd stanza :

C : (17*b*, 5-8) :

« Oh Lo-yün : bodily deeds, vocal and mental deeds,
They are meritorious or demeritorious,
You should reflect over them.
Knowingly telling a lie, Oh Lo-yün, you should not speak (falsehood).
Danger comes from telling lie. So why do you speak (lies) ?
Covering the dharma of the recluse,
Empty, devoid of truthfulness, is called telling lies.
Due to not protecting oneself's mouth,

That one speaks of falsehood.

Oh son of the Enlightened One, this is the dharma of the Recluse;

Lo-yün you should learn; in every direction (you would be) prosperous and happy, secure and fearless.

Lo-yün, to attain all these, you should not harm others ».

Again in *C. S. N°* 55, 2 verses are available in the C, but not in the P:

C N° 67 : (v, 79b, 9) :

King Ta-t'ien took these white hairs and said:

« My head has grey hair, my life is growing weak and old,

The heaven-messenger has come. It is time for me to study the Dharma ».

C : (80b, 10-11) :

King Ni-mi told the deities of the Thirty-three Heaven:

« It is like borrowed carriage, to be ridden temporarily for one time.

This place is like that, that is it belongs to others.

I shall return to Mi-sa-lo and practise countless meritorious deeds there.

Due to that, (I) shall be born in heaven.

I store meritorious deeds as food (for a journey) to heaven.

In *C. S. N°* 89, there is another C verse not available in the P:

C N° 170 : (vii, 16b, 2):

« The brāhmaṇas due to over-pride,

After death from this world will be born in 6 states:

As hen, dog, pig, jackal,

Donkey and in the Hell as the 6th».

There are 15 sūtras in which both C and P have their respective gāthas as seen in *C. S. N°* 6; *N°* 22; *N°* 35; *N°* 36; *N°* 39; *N°* 48; *N°* 54; *N°* 60; *N°* 83; *N°* 85; *N°* 86; *N°* 87; *N°* 88; *N°* 96; *N°* 97.

Some verses are almost the same in both versions. Thus in *C. S. N°* 35, both gāthas are as follows:

C N° 78 : (v, 107b, 8) :

« To see danger in becoming, not to be afraid of non-becoming,

Thus not to delight in becoming,

What becoming cannot be eradicated of ? ».

P N° 49 : (i, 330, 13-14) :

« Having seen the danger of becoming,
Becoming, I seek the non-becoming
I do not enjoy becoming,
I do not grasp any delight ».

In *C. S. N°* 48, we have the following 2 gāthas :

C N° 153 : (vi, 91b, 1) :

« No sickness is the highest gain »
Nirvāṇa is the highest happiness.
Among the ways, there is the 8 fold right Path,
Which dwells in security and deathlessness ».

P N° 75 : (i, 508, 30-31) :

« No-sickness is the highest gain,
Nibbāna is the highest happiness.
Of the ways, the 8 fold Path
Leads to security and deathlessness ».

In some cases, the C sūtra contains up to 3 gāthas, while the P has only one, as seen in *C. S. N°* 36, and the only one P gāthā holds only 96 lines, while its C counterpart has up to 122 lines. The same can be said of *C. S. N°* 39, in which the C contains 2 gāthas extra, one of 6 lines and one of 4 lines ; while in the gāthā in common, the C exceeds the P one of 8 lines. In *C. S. N°* 6, the C gāthā contains 32 lines while the P contains only 22. In *C. S. N°* 60, the C sūtra has 4 gāthas while the P contains only 3 gāthas. In the 1st gāthā, the P exceeds the C by 4 lines only ; the 2nd gāthā has equal number of 12 lines in both versions, while the C exceeds the P by 10 lines in the 3rd gāthā. The 4th gāthā, which is found in the C only, contains 10 lines and is quoted under.

C N° 161 : (vii, 4b, 13-14) :

« Among sacrifices, fire is the highest.
The penetrating voice is the foundation of all voices.
Among men, king is the supreme chief.
The ocean is bigger than rivers.
The moon is brighter than the stars ;
But no light can exceed the sun.
The above, the below,
The four alternates and the four directions,
Together with all the worlds,
From mankind up to deities,
Only Buddha was supreme. »

About this gāthā, these observations of Dr ANESAKI (1) are noteworthy : « In the C Āgamas, the following verses are repeated at least 12 times : « Among sacrifices, fire is the highest ; among chandas the Sāvittī ; among men kings..., among all beings, men and devas, Buddha alone is highest ». I could not find these in the P Nikāyas. In all the P suttas, agreeing with the Chinese in other respects, in which these verses are found, they are wanting. I find them, with the exception of the last part, in the Selasutta of the Suttanipāta. Were they added later to the Āgamas and the Suttanipāta, or were they excluded from Pāli Nikāyas ? »

Similarly in *C. S. N°* 96, only one gāthā is available ; and the C gāthā has 24 lines and the P 20 lines only. In *C. S. N°* 97, the C contains 2 gāthas extra, one of 16 lines, one of 8 lines, while the P counts one gātha extra of 16 lines. This difference is due rather to the difference in contents of these 2 sūtras. In the C, while relating the sickness of Kei-ku-tu, the C adds a story related by Kei-ku-tu of his first meeting with the Buddha and the 2 gāthas belong to this story. The 1st gāthā is spoken by a deity, Kei-ku-tu's former friend, urging him to go and meet the Buddha. The 2nd one was spoken by Kei-ku-tu himself, by way of greeting the Buddha. And the P gāthā which is omitted in the C was spoken by the deity Anāthapiṇḍika in praise of the Buddha, the Dhamma and of elder Sāriputta. Anāthapiṇḍika after his death was reborn as a deity, came to the Buddha and recited this gāthā in praise of the Blessed One. But as the C sūtra related another anecdote in the life of Kei-ku-tu, who was not reported dead, of course, that gāthā is found missing.

But there are cases in which the P contains more gāthas than the C and that the P verses are longer. Thus in *C. S. N°* 22, the P has 3 gāthas extra, one of 8 lines, one of 14 lines and one of 4 lines. The 1st gāthā depicts the Buddha's hesitation to preach the d'harma ; and the 2nd gāthā describes Brahmā Sahampati's request to preach the dhamma ; and the Buddha acceeded to the Brahmā's request in the 3rd gāthā. All these 3 gāthas are not available in the C version, because the C drops the whole passage. In *C. S. N°* 54, in the 1st gāthā, the C one of 22 lines, is short of 2 lines to compare with the P one ; while the P 2nd gāthā exceeds by 4 lines that of the C of 48 lines.

In order to show clearly similarities and differences between the C and the corresponding P gāthas, we propose to analyse line by line the comparative study of the gāthas in C. S. N° 6, N° 39 and N° 96.

In *C. S. N°* 6, the Buddha replied to brāhmaṇa Shui-ching, when the latter requested him to go take bath in the holy water :

C N° 93 *: (vi,* 13*a,* 20 ; 13*b,* 1-3) *:*

« Oh brāhmaṇa Miao-hao-shou, to enter To-shui river,
Is the sport of the fool ; black deeds cannot be purified.

---

(1) *JRAS*, 1901, p. 898.

Hao-shou, what is the use of going to the stream ?
What meaning (benefit) does To-shui river possess ?
When people commit demeritorious deeds ?
What is the benefit of pure water ?
The pure ones are without defilements,
The pure ones always speak of rules of conduct,
The pure ones are of pure and white deeds,
Who always perform pure actions.
If you do not kill living beings,
Never take what is not given,
Truthful, do not tell lies,
Are always with right mindfulness, right understanding.
Oh Brāhmaṇa, with such a learning (training),
All living beings will live secure,
Oh brāhmaṇa, what is (the use) of going back to family ?
The family water possesses no purity.
Oh brāhmaṇa, you should learn,
To cleanse with meritorious dharmas.
What is the need of bad, evil water,
Which can cleanse only physical dirt ? »

P N° 7 : (i, 39, 14-25) : Almost the same. The P mentions the name of 7 rivers : Bāhukā, Adhikakkā, Gayā, Sundarikā, Sarassatī, Payāgo and Bāhumatī, which are useless because they cannot cleanse black deeds. To the pure one, every day is Phaggu, auspicious day ; every day is Uposatha day, as he is always observing the rules. While the C adds: Always with right mindfulness, with right understanding to the Buddha's admonition, the P omits the two terms but adds : saddahanā (with faith) and amaccharī (without stinginess). In the last line, the P mentions the Buddha as saying : « What will you do by going to Gayā, when any well is your Gayā ? ».

While the P ends the gāthā here and reverts to the prose form, the C still continues in the gāthā form :

C : (13a, 3-6) :

Then the brāhmaṇa said to the Buddha :

« I now also think, to cleanse with meritorious dharmas.
What is the use of bad evil water ?
The brāhmaṇa after listening to the Buddha's instruction,
His mind was filled with joy.
Then he bowed down at the Buddha's feet,
And took refuge in the Buddha, Dharma and Sangha ».

In *C. S. N° 39*, it is the important and well-known Yu-p'o-li's gāthā, the remains of which in original Sanskrit were found in Central Asia. (1).

(1) See Appendix N° 9.

C N° 133 : (*vi*, 58*b*, 20; 59*a*, 1-9) : Then Ch'in-tzu asked Yu-p'o-li that all Na-lan-t'o knew that Yu-p'o-li was a disciple of the Ni-chien; but now of whom was he a disciple ? Yu-p'o-li replied to Ch'in-tzu in a very long gāthā, while kneeling down with his right knee touching the ground and with his hands joined towards the direction where the Buddha was staying :

1/ a) Of the brave, free from ignorance, who has eradicated blemishes and rightly overcome (them) P 1a,

b) Peerless, of subtle pondering, trained in discipline, in meditation, in wisdom, P 1b.

c) Secure stainless, of the Buddha, Yu-p'o-li is the disciple. P 1c.

2/ a) Of the great Noble One, with self-training (completed) ; with holiness obtained, with mastery of speech. P 7a.

b) With good mindfulness, with subtle and right contemplation, not high and also not low, P 7b.

c) Impassible, always mastery of oneself,
Of the Buddha, Yu-p'o-li is the disciple. P 7c.

3/ a) Of Him who is without crookedness, always contented,
With stinginess removed, well satisfied, P 2a,

b) Having become a recluse, he obtained enlightenment,
With the present body as the last one, the W.H. One. P 2b.

c) Peerless and dustless,
Of the Buddha, Yu-p'o-li is the disciple. P 2c.

4/ a) Of Him who is without jealousy, immeasurable,
Very deep, with sageness obtained, P 4a.

b) Always secure and energetic,
Abided in dharma, of subte thinking, P 4b.

c) Tamed, always without sporting,
Of the Buddha, Yu-p'o-li is the disciple. P 5c.

5/ a) Of Him who is a great dragon, (1), delighted in dwelling high, with fetters extinguished, with emancipation obtained P 5a.

b) Clever in discussion, pure,
Wisdom born, sorrow and grief removed, P 5b.

c) No returner to existence, the Sakya,
Of the Buddha, Yu-p'o-li is the disciple. P 6c.

6/ a) Of Him, who has gone rightly, with concentrated thoughts, without disturbances, pure, P 8a,

b) Always smiling, without anger,
Delighted in seclusion, with supreme state obtained. P. 8b.

---

(1) It should be interpreted as elephant.

c) Fearless, always eager and energetic,
Of the Buddha, Yu-p'o-li is the discipel.

7/ a) Of Him who is the 7th of the Great Sage (Isisattama), incomparable,
With 3 attainments, with brahma-state obtained, P 6a.

b) Spotless and pure like a bright lamp,
With calmness obtained, with hatred and enmity stopped,

c) Energetic and extremely pure,
Of the Buddha, Yu-p'o-li is the disciple.

8/ a) Of Him who has obtained quietude, with wisdom like earth, with great wisdom, with worldly attachment removed, P 9a.

b) Having well reflected with supreme eye,
A superman without equal, P 10b.

c) A master of oneself, without hatred,
Of the Buddha, Yu-p'o-li is the disciple.

9/ a) Of Him who is with hope eradicated, of supreme good,
Good leader, with matchless mastery, P 3a.

b) Supreme and always happy,
Without doubt, with light shining, P 3b.

c) With pride eradicated, of supreme enlightenment,
Of the Buddha, Yu-p'o-li is the disciple. P 3c.

10/ a) Of Him whose craving is eradicated, with matchless enlightenment, without smoke, without flame, P 10a.

b) The Tathāgata is the Well-farer,
Matchless, and peerless,

c) Of great fame, with righteousness attained,
Of the Buddha, Yu-p'o-li is the disciple. P 10c.

11/ a) Thus in one hundred (words), he praised the Buddha,
These (words) were never premeditated.

b) Yu-p'o-li had said them.
The deities had come to him,

c) Helped him well in the discussion,
In accordance with dharma, appropriate to such a man.
Ch'in-tzu had asked,
The disciple of the Buddha, possessor of 10 strengths.

P N° 56: (i, 386, 3-32): Upāli's gāthā consists of 11 stanzas in the C and 10 stanzas in the P. The P omits the 11th one. Each stanza ends with the same refrain : C : Of the Buddha, Yu-p'o-li is the disciple = P : Of Him, the Blessed One, I am the disciple. Although both poems in the main are identical, they differ a good deal as to the consecutive order of the stanzas and in the position of the verses which constitute the stanzas.

C 1 = P 1; C 2 = P 7; C 3 = P 2; C 4a = P 4a ; C 4b = P 4b ; C 4c = P 5c ; C 5a = P 5a ; C 5b = P 5b; C 5c = P 6c ; C 6a = P 8a ; C 6b = P 8b ; C 6c = P no ; C 7a = P 6a ; C 7b = P no. C 7c = P no; C 8a = P 9a ; C 8b = P 10b; C 8c = P no ; C 9a = P 3a ; C 9b = P 3b ; C 9c = P 3c ; C 10a = P 10a ; C 10b = P no ; C 10c = P 10c ; C 11 = P no.

Thus C 6c, C 7b, C 7c, C 8c, C 10b, C 11 are not available in the P; and P 4c, P 6b P 8c and P 9c are not available in the C version.

Even in corresponding verses, the C and the P readings differ considerably. Thus in *C 1b*, C : peerless = P : anighassa (without suffering) ; in *C 1c*, C : secure = P : vessantarassa (poised); in *C 2a*, C: with holiness attained = P : pattipattassa (who has obtained what can be attained); in *C 2b*, C: not high and not low = P : anabhinatassa no apanatassa (not bent on passion, without hatred) ; in *C 3a*, C : of Him who is without crookedness = P: akathaṅkathissa (without doubt) ; C: with stinginess removed = P: vantalokāmisassa (renouncing the worldly material things) ; In *C 3b*, C: he obtained enlightenment = P: manujassa (a human being) ; C : The W.H. One = P : narassa (a man) ; in *C 4a*, C : of Him who is without jealousy = P nisabhassa (the best man, the highest bull) ; in *C 4b*, C: energetic = P: vedassa (knower) ; C: of subtle thinking = P : saṃvutattassa (self-controlled); in *C 4c*, C: always without sporting = P: nippapañcassa (without hindrance); in *C 5a*, C: of Him who is a great dragon = P: nāgassa (of Him who is an elephant); C: delighted in dwelling high = P: pantasenassa (who lives far away from men's places); in *C 5b*, C: clever in discussion = P: paṭimantakassa (who speaks gently); C: wisdom born = P: pannadhajassa (banner put down); C: sorrow and grief removed = P: Vītarāgassa (free from passion); in *C 5c*, C: no returner to existence = P: purindadassa (foremost giver); in *C 6a*, C: of Him who has gone rightly = P: sammaggatassa; in *C 6b*, C: always smiling = P asitassa (without fetter); C: without anger = P : appahīnassa (not bend on anything ?) ; in *C 7a*, C: of Him who is the 7th deity = P: isisattamassa (of the 7th sage) ; C : incomparable = P : akuhassa (not hypocrite); in *C 8a*, C: with wisdom like earth = P: Bhūripaññassa (of extensive wisdom); in *C 8b*, C : having well reflected = P : āhuneyyassa (worthy of offering) ; C : with supreme eye = P : yakkhassa (the spirit) ; The P adds one y extra and the meaning is distorted ; in *C 9a*, C : of Him who is with hope eradicated = P : asaṃsayassa (of Him who is sure) ; C : good leader = P : venayikassa (leader) ; *in C 9c*, C : of supreme enlightenment = P : virassa (the hero, the energetic one) ; in C 10c, C : of great fame = P : mahato (the great) ; C : with righteousness attained = P : yasaggapattassa (of highest fame attained).

In the corresponding stanzas, the remaining ones are more or less the same.

Remarks : « The presence of the epithet *yakkhassa* in verse 10b of the P version is puzzling. Buddha could not, with any propriety be called a Yakkha, particularly in a hymn in his praise. The Chinese translation which says « who has highest eyes » supplies the solution. Its Sanskrit original must have had the word akṣasya, eye... The Pāli yakkhassa, therefore, is clearly akkhassa with an initial euphonic y just as we have it in *na yimassa, yaci yeva, kiñci yiṭṭham* etc (1).

In *C. S. N°* 96, the C gāthā and its corresponding P gāthā are referred to as follows :

C N° 180 : (*vii*, 31*a*, 15-19) = *P N°* 143 : (*iii*, 257, 4-27) :

The Buddha recited a gāthā of 6 verses in C and of 5 verses in P :

1) C : The diligent gives to the negligent, a gift acquired in accordance with dharma, with a joyful heart. He believes in actions and in the fruit of the actions ; thus this offering is purified by the donor.

P : Almost the same. C : diligent = P : of moral habit. C : negligent = P : of bad moral habit. C : he believes in actions and in the fruits of actions = P : he firmly believes in the rich fruit of actions.

2) C : The negligent gives to the diligent, a gift acquired not accordance with dharma and not with a joyful heart, he does not believe in actions and in the fruit of the actions, thus this offering is purified by the recipient.

P : Almost the same with the same differences as above.

3) C : The lazy gives to the negligent, a gift acquired not in accordance with dharma and not with a joyful heart ; he does not believe in actions and in the fruit of the actions ; thus this offering has no big result.

P : Almost the same, with the same differences. C : has no big result — P : is not purified by both (the donor and the new recipient).

4) C : The diligent gives to the diligent, a gift acquired in accordance with dharma and not with a joyful heart; he believes in actions and in the fruit of the actions ; thus this offering has big result.

P : Almost the same, with the same differences as seen above.

5) C : The servants and the poor, who gladly share their own part to be given as a gift, they believe in actions and in the fruit of the actions, such a material gift is praised by the wise.

P : Not available.

6) C : With body and speech well and rightly protected; stretching his arms to beg in accordance with dharma, one without desire, gives to one without desire, this gift is supreme.

---

(1) *M.R.E.T.* p. 34.

P : Not exactly the same : « One without attachment gives to one without attachment, a gift rightly acquired with a joyful heart, firmly believing in the rich fruit of action, I said that this gift is abundant in gain.

Thus a general review of the comparative study of the Gāthas in the C and the P versions shows us that the C version is richer in Gāthas than its P counterpart ; and the C gāthas are generally longer than the P ones. We notice also that the common ground between the C and the P is fairly extensive and this bespeaks the same source from which both versions draw their materials. A close study of the corresponding gāthas of the 2 versions reveals many dissimilarities and differences and this points out to the independent attitude of the C and of the P compilers as far as the collections and the arrangements of materials are concerned.

Chapter VIII. — SIMILES OR PARABLES

Similes abound in the Buddha's preachings, and so we witness a rich collection of parables or similes in both the C and the P versions. A comparative study of these similes of the two versions shows these distinctive features: 1) Some similes are almost the same in both versions; 2) some have the same purport but their wordings are different; 3) in some cases, the P simile is simpler; 4) in some cases, the contrary is the case, that is the C simile is simpler than the P; 5) some similes available in C are found missing in the P; 6) in some cases, the C simile is found wanting; 7) there are cases where the P similes are more appropriate and clearer than the C ones and 8) some similes are different altogether in both versions.

1. — *The similes are almost the same :*

In some cases, there are almost no difference between the 2 similes as far as purport and wording are concerned.

Thus in *C. S. N°* 4, Ven. Ta-mu-chien-lien (Mahāmoggallāna) related a simile to show how well Ven. Shê-li-tzu knew the listeners' mind so that he could preach to them heart to heart :

C N° 87 *:* (*vi*, 8*a*, 7-12): « I came to the house of a naked ascetic named Man-tzu who was formerly a carriage-maker. At that time, adjacent to his house, there was a carriage-maker who was chopping (wood) and making the carriage axle-tree. At that time, the naked Man-tzu, who was formerly a carriage-maker went to that house and he saw that carriage-maker busy shaping the axle-tree. Then such a thought occurred to him : « If that carriage-maker takes an axe and chops off those defective places, then that axle-tree will be extremely fine ». At that time, according to what the former carriage-maker, the naked Man-tzu had thought, that carriage-maker took an axe and chopped off those defective places. Then the ex-carriage-maker, the naked Man-tzu was greatly delighted and said : « Oh carriage-maker, thus your heart knows my heart. Why is it so ? because you took the axe and chopped off those defective places to shape the axle-tree just as I thought. »

P N° 5 *:* (*i*, 31, 30-37 *:* 32, 1-6) : Almost the same. C : a naked ascetic, named Man-tzu who was formerly a carriage-maker = P : purāṇayānakāraputto Paṇḍuputto ājīviko. C : there was a carriage-maker who was chopping (wood) and making the axle-tree of a carriage = P : at that time, Samīti, a carriage-maker was chopping thin the rim (nemi) of a wheel. C : if that carriage-maker takes an axe and chops off those defective places = P : iman ca vaṅkaṃ imañ ca jimham imañ ca dosaṃ taccheyya (May he chop off this crookedness, this twist, this defect). C : thus your heart knows my heart = P : hadayā hadayaṃ maññe aññāya tacchatīti (It seems as if he is shaping it, with (his) heart knowing (my) heart).

In *C. S. N°* 13, the Buddha quoted a simile of the hen to show that any person endowed with the 15 qualities would surely attain complete enlightenment :

C N° 206 *:* (*vii,* 78*a,* 15–16) *:* «It is just like a hen which lays 10 eggs, or 12 eggs and timely covers them, timely hatches them, timely watches them. The hen may be heedless, (but) in those eggs, the chickens with beaks, with claws will peck and break through the egg and safely come out».

P N° 16 *:* (*i,* 104, 3–10) *:* Almost the same. C : 10 eggs or 12 eggs = P : 8 eggs, 10 eggs or 12 eggs. C : timely covers them, timely hatches them, timely watches them = P : rightly sits on them, rightly hatches them, rightly takes good care of them. C : the hen may be heedless = P : although the hen does not formulate the wish that the chicken may break through the shell with their claws or with their beaks.

2. — *Purport is the same, but wording is different :*

In most of the similes, we observe that the purport conveyed by the simile to illustrate some teachings is the same in both versions, but the wording of the simile is not exactly the same. The majority of the similes fall into this category and this shows that the compilers are quite independent in the selection of words and manners of expressions.

Thus in *C. S. N°* 16, the Buddha quoted the simile of the herd of deer to illustrate the benefit brought about by the Buddha's teachings to the people in general :

C N° 102 *:* (*vi,* 24*b,* 10–11) *:* Suppose there is a place without trouble, where there is a great stream of water. There lives and roams about a herd of deer. If there is a man who comes, not seeking meaning (good) and well-being for that herd of deer, does not seek security and happiness. He blocks the main path, opens up a dangerous road, digs up a pit and orders a man to keep watch over it. Thus the whole herd of deer will come to total death and destruction. Again, if there is a man who comes, desiring meaning (rather good) and well-being for that herd of deer, seeks security and happiness for that herd of deer, he opens and levels up the main path, blocks the dangerous path and drives away the watchman. Thus the herd of deer will live secure and safe.

P N° 19 *:* (*i,* 117, 23–36) : The P simile offers some differences in details. The place referred to is a low deep marshy ground; in the forest near by lives a large herd of deer. The safe road is described as khemo sovatthiko pītigamanīyo, the treacherous road as kumaggo. Here there is no mention of digging a pit and posting a watchman but a male decoy (okacaram), a female decoy (okacārikam) are put there to lure the deer.

C: (24*b*, 11–18) : « Oh monks you should know that I speak of the simile in order to illustrate some meaning. The intelligent man hears the simile and understands its meaning. This simile illustrates the following meaning: The great stream of water represents the 5 kinds of desire, which are attractive, pleasant. What are the 5 ? Material forms perceived by eyes; sound perceived by ears ; odour perceived by nose ; taste perceived by tongue; touch perceived by body. (You) should know that the great stream of water illustrates the 5 kinds of sense-desire. The great herd of deer illustrates the recluses, the brāhmaṇas. The man who comes, not desiring meaning and well being for that herd of deer illustrates Māra, the Evil One. Blocking the main road, opening up the dangerous road illustrates the 3 evil, demeritorious thoughts, thoughts of sense-desire, thoughts of malevolence, thoughts of harming. The dangerous road illustrates the 3 evil, demeritorious thoughts. Again the dangerous road illustrates the 8 fold wrong path from wrong understanding up to wrong concentration as the 8th. Digging up a big ditch illustrates ignorance; putting a man to watch over illustrates the relatives of Māra. Again there is a man who comes, desiring meaning and well being for that herd of deer, seeks security and happiness for that herd of deer, illustrates the Tathāgata, fully emancipated, supremely enlightened. Blocking the dangerous road, opening up the safe and main road illustrates the 3 meritorious thoughts, thoughts of no-desire, thoughts of no-malevolence, thoughts of no-harming. The road illustrates the 3 meritorious thoughts and also the 8 fold right path from right understanding up to right concentration as the 8th ».

P: (117, 37; 118, 1–20): The deep marshy ground is a synonym for sense-desire ; the great herd of deer represents living beings; the man who wishes them harm represents Māra, the evil one. The dangerous road is a synonym for the 8 fold wrong path; the male decoy represents the passion for delight (nandīrāga). The female lure illustrates ignorance; the man who desires good for the herd of deer is a synonym for the Tathāgata, the Perfect One; the road which is secure, safe represents the 8 fold noble Path.

In *C. S. N°* 19, the Buddha used the simile of a raft to show that the dharma taught by Him is to be given up after having made use of it, but not to be kept with.

C N° 200 *:* (*vii*, 64*b*, 16–20; 65*a*, 1–5) = *P N°* 22 *:* (*i*, 134, 30–37 ; 135, 1–26) *:*

« I, *for your sake,* (not in P), have talked about the simile of the raft *for a long time* (not in P), to be given up but not to be kept with. Just as there is a stream from the mountain, very deep and very large, the current is swift and lots of things floating upon it. On this stream, there are no boats and no bridge. Suppose there is a man who comes and wants to cross over to the other shore, as he has some work there. (The P mentions a man on a journey sees a great stretch of water, the hither shore is full of dangers and fear, the other shore is secure and without fear ; there is no boat to cross over, no bridge to lead from one shore to the other). Wishing to cross over, he thinks : « Now this mountain-stream is very deep and very large ; its current is swift and there are lots of things floating upon it. On this stream, there are no boats and no bridge which can be crossed over. Now I have works on that shore and want to cross over. What means, what expedient (I have to resort to) in order to cross over to that shore safely ? (P : same differences as noted in previous passage ; the last passage : what means... safely, is missing). Then he thinks : « Now I would at this hither shore gather grass and trees, tie them together to make a raft and ride this raft to cross over. » Then at this shore, he gathers, collects grass and woods, binds them into a raft, rides this raft and safely crosses over to the other shore (P : it adds sticks, branches and leaves but omits woods. It adds also : depending on this raft, striving with hands and feet). Then he thinks : « This raft is very useful to me. Riding this raft, I, from that shore safely reached this shore. I would carry it over my right shoulder or over my head and depart ». Then that man carries the raft over his right shoulder or over his head and departs. What do you think ? Having done about the raft like that, does he obtain the usefulness (of the raft) ? The monks replied : « No ». (P : almost the same, with the same differences already stated. It mentions simply shoulder but not right shoulder). The W. H. One said : « How should that man do about the raft so as to obtain the usefulness (of the raft) ? That man should think : « This raft is very useful to me. Riding this raft, I, from that shore reached this shore. Now I should immerse this raft into the water or leave it on the bank and depart ». Then that man immerses this raft into the water or leaves it on the bank and departs. What do you think ? Does that man, having done thus about the raft obtain the usefulness (of the raft) ? Then the monks replied : « Yes, there is usefulness ». (P : almost the same, with the same differences already listed. Here the P mentions simply to uplift the raft on the shore or to immerse it in the water). The W.H. One said : « Thus for a long time, I have preached for you the parable of the raft for the sake of giving it up but not for the sake of keeping it. If you have understood the parable of the raft which for a long time I have taught, you should give up that dharma, not to speak of the wrong dharma ».

In *C. S. N*° 32, the Buddha used the simile of the seed of a creeper, which grew up and became a danger to a tree to illustrate the danger of sense-desire.

C N° 174 : (*vii*, 22*a*, 12-20 ; 22*b*, 1-4) = *P N*° 45 : (*i*, 306, 1-37 ; 307, 1-4) :

« Just as in the last month of spring, when days are extremely hot (P : in the last month of summer), a seed of a creeper called Chih-i (?) cracks and falls down at the feet of a so-lo tree (Sāla) P : a creeper's seed-pod cracks and a seed falls down at the foot of a certain Sāl tree). At that time, the deity of the Sāl tree, due to this becomes frightened (The P adds : the deity residing in this Sāl tree becomes afraid, agitated and trembles all over. It omits: due to that). Then the deities of village, of trees in the neighbourhood, of hundred kinds of corn, of medicinal trees (?), who are relatives and friends of this tree deity, who see the future fear and danger of the seed, come to this tree-deity's place and comfort him saying: (P omits deities of village, of trees in the neighbourhood, of hundred kinds of corn, of medicinal trees; it speaks instead: grove-deities, forest-deities, trees-deities, deities residing in medicinal herbs and forests. It omits : who see the future fear and danger of this seed): Deity of the tree, do not be afraid, deity of the tree, do not be afraid. Now this seed may be eaten by deer, or may be eaten by peacock, or may be blown away by wind, or may be burnt by village fire, or may be burnt by wild fire, or may be rotten not to be a seed any more (P omits: deity of the tree, or may be blown away by wind or may be burnt by village fire. It adds: or it may be picked up by forest workers, or it may be eaten by white ants. C: or it may be rotten not to be a seed any more = P: or it may become no-seed). You will be safe (P: no). But this seed is not eaten by the deer, is not eaten by peacock, is not blown away by wind, is not burnt by village fire, is not burnt by wild fire, is not rotten not to be a seed. This seed has nothing lacking, is not pierced through, is not cut through, is not burnt by wind, rain and sun. It meets with heavy rain and germinates quickly. (P omits : this seed has nothing lacking... by wind, rain and sun). This tree-deity thinks: « For what reason the deities of village, of trees in the neighbourhood... is not hurt by wind, rain and sun (with *you* replaced by *me*). It becomes stems, branches, leaves, soft and pleasant to the touch. (The P refers first to the growth of the seed into a creeper, which is tender, soft, hairy and clinging to the Sāl tree. Then the tree-deity thinks why these deities-friends of his gather and comfort him, while he himself finds the touch of this creeper pleasant). These stems, branches, leaves, pleasant to the touch offer pleasant feelings. This (creeper) depending on the tree becomes great stems, with knots and leaves, intertwines itself round this tree and makes a covering above it. When (the creeper) has covered above (the tree), then the deity of this tree thinks: « These deities of village... it meets with heavy rains and germinates quickly. I, due to the seed, depending upon the seed, experience this acute suffering, extremely severe suffering. (P: the creeper covers that Sāl tree, forms a canopy above it, gives birth to a flood of undergrowth and every great branch of this Sāl tree is destroyed. Then the deity thinks that his friends and relatives are right in warning him of the danger of this seed).

3. — *The P simile is simpler :*

There are cases when the P similes are simpler than those of the C as seen in the following examples :

In *C. S. No* 4, the P simile proves to be simpler than the C:

C N° 87 *:* (*vi*, 8*a*, 15–18) : It is like a khattiya-girl, a brāhmaṇa-girl, a householder-girl, a worker's girl, who is good mannered, beautiful, who has taken an exceedingly clean and pure bath, who puts perfumed powder over the body, who wears pure and clean dress. She wears various jewels to enhance her beauty. If there is a man who thinks of that girl, who wishes (her) advantage, benefit, security and happiness. He takes a garland of blue lotuses, of flowers of chan-po (薝蔔 ?), of hsiu-mo-na (修摩那 : jasmine) of p'o-shih-hua (婆師花 ?), of a-t'i-mou-to (阿提牟哆 : acacia flower), and offers this garland to her. That girl, delighted receives the garland with both hands and adorns her head with it.

P N° 5 (*i*, 32, 26–32) : The simile here is simpler. It states the case of a woman, or a man, or a young man, who is fond of ornaments, with his or her head washed. If he or she obtains a garland of uppala flowers (lotuses), or of vassika flowers (jasmine), or of atimuttaka flowers (acacia creeper), he or she will take it with both hands and place it on his or her head.

The same can be said of the following simile in *C. S. N*° 18 :

C N° 193 *:* (*vii*, 48*b*, 16–19) : It is just like a sāl-wood on a good land. The forester is intelligent, clever and not lazy. He, according to season, nurses the root of the Sāl trees. He frequently hoes, puts manure and waters them. If it is too high, he digs it down ; if it is too low, he fills it up. If weeds grow near by, he removes them If the trees growing together are crooked, knotty, not straight, he uproots them and throws them outside. If some branches are bent and crooked, then he chops them off. If near the trees, there are new sāḷ trees, which are straight and sound, he nurses them according to season, frequently hoes, adds manure and waters them. Thus that Sāl forest on a good land, will grow up luxuriant and exuberant.

P N° 21 *:* (*i*, 124, 23–37 ; 125, 1–2) : Not exactly the same. It mentions a great salwood in the vicinity of a village of a county-town. This sal-wood is invaded by parasite creepers. Some people, wishing it good, its welfare and its security, chop off the stems which are eaten up by the creepers, drag them outside the wood. But they would tend carefully those stems which are straight and sound. Thus this sal-wood will grow up luxuriant and abundant.

4. — *The C simile is simpler :*

In some cases, we find that the simile in the C version proves to be simpler than the simile in the P version.

The following simile in *C. S. N*° 18 serves as an example :

C N° 193 *:* (*vii*, 48*b*, 15–16) : It is just like a horse-cart with a charioteer riding on it. His left hand holds the reins, his right hand grasps a riding whip. He drives the cart following the 8 right roads and reaches any destination he likes.

P N° 21 *:* (*i*, 124, 18–23) : It refers to a cart yoked with well-bred horses, standing on a cross-road, on a smooth ground and with a goad held ready ; a skilled trainer, a charioteer to tame the horse mounts it, and holding the rein in his left hand and the goad in his right hand, he can drive the cart up and down, to whatever direction he likes.

5. — *Similes not found in P :*

Sometimes some similes, which are available in the C version are found missing in the P version. Thus in *C. S. N°* 90, there is a simile which is wanting in P, but available in C:

C N° 171 *:* (*vii*, 19*b*, 20; 20*a*, 1–2): There are 4 kinds of people, some have no results, but apparently have results, some have results but apparently have no results, some have no results and also apparently have no results, some have results and also apparently have results. Just like the 4 kinds of Nai fruit (㮈 : jack), some are not ripe but apparently look ripe, some are ripe but apparently look unripe, some are unripe and look unripe, some are ripe and look ripe.

P N° 136 *:* (*iii*, 214, 15–18) : The P refers to kamma but not to people. There are actions which are inoperative and seem to be inoperative; there are actions which are inoperative but seem to be operative ; there are actions that are operative and seem to be operative; there are actions that are operative but seem to be inoperative. The simile is missing here.

6. — *Similes not found in the C :*

Sometimes a reverse situation takes place, in which the C version is found wanting in the similes, which exist in its Pāli counterpart.

Thus in *C. S. N°* 8, this case occurs as follows:

C N° 98 *:* (*vi*, 19*a*, 2–4): Here the C deals with a phase in the contemplation of the body when the monk is well aware of, while inhaling or exhaling. It omits the simile.

P N° 10 *:* (*i*, 56, 11–32): Here the P adds the simile of a turner who is well aware of, when he gives a short or a long turn to the lathe.

In *C. S. N°* 74, the *P N°* 119 : (*iii*, 96, 16–31 ; 97, 1–14) proceeds further and says that mindfulness of body is developed further with the mind bent on this or that realization by super-knowledge and he can achieve this and be a witness of this achievement, whatever may be the plane. Then the P quotes 3 similes to illustrate the Buddha's explanation:

a) Just like a water-pot full to the brim so that one crow may drink from it and this pot is placed on its support. If a strong man comes and shakes the pot, he can spill the water out;

b) Just like a tank on an even plot of land, its four sides bound by dykes. This tank is full of water to the brim so that a crow may drink from it. If a strong man comes and releases the dyke, he is able to drive out the water;

c) Just as at a cross-road, on a level ground, a chariot is standing harnessed with thorough-breds. A clever charioteer of horses to be tamed mounts the chariot, takes the reins in his left hand, takes the goad in his right hand, he is able to drive the chariot to whatever place he likes.

7. — *The P similes are more appropriate :*

In some cases, we find that the P similes are more appropriate and clearer than those in the C version. This is due either to a faulty translation of the C version or to an unhappy interpretation of the Sanskrit originals.

Thus in *C. S. No* 17, in order to illustrate the first method of turning the mind from one characteristic to another characteristic so as to get rid of demeritorious thoughts, the Buddha resorted to the following simile, in which we observe that the P interpretation is more appropriate.

C N° 101 *:* (*vi*, 24*a*, 13) : It is like a carpenter or a carpenter's apprentice, who with an ink-string draws a line on the wood. Then he uses a sharp axe and chops off the wood, making it straight.

P N° 20 *:* (*i*, 119, 14-16) : Not exactly the same. The P refers also to a carpenter or a carpenter's apprentice but adds the expression dakkho. It mentions here that this carpenter or carpenter's apprentice knocks out, drives out a rough peg with the help of a smooth one.

The same can be said of the simile in *C. S. N°* 43, about the taming of a horse.

C N° 194 *:* (*vii*, 52*b*, 7-19) : The Buddha asked P'o-t'o-ho-li if he remembered for what reason formerly the Buddha related the simile of a pure horse ? P'o-t'o-ho-li replied that this was due to his not observing the one-sessioner's practice, when the other monks were observing it. The Buddha said that this was not the only cause. When he was relating the simile of a pure horse, P'o-to-ho-li might not be of one-pointed-mind, not very respectful, not be attentive to listen to. This was the added reason. Then at P'o-t'o-ho-li's request, the Buddha related the simile. There is a horse-trainer who gets a pure, thorough-bred horse. At first he trains the horse in the mouth. While training, the horse may not be pleased to be trained, willing or not willing, because the horse is not yet used to be trained. Having finished the first stage of training, he trains the horse in bridle to make it go. Here the C is rather confusing about the various stages of training to make the horse thoroughly trained, worthy of the name of a king's horse.

P N 65 : (*i*, 445, 16–36 ; 446 ; 447, 1–6) : The P is very clear on the various stages of training. First, the horse is trained in wearing the bridle, and while being trained, the horse might wrangle, caper as it is not used to it. When it is trained in wearing the bit, the horse is further trained in wearing the harness, in going forward, going round, going on the point of its hoofs (khurakāye), in galoping, neighing, in royal tricks, royal acrobatic feat, in utmost speed, utmost swiftness, utmost gentle manners. Then the horse-trainer gives the horse a beautiful appearance (vaṇṇiyañ ca valiyañ ca anuppavecchati). When the horse is endowed with these 10 qualities, it becomes worthy to be used by a king.

8. — ***Both similes are not the same :***

We observe also that sometimes the similes in both versions are not the same as clearly seen in C. S. N° 19, N° 23, N° 39.

Thus in *C. S. N°* 19, the following simile was used by the Buddha when he exhorted his disciples to be aloof from blame and praise :

C N° 200 : (*vii*, 66*a*, 11–13) : It is just like in this Shêng-lin forest (Jetavana) ; outside the gate there are dry leaves and dry wood ; suppose a man comes, takes them away, burns them in fire and uses them as he likes. What do you think ? Do those dry leaves and woods think : « That man takes us, burns us in fire and uses us as he likes ? » The monks replied : « W.H. One, it is not so. » In the same way, if there are people who abuse you, beat you, are angry, are displeased with you, frequently blame you; if other people respect, present offerings, worship and honour you, you should not harbour anger, hatred, ill-will, dislike, harmful thoughts; you also should not be joyful and glad, your mind should not be elated.

P N° 22 : (*i*, 140, 33–37; 141, 1–19): Not the same. Here the Buddha advised the monks to put away what did not belong to them, as this would result in happiness, in welfare for the monks for a long time. What did not belong to the monks here were material forms, feelings, perceptions, mental tendencies and consciousness. All these were not the self, did not belong to the self, so they should be put away by the monks. Then the Buddha quoted the same simile to illustrate his teachings. The P omits the adjective dry and the term wood, but adds grass, stems, branches. While in the C version, the Buddha asked the monks if these dry leaves and wood thought that this man had taken them away, in the P version, the Buddha asked the monks if the monks themselves thought that this man had taken them away.

In *C. S. N°* 39, a series of similes which offer differences between the two versions is seen as under. Here Yu-p'o-li (Upāli) cited 4 similes to show how he would drag recluse Ch'ü-t'an in his controversy.

C N° 133 : (*vi*, 56*a*, 12-13) : Just like a strong man who takes hold of a ram by its long fleece and drags him along, according to his wish.

P N° 56 : (*i*, 374, 36-38) : C : Drags him along according to his wish= P : ākaḍḍheyya parikaḍḍheyya samparikaḍḍheyya. The rest is almost the same.

C : (56*a*, 13-14) : Just like a strong man who with his hand holding a fleeced cloth, beats it to remove dust.

P : (374, 29-32) : Not the same. Just like a seller of liquor (soṇḍikākammakaro) who sinks a big soṇḍikākilañjaṃ (a mat of rushes or a cask of liquor ?) in a deep lake ; he takes hold of its corner and drags it.

C : (56*a*, 14-15) : Just like a seller of alcohol, who sinks a bag of alcohol liquor into deep water and drags it according to his wish.

P : (374, 34-36) : Not the same. Just like a strong soṇḍikādhutto (a dissipated drunkard), who takes hold of a vālaṃ (a hair-sieve) by the corner and shakes it, tosses it over and over.

C : (56*a*, 15-16) : Just like an elephant king of 60 years old, a proud big elephant, with matured tusk, feet and body, in full strength, is taken by a strong man, to take bath, washing its hip, its back, its belly, its tusks, its head and makes it play in the water.

P : (375, 1-3) : It refers to an elephant kuñjaro, 60 years old, who plunges into a deep pond and plays the game called saṇadhovikam (washing play, saṇa may mean a kind of reed, which the elephant pulls out and thrashes it against the water).

Again in the same *C. S. N°* 39, Ch'in-tzu (P : Nātaputta) reproached Yu-p'o-li to have gone to recluse Ch'ü-t'an to defeat him in arguments but was defeated instead and he used two similes to blame Yu-p'o-li.

C : (58*a*, 19-20) : Just like a man who enters the forest to obtain eyes but comes back with his eyes lost ; just like a man due to thirst enters a lake but comes back still thirsty.

P : (383, 24-27) : The first simile is not the same. It refers to a man who is a gelder (aṇḍahārako) and who comes back with his testicles removed. The 2nd simile is the same as the first simile of the Chinese version.

Remarks : Thus a comparative study of the similes in both versions shows us that both compilers drew their documents from a common source as seen by the common data collected from both versions. But although the illustrations conveyed by these similes are more or less the same, the wording of the similes, the selection of details offer some striking differences and this testifies to the ample latitude given to the compilers in the choice of documents. If some discrepancies crept into some similes, this is due perhaps to a faulty interpretation of the simile or to a defect in the translation. On the whole, the study of the similes in both versions helps us to see clearly the similarities as well as the dissimilarities between the Chinese and the Pāli versions.

Chapter IX. — CONCLUSIONS OF SŪTRAS

At the end of the discourse, either C or P, there is generally a conclusion to indicate the end of the discourse and to describe the rejoicements of the listeners at the Buddha's or one of his disciples' sermon. A comparative study of the conclusions of the 98 sūtras shows the following features : 1) 36 sūtras have almost the same conclusions ; 2) 26 sūtras have slightly different conclusions in which the C ones add either the monks, or some disciples, or some personages ; 3) 13 sūtras have not the same conclusions and 4) there are 23 sūtras in the P version where conclusions are missing.

1. — 36 *sūtras with almost the same conclusions :*

The following C. S. show the same conclusion of the sūtras : N° 2, N° 5, N° 8, N° 9, N° 10, N° 12, N° 13, N° 14, N° 16, N° 17, N° 18, N° 19, N° 21, N° 24, N° 26, N° 27, N° 28, N° 29, N° 32, N° 33, N° 34, N° 44, N° 47, N° 49, N° 58, N° 65, N° 70, N° 71, N° 73, N° 74, N° 75, N° 84, N° 91, N° 92, N° 93, N° 95.

Thus in *C. S. N°* 2, the conclusion is as follows :

C N° 10 : (*v*, 13*b*, 17–18) : Thus spoke the Buddha. Those monks having heard the Buddha's speech, became delighted and abided by.

P : N° 2 : (*i*, 12–7–8) : Thus spoke the Lord. Delighted those monks rejoiced at the Lord's speech.

In *C. S. N°* 12, it was elder Mu-chien-lien (P : Moggallāna) who delivered the discourse and the monks rejoiced at elder Mu-chien-lien's speech. In *C. S. N°* 24, it was elder Shê-li-tzu (P : Sāriputta) who spoke on the occasion and the monks rejoiced at elder Shê-li-tzu's speech.

2. — 26 *sūtras of slightly different conclusions :*

The following C. S. present slightly different conclusions :

N° 7, N° 11, N° 15, N° 22, N° 25, N° 40, N° 42, N° 43, N° 45, N° 50, N° 53, N° 55, N° 57, N° 60, N° 66, N° 67, N° 72, N° 76, N° 77, N° 80, N° 81, N° 83, N° 86, N° 87, N° 88, N° 90.

In these sūtras, among the people who rejoiced at the Buddha's speech or one of his disciples' speech, the C adds either « those monks » or some personages. Thus in *C. S. N°* 7, the P mentions only Mahācundo who rejoiced at the Lord's speech, the C counterpart, besides Ven. Ta-chü-na, adds those monks as well. In *C. S. N°* 25, the P mentions only Dīgho parajano yakkho who rejoiced at the Lord's speech, the C besides Ch'ang-kuei-t'ien adds « These 3 sons of good families » as well. In *C. S. N°* 57, the P mentions only those monks, the C adds the name of Ven. A-nan. In *C. S. N°* 60, the P quotes only those monks, the C adds also Fan-mo. This is rather strange, in the sense that Fan-mo was already mentioned dead in the preceding paragraph. In *C. S. N°* 83, the P mentions Anuruddha alone who rejoiced at the Lord's speech, the C adds elders Nan-t'i and Chin-p'i-lo as well.

3. — 13 *sūtras have not the same conclusions:*

The following C. S. have not the same conclusions :

N° 1, N° 3, N° 4, N° 20, N° 30, N° 31, N° 41, N° 78, N° 85, N° 94, N° 96, N° 97, N° 98.

In *C. S. N°* 1, the conclusions are as follows :

C N° 106 *:* (*vi,* 30*a,* 11) : Thus spoke the Buddha. Those monks having heard the Buddha's speech were delighted and abided by.

P N° 1 *:* (*i,* 6, 24-25) : Thus spoke the Lord. Delighted those monks rejoiced at the Lord's speech (according to Roman Script edition).

Remarks : According to the Singalese tradition and the Singalese text, the monks were ***not*** pleased with this discourse. « Na te bhikkhū Bhagavato bhāsitaṃ abhinandunti ». The Burmese 6th Council Edition also follows the Singalese tradition. It is stated in the Commentary (1) that 500 monks found no pleasure in listening to this discourse. The Buddha realizing this, preached to them the Mūlapariyāya jātaka. Their pride was thereby vanquished and they begged the Buddha for a subject for meditation. Later on, when the Buddha was at the Gotamacetiya in Vesāli, he preached to them the Gotamakasuttaṃ and they attained Arahantship (2).

But the Pāli text Society edition and the Chinese version adopt the usual conclusion, mentioning that those monks were delighted at the Buddha's speech. From the unusual conclusion of this discourse, the distinction between the Tathāgata and the Arahant, and the idea not to cling even to Nibbāna in this discourse, can we consider this sutta which bears some Mahāyānic spirit, as one of those rare suttas which escaped the vigilance of the Ther. compilers and was included in the Pāli Tipiṭaka, possibly by mere inadvertence. ? There is possibility that the addition of the term *na* might have been used to earmark its expunging from the Pāli Tipiṭaka, but the later P compilers forgot to do so.

(1) *M.A.* ii, 46 ff.
(2) *D.P.P.N.* ii, p. 649.

In *C. S. N*° 3, the C mentions that it was elder Shê-li-tzu who rejoiced at the Buddha's speech, but in the P version, those monks rejoiced at elder Sāriputta's speech. This difference is explained by the addition in the C version of one passage in which the Buddha praised Ven. Shê-li-tzu and ended the discourse, while in the P, it was elder Sāriputta who concluded the discourse.

In *C. S. N*° 4, the 2 conclusions are as below :

C N° 87 : (*vi*, 8*a*, 20 ; 8*b*, 1) : The 2 venerables, having thus talked and praised each other got up from their seat. Ven. Shê-li-tzu had thus spoken. Ven. Ta-mu-chien-lien, together with the monks were delighted in what Ven. Shê-li-tzu had said and abided by.

P N° 5 : (*i*, 32, 33-34) : Thus the two great monks (Mahānāga) rejoiced mutually in their good speech.

In *C. S. N*° 20. the following conclusions are mentioned :

C N° 9 : (*v*, 12*b*, 19) : Thus the 2 venerables discussed together and having praised each other, they gladly abided by. Then they got up from their seat and returned to their respective abodes.

P N° 24 : (*i*, 151, 4-5) : Thus the 2 great beings mutually were satisfied with their speech.

In *C. S. N*° 30, the difference between the 2 conclusions is as follows :

C N° 211 : (*vii*, 87*a*, 8-9) : Thus those two elders praised each other, saying : « Very good, very good », spoke to each other, were delighted and abided in. Then they got up from their seat and departed.

P N° 43 : (*i*, 298, 28-29) : Thus spoke elder Sāriputta. Well pleased, elder Mahākoṭṭhito was delighted in what elder Sāriputta had said.

In *C. S. N*° 31, the C refers to Bhikṣuṇī Fa-lo and the monks who were delighted at the Buddha's speech ; while the P mentions that it was the layman devotee Visākha who was delighted at the Lord's speech. This difference is due to the fact that in the C version, it was bhikṣuṇī Fa-lo who reported the conversation to the Buddha, while in the P version, it was the layman Visākha who approached the Blessed One.

In *C. S. N*° 41, in the C, it was those monks who were delighted by the Buddha's speech, while in the P, it was elder Mālunkyaputta who rejoiced at the Blessed One's discourse.

In *C. S. N*° 78, it was Ven. A-nan and the monks who were delighted by the Buddha's speech, while in the P version, the last portion of the discourse was spoken by elder Ānanda and those monks rejoiced at elder Ānanda's discourse.

In *C. S. N°* 85, in the C version, those monks rejoiced at the Buddha's speech, while in the P, the discourse ended with one gāthā recited by the Master without the usual conclusion.

In *C. S. N°* 94, in the C version, Ven. Fu-chia-lo-so-li was delighted at the Buddha's speech, while in the P, those monks were rejoiced at the Blessed One's speech.

In *C. S. N°* 96, while the C mentions Ven. A-nan and the monks rejoicing over the Buddha's discourse, in the P, the Blessed One ended the discourse and the Master recited a gāthā as a conclusion to the discourse.

In *C. S. N°* 97, in the C version, those monks rejoiced at the Buddha's speech, while in the P, it was elder Ānanda.

In *C. S. N°* 98, the C mentions that Ven. A-nan and the young monks were delighted by the Buddha's discourse while the P mentions simply those monks. The P adds that while the discourse was being delivered, 60 monks obtained freedom from cankers, without graspings.

4. — 23 *sūtras in which the P conclusions are missing :*

They are as follows : N° 6, N° 23, N° 35, N° 36, N° 37, N° 38, N° 39, N° 46, N° 48, N° 51, N° 52, N° 54, N° 56, N° 59, N° 61, N° 62, N° 63, N° 64, N° 68, N° 69, N° 79, N° 82, N° 89.

Thus in *C. S. N°* 6, the C mentions that brāhmaṇa Hao-shou-shui-ching and the monks rejoiced at the Buddha's speech, but the P stops short with Bhāradvājo's attainment of arahantship.

In *C. S. N°* 23, the C mentions that brāhmana Shêng-wên and the member of different sect Pi-lu rejoiced at the Buddha's speech, while the P omits the conclusion, after brāhmaṇa Jāṇussoṇī asking to take refuge in the Triple Gem and to become a lay-disciple.

In *C. S. N°* 35, Brahmā and Brahmā's followers rejoiced at the Buddha's speech.

In *C. S. N°* 36, the C mentions that Māra the Evil One rejoiced at Ven. Ta-mu-chien-lien's speech. This is rather strange for Māra to be delighted at Ta-mu-chien-lien's discourse, as the Elder's sermon aimed rather at subduing him. Moreover, in the discourse, Māra was mentioned as having vanished away already. The P silence is significant and points out to the high degree of accuracy in its compilation.

In *C. S. N°* 39, Yu-p'o-li rejoiced at the Buddha's speech, according to the C version, while the P refers simply to Nātaputta vomiting blood.

In *C. S. N°* 59, in the C version, king Po-ssu-ni, elder A-nan and the great Assembly rejoiced at the Buddha's speech ; but in the P, king

Pasenadi rejoiced at the Blessed One's speech, got up from his seat, paid homage to the Blessed One, went round him and departed.

In *C. S. N*° 63, Ven. Shê-li-tzu and innumerable hundred thousand (people) in the Assembly rejoiced at the Buddha's speech, according to the C version. But the P mentions simply that the Blessed One told Sāriputta that brāhmaṇa Dhānañjāni was dead and was born in the Brahma-world.

In *C. S. N*° 79, in the C version, the member of different sect and the monks rejoiced at Ven. Po-chü-lo's speech. But there is no conclusion in the P version, which mentions that elder Bakkula while sitting in the middle of the Sangha entered into Nibbāna.

In *C. S. N*° 89, Young Ying-wu, son of Tu-t'i and innumerable people in the Assembly rejoiced at the Buddha's speech in the C version; but the P ignores the conclusion and mentions simply Todeyyaputta asking the Blessed One to accept him as one of his lay-disciples.

Remarks : Thus a comparative study of the conclusions of the 98 corresponding sūtras shows that the C compilers are rather too systematic in their compilations as not a single sūtra out of 222 sūtras was left without a conclusion, while the P contains 23 sūtras without proper conclusions. 36 sūtras of almost the same conclusion along with 26 sūtras of slightly different conclusions point out to a common source from which both compilers derived their materials. But the omission of the conclusion in some P suttas shows the high degree of reliability of the P version. Thus it is rather strange that Māra the Evil One rejoiced at Ven. Mu-chien-lien's speech as seen in *C. S. N*° 36; and we are no less puzzled when the C adds Fan-mo rejoicing over the Buddha's speech, when he was reported dead already in the previous paragraph as seen in *C. S. N*° 60. We observe also that the C has mentioned in *C. S. N*° 63 up to innumerable hundred thousand people in the Assembly rejoicing at the Buddha's speech. This seems to have some Mahāyānic ideas and testifies to a rather late compilation. But we have to recognise that there is possibility of later compilers or rather editors adding these conclusions so as to give a better uniformity to the whole Āgama, thereby causing some discrepancies to creep in.

PART THREE

15 SPECIMENS OF COMPARATIVE STUDY OF CHINESE AND PĀLI CORRESPONDING SŪTRAS.

C. S. N° 1

CHINESE : No. 100. Hsiang-ching (想經) (Tsê vi, 29b–30a)
PĀLI : No. 1. Mūlapariyāyasuttaṃ (P.M.N. i, 1–6)

A. — GIST OF THE C SŪTRA

The Buddha enumerated different attitudes of different people towards various dharmas, the cause which determined these attitudes and their degree of emancipation due to these attitudes.

P : Almost the same.

B. — TITLES

C: *Hsiang ching*, discourse on perceptions, which refers to the attitude of different people towards various dharmas.

P: *Mūlapariyāyasuttaṃ*, discourse on the Fundamentals, which refers to the basic method of approach towards the Dhammas.

C. — PLACE OF OCCURRENCE

C: Shê-Wei, Shêng-lin, Kei-ku-t's park (Sāvatthi, Jetavana, Anāthapiṇḍikārāma).

P : Ukkaṭṭhā, Subhagavana, at the foot of a Sālarāja tree.

Remarks : Ukkaṭṭhā is a town in Kosala, near the Himālayas. It was given free of taxes to Pokkarasāti by the king of Kosala, in recognition of the former's skill (1).

Subhagavana is a wood in Ukkaṭṭhā, so called because of its beauty (2).

The C translates the term Viharati as travelling in this sūtra as well in other sūtras. The P uses it in the original sense of dwelling, staying.

D. — CONTENTS OF THE SŪTRAS

I) *Circumstances leading to the deliverance of the discourse :*

C : (29*b*, 20) : The Buddha delivered the discourse without any preamble.

---

(1) D.P.P.N. i, p. 329.
(2) D.P.P.N. ii, p. 1230.

P : (*i*, 4–9) : The Buddha called the monks, announced his intention of preaching the Sabbadhammapariyāya, asked the monks to be attentive and the monks answered in readiness. Then the Buddha delivered the discourse.

II) *Attitude of the ignorant recluses and brāhmaṇas :*

C : (29*b*, 20 ; 30*a*, 1–4) : There are recluses and brāhmaṇas who towards the earth have the earth-perception, that earth is the soul, earth belongs to the soul, the soul belongs to earth. When they hold the view that earth is the soul, then they are not knowing the earth. In the same way towards water, fire, wind, spirits, deities, Lord of beings, Brahmā, No-worry-plane, no distress-plane, purity, plane of infinite space, plane of infinite consciousness, plane of nothingness, plane of neither perception nor non-perception, oneness, diversity, plurality, the seen, the heard, the sensed, the cognised, the obtained, the contemplated, mindfulness, thought, from this world to that world, from that world to this world, all. They towards all have the all-perception, that all is the soul, all belongs to the soul, the soul belongs to all. When they hold the view that all is the soul, then they are not knowing all.

P : (1, 11–26 ; 2 ; 3 ; 4 ; 1–6) : Not exactly the same. While the C refers simply to recluses and brāhmaṇas in general, the P refers to an ignorant worldling, who has no consideration for the ariya and for the Sappurisa, who is not versed, not trained in the Ariyadhamma and in the Sappurisa-dhamma. C : « who towards the earth has the earth-perception, that earth is the soul, earth belongs to the soul, the soul belongs to the earth = P : He perceives earth as earth. Having perceived earth as earth, he thinks of the earth, he thinks (of self) in the earth, he thinks of earth (in the self or of self as the earth). He thinks : « earth is mine. » He rejoices in the earth. C : when they hold the view that earth is the soul, then they are not knowing the earth = P : Why is it so ? I said : « Earth is not completely understood by him ». While the C enumerates up to 29 dharmas, the P refers only to 24 dhammas which are in the following order : Earth, water, fire, wind, beings, deities, Pajāpati, Brahmā, Ābhassarā, Subhakiṇhā, Vehapphalā, Abhibhū, plane of infinite space, plane of infinite consciousness, plane of nothingness, plane of neither perception nor non-perception, the seen, the heard, the sensed, the cognised, oneness, diversity, all, Nibbāna... 11 *dharmas* are not found in P : spirits, no worry-plane, no distress-plane, purity, plurality, the obtained, the contemplated, mindfulness, thought, from this world to that world, from that world to this world. 6 dharmas are not found in C : Beings, Ābhassarā, Subhakiṇṇā, Vehapphalā, Abhibhū, Nibbāna.

Remarks : The C omits the term Nibbāna which is interpreted in Papañcasūdanī as enjoyments of 5 kinds of sense-pleasures. This was the interpretation of the materialist who considered that the enjoyment of sense-pleasures in this very life was Nibbāna.

III) *Attitude of the wise recluses and brāhmaṇas :*

C : (30*a*, 4-7) : This passage is nothing but the reverse of the attitude of the ignorant recluses and brāhmaṇas with appropriate changes.

P : (4, 7-22) : Not exactly the same. Here the Pāli refers to a sekha, the learner, not yet attained to perfection, who is striving for the supreme security from bondage. He knows the earth as the earth and does not perceive it like the ignorant worldling. He tries to refrain from thinking of the earth, from thinking earth as mine, and not to take delight in earth. The reason for this attitude is that « the true nature of the object is knowable to him (Pariññeyyaṃ tassāti).

Here the P adds the attitude of the Asekha (4, 23-37 ; 5, 1-33) : who is an arahant, whose cankers are destroyed, who has lived the life, who has done what should be done, who has laid down the burden, has attained the goal, whose fetters of becoming is completely eradicated, who is freed by perfect knowledge. He has succeeded not to think of the earth, not to consider earth as « mine », not to take delight in earth. The reason of his attitude is that he has already understood the earth, he has already got rid of attachment, of aversion and of delusion.

IV) *Attitude of the Tathāgata :*

C : (30*a*, 7-11) : Almost the same as with the case of wise recluses and brāhmaṇas, with recluses and brāhmaṇas replaced by « myself » that is Lord Buddha.

P : (5, 34-37 ; 6, 1-23) : Here the Pāli refers to a Tathāgata, arahant, fully Enlightened. He has succeeded not to think of the earth, not to consider earth as « mine », not to take delight in earth. The reason of his attitude is that he has thoroughly understood. He knows that delight is the root of suffering ; from becoming birth arises and there are old age and death for the being. The Tathāgata by the eradication of all cravings, by no-attachment, by cessation, by giving up, by complete renunciation, has attained the supreme Enlightenment.

Remarks : Here the P offers a clear-cut definition of different categories of people with their different attitudes and the reason for their doing so, while the Chinese is rather over-simple. The P refers to the distinction between the 2 last categories of people, between the monk who is an arahant with all the qualifications of arahantship and the Tathāgata who is an arahant but sammāsambuddho. Here the C translates the term ātman as soul.

E. — CONCLUSION

C : (30*a*, 11) : Thus spoke the Buddha. Those monks having heard the Buddha's speech were delighted and abided by it.

P : (6, 24-25) : Thus spoke the Lord. Delighted those monks rejoiced at the Lord's speech.

Remarks : According to the Singalese tradition and the Singalese text, the monks were ***not*** pleased with this discourse. « Na te bhikkhū Bhagavato bhāsitaṃ abhinandunti ». The Burmese 6th Council edition also follows the Singalese tradition (1).

---

(1) See ante, p. 204. Remarks.

C. S. N° 2

CHINESE : N° 10. *Lou-chin-ching*, (漏盡經) (Tsê, v, 13a-13b).
PĀLI : N° 2. Sabbāsavasuttaṃ, (T.M.N. i, 6-12).

A. — GIST OF THE CHINESE SŪTRA

The Buddha stressed upon the importance of knowledge and right thinking that lead to the extinction of cankers, and upon dangers of wrong thinking which nurtures and increases cankers. Then he pointed out 7 ways of eradicating cankers.

P : Almost the same.

B. — TITLES

C : Lou-chin-ching, discourse on extinction of cankers which refers to the cessation of cankers by 7 ways of eradicating them.

P : Sabbāsavasuttaṃ, discourse on all the cankers which refers to all the cankers to be got rid of by 7 ways.

C. — LOCATION

C : Among the Chü-lou-shou (P : Kuru), at the market-town of the Chü-lou called Chien-mo-sê-t'an P: Kammassadamma.

P : At Sāvatthi, Jetavana, Anāthapiṇḍikārāma.

Notes : Kuru is one of the 16 mahājanapada. Its people had a reputation for deep wisdom and most profound discourses were delivered there by the Buddha. Kammassadama is a nigama of the Kurus where the Buddha resided from time to time (1).

D. — CONTENTS OF THE SŪTRA

I) *Circumstances leading to the deliverance of the discourse :*

C : (13*a*, 2) : The Buddha delivered the discourse without preamble.

P : (6, 28-31 ; 7, 1-3) : The Buddha called the monks, announced his intention of preaching the Sabbāsavasaṃvarapariyāyaṃ, asked the monks to

(1) D.P.P.N. i, p. 641-642.

be attentive. The monks answered in readiness and the Buddha delivered the discourse.

II) *Knowledge and vision lead to the extinction of cankers :*

C : (13*a*, 2–4) : It is through knowledge, through vision that cankers are extinguished, not without knowledge, without vision. How is it that through knowledge, through vision that cankers are extinguished, not without knowledge, without reason. There are right consideration and wrong consideration. With wrong consideration, the not yet arisen cankers of sense-desire arise, the already arisen cankers increase; the not yet arisen cankers of becoming, cankers of ignorance arise, the already arisen cankers increase. With right consideration, the not yet arisen cankers of sense-desire do not arise ; the already arisen cankers then disappear; the not yet arisen cankers of becoming, cankers of ignorance do not arise, the already arisen cankers then disappear.

P : (7, 4–10) : Almost the same. C : through knowledge, through vision = P : jānato passato. C : right consideration, wrong consideration = P : yoniso manasikāro, ayoniso manasikāro. The Pāli mentions simply āsavā (cankers) in general.

III) *Attitude of the ignorant worldling and of the learned noble disciple :*

C : (13*a*, 4–10) : But the ignorant worldling cannot hear the right dharma, cannot meet the truly learned people, does not know the noble dharma, is not versed in the noble dharma, does not know the dharma as it really is. With wrong consideration the not yet arisen cankers of sense-desire arise... (as above up to)... the already arisen cankers then disappear. As he does not know the dharma as it really is, he thinks of the dharmas which should not be thought of, he does not think of the dharmas which should be thought of. As he thinks of the dharmas which should not be thought of and as he does not think of the dharmas which should be thought of, then the not yet arisen cankers of sense-desire arise, the already arisen cankers increase, the not yet arisen cankers of becoming, cankers of ignorance arise, the already arisen cankers increase. The learned noble disciple can hear the right dharma, can meet the truly learned people... (just the reverse of the case of the ignorant worldling).

P : (7, 16–37 ; 8, 1–3 ; 32–37 ; 9, 1–17) : (The P includes this passage in the paragraph of cankers to be eradicated by vision). Here the unlearned worldling is described as having no consideration for the ariya (noble ones) and for the Sappurisa (true ones), being not versed, not trained in the ariyadhamma and in the sappurisadhamma. It omits : « with wrong consideration... up to... the already arisen cankers then disappear ». The Pāli mentions that this worldling does not know the dhamma which should be considered and the dhamma which should not be considered. The dhammas which should not be considered are the dhammas on the consideration of which, cankers of sense-desire, of becoming, of ignorance which are not yet arisen will arise, those which are already arisen will increase. The dhammas which should be considered are the dhammas on the consideration of which, cankers of sense-desire, of becoming, of ignorance which are not yet arisen will not arise, those which are already arisen will disappear. As this worldling considers the dhammas which should be considered, the not yet arisen cankers arise, and the already arisen cankers increase. The case of the learned noble disciple is just the reverse.

IV) *Seven ways of eradicating cankers :*

C : (13*a*, 11-12): There are 7 ways of eradicating cankers, distress, vexation, grief and sorrow. There are cankers which are eradicated by vision ; there are cankers which are eradicated by protection ; there are cankers which are eradicated by avoidance ; there are cankers which are eradicated by use ; there are cankers which are eradicated by forbearance ; there are cankers which are eradicated by elimination ; there are cankers which are eradicated by reflection.

P : (7, 10-15): Almost the same. The order in the P is as follows: 1) dassana, by vision, 2) saṃvara, by protection, 3) paṭisevana, by use, 4) adhivāsanā, by forbearance, 5) parivajjana, by avoidance, 6) vinodana, by elimination and 7) bhāvanā, by reflection.

Remarks : The P order is more systematic as it places patisevana near adhivāsana and parivajjana near vinodana. In the 7th method, the C uses the term reflection, while the P uses the term bhāvanā which means both reflection and meditation.

V) *Cankers to be eradicated by vision :*
P : dassana :

C : (13*a*, 12-20): How are cankers eradicated by vision ? The ignorant worldling cannot hear the right dharma... does not know the dharma as it really is. As he is with wrong consideration, he thinks : « I had the past life; I had no past life ; By what cause I had the past life ? How was my past life ? I shall have a future life; I shall have no future life ? He himself doubts what his body is, it is, how it is ? Now these living beings when do they come and where will they go ? By what previous causes, did they come into being ? By what future cause will they come into being ? » Having made such a wrong consideration, towards the 6 views, following any of his views, the view arises that really there is a soul; the rise of this view begets the view that really there is no soul; the rise of this view begets the view that the soul sees the soul; the rise of this view begets the view that the soul sees the no-soul; the rise of this view begets the view that the no-soul sees the soul; the rise of this view begets the view that this is the soul which can speak, can understand, can act, causes to act, can teach, causes to teach ; (The text is rather misleading ; it should read : « nêng-tso, tso-ch'i, nêng-chiao, chiao-ch'i 能作作起能教教起) » born here and there, it receives good and bad results, it surely comes from nowhere, surely it does not exist, surely it will not exit. This is called veil of views, wriggling of views, bondages of views. The ignorant worldling for this reason receives suffering of birth, old age, sickness and death.

The learned noble disciple can hear the right dharma, can meet truly learned people ; he knows the dharma as it really is, he knows suffering as it really is, knows the cause of suffering, knows the cessation of suffering, knows the path (leading) to the cessation of suffering as it really is. (Having thus known in accordance with truth), then the 3 fetters extinguish. The 3 fetters of view on body, of clinging to rules and of doubt being extinguished, he obtains the stream-attainment stage, not to fall into evil dharmas, surely he will proceed to right enlightenment. At the utmost after 7 births, having gone and come 7 times in the deities' realms and in the human world, then he obtains the end of suffering. If he does not know (proper) vision, then distress, vexation, grief and sorrow arise ; if he knows (proper) vision, then distress, vexation, grief and sorrow do not arise. This is called cankers which are eradicated by vision.

P : (8, 3-32 : 9, 17-23) : (The P includes the passage of the attitude of the worldling and of the noble disciple in this paragraph). Almost the same. What the ignorant worldling thinks of the past and of the future is the same with the Chinese. As to the present, C : He himself doubts what his body is, it is, how it is ? = P : Now am I ? Now am I not ? Now what am I ? Now, how am I ? The Pāli omits : « By what previous cause did they come into being ? By what future cause will they come into being ? » The 6 views which arise due to his wrong consideration are almost the same. *1st view :* C : the view arises that really there is a soul = P : the view arises as though it were true, as though it were real : « There is for me a self ». *2nd view :* same remarks. *3rd view :* C : the view arises that the soul sees the soul = P : Pāli uses the term sañjānāmi instead of see, and atta instead of soul. *4th and 5th views :* same remarks. *6th view :* C : This is the soul which can speak, can understand, can act, causes to act, can teach, causes to teach ; born here and there, it receives good and bad results ; it surely comes from nowhere, surely it does not exist, surely it will not exist = P : « The self I have is the speaker, the experiencer, who enjoys here and there fruits of good and bad actions. This self to me is permanent, firm, eternal, not subject to change, everlasting. » C : This is called veil of views, wriggling of views, bondages of views = P : diṭṭhigatam̩, diṭṭhigahanam̩, diṭṭhikantāram̩, diṭṭhivisūkam̩, diṭṭhivipphanditam̩, diṭṭhisamyojanam̩ (going to wrong views, thicket of wrong views, wilderness of wrong views, wriggling of wrong views, struggling of wrong views, fetters of wrong views). As to the attitude of the learned noble disciple, the P inserts the whole passage in paragraph III as seen above. It mentions also the knowledge of the 4 noble Truths in accordance with right consideration and the eradication of the 3 fetters : sakkāyadiṭṭhi, vicikicchā and sīlabbataparāmāso (not in the same order as the Chinese). It omits the attainment of sotapatti and the extinction of suffering, distress, vexation, grief and sorrow.

VI) *Cankers to be eradicated by protection:*
P : saṃvara :

C: (13*a*, 20; 13*b*, 1-2): The monk, when he sees material objects protects his eye-faculties. With right consideration, he contemplates them as impure. He does not protect his eye-faculties when, with wrong consideration, he contemplates them as pure. When there is no protection, then distress, vexation, grief, sorrow arise; when there is protection, then distress, vexation, grief and sorrow do not arise. In the same way with ears, nose, tongue, body and mind cognizing objects. He protects his mind-faculty. With right consideration, he contemplates them as impure; he does not protect his mind-faculty when with wrong consideration, he contemplates them as pure. When there is no protection, then distress, vexation, grief, sorrow arise; when there is protection, then distress, vexation, grief, sorrow do not arise.

P : (9, 24-37; 10, 1-3) : Not exactly the same. Here the P says that the monk with right consideration lives protected with the protection of eye-faculties. If he lives unprotected with the protection of eye-faculties, then those cankers which are destructive and consuming arise; if he lives protected with the protection of eye-faculties, then those cankers which are destructive and consuming do not arise. In the same way with the other faculties. The rest not available.

VIII) *Cankers to be eradicated by avoidance :*
P : parivajjana :

C: (13*b*, 2-5) : When the monk sees evil elephant, he should avoid it, evil horse, evil bull, evil dog, poisonous serpent, evil path, trench, pit, covered cess-pool, river, deep pool, precipice, evil learned man, evil friend, evil heretic, evil neighbour, evil dwelling place (he should avoid them). When living together with those brahma-farers, if people who have no suspicion will have suspicion, therefore the monk should avoid evil dwelling places. In these places, if people who have no suspicion will have suspicion, all these should be avoided completely. When there is no avoidance, then distress, vexation, grief, sorrow arise; when there is avoidance, then distress, vexation, grief, sorrow do not arise. This is called cankers which are eradicated by avoidance.

P : (10, 34-37; 11, 1-9) : Among animals and places to be avoided, the Pāli omits : evil path, covered cess-pool, rivers, deep pool but adds : khāṇuṃ (stumps of tree), kaṇṭakadhānaṃ (thorny edge), oligallaṃ (rubbish pit). For the C: « When living together... all these should be avoided completely », the P writes : « Whatever sitting places he sits, whatever place he resorts to, whatever evil companions he is associated with, if by doing so, his learned co-religious brahma-farers would suspect him of depraved qualites (pāpakesu ṭhānesu okappeyyuṃ), then the monk with right consideration, should avoid these places, these people. The rest, same remarks as in the above paragraph.

VIII) *Cankers to be eradicated through use :*
P : paṭisevana :

C : (13*b*, 5-9) : How are cankers eradicated by use ? If a monk uses robe, it is not for the sake of gain, not for the sake of pride, not for adornment, but only for protection against mosquitoes, gad-flies, wind, rain, cold, heat, for the sake of shame. If he uses food and drink, it is not for the sake of gain, not for pride, not for joy of becoming fat, but only for the sake of maintaining the body for a long time, of eliminating distress, vexation, grief, sorrow, for the sake of carrying the brahma-life, of getting rid of old disease and preventing new disease to arise, for the sake of living long, secure, without disease. If he uses residential quarters, rooms, houses, beds, mattresses, beddings, it is not for the sake of gain, not for pride, not for adornment, but only for the sake of stopping weariness, of sitting in meditation. If he uses lotion, medicine, it is not for the sake of gain, not for pride, not for joy of becoming fat, but only for the sake of eliminating distress (generated by) disease, for the sake of preserving life, for living secure, without sickness. When there is no use, then distress, vexation... do not arise. This is called cankers which are eradicated by use.

P : (20, 4-23) : Not exactly the same. For the use of robe, the P adds yoniso paṭisaṅkhā (wise reflection) to the attitude of the monk and siriṃsapa to the list of mosquitoes and flies. It omits : « Not for the sake of gain, not for pride, not for adornment. For the use of food and drink, C : food and drink = P : alms-food. Here the Pāli mentions that the monks uses alms-food not for the sake of sport (davā), not for indulging (madā), not for decorating, not for personal beauty but for the sake of maintaining life, of keeping it from harm, for carrying on the brahma-life, for destroying old feelings, for preventing new feelings, for living without fault, with ease and comfort.

For the use of dwelling places, the P uses the term senāsanam only. It omits : « Not for the sake of... », and mentions for the sake of protection against cold, heat, for warding off mosquitoes, flies, wind, sun, creeping creatures, for removing hardship of the season, for enjoying seclusion.

For the use of medicine, the P uses the term gilānapaccayabhesajjaparikkharā. It omits : « Not for the sake of... » but mentions for the sake of eradicating the arising feelings which are causing pain, for the sake of the utmost well-being.

Remarks : For « siriṃsapa, its place is rather queer as it should be placed near ḍaṃsa, makasa. In the « Uttaradhyayanasūtraṃ (1), the enume-

(1) p. 5, Verse 3-5.

ration follows the order vāta, ātapa, ḍaṃsa, makasa, sirimsapa. In the P tradition, only positive necessities of cīvara are stated, but no occasions of misuse are enumerated. In the C version, the term *pride* is used to translate the term *madā*, which means both pride and intoxication. Here the term intoxication suits better. As to the use of alms-food, the P mentions : « Not for the sake of adornment (vibhūsana), not for the sake of decoration », it looks forced here. The C version seems more plausible.

IX) *Cankers to be got rid of by forbearance :*
P : adhivāsanā :

C : (13*b*, 9–12) : How are cankers eradicated by forbearance? For the sake of energetically eradicating evil, demeritorious dharmas and developing meritorious dharmas, the monk frequently sets his mind thinking: (I) shall be energetic with all my heart, even if my body, skin, flesh, sinews, bone, blood and marrow dry up and become exhausted, (I) shall never give up exertion; only when (I) obtain what (I) want, do (I) give up exertion. The monk again should endure hunger, thirst, cold, heat, mosquitoes, gad-flies, flies, louse, fleas, oppression of wind and sun, evil words, stick beating. He forbears all. When the body suffers disease of acute pain even up to near dying and towards all unpleasant feelings, he can forbear all. When there is no forbearance, then distress... do not arise. This is called cankers which are eradicated by forbearance.

P : (10, 24–33): The P mentions only that the monk with right consideration, should forbear cold, heat, hunger, thirst, gad-flies, mosquitoes, wind, sun, creeping creatures, insulting and abusive languages. He should endure arising physical feelings which are miserable, piercing, acute, severe, shooting, unbearable, taking away life.

Remarks: The P omits the practice of exertion even up to drying of body, blood, flesh etc...

X) *Cankers to be got rid of by elimination :*
P : vinodana :

C : (13*b*, 12–13) : How are cankers eradicated by elimination ? When thoughts of desire arise, the monk should eliminate, eradicate, get rid of them. When thoughts of hatred, thoughts of harming arise, he should eliminate, eradicate, get rid of them. When there is no elimination, then distress... do not arise. This is called cankers eradicated by elimination.

P: (11, 11–21) : Almost the same. The P adds demeritorious dharmas to thoughts of desire, hatred and harming.

XI) *Cankers to be got rid of by reflection :*

P : bhāvanā :

C : (13*b*, 13–15) : How are cankers eradicated by reflection ? The monk reflects upon mindfulness the first factor of wisdom, which depends upon aloofness, upon no–desire, upon complete cessation, leading to emancipation. (In the same way), he reflects upon (discrimination of) dharma, exertion, joy, tranquillity, concentration and equanimity the 7th factor of wisdom, which depends upon aloofness, no–desire, complete cessation, leading to emancipation. When there is no reflection... do not arise. This is called cankers eradicated by reflection.

P : (11, 21–32) : Almost the same. The P adds : with wise reflection. Here the 7 factors of wisdom depend upon aloofness (viveka), absence of lust (virāga), cessation, leading to renunciation (vossaggapariṇāmin).

Remarks : The C speaks of the 2nd factor of wisdom as dharma only, omiting the term chê (擇 P: vicaya) meaning discrimination.

XII) *Removal of all cankers :*

C : (13*b*, 15–17) : If a monk succeeds in eradicating by vision all cankers to be got rid of by vision, by protection all cankers to be got rid of by protection, by avoidance all cankers to be got rid of by avoidance, by use all cankers to be got rid of by use, by forbearance all cankers to be got rid of by forbearance, by elimination all cankers to be got rid of by elimination, by reflection all cankers to be got rid of by reflection, then this monk has eradicated all cankers, is emancipated from fetters, is able to use right wisdom to put an end to suffering.

P : (11, 33–37 ; 12, 1–6) : The first portion is the same with the Chinese. The 2nd portion is as follows : « This monk is said to have dwelt controlled with the control of all cankers, having destroyed craving, removed fetters and fully realising pride, he puts an end to suffering.

E. — CONCLUSION

C : (13*b*, 17–18) : Thus spoke the Buddha. Those monks having heard the Buddha's speech, became delighted and abided by.

P : (12, 7–8) : Thus spoke the Lord. Delighted, those monks rejoiced at the Lord's speech.

C. S. N° 5

CHINESE : N° 105, *Yüan-ching*, (願 經) (Tsê, vi, 29a-29b).
PĀLI : N° 6, Ākaṅkheyyasutta, (T.M.N. i, 33-66).

A. — GIST OF THE CHINESE SŪTRA

The Buddha enumerated a number of wishes (13 in Chinese and 17 in Pāli). These wishes are to be fulfilled by the monks by observing the rules of moral code and by exercising themselves in meditation and in insight.

P: Almost the same.

B. — TITLE

C: Yüan-ching, discourse on wishes, which refers to the wishes formulated by the monks.

P: Ākaṅkheyyasuttaṃ, discourse on what one may wish, which refers also to the wishes to be formulated by the monks.

C. — LOCATION OF THE SŪTRA

The same in both versions: Sāvatthi, Jetavana, Anāthapiṇḍika's park.

D. — CONTENTS OF THE SŪTRA

I) *Circumstances leading to the deliverance of the sūtra :*

C: (29*a*, 18-20) : At that time a certain monk, lived aloof, alone, in a secluded quiet place. While sitting in meditation, these thoughts occurred to him : « The W.H. One comforts (me), talks to me, preaches the doctrine for me (so that I) obtained the Complete (ordination) rules, but not neglecting meditation, fulfilled the practice of insight, in an empty secluded place ». Having thought thus, towards evening, this monk got up from his meditation-seat, and went to the Buddha's place. The W.H. One, having seen that monk coming from afar, on account of that monk, said to the monks » :

P: No particular circumstances. The Lord addressed the monks without preamble.

II) *The wishes :*

(*C :* 29*a*, 20 ; 29*b*, 1-13) = (P : 33, 15-35 ; 34 ; 35 ; 36, 1-3).

The wishes are 13 in C and 17 in P. Purport of the wishes is almost the same in both versions, but in wording, in details, they offer some differences. The P before enumerating the wishes quotes the Buddha admonishing the monks to observe the moral precepts, to practise the Pāṭimokkha, to live well controlled by the control of Pāṭimokkha, to observe correct behaviour and correct frequentation, to see dangers in small faults and to train themselves in spiritual precepts. The C omits it. In the P version, after every wish, there is the same formula, a kind of refrain stating conditions to be observed for the fulfilment of the wish as follows : « He should be one who is a fulfiller of moral precepts, who is engaged in inner mental tranquillity, whose concentration is never broken off, who is endowed with insight, who is a frequenter of empty places». In the C version, there is also a kind of refrain at the end of every wish, but it is not separated from the wish itself, and its wording is such that it is difficult to ascertain it as conditions to be fulfilled as seen in the P versions. This refrain is as follows : « Observe the complete (ordination) rules, but not neglecting meditation, fulfil the practice of insight by dwelling in a secluded place ».

C 1 = *P* 1 :

C : (29*a*, 20) : You should wish that : « May the W.H. One comfort (me), talk to me, preach the doctrine to me »...

P : (33, 9-12) : May I be dear to my fellow-monks, liked, honoured and respected by them »

C 2 = *P* 4 :

C : (29*b*, 1) : « I have relatives. May they on account of me, when they pass away, go to good places up to be born in heaven.

P : (33, 21-24) : « May these relatives of mine, when they are dead and born into some other species remember (me), with a pleasant mind, (and thereby obtain) this great fruit, this great profit ».

Remarks : Miss Horner (1) translates as follows : « May this be a great fruit, a great advantage to those of my kith and kin who, their mind pleased recollect the departed who have passed away... » But in Papañcasūdanī (2), it is mentioned that the relatives when they are dead, recollect the monk's good qualities and thereby pass away with their mind pleased (Tesaṃ tan ti. Tesaṃ taṃ mayi pasannacittaṃ vā pasannena cittena anussaranaṃ vā).

C 3 = 3 *P :*

---

(1) M.L.S. i, p. 41-42.
(2) i, p. 144. Singalese edition.

C : (29*b*, 2) : « To those who offer me robes, mattresses, food, drink, beds, couches, lotion, medicine, the requisites for life, may they due to these charities obtain great merit, great light (fame), and reap great fruit ».

P : (33, 17–20) : The same. It enumerates as usual cīvara, piṇḍapātasenāsanagilānapaccayabhesajjaparikkhāraṃ. It mentions only great fruit and great benefit.

C 4 = *P* no.

C : (29*b*, 3–4) : « May I be able to bear hunger, thirst, cold, heat, mosquitoes, gad-flies, flies, louse, fleas, oppression of wind and sun, evil words, stick beating. (When) the body suffers disease of acute pain even up to near dying and towards all unpleasant feelings, (may I be able) to bear them all.

C 5 = *P* 5 :

C : (29*b*, 4–5) : « May I be able to endure unpleasantness If unpleasantness happens, may my heart ultimately not to be affected ».

P : (33, 24–26) : « The same. C : unpleasantness = P : aratiratisaho ».

C 6 = *P* 6 :

C : (29, 5) : « May I be able to endure dread and fear. If dread and fear occur, may my heart ultimately not to be affected ».

P : (33, 27–31) : The same. C : dread and fear = P : bhayabherava.

C 7 = *P no.*

C : (29*b*, 6) : « If three evil demeritorious thoughts arise in me, thoughts of desire, of hatred and of harming, ultimately may I be able not to be affected ».

C 8 = *P* 7 :

C : (29*b*, 7) : « May I be able to be aloof from desire, from evil, demeritorious dharmas, up to obtaining the 4th stage of dhyāna and abide by it ».

P : (33, 31–34) : « May I be able to obtain without difficulty, without pain, without trouble, the 4 jhānic stages which are of high mentality and enable me to dwell in happiness here-now ».

C 9 = *P* 9 :

C : (29*b*, 7–8) : « May I be able, with 3 fetters extinguished to obtain the stream-attainer's stage, not fall into evil dharmas, surely to obtain enlightenment, at the utmost to have only 7 becomings in heaven or in human world, and having gone and come 7 times, to put an end to suffering ».

P : (34, 1-3) : Almost the same. C : not to fall into evil dharmas = P : avinipātadhammo. The P omits : and having gone and come 7 times, to put an end to suffering ».

Remarks : For the P term avinipātadhamma, the Chinese translates the term dhamma by *fa* (法), while the meaning here is « is liable to ».

C 10 = *P* 10 :

C : (29*b*, 9) : « With 3 fetters already extinguished, with lust, anger and delusion thinned out, may I be able to go and to come only once to the heaven or to the human world, and after having gone and come once, be able to put an end to suffering ».

P : (34, 4-7) : The same. C : to the world of deities and to the human world = P : imaṃ lokaṃ (this world).

C 11 = *P* 11 :

C : (29*b*, 10) : « May I be able, with 5 fetters binding to the lower world extinguished, to be born in that plane and from there, to attain Nirvāṇa, to obtain non-retrogressive dharma, not to return to this world ».

P : (34, 7-10) : The same. The P adds : opapātiko (to be born spontaneously). C : to obtain non-retrogressive dharma, not to return to this world = P : anāvattidhammo tasmā lokā ».

C 12 = *P* 8 :

C : (29*b*, 10-11) : « May I be able (to realize) the tranquil deliverances, which transcend the corporeal, which obtain the incorporeal, similar (to those obtained in) meditation (?) with the body attained and abided by, to reflect with the help of wisdom, to eradicate cankers, to know cankers ».

P : (33, 33-35) : The P omits : « similar (to those obtained in) meditation » and « to reflect with the help... cankers. » The Pāli uses the term *phassitvā* for the Chinese « *realize* », which is correct as the term phassitvā here has not the meaning of touch as it usually has.

C 13 = *P* 12 + *P* 13 + *P* 14 + *P* 15 + *P* 16 + *P* 17 :

C : (29*b*, 12-13) : « May I be able to obtain the psychic powers, the divine ear, the knowledge of others' mind, the knowledge of previous births, the knowledge about birth and death. May all cankers be extinguished, (the stage of) no cankers be reached and by self-knowledge, by self-enlightenment, by self-realization to attain here-now emancipation of mind, emancipation of wisdom. Birth is destroyed, the brahma-life is established, what should be done is done, there will be no more becoming, true is the knowledge.

P : (34, 10-37 ; 35 ; 36, 1-3) : Here the P treats the same subject, but divides it into 6 wishes. 12th for iddhividhaṃ, 13th for dibbasotañāṇaṃ, 14th for cetopariyañāṇaṃ, 15th for pubbenivāsānussati, 16th for dibbacakkhuñāṇaṃ, 17th for the destruction of all cankers. C : knowledge about birth and death (Cutūpapātañāṇaṃ) = P : dibbacakkhuṃ. These knowledges are described in details in the P version.

P 2 = *C no.*

P : (33, 13-17) : « May I be the one who receives robes, alms-food, dwelling places, medicine for the sick ».

Remark : The 4th wish here is found also in the Lou-chin-ching N° 10, discourse on extinction of cankers, but the first portion in Lou-chin-ching in which a monk exerts himself even up to drying of his body, bones, blood, etc. without giving up his exertion is missing here. It shows that this portion might have been added later on as evidenced by the Pāli passage.

III) *The monks' training and attainment :*

C : (12*b*, 13-16) : « Then those monks having heard the Buddha's speech, well received and well abided by. Then they got up from their seat, bowed down their head at the Buddha's feet, went round him 3 times and departed. Those monks having received this instruction from the Buddha, lived aloof in a secluded place, sat in meditation and engaged in (spiritual) training energetically, with their mind not scattered. Due to their living aloof in a secluded place, their sitting in meditation and engaging in (spiritual) training energetically, with their mind not scattered, by self knowledge, by self-enlightenment, by self-realization, they attained and dwelt in this supreme goal of the brahma-life which sons of clans and families were engaged themselves to, having shaved off beard and hair, donned the yellow robe, given up the home-life, adopted the homeless life and learnt the dharma. Birth was destroyed ; the brahma-life was established ; what should be done was done ; there would be no more becoming. True was the knowledge. Those venerable ones, having known the Dharma attained Arahantship.

P : (36, 4-7) : Not available. Here the P repeats the Buddha's admonition at the beginning of the sutta.

E. — CONCLUSION

As usual in both sūtras.

C. S. N° 6

Chinese : N° 93, *Shui-ching-fan-chih-ching* (水淨梵志經) (Tsê vi, 12b-13b).

Pāli : N° 7, Vatthūpamasutta (T.M.N. i, 36-40).

A. — GIST OF THE C SŪTRA

The Buddha enumerated 21 kinds of defilements and compared a defiled mind with a dirty soiled cloth, an undefiled mind with a clean cloth. Then he pointed out the way to get rid of defilements and explained the practice of 4 brahma-vihārā. After that, the Buddha showed to brāhmaṇa Shui-ching the uselessness of taking bath in the supposed holy water to wash away sins and pointed out that only by doing meritorious actions that evil actions could be eradicated. *P :* Almost the same. Here the Buddha gave the simile of the cloth first, then enumerated 16 kinds of defilements.

B. — TITLES

C : Shui-ching-fan-chih-ching, discourse on brāhmaṇa Shui-ching. for whom the discourse was intended.

P : Vatthūpamasuttaṃ, discourse on the simile of the cloth, which refers to the simile used by the Buddha in his discourse.

C. — LOCATION OF THE SŪTRA

C : Yü-pei-lo (P : Uruvelā), on the bank of river Ni-lien-jan (P : Nerañjarā), under the A-yê-ho-lo-ni-chü-lei tree (P: Ajapālanigrodha).

P : Sāvatthi, Jetavana, Anāthapiṇḍikārāma.

D. — CONTENTS OF THE SŪTRA

I. — *Circumstance leading to the deliverance of the sūtra :*

C : (12*b*, 18-19) : At one time, the Buddha was travelling in Yü-pei-lo, on the bank of river Ni-lien-jan at the root of the A-yeh-ho-lo-ni-chü-lei tree, when he just got enlightenment. At that time, a Shui-ching brāhmaṇa was wandering in the after-noon ; he came to the Buddha's place... The W.H. One on account of brāhmaṇa Shui-ching said to the monks ».

P : (36, 12–14) : No special circumstances. The Buddha called the monks and delivered the discourse.

Remarks : The Chinese mentions here : « When he (the Buddha) just got enlightenment. » We do not know whether this discourse was delivered before the Buddha's going to Bārānasī or after his preaching the first sermon when he returned to Uruvelā to convert the 3 Kassapa brothers.

Shui-ching brāhmaṇa may mean a brāhmaṇa who practises washing away sin by taking bath in the holy water.

II. — *Enumeration of defilements :*

C : (12*b*, 19–20 ; 13*a*, 1–3) : « There are people whose mind is defiled by 21 defilements. They surely come to evil places and are born in the hell. What are the 21 defilements ? 1) wrong view is a defilement of mind, 2) desire for wrong dharma, 3) evil greed, 4) wrong dharma, 5) greed, 6) hatred, 7) sloth and torpor, 8) agitation, remorse, 9) doubt, disbelief, 10) ill-will, fetter of mind, 11) not speaking bondage (Pu-yü-chieh-hsin-wei : 不語結心穢?), 12) stinginess, 13) envy, 14) deceit, fraud, 15) flattery, fawning, 16) shamelessness, 17) unscrupulousness, 18) pride, 19) over-pride, 20) arrogance, 21) negligence is a defilement of mind. If people possess these 21 defilements which defile the mind, they surely come to evil places and are born in the hell.

P : (36, 27–31 ; 37, 1–2) : It mentions only 16 defilements as follows: 1) abhijjhāvisamalobho (greed), 2) byāpādo (ill-will), 3) kodho (anger), 4) upanāho (malevolence), 5) makkho (hypocrisy or depreciation of others' worth), 6) paḷāso (spite), 7) issā (envy), 8) macchariyaṃ (stinginess), 9) māyā (deceit), 10) Sāṭheyyaṃ (fraud), 11) thambho (obduracy), 12) sārambho (impetuosity), 13) māno (pride), 14) atimāno (over-pride), 15) mado-intoxication, conceit), 16) pamādo (negligence).

Remarks : If we compare this list with the list in the Chinese Ch'iu-fa-ching and in the Pāli Dhammadāyādasuttaṃ, we remark that the 2 Chinese lists are not exactly the same (number different, order not the same etc...), while the Pāli lists are the same except that the first defilement here is abhijjhāvisamalobho, while in the other sutta, it is lobho. Thus the Pāli compiler seems to be more systematic, more faithful and more consistent in his compilation.

III. — *Simile of the cloth :*

1) *Dirty cloth :*

C : (13*a*, 2–3) : It is like a dirty soiled cloth taken and given to a dyer. That dyer uses either clean ashes, or washing beans, or soaked earth to wash it thoroughly clean. Although that dirty soiled cloth is washed clean by the dyer, with clean ashes, or with washing beans, or with soaked earth, that soiled cloth still wears its former dirty colour.

P : (36, 15–21) : The P does not mention the dyer washing clean the cloth with various ingredients but it mentions the dyer plunging the soiled cloth in a dye of blue colour, of yellow colour, of red colour, of crimson colour. But the cloth does not take colour because it is stained already.

2) *Clean cloth* :

C : (13*a*, 6–13) : (The C refers to the case of people whose mind is not defiled by the 21 defilements. It is the reverse of the case of people whose mind is defiled by the 21 defilements with proper changes. Then it related the simile of a clean cloth). It is like a white, clean Po-lo-nai (Bārāṇasī) cloth which is taken and given to a dyer. That dyer uses either clean ashes, or washing beans, or soaked earth to wash it thoroughly clean. That white, clean Po-lo-nai cloth is washed clean by the dyer, either with clean ashes or with washing beans, or with soaked earth. Thus that white clean Po-lo-nai cloth which is already clean becomes cleaner.

P : (36, 21–26) : Same differences as seen in the previous simile.

IV. — *Eradication of defilements and its numerous advantages* :

1) *Knowledge of defilements and their eradication* :

C : (13*a*, 13–15) : If he knows that wrong view is a defilement of the mind, having known thus he eradicates wrong view. (In the same way with the other 20 defilements).

P : (37, 9–15) : The same, with the differences only in the defilements as observed before.

2) *Faith in the Triple Gem* :

P : (37, 16–28) : With the eradication of the defilements, there develops faith in the Triple Gem, Buddha, Dhamma and Sangha. Here are enumerated all the qualities of the Triple Gem in a stereotyped way.

C : not available.

3) *Advantages of having faith in the Triple Gem* :

P : (37, 28–37) : With the faith in the Triple Gem, the monk obtains advantages from atthavedaṃ, dhammavedaṃ to pāmujjaṃ, pīti, passaddhakāyo, sukhaṃ, cittaṃ samādhiyati (Knowledge of goal, knowledge of dhamma, delight, joy, composure of body, happiness, concentrated mind).

C : not available.

4) *Advantages of being endowed with such conduct, such merit :*

P : (38, 10-19) : A monk endowed with such a conduct, merit and knowledge, although partaking of rich, luxuriant food will not be adversely influenced, just as a dirty cloth put into clean water becomes clean, just as gold put into smelting pot becomes pure.

C : not available.

5) *Practice of brahmavihārā :*

C : (13, 15-17) : He dwells, suffusing one direction with a mind endowed with benevolence, in the same way the 2nd direction, 3rd direction, 4th direction, 4 intermediate directions, the above, the below, suffusing all over, everywhere, with a mind endowed with benevolence, (which is) without bondage (Chieh : 結 ?), without enmity, without hatred, without quarrel, extremely extensive, excessively big, immeasurable, suffusing it all over the world he well develops it and abides by. In the same way with compassion, sympathetic joy and a mind endowed with equanimity, without bondage, without enmity, without hatred, without quarrel, extremely extensive, excessively big, immeasurable, suffusing it all over the world he well develops it and abides by.

P : (38, 20-30) : Almots the same. C : 4 alternate directions = P : across. C : without bondage, without enmity, without hatred, without quarrel = P: without enmity, without ill-will (averena abyābajjhena). C : extremely extensive, excessively big, immeasurable = P : vipulena, mahaggatena appamāṇena (almost the same with the terms : extremely, excessively omitted). C : he well develops it = P : (missing).

6) *The attainment of Arahantship :*

P : (38, 31-36 ; 39, 1-2) : The Pāli adds also the attainment of Arahantship with the knowledge of idaṃ (arahantship), of hīṇaṃ (defilement, literally inferior) and paṇītaṃ (the means of rejecting defilements, literally superior). Such a knowledge leads to the eradication of the 3 cankers, the destruction of birth, the establishment of holy life, the accomplishment of his duty and the elimination of rebirth.

C : not available.

Remarks : This passage is not found in the Chinese version which contains only one sentence to conclude this paragraph and to serve as opening to the next paragraph. This sentence is as follows : « This is called washing clean the inner mind but not the outer body ». The Pāli writes : « This is called a monk who is bathed with an inner bath ». In this paragraph, the Chinese omission of the faith in the Triple Gem may mean a later interpolation in the Pāli version.

V. — *Intervention of brāhmaṇa Shui-ching and his conversion :*

1) *Intervention of brāhmaṇa Shui-ching :*

C : (13*a*, 17–19) : At that time, the brāhmaṇa said to the W.H. One : « Oh Ch'ü-t'an, please go to To-shui river (P : Bāhukā) to take bath. » The W.H. One asked : « If one comes to To-shui river to take bath, what will he obtain ? » The brāhmaṇa replied : « Oh Ch'ü-t'an, that To-shui river is considered by the people as having cleansing, purifying nature, emancipating nature and merit-giving nature. If anyone comes to To-shui river to take bath, that river will purify and cleanse away all the evils.

P : (39, 3–12) : Here the brāhmaṇa is named Sundarikabhāradvāja. The power attributed to Bāhukā river is : mokkhassammatā (a means for deliverance), puññasammatā (a means for merit), and removing sins. Only here the P mentions the presence of the brāhmaṇa, while the C mentions him already at beginning of the discourse.

2) *The Buddha's reply :* (Please see ante Chapter VII on Gāthā, page 186 from : « Oh Brāhmaṇa Miao Hao Shou to page 187 up to « and took refuge in Buddha, Dhamma, Sangha »).

(Then the prose continues) : Oh W. H. One, I have known, Oh Well Farer, I have understood. Now I will take refuge in the Buddha, Dharma and Sangha. May the W.H. One receive me as a lay disciple. From now on to the end of my body, I will take refuge up to my death ».

P : (39, 26–36 ; 40, 1–8) :

Not exactly the same. Here brāhmaṇa Sundarika Bhāradvāja after listening to the Buddha's explanation exclaimed his wonder and poured forth his praise in the usual way, then he declared his taking refuge in the Triple Gem and asked the Buddha to allow him to adopt the monk's life and receive higher admonition. When all these were granted to him, he exerted himself strenuously in the spiritual training and at the end attained arahantship.

Remarks : Here the moderation of the brāhmaṇa's conversion in the Chinese version is rather significant. May be it is close to the truth when it relates this simple form of conversion secured during the Buddha's time. We remark also that according to the Chinese version, this incident happened when the Buddha recently attained enlightenment ; so the restraint in the Chinese version is appropriate.

E. — CONCLUSION

In the Pāli, there is no conclusion. The discourse stops with the attainment of arahantship of Sundarika-bhāradvājo, while the Chinese has its usual conclusion.

C. S. N° 15

CHINESE : N° 115, *Mi-wan-yü-ching* (蜜丸喩經) (Tsê vi, 35b–37a).
PĀLI : N° 18, Madhupiṇḍikasuttaṃ (T.M.N. i, 108–114) :

A. — GIST OF THE CHINESE SŪTRA

The Buddha said to a Sakyan that his teachings aimed at creating no conflict among the world of Devas and men and at eradicating sense-desire and attachment. Afterwards the Buddha explained in brief to the monks the meaning of his reply to the Sakyan. Then Ven. Ta-chia-chan-yen elaborated the Buddha's speech at the monks' request. Ta-chia-chan-yen's explanations were reported to the Buddha who praised him and approved Ta-chia-chan-yen's explanation. Then the Buddha quoted the simile of a honey ball to the monks.

P : Almost the same but in the Pāli it was Ānanda who quoted the simile of the honey-ball.

B. — TITLES

C : Mi-wan-yü-ching, discourse on the simile of the honey-ball,

P : Madhupiṇḍikasuttaṃ, discourse on the honey-ball.

C. — LOCATION OF THE SŪTRA

C : The Buddha was travelling among the Sakyas, at Chia-wei-lo wei (Kapilavatthu).

P : The same. It adds : in the Nigrodha grove.

D. — CONTENTS OF THE SŪTRA

I. — *Meeting of the Buddha with the Sakyan :*

1) *Encounter of the Buddha and the sakyan's question :*

C : (35*b*, 15–17) : At that time, the W. H. One, when night was over, in the morning, put on the robe, took the begging bowl, and entered Chia-wei-lo-wei for alms. Having finished his meal, in the after-noon, having put back bowl and robe, washed feet and hands, he put the sitting mat on his shoulder, went to the Sakyan Bamboo grove temple, entered that Great Forest, came to a tree, spread his sitting mat and sat down cross-legged. At that time, a stick-in-hand Sakyan went about leaning on a stick ; in the after-noon, he wandered about, came to the Buddha's place, exchanged greetings with him, stood leaning on the stick before the Buddha and asked the W. H. One : « Oh recluse Ch'ü-t'an, what are your fundamental principles ? What doctrine have you preached ?

P : (108, 14-27) : Almost the same. It omits : « The night was over, put back bowl and robe, and washed feet and hands ; he put the sitting mat on his shoulder, the Sakyan Bamboo grove monastery, he spread his sitting mat ». It adds : Divāvihārāya (for the day's rest) ; Beluvalaṭṭhikāya mūle divāvihāraṃ (nisīdi). Here the Sakyan asked the Buddha : « What is your teaching, what have you preached ?

2) *The Buddha's reply and the Sakyan's reaction :*

C : (35*b*, 17-19) : The W. H. One replied : « Oh Sakya, in all the worlds with its deities, māra, brahmā, recluses and brāhmaṇas, from men to deities, to prevent from fighting, quarrelling, to cultivate, to practise the desire-free and pure brahma-life ; to get rid of flattery and crookedness, to remove remorse, not to have attachment, not to have perception of becoming, of non-becoming. This is my fundamental principle, this is what I preached ». Then the stick-in-hand Sakyan, having heard the Buddha's words, did not approve, did not reject, raised his head and went away.

P : (108 27-33 ; 100, 1-2) : Almost the same. C : to prevent from fighting, from quarrelling = P : not to have contention with anyone in the world. C : to train to be aloof from desires = P : kāmehi visaṃyuttaṃ. C : to cultivate, to practise the desire-free and pure brahma-life = P : viharantaṃ taṃ brāhmaṇaṃ. C : to remove remorse = P : akathaṃkathiṃ chinnakukkuccaṃ (having no doubt, with remorse cut off). C : not to have attachment, grasping, not to have perception of becoming, of non-becoming = P : bhavābhave vītataṇhaṃ saññā nānusenti (no craving for becoming and non-becoming). The P omits : to get rid of flattery and crookedness. As to the reaction of the Sakyan, the P omits : did not approve, did not reject. It adds : lolling his tongue, with his brow lined up with 3 wrinkles and leaning on the stick.

II. — *The Buddha's explanation of his reply to the Sakyan :*

C : (35*b*, 19-20 ; 36*a*, 1-7) : « Then the W.H. One, when the stick-in-hand Sakyan had gone not for a long time, in the evening, got up from his meditation-seat, came to the preaching hall, in front of the monks, spread his seat, sat down and said to the monks : « To-day, in the morning, I donned the robe... (as above with the Buddha replaced by I, up to)... shook his head and went away. » Then one monk got up from his seat, wore his robe showing bare one shoulder, joined his hands towards the Buddha and said : « Oh W.H. One, what is (the meaning of) : « In all the worlds.,. and non-becoming ? » The W.H. One said : « Oh monks, there is a man who, due to thinking, goes forth from home, learns the dharma, ponders and trains himself. He does not crave for, does not delight in, is not attached to, does not dwell in Dharmas of the past, future, present. This is called the end of suffering. Fetter of desires, fetter of hatred, fetter of becoming, fetter of pride, fetter of ignorance, fetter of views, fetter of doubts, fight and quarrel, dislike and envy, flattery and fawning, fraud and deceit, telling lies, double tongues, and innumerable evil, demeritorious dharmas. This is called the end of suffering. » Having said thus, the Buddha got up from his seat, entered the house and sat in meditation.

P : (109, 34-47; 110, 1-5) : The P interpretation is somewhat different : « If from any cause, a number of obstructing perception (papañcasaññāsaṅkhā) lay hold on a man, if there is neither delight (abhinanditabbaṃ), nor response (abhivaditabbaṃ), nor clinging (ajjhositabbaṃ) in him, then this is an end of tendencies of lust, malevolence, view, doubt, pride, attachment to, becoming, ignorance (rāga-paṭigha-diṭṭhi-vicikicchā-māna-bhavarāga-avijjānusayaṃ), this is also an end to taking up stick, taking up sword, to quarrel, to dispute, to contention, to strife, to back-biting, to lies, all these evil demeritorious dharmas are destroyed without a remainder ».

III. — *The monks' request to Ven. Ta-chia-chan-yen and the latter's explanation :*

1) *The monks' request :*

C : (36*a*, 7-16): Then the monks thought thus: « Rev. fr., (you) should know. The W.H. One spoke in brief of this meaning, did not analyse it in details, then got up from his seat, entered the house and sat in meditation. « There is a man who due... this is called the end of suffering ». They again thought: « Rev. Fr., who is able to analyse in details the meaning spoken in brief by the W.H. One and by the learned brahma-farers ? Ven. Ta-chia-chan-yen is able to analyse in details the meaning spoken in brief by the W.H. One. Let the Rev. Fr. come together to Ven. Ta-chia-chan-yen's place and request him to explain this meaning. And what Ven. Ta-chia-chan-yen will analyse, we shall well keep in mind ». Then the monks came to Ven. Ta-chia-chan-yen's place, exchanged greetings with him, sat on one side and said : « Ven. Ta-chia-chan-yen should know ! The W. H. One spoke in brief this meaning and did not analyse it in details, got up from his seat, entered the house and sat in meditation : « If there is a man who... this is called the end of suffering. » We then thought : « Rev. fr., who is able... Ven. Ta-chia-chan-yen is able to analyse in details, the meaning spoken in brief by the W. H. One. » May Ven. Ta-chia-chan-yen, out of compassion, explain it in details ! Then Ven. Ta-chia-chan-yen said : « Rev. fr., please listen to my parable. The wise man, having listened to the parable realized its meaning ».

P : (110, 6-37 ; 111, 1-5) : Almost the same with the same differences seen in the precedent paragraph.

2) *Ven. Ta-chia-chan-yen's simile:*

C : (36*a*, 16-20) : « Rev. fr., suppose a man who wants to go in search of a pith. For the sake of seeking the pith, he takes an axe and enters the forest. He sees a big tree which has roots, branches, knots, stems, leaves, flowers, fruits. He does not touch roots, branches, knots, fruits but touches only stems, leaves. Rev. fr., your talk is like that. You left the W. H. One and approached me to ask this meaning. Why is it so ? Rev fr., should know ! the W. H. One is the eye, is knowledge, is meaning, is Dharma, Lord of Dharma, Captain of Dharma ; the W. H. One expounds meaning of real truth, shows the meaning of everything. Rev. fr., (you) should go to the W. H. One's place and ask this meaning : « Oh W H. One, what is this ? what is the meaning of this ? According to what the W. H. One speaks, Rev. fr., (you) should well accept and bear (in mind) ».

P : (111, 6-7) : The simile is the same, but details are different. It omits : taking an axe, entering the forest, stems, flowers, fruits and mentions only that « a man who is in need of a pith, in search of a pith, looking for a pith, comes up to a big tree with pith. But he bypasses the root, the trunk and thinks that the pith is to be found among branches and foliage. Thus is what you have done The Master is before you, yet you bypass him, thinking to ask me for this meaning. » Here the P is more prolix in its praise of the Buddha : « He knows what should be known, he sees what should be seen, he is endowed with eyes, with knowledge, with Dhamma, with Brahmā, the speaker (vattā), the expounder (pavattā), the guide to the meaning (atthassa ninnetā), the Giver of the Deathless (amatassa dātā), the Lord of Dhamma (Dhammassāmī), the Tathāgata » Then he advised the monks that it was time to approach the Buddha and ask the meaning of this sermon, and what the Buddha explained, the monks should bear it in mind.

3) *The monks' insistence :*

C : (36*a*, 20 ; 36*b*, 1-2) : At that time, the monks said : « Yes, Ven. Ta-chia-chan-yen, the W H. One is the eye, is knowledge, is meaning, is Dharma, Captain of Dharma ; the W. H One expounds meaning of real truth, shows the meaning of everything. We should go to the W. H. One and ask this meaning. What the W. H. One has spoken, we should bear in mind. But Ven. Ta-chia-chan-yen was praised by the W. H. One and by the learned brahma-farers. Ven. Ta-chia-chan-yen is able to analyse in details the meaning spoken in brief by the W. H. One. May Ven. Ta-chia-chan-yen out of compassion explain it in details ».

P : (111, 17-29) : Almost the same, with the same differences as seen in the preceding paragraph.

4) *Ven. Ta-chia-chan-yen's explanation :*

C : (36*b*, 2-17): Ven Ta-chia-chan-yen said to the monks : « Rev. fr., listen to what I shall speak. With eyes and material forms as conditions, eye-consciousness arises. When the 3 things come together then there is touch. Conditioned by touch, feelings arise. What one feels, one perceives. What one perceives, one thinks ; what one thinks one formulates ideas ; what one formulates ideas, one discriminates. The monks due to these ideas, go forth from home, learn the dharmas, well ponder over and practise them. Towards the past, the future and the present dharmas, there will be no craving for, no delight in, no attachment to, no dwelling in ; this is called the end of suffering. Fetter of desire, fetter of hatred, fetter of becoming, fetter of pride, fetter of ignorance, fetter of views, fetter of doubts, fight and quarrel, dislike and envy, flattery and fawning, fraud and deceit, speaking lies, double tongue and innumerable evil and demeritorious dharmas, this is called the end of suffering (In the same way with the other faculties). Rev. fr., with eyes removed, material forms removed, eye consciousness removed, touch cannot arise, touch cannot come into being; when touch does not arise, feelings cannot arise ; if feelings do not arise, (here thoughts are omitted) there is no possibility of ideas to arise, of going forth from home, of learning the doctrine, of pondering over and of practice (in the same way with the other faculties with their respective objects and consciousness). Rev. fr., due to eyes, due to material forms, due to eye-consciousness, there is possibility of the rise of touch. Due to the rise of touch, there is possibility of the rise of feelings. Due to the rise of feelings, there is possibility of the rise of ideas, of going forth from home, of learning the doctrine, of pondering over, and of practice (In the same way with the other faculties with their respective objects and consciousnesses). Rev. fr., this is called the W. H. One speaking of this meaning in brief, not analysing it in details ; then he got up from his seat, entered the house and sat in meditation. The monks, due to ideas, go forth from home, learn the doctrine, well ponder over and practise. Towards dharmas of the past... this is called the end of suffering Rev. fr., this meaning which the W. H. One has spoken in an abridged form, not analysed it in details, I have used these sentences, these contexts to explain it in details. Thus Rev. fr., please go to the Buddha and report all (to him). What meaning is explained by the Buddha, you should bear it in mind ».

P : (111, 36-38; 112; 113, 1-7): Almost the same. C: thoughts arise = P : vitakketi ; C : Ideas arise = P: papañceti ; C: from ideas arises distinction = P: yaṃ papañceti tato nidānaṃ purisaṃ papañca-saññāsaṅkhā samudācaranti atītānāgatapaccuppannesu cakkhuviññeyyesu rūpesu (What obsesses one is the cause of a number of perceptions and obsessions which lay hold on a man's attitude towards past, future, present mental objects cognisable by mind. (In the same way with the other faculties). The other differences are almost the same as seen in the precedent paragraph. At the end, elder Mahākaccāna asked the monks if they desired to approach the Enlightened One and ask the same meaning, and he advised them to bear in mind what the Enlightened One had spoken ».

IV. — *The Monks' report to the Buddha and the latter's praise :*

1) *The monk's report :*

C : (36*b*, 17–19) : Then the monks, having heard Ven. Ta-chia-chan-yen's speech, well received, kept in mind and recited, got up from their seat, went round Ven. Ta-chia-chan-yen 3 times and departed. They came to the Buddha's place, bowed down their head to pay respect, sat on one side and said : « This meaning was spoken in brief but not in details by the W.H. One, who then got up from his seat and entered the house and sat in meditation, Ven. Ta-chia-chan-yen has taken these sentences, these contexts to explain it in details ».

P : (113, 8–37 ; 114, 1–3) : Almost the same, with the same differences as seen in the precedent paragraph. Here the P mentions only that these monks were delighted and rejoiced at Mahākaccāna's speech. Then they reported his explanations to the Buddha.

2) *The Buddha's praise :*

C : (36*b*, 19–20) : The W.H. One having heard (this) uttered praises saying : « Very good, indeed, very good indeed : My disciple possesses eyes, possesses knowledge, possesses dharma, possesses meaning. Why is it so ? Because what the Master explained in brief to the disciples, the meaning of which was not analysed in details, the disciple used such a sentence, such a context in order to explain it in details. In what way Ta-chia-chan-yen has told you, in that way you should receive and bear in mind. Why is it so ? If we take the speech and see its meaning, it should be like this ».

P : (114, 3–7) : Almost the same. The Buddha praise Mahākaccāna as mahāpaṇḍita and mahāpañña. And he said that if the monks asked him this question he would reply in the same way as Mahākaccāna had done.

V. — *Simile of the honey-ball :*

C : 36*b*, 20 ; 37*a*, 1–2) : « Oh monks, just as a man who is going through a troublefree place, among the trees, suddenly obtains a honey-ball ; from whatever morsel he eats, he would get the taste of it. In the same way, the son of clans, of families towards this dharma and vinaya of mine, whatever he reflects upon, he would get the taste of if. Reflecting upon the eye, he obtains the taste. Reflecting upon the ear, nose, tongue, body, mind, he obtains the taste ».

P : (114, 8–14) : In the P, it was elder Ānanda who quoted the simile to illustrate the Buddha's teachings. The simile is slightly different : « A man overcome by hunger and exhaustion obtains a honey-ball, and whatever morsel he eats he gets the sweet and savourous taste ». The P replaces the son of clans, of families by a monk who is intelligent. C : towards that dharma-vinaya of mine = P: towards that dhamma-pariyāya that is what the Buddha just preached. The P drops: reflecting upon the eye, he obtains the taste, reflecting upon ear, nose, tongue, body, mind he obtains the taste.

VI. — *Name of the sūtra :*

C : (37*a*, 2-3): At that time, Ven. A-nan was attending upon the Buddha with a whisk of hair. Then Ven. A-nan joined his hands towards the Buddha and said: « Oh W. H. One, what is the name of this dharma ? How do we respect and abide by? Then the W. H. One spoke to the monks: « Oh A-nan, this dharma is called the simile of the honey-ball ; thus you should respect and abide by ».

P : (114, 13-15): Here elder Ānanda asked the same question and the Buddha gave the name as « Madhupiṇḍikapariyāya ».

VII. — *The Buddha's exhortation : (While the Pāli version ends here, the C adds this exhortation of the Buddha) :*

C : (37*a*, 3-4): Then the W. H. One spoke to the monks: « Having received that dharma of the simile of the honey-ball, you should recite it, intone it, read it. Why is it so? Oh monks, this sūtra of the simile of the honey-ball possesses dharma, possesses meaning, is the foundation of the religious life, leading to psychic attainment, to enlightenment, to Nirvāṇa. If there are sons of clans, of families who shave off hair and beard, don the yellow robe, out of faith have gone forth from home to the homeless life, to learn the dharma, they should well receive and abide by that simile of the honey-ball ».

E. — CONCLUSION

While the Pāli mentions only elder Ānanda rejoicing at the Blessed One's speech, the C adds the monks as well.

C. S. N° 17

CHINESE : N° 101, *Tsêng-shang-hsin-ching* (增上心經) (Tsê vi, 23a-24a).

PĀLI : N° 20, Vitakkasanthānasutta (T.M N. i, 118-122) :

A. — GIST OF THE CHINESE SŪTRA

The Buddha told the monks that to obtain high and noble thoughts, the monk should frequently exert his mind according to the 5 following methods : 1) to turn his mind from one characteristic to another, 2) to meditate upon the dangers of demeritorious thoughts, 3) to avoid thinking of demeritorious thoughts, 4) to reflect over, act upon and gradually reduce these thoughts, 5) to train, to subdue the mind with the mind.

P : Almost the same. The 4th method is slightly different.

B. — TITLES

C : Tsêng-shang-hsin-ching : Discourse on high and noble thoughts.

P : Vitakkasanthānasutta, discourse on the origin of thoughts.

C. — PLACES OF OCCURRENCE

The same in both versions : Sāvatthi, Jetavana, Anāthapiṇḍikārāma.

D. — CONTENTS OF THE SŪTRAS

I. — *How to obtain high and noble thoughts :*

C : (23*a*, 10-11) : « At that time, the W H. One said to the monks : « If a monk wants to obtain high and noble thoughts, he should frequently reflect upon 5 characteristics. By frequently reflecting upon 5 characteristics, demeritorious thoughts which have already arisen, cease ; demeritorious thoughts having ceased, his mind becomes fixed, innerly tranquil, oneminded and concentrated.

P : (119, 3-4) : Almost the same C : high and noble thoughts = P : adhicittaṃ. C : characteristics = P : nimittaṃ. It omits : « By frequently reflecting... concentrated ».

II. — *The first characteristic :*

1) *Turning the mind from one characteristic to another characteristic :*

C : (23*a*, 11–16) : What are the five? The monk reflects upon a characteristic, which is meritorious ; if demeritorious thoughts arise due to this characteristic, he should reflect upon another meritorious characteristic different from this characteristic so that evil, demeritorious thoughts do not arise. Due to his reflection upon another meritorious characteristic different from this characteristic, demeritorious thoughts which have already arisen cease. Demeritorious thoughts having ceased... (as above)... and concentrated.

P : (119, 5–14) : In the P version, the characteristic is mentioned simply as nimittan, not meritorious as in the C. The evil thoughts which arise are enumerated as pāpaka akusalā vitakkā chandūpasaṃhitā dosūpasaṃhitā pi mohūpasaṃhitā pi (evil demeritorious thoughts associated with desire, malevolence and delusion). The inner thoughts, with the destruction of demeritorious thoughts are described as: ajjhattaṃ eva cittaṃ santiṭṭhati, sannisīdati, ekodi hoti samādhiyati (the inner mind steadies, becomes tranquil, onepointed and concentrated).

2) *Simile to illustrate the first characteristic :*

C : (23*a*, 13) : It is like a carpenter or a carpenter's apprentice who with an ink-string draws a line on the wood. Then he uses a sharp axe and chops off the wood, making it straight.

P : (119, 14–16) : Not exactly the same. The P refers also to a carpenter or a carpenter's apprentice, but adds the expression dakkho (skilful). It mentions here that this carpenter or carpenter's apprentice knocks out, drives out a bigger peg with the help of a smaller one.

Remarks : Here the P simile is more appropriate while the C repeats the simile of *C. S. N°* 8, in the paragraph of contemplation of the body.

III. — *The 2nd characteristic :*

a) *Considering demeritorious thoughts as evil :*

C : (23*a*, 16–18) : « Again the monk reflects upon a characteristic which is meritorious; if demeritorious thoughts arise, he should consider these thoughts as evil, these thoughts are despised by the wise ; one endowed with these thoughts fully and abundantly cannot obtain enlightenment, cannot obtain Nirvāṇa, because they cause evil, demeritorious thoughts to arise. » Having contemplated these (thoughts) as evil, then demeritorious thoughts, which have already arisen cease. Demeritorious thoughts having ceased... (as above).

P : (119, 27–35) : Almost the same. Here the P says clearly that if he turns his mind to meritorious thoughts, but still demeritorious thoughts arise, then the monk is asked to consider the dangers of these thoughts, that they are demeritorious, blamable and are of painful results.

b) ***The simile :***

C : (23*a*, 18–19) : It is like a young man, of good manners, lovely, who has taken his bath and his wash, dons clean, pure clothes, with body smeared with perfume, with hair and beard well-groomed, extremely clean and pure. Suppose he takes a dead serpent, a dead dog, a dead human body, which is partly eaten, of bluish colour, swollen, festering, cracking, with loathsome liquid pouring out, and puts it round his neck, then he would become disgusted, revolted, not pleased and not happy.

P : (119, 36–37; 120, 1–3) : Almost the same. Here the P mentions the case of a woman or a man or young man, who is fond of ornaments, and omits all the other details. It mentions only the corpse of a serpent, a dog or of a dead body, hanging round the neck but omits all the other details. C : he then would become disgusted, revolted, not pleased and not happy= P : he would revolt, be depressed and disgusted ».

IV. — *The 3rd characteristic :*

a) ***Not to consider these thoughts :***

C : (23*b*, 2–3) : Again when the monk reflects upon meritorious characteristic but demeritorious thoughts arise ; when he reflects upon the dangers, again demeritorious thoughts arise, this monk should not reflect upon these thoughts which cause the arising of demeritorious thoughts. By not reflecting upon these thoughts, demeritorious thoughts which have arisen cease. Demeritorious thoughts having ceased... (as above)... and concentrated.

P : (120, 4–10) : It is almost the same. Here the Pāli uses the expression : « Vitakkānaṃ asati-amanasikāro. »

b) ***A simile :***

C : (23*b*, 3–4) : It is like a man with eyes, who does not want to look at the material forms which are in open daylight. He either shuts his eyes or turns his body away. What do you think ? Although material forms are in open daylight, does that man receive the image of material forms ? (The monks) replied : « No, he cannot. »

P : (120, 10–14) : Almost the same. C : turns his body away = P : he looks to another direction. C : in open daylight = P : in his vision. And it omits the last portion about the question : What do you think... he cannot.

V. — *The 4th characteristic :*

a) *Reflecting over the process of thoughts and gradually reduce these thoughts :*

C : (23*b*, 6–8) : Again even when the monk reflects upon meritorious characteristic, demeritorious thoughts arise, when (the monk) reflects upon the dangers of thoughts, again demeritorious thoughts arise ; when (the monk) does not reflect upon the thoughts, again demeritorious thoughts arise, this monk should ponder over and act upon it and gradually reduce his thoughts, so that demeritorious thoughts which have already arisen cease. Demeritorious thoughts having ceased... (as above)... concentrated.

P : (120, 15–21) : Slightly different. The P mentions only that although the monk does not reflect, does not keep in mind these thoughts, still evil demeritorious mental states keep arising, then he should reflect over the process and the origin of these thoughts (vitakkasaṅkhārasanthānaṃ).

b) *A simile :*

C : (23*b*, 8–10) : It is like a man walking quickly on the road, he thinks : « Why should I walk so fast, now I should walk slowly. » Then he walks slowly. Again he thinks : « Why should I walk slowly, it is better to stop. » Then he stops. Again he thinks : « Why should I stop, it is better to sit down. » Then he sits down. Again he thinks : « Why should I sit down, it is better to lie down. » Then he lies down. Thus that man gradually stops the coarse posture of his body.

P : (120, 22 32) : Almost the same. Only the final sentence is slightly different and is as follows : « Thus this man gets rid of coarse posture and keeps up with smooth, easy posture. »

VI. — *The 5th characteristic :*

a) *Controlling the mind :*

C : (23*b*, 13–16) : Again, even when the monk reflects upon meritorious characteristic, still demeritorious thoughts arise ; when... ponders, acts upon and gradually reduces the thoughts, again demeritorious thoughts arise. Then this monk should reflect thus : « Due to these thoughts, demeritorious thoughts arise. » Then this monk should set teeth upon teeth, press his tongue upon the upper palate, he uses his mind to cultivate his mind, he restrains, holds on, subdues so that evil, demeritorious thoughts do not arise.

P : (120, 33–37 ; 121, 1–5) : Almost the same. The P uses these expressions : cetasā cittaṃ abhiniggaṇhitabbaṃ abhinippīḷetabbaṃ abhisantāpetabbaṃ (to check, to subdue, to overpower).

b) *A simile :*

C : (23*b*, 16–18) : It is like 2 wrestlers who catch hold of a weak man, they restrain, hold on and subdue him.

P : (121, 5–7) : Almost the same. It mentions about a strong man who takes hold of the head or the shoulders of a weak man and checks, subdues and overpowers him.

VII. — *Summing up :*

C : (23*b*, 18–20 ; 24*a*, 1) : If a monk wants to obtain high and noble thoughts, he should frequently ponder over these 5 characteristics. If he ponders over these 5 characteristics, then arising demeritorious thoughts will cease. With the cessation of the arising demeritorious thoughts, his mind becomes fixed, inwardly tranquil, oneminded and concentrated. When the monk ponders over meritorious characteristics, evil thoughts do not arise ; when he ponders over the dangers of thoughts, evil thoughts also do not arise ; when he ponders over, acts upon and gradually reduces these thoughts, evil thoughts also do not arise ; when he trains his mind with his mind, restrains, holds on and subdues it, evil thoughts also do not arise, then he obtains mastery over himself. If he wants to think, he thinks ; if he does not want to think, he does not think. If a monk can think if he wants to think, does not think when he does not want to think, then that monk is called controller of thoughts, a master of the process of thoughts.

P : (121, 18–37 ; 122, 1–3) : The summing up in the P version is almost the same with that of the C version ; but the last portion presents some differences : C : is called a controller of thoughts, a master of thoughts = P : he is master in the method and in the path of thoughts (Vasī vitakkapariyāyapathesu). It adds : « He has destroyed craving, removed fetters, fully subdued pride and put an end to suffering).

E. — CONCLUSIONS

Both versions have their usual conclusion.

C. S. N° 22

CHINESE : N° 204, *Lo-mo-ching* (羅摩經) (Tsê, vii, 73b-76b).
PĀLI : N° 26, Ariyapariyesanasutta (T.M.N. i, 160-175).

A. — GIST OF THE C SŪTRA

The Buddha advised the monks when they met together either to discuss about the dharma or to keep silent. Then he explained the ariyan quest, the unariyan quest and he related his own life of ariyan quest, from the moment he approached the 2 sages for initiation into the dharma up to his preaching his first sermon at Bārāṇasī to the 5 monks. Further he explained the 5 objects of sense-desires and depicted 2 attitudes of 2 kinds of people towards them.

P : Almost the same, with some differences in the accounts of the Buddha's life.

B. — TITLE

C : Lo-mo-ching, the Lo-mo discourse, Lo-mo being the name of the brāhmaṇa in whose house the Buddha preached the discourse.

P : Ariyapariyesanasutta : discourse on the Ariyan quest, which refers to the explanation given by the Buddha about the ariyan quest. Pāli has also the title Pāsarāsisutta.

C. — LOCATION OF THE SŪTRA

C : The Buddha was travelling in Shê-wei (and staying) at Lu-tẓu-mu at (Migāra's mother) palace. Toward evening, he went with Ven. A-nan to A-i-lo-p'o-t'i river (Aciravatī) to take bath. From there, they proceeded to Lo-mo's house where the Buddha delivered the discourse.

P : The Buddha was staying in Sāvatthi, in Jetavena at Anāthapiṇḍika's monastery. Then he went to Pubbārāma Migāramātu palace for a day rest. From there, he went to Pubbakoṭṭhaka to bathe his limbs, then at the request of Elder Ānanda, he proceeded to Rammaka's house, met the monks and delivered the discourse.

D. — CONTENTS OF THE SŪTRA

I. — *Circumstances leading to the deliverance of the discourse :*

1) *The Buddha's going to take bath :*

C : (73*b*, 14–17) : At one time the Buddha was travelling in Shê-wei and (staying) at the Eastern Park, the Lu-tzu-mu palace. At that time, the W. H. One towards the evening, rose from his meditation seat, came down from the upper palace and said to Ven. A-nan : « Now I shall go with you to A-i-lo-p'o-t'i to take bath. » Ven. A-nan replied : « Yes, (the W. H. One). » Ven. A-nan in the afternoon took out a key, went wandering to many houses (or huts) saw the monks and said : « Your reverences should go to the brāhmaṇa Lo-mo's house. » The monks having heard thus went together to brāhmaṇa Lo-mo's house. The W.H. One went with Ven. A-nan to A-i-lo-p'o-t'i river, took off the (upper) garment on the bank and entered the river to take bath. Having finished bathing, he came out, wiped dry the body and donned his robe.

P : (160, 16-32 ; 161, 1-10) : Not exactly the same. The P starts with the Buddha staying at Sāvatthi in Jetavana at Anāthapiṇḍika's monastery. Then the Buddha entered Sāvatthi for alms. Many monks came to Elder Ānanda telling him that they wanted to hear a discourse from the Buddha face to face, as for a long time, they had no such occasion. Elder Ānanda then asked them to go to Brāhmaṇa Rammaka's house. When the Buddha came back from his begging round and finished his meal, he with Elder Ānanda went to Pubbārāma at Migāramātu's palace for the day's rest. In the evening, the Buddha rose from his seclusion and with Elder Ānanda went to Pubbakoṭṭhaka to bathe his limbs. Having bathed his limbs, the Buddha came out of the water, stood with a single cīvara, drying his limbs.

2) *Elder Ānanda's request to go to Brāhmaṇa Rammaka's house :*

C : (73*b*, 17-18) : At that time Ven. A-nan stood behind the W.H. One and fanned him with a fan. Then Ven. A-nan joined his hands towards the Buddha and said : « Oh W.H. One, the house of Brāhmaṇa Lo-mo is extremely well arranged, very lovely and pleasant. May the W.H. One, out of compassion, come to Brāhmaṇa Lo-mo's house. » The W.H. One for the sake of Ven. A-nan accepted by remaining silent. Then the W. H. One along with Ven. A-nan went to Brāhmaṇa Lo-mo's house.

P : (161, 10-16) : Almost the same. The P omits Elder Ānanda standing behind the Buddha and fanning him with a fan. Elder Ānanda praised Rammaka's house as « not far, pleasant, lovely. »

C : house. P : assamo (hermitage).

3) *The Buddha's meeting with the monks :*

C : (73*b*, 18–19 ; 74*a*, 1–3) : At that time, at Brāhmana Lo-mo's house, a great number of monks assembled and discussed about the dharma. The Buddha stood outside the door, waiting for the monks to finish discussing the dharma. This great number of monks finished discussing about the dharma and remained silent. The W. H. One knew (it), coughed and knocked at the door. The monks having heard, came to open the door. Then the W. H. One entered Brāhmaṇa Lo-mo's house, and in front of the monks, spread his seat, sat down and asked the monks : « Oh monks, what are you discussing about ? For what purpose did you assemble and sit here ». Then the monks replied : « W. H. One hitherto (we) are discussing about the dharma. For that dharma work, we assemble and sit there. » The W.H. One praised saying : « Very good, very good, the monks when they assemble should either discuss about the dharma or keep silent. »

P : (161, 17–33) : Almost the same. C : in front of the monks, the Buddha spread his seat and sat down = P : he sat down on the prepared seat. C : for what purpose did you assemble and sit here = P : what was your conversation that was interrupted. C : for that dharma work that we assembled here = P : our dharma conversation with reference to the Blessed One was interrupted with the arrival of the Blessed One. C : to keep silent P = to keep the ariyan silence.

II. — *Two kinds of quest :*

1) *The unariyan quest :*

C : (74*a*, 3–8) : There are 2 quests : one is the ariyan quest, one is the unariyan quest. What is the unariyan quest ? There are people who are really liable to disease and seek what are liable to disease, really liable to old age, to death, to sorrow, to grief, to despair, really liable to blemishes and seek what are liable to blemishes. What are really liable to disease and seek what are liable to disease ? What are liable to disease ? Children, brothers are liable to disease ; elephants, horses, cows, goats, women-slaves, riches and properties, jewels and precious stones, crops, are liable to disease, to dangers. Living beings are enamoured of, addicted and attached to them, become proud and engrossed in them, do not see (their) dangers, do not know the way of escape (from them) but grasp and make use of them. What are the matters liable to old age, to death, to sorrow, to grief, to despair, liable to blemishes ? (same as above) up to... but grasp and make use of them ? Those people, if they want to seek the diseaseless, the supreme peacefulness, Nirvāṇa, are not likely to obtain the diseaseless, the supreme peacefulness, Nirvāṇa, seek the ageless, deathless, sorrowless, griefless, despairless, blemishless, the supreme peacefulness, Nirvāṇa are not likely to obtain the blemishless, the supreme peacefulness, Nirvāṇa. This is called the unariyan quest.

P : (161, 34-37 ; 162, 1-35) : Almost the same. These differences are to be noted : C : liable to disease, to old age, to death, to sorrow, to grief, to despair, to blemishes = P : liable to birth, to old age, to disease, to death, to sorrow, to blemishes. C : what are liable to disease ? Children, brothers, elephants, horses, cows, goats, women-slaves, riches and properties, jewels and precious stones, crop = P : sons and wives, women-slaves and men slaves, goats and sheep, cocks and pigs, elephants, cows, horses, mares. C : living beings are enamoured of, addicted and attached to them, become proud and engrossed in them, do not see (their) dangers, do not know the way of escape while making use of them = P : these graspings (upadhayo) are liable to birth, but this (man) is tied, infatuated, attached to them, being himself liable to birth seek what are liable to birth. The Pāli omits : « These people, if they want to seek the diseaseless... Nirvāṇa ».

2) *The ariyan quest :*

C : (74*a*, 8-11) : « What is the ariyan quest ? There is some one who sets himself thinking : « I am really liable to disease, why should I foolishly seek what are liable to disease ? I am really liable to old age... to blemishes, why should I foolishly seek what are liable to old age... to blemishes ? What if now I seek the diseaseless, the supreme peacefulness, Nirvāṇa, seek the ageless... the supreme peacefulness, Nirvāṇa, is likely to obtain the ageless... the supreme peacefulness, Nirvāṇa.

P : (162, 36-37; 163, 1-8) : Almost the same with the same differences as noted in the preceding paragraphs. The P here is very simple : someone being liable to birth, knows the dangers of what is liable to birth, seeks the unborn, the supreme release from attachment, Nirvāṇa (the same way with the rest).

III. — *Reminiscences of the past :*

(Please see ante chapter V Accounts of the Buddha's life page 153 from a) going forth... to page 159 up to : Pāli : (173, 2-20)... the rest is almost the same).

IV. — *The five objects of sense-desire :*

1) 5 *objects of sense-desire :*

C : (75*b*, 10-11) : Then the W. H. One spoke : « Oh five monks ! there are five objects of sense-desire which are pleasant, agreeable, to be remembered by the mind, well connected with sense-desire. What are these five ? Forms cognisable by the eyes, sound cognisable by the ears, smell cognisable by the nose, taste cognisable by the tongue, touch cognisable by the body.

P : (173, 21-26) : Almost the same. « Oh monks, there are five objects of sense-desire : material forms cognised by the eyes, which are pleasant, lovely, charming, enticing, connected with desire, alluring... (the same with sounds up to touch).

2) *Attitude of the worldling :*

C : (75*b*, 11-13): « Oh five monks, the ignorant worldly beings, unlearned, who do not frequent meritorious friends, who do not know the ariyan norm, who are not trained in the ariyan dharma, become enamoured, infatuated, attached, are proud, enjoy them, do not see their danger, do not see the way of escape (from them) and make use of them. You should know that these people follow Māra the evil one, and themselves become the evil Māra, fall into the hands of Māra, are trapped into Māra's net, are caught in Māra's trap, are not able to get free from Māra's trap.

P : (173, 26-30): Not exactly the same. « Oh monks, those recluses, brāhmaṇas who indulge in five objects of sense-desire, not seeking their danger, not realizing the way of escape from desire, are infatuated, addicted to them, these people should be understood to have fallen into misfortune, into ruin, they are dealt with by the Evil One as he wishes.

3) *Simile :*

C : (75*b*, 13-15): « Oh five monks, it is like a wild deer which is caught in a trap. You should know, this deer follows the hunter, will be dealt with by the hunter, will fall into the hunter's hands, is caught in the hunter's trap, and when the hunter comes, it cannot get itself free. Thus « Oh five monks, it is the same with the ignorant wordling. . . (as above). . . from Māra's trap ».

P : (173, 30-35) : Almost the same : « Just like a forest deer which is caught in a snare, it should be understood that it has fallen into misfortune, into ruin, it is done by the hunter as he wishes ; when the hunter comes, it cannot go away where it wishes. »

4) *Attitude of the learned ariyan disciple and simile :*

C : (75*b*, 15-20) : This passage is the reverse of the previous C passage of the unlearned worldling.

P : (173, 35-37 ; 174, 1-8) : This passage is also the reverse of the previous P passage of the recluse and brāhmaṇa who indulge in the 5 objects of desire.

5) *Emancipation of the Tathāgata :*

C : (75*b*, 20 ; 76*a*, 1-5) : « Oh five monks, when the Tathāgata comes to the world, fully emancipated and completely enlightened, endowed with wisdom and virtue, well gone, knower of the world, the peerless, a tamer of the Path and of the Dharma, Teacher of Gods and men, the Enlightened, the Protector of all. He gets rid of 5 hindrances, is aloof from desires, from demeritorious dharmas, reaches and abides up the 4th dhyāna. Thus with such a concentrated mind, pure, stainless and troublefree, fit and flexible, he well abides in and obtains the unshakable mind. He engages in mental training, cankers vanish, knowledge dawns, realization matures. He knows suffering as it really is, the origin of suffering, the cessation of suffering, the path leading to the cessation of suffering as it really is. He knows cankers as it really is, the origin of the cankers, the cessation of the cankers, the path leading to the cessation of the cankers as it really is. Such is his knowledge, such is his vision, his mind is free from cankers of sense-desire, of existence and of ignorance. When he is emancipated, he knows that he is emancipated. Birth is destroyed... True is his knowledge. At that time, he walks freely, stands freely, sits freely, lies down freely ; why is it so ? Because he perceives that innumerable evil dharmas, demeritorious dharmas are destroyed. That is why he walks freely, stands freely, sits freely, lies down freely.

P : (not available).

6) *Emancipation of a monk* :

C : (76*a*, 5-9) : « Oh five monks, it is like a place where there is no disturbance, no people, a deer walks freely, stands freely, sits freely, lies down freely. Why is it so ? The wild deer does not enter the realm of the hunter, that is why it walks freely, stands freely, sits freely, lies down freely. Thus, « Oh 5 monks, a monk whose cankers are destroyed obtains the state of no cankers. His mind is free, his knowledge is free. His self knowledge, his self penetration, his self realization are thoroughly obtained and he abides in them. Birth is destroyed... True is his knowledge. This monk at that time walks freely, stands freely, sits freely, lies down freely. Why is it so ? He himself sees that innumerable evil, demeritorious dharmas are destroyed, that is why he walks freely, stands freely, sits freely, lies down freely. Oh 5 monks, this is called emancipation without any remainder. This is called the diseaseless, the supreme peacefulness, Nirvāṇa.

P : (174, 9-37 ; 175, 1-9) : Not the same. While the simile is almost the same in both, the Pāli explains the freedom of the monk when he walks, stands, sits and lies down as due to his being able to practise and attain the 4 rūpa jhānā, the 4 arūpajhānā, to go beyond the nevasaññānāsaññā up to the cessation of all perceptions and feelings, up to the destruction of all cankers. In doing so, the monk is said to have made Māra blind, to go outside the range of vision of the Māra, to cross over the bondage of the world.

E. — CONCLUSION

C : = Thus spoke the Buddha. Ven. A-nan and the monks rejoiced at the Buddha's speech and abided by.

P : = Idaṃ avoca Bhagavā. Attamanā te bhikkhū Bhagavato bhāsitaṃ abhinandun ti.

C. S. N° 26

CHINESE : N° 184, *Niu-chioh-so-lo-lin-ching* (牛角娑羅林經)
(Tsê vii, 34b-36b).

PĀLI : N° 32, Mahāgosiṅgasuttaṃ (T.M.N. i, 212-219).

A. — GIST OF THE CHINESE SŪTRA

Seven elders, Shê-li-tzu (P : Sāriputta), Ta-mu-chien-lien (P : Mahāmoggallāna), Ta-chia-yeh (P : Mahākassapa), Ta-chia-chan-yen (P : Mahākaccāna), A-na-lü-t'o (P : Anuruddha), Li-yüeh-to (P : Revata), and A-nan (P : Ānanda) were staying together with the Buddha in Niu-chioh-so-lin (P : Gosiṅgasālavana). One day, these elders came to Ven. Shê-li-tzu to have a dharma talk with him and elder Shê-li-tzu asked them what kind of monk would lend charm to the Niu-chioh-so-lo grove. These elders stated their own view and the matter was brought up before the Buddha who approved their answers and gave his own answer to the question.

P : Almost the same. Only 6 elders. It omits elder Mahākaccāna and assigns a different answer to Mahāmoggallāna.

B. — TITLE

C : Niu-chioh-so-lo-lin-ching, discourse on the So-lo forest called Horn of the cow, which refers to the forest in which the 5 elders were living.

P : Mahāgosiṅgasutta, greater discourse on Gosiṅga, which refers to the same forest.

C. — PLACE OF OCCURRENCE

C : In Pa-ch'i-shou (P : Bhagga), and in the So-lo forest called Cow Horn.

P : Gosiṅgasālavana.

D. — CONTENTS OF THE SŪTRA

I. — *Circumstances leading to the deliverance of the sūtra :*

C : (34*b*, 9-15) : At one time, the Buddha was travelling among the Pa-ch'i-shou and staying in the So-lo forest called Cow-Horn, together with a number of great disciples who were well-known and elder such as elders Shê-li-tzu, Ta-mu-chien-lien, Ta-chia-yeh, Ta-chia-chan-yen, A-na-lü-t'o, Li-yüeh-to and elder A-nan. These great disciples who were well-known and elder were also travelling among the Pa-ch'i-shou and staying in the So-lo forest called Cow-Horn, dwelling near the leafy hut of the Buddha. At that time, elder Ta-mu-chien-lien, elder Ta-chia-yeh, elder Ta-chia-chan-yen, elder A-na-lü-t'o, when night was over and early in the morning, came to elder Shê-li-tzu's place. Elder A-nan saw from afar those elders coming and said: « Rev. fr. Li-yüeh-to, you should know that these elders Ta-mu-chien-lien, Ta-chia-yeh, Ta-chia-chan-yen and A-na-lü-t'o, when night was over and early in the morning had come to elder Shê-li-tzu's place. Rev. fr. Li-yüeh-to, now we should together with those elders go to elder Shê-li-tzu's place to be able to listen to a few dharma talk from elder Shê-li-tzu». Then elder Ta-mu-chien-lien, Ta-chia-yeh, Ta-chia-chan-yen, A-na-lü-t'o and A-nan, when night was over, early in the morning, came to elder Shê-li-tzu's place.

P : (212, 1-26): Almost the same. The P omits: among the Pa-ch'i-shou, great disciples, elder Ta-chia-chan-yen. It omits also: « These great disciples... dwelling near the leafy hut of the Buddha ». C: when night was over, early in the morning = P: in the evening. The P adds that it was elder Mahāmoggallāna who got up from his meditation and called Mahākassapa to go to elder Sāriputta and the 3 elders Mahāmoggallāna, Mahākassapa and Anuruddha went together to elder Sāriputta's place. The P adds that elder Ānanda called the 3 elders as sappurisa, which is missing in the Chinese.

II. — *Elder Shê-li-tzu's question :*

C : (34*b*, 15-17): Elder Shê-li-tzu from afar saw those elders coming. Elder Shê-li-tzu for the sake of those elders said: « Welcome, Rev. A-nan, welcome, Rev. A-nan, who is an attendant of the W. H. One, who understands the W.H. One's mind, who is always praised by the W. H. One and by the learned brahmafarers. Now I ask Rev. A-nan: « This So-lo forest called Cow-Horn is extremely pleasant, the night is moonlit, the So-lo trees are breathing forth sweet fragrance, like heavenly flowers. Rev. fr. A-nan, what type of monks is able to lend charm to the So-lo forest called Cow-Horn ?

P: (212, 27-34): Almost the same. C: Elder Shê-li-tzu from afar saw those elders coming = P adds: saw elder Ānanda and Revata. C: Rev. A-nan is an attendant... and by the learned brahmafarers = P: Ven. Ānanda who is the Blessed One's attendant and intimate companion. C: The So-lo trees are breathing forth sweet fragrance like heavenly flowers = P: The Sāla trees are in full blooms, methinks heavenly fragrance is blowing. C: What type of monk is able to elevate the Niu-chioh forest = P: What type of monk can lend charm to the Gosinga forest.

III. — *Elder A-nan's reply :*

C : (34*b*, 17-19) : Elder A-nan replied : « Elder Shê-li-tzu, if there is a monk who has learnt much, who has heard much, keeping in mind and not forgetting, accumulates and hears the dharma which is lovely at the beginning, lovely in the middle, lovely also at the end, with meaning, with letter, which shows the brahma-life complete and pure, such dharma is broadly learnt, much heard, well trained, well repeated, reflected by mind, well lighted with view and deeply realized He preaches the dharma simply and fluently, rightly for the sake of eradicating fetters. Elder Shê-li-tzu, such a monk will lend charm to the Niu-chioh forest.

P : (212, 35; 213, 1-9) : Almost the same. It omits : « Who has learnt much, not forgetting, broadly learnt, well trained, deeply realized, he preaches the dharma simply, rightly. It adds : Absolutely complete, he preaches the dhamma *to the four assemblies*, with correct and fluent *letters and sentences.* C : For the sake of eradicating fetters = P : for removing latent tendencies.

IV. — *Elder Li-yüeh-to's reply :*

C : (34*b*, 19-20; 35*a*, 1-2) : Elder Shê-li-tzu again asked : « Rev. Li-yüeh-to ! Rev. A-nan has spoken according to his knowledge, now again I ask Rev. Li-yüeh-to : « This So-lo forest... called Cow-Horn ? » Elder Li-yüeh-to replied : « Ven. Shê-li-tzu, if there is a monk who is happy in sitting in meditation, who is engaged in inner mental tranquillity, not neglecting dhyāna, endowed with insight, always lives in seclusion and enjoys quiet places. Elder Shê-li-tzu, such a monk will lend charm to the So-lo forest called Cow-Horn... ».

P : (213, 10-19) : Almost the same. C : According to his knowledge = P : according to his own knowledge. C : He always lives in seclusion = P : who delights in seclusion. C : enjoys quiet places = P : who frequents empty places (Brūhetā Suññāgārānaṃ).

V. — *Elder A-na-lü-t'o's reply :*

C : (35*a*, 2-6) : (Elder Shê-li-tzu asked elder A-na-lü-t'o in the same way as he asked elder Li-yüeh-to and elder A-na-lü-t'o replied as follows) : « Elder Shê-li-tzu, if there is a monk who has attained the heavenly eye, who is endowed with heavenly eye, he with a little effort can see in one moment all thousand worlds. Elder Shê-li-tzu, just like a man with eyes, standing upon the upper story and looking down at the open ground below, with thousand mounds, he with a little effort, in a moment, can see them all. Elder Shê-li-tzu, such a monk will lend charm to the So-lo forest called Cow-Horn. »

P : (213, 20-32) : Almost the same. It omits : « Who has attained the heavenly eye, with a little effort, in one moment. » It adds : « With a heavenly eye, *pure, surpassing that of men.* » C : Standing upon the upper story = P : Who has gone to the top of an excellent palace. C : Looking down at the open ground below, with thousand mounds = P : He looks down at 1000 concentric circles (Nemimaṇḍālā).

VI. — *Elder Ta-chia-chan-yen's reply :*

C : (35*a*, 6-9) : Being asked by Ven. Shê-li-tzu, elder Ta-chia-chan-yen replied as follows : « Elder Shê-li-tzu, just like two monks, master of the dharma, who are discussing about the very deep A-p'i-t'an (P : Abhidhamma). What they ask is well understood and well known. Their reply is without hindrance and his talk on dharma is fluent. Elder Shê-li-tzu, such a monk will lend charm to the So-lo forest called Cow-Horn ».

P : Not available.

Notes : Here the term A-p'i-t'an (Abhidhamma) is referred to, meaning simply deep dharma.

VII. — *Elder Ta-chia-yeh's reply :*

C : (35*a*, 9-14) : (Being asked by elder Shê-li-tzu, elder Ta-chia-yeh replied as follows) : « Rev. friend Shê-li-tzu, if there is a monk who follows aloofness and speaks in praise of aloofness ; being with few desires, speaks in praise of few desires ; being with contentment, speaks in praise of contentment ; being delighted in living secluded and alone, speaks in praise of living secluded and alone ; being energetic in spiritual training, speaks in praise of being energetic in spiritual training ; being established in right mindfulness, in right wisdom speaks in praise of right mindfulness, of right wisdom ; having obtained concentration, speaks in praise of the attainment of concentration ; being with wisdom, speaks in praise of wisdom ; having eradicated cankers, speaks in praise of the eradication of cankers ; having advised, incited, gladdened, speaks in praise of advising, inciting, gladdening. Rev. fr. Shê-li-tzu, such a monk will lend charms to the So-lo forest called Cow-Horn. »

P : (213, 33-37 ; 214, 1-17) : Not exactly the same. It omits : « Having eradicated the cankers, speaks in praise of the eradication of cankers ; having advised, incited, gladdened, speaks in praise of advising, inciting, gladdening. It adds : « Being a dweller in the forest, speaks in praise of dwelling in a forest ; being an almsman, speaks in praise of an almsman ; being a ragwearer, speaks in praise of being a ragwearer ; being a three-robes holder, speaks in praise of being a three-robes holder ; having possessed knowledge and vision of emancipation, speaks in praise of being possessed of knowledge and vision of emancipation ; having possessed emancipation, speaks in praise of emancipation. » C : who follows aloofness = P : asaṃsaṭṭho (not mixed with the world). C : being delighted in living secluded and alone = P : living secluded. C : Being energetic in spiritual training = P : Being energetic : C : Being established in mindfulness, in right wisdom = P : Being endowed with moral practice. In the C version, Mahākassapa called Sāriputta as Rev. Fr. (Āvuso) and Sāriputta called Mahākassapa as Venerable (P : Bhante). But in the P version, Sāriputta and Mahākassapa addressed each other as Āvuso.

VIII. — *Elder Ta-mu-chien-lien's answer:*

C : (35*a*, 14–19) : (Being asked by elder Shê-li-tzu, elder Ta-mu-chien-lien replied as follows) : « There is a monk who possesses great psychic power, great merit, great blessedness, great supernatural power, who masters innumerable psychic powers and performs innumerable psychic powers : Being one, he becomes many, being many he becomes one ; being one, he becomes one endowed with knowledge, with vision ; he goes through stone, through walls without hindrance as through empty space ; he comes out, he enters the earth as through water ; he walks on the water without sinking as on the earth ; he flies up the sky and sits cross-legged there like the birds. Now these sun and moon that possess great psychic powers, great merit, great blessedness, great supernatural powers, he with his hand touches, rubs the body of the sun, the moon, up to the Brahma-world. Elder Shê-li-tzu, such a monk will lend charm to the So-lo forest called Cow-Horn ».

P : (214, 18–28) : Totally different. The P puts elder Ta-chia-chan-yen's reply (Mahākaccāna) as we have seen in the C version here and does not mention anything of the psychic powers of elder Mahāmoggallāna. The reply is as follows : « Here the 2 monks are talking about the Abhidhamma, they put questions to each other and reply them without being tired out and the dhamma talk proceeds on. »

Remarks : Here the C version is more faithful and reliable than the P version as Mahākaccāna is well known as being expert in dharma discussion and Mahāmoggallāna is well known as being expert in supernatural powers.

IX. — *Elder Shê-li-tzu's reply :*

When elder Ta-mu-chien-lien ended his reply, he requested elder Shê-li-tzu to give his own reply to the question and here is elder Shê-li-tzu's reply :

C : (35*a*, 19–20 ; 35*b*, 1–5) : « Rev. Mu-chien-lien, if there is a monk who masters his own mind, but is not under the domination of his mind. Whatever attainment, abiding he wishes to practise in the morning, he practises that attainment, that abiding in the morning ; whatever attainment, abiding he wishes to practise at noon, in the evening, he practises that attainment, that abiding at noon, in the evening. Rev. Mu-chien-lien, just like a king or a king's minister who has plenty of garments, who has plenty of robes of various beautiful colours ; (whatever robes) he wishes to wear in the morning, he takes and wears it ; (whatever robes) he wishes to wear at noon, in the evening, he takes and wears it Rev. Mu-chien-lien, in the same way with the monk who masters his own mind, but is not under the domination of his mind... (as above up to)... in the evening. Rev. Mu-chien-lien, such a monk will lend charm to the So-lo forest called Cow-Horn ».

P : (214, 29-37; 215, 1-24) : Almost the same with the following minor differences : While the C puts the practice at noon and in the evening in the same sentence, the P separates them in two sentences. In the simile, the P adds: the king, the king's minister possesses a cloth-chest full of clothes of various nice colours C : robes = P : pair of clothes.

X. — *The elders' approach to the Buddha and the Buddha's reply :*

C : (35*b*, 5-20; 36*a*; 36*b*, 1-12) : (Elder Shê-li-tzu asked all the other elders to approach the Buddha and all agreed. They approached the Buddha and reported to Him the whole conversation and asked him to judge which answer was the best. The Buddha approved all answers saying that each elder had replied according to his own practice, as elder A-nan was well learnt, elder Li-yüeh-to liked to sit in meditation, elder A-na-lü-t'o possessed the divine eye, elder Ta-chia-chan-yen was master in analysing the dharma, elder Ta-chia-yeh was a follower of aloofness, elder Ta-mu-chien-lien had great psychic powers and elder Shê-li-tzu was master of his own mind. Then the Buddha gave his own answer to the question as follows) : « Shê-li-tzu, all the replies are good. Why is it so ? All these dharmas are spoken by me. Shê-li-tzu, please listen to what I shall speak about the type of monk who lends charm to the So-lo forest called Cow-Horn. Shê-li-tzu, there is a monk who is staying in the town, in the village, in the market-town; he when night is over, early in the morning, dons his robe, takes his bowl and enters the village for alms. With body well controlled, with faculties well protected, he establishes himself in mindfulness. When the meal is over, in the afternoon, he puts back his robe and bowl, washes hand and feet, puts the sitting mat over his shoulder, he goes either to a troublefree place, or to the foot of a tree, or to an open and tranquil place. There he spreads his sitting mat, sits cross-legged, making vow not to leave his cross-legged position up to the time when he eradicates the cankers. He does not leave his cross-legged position and eradicates the cankers. Oh Shê-li-tzu, such a monk will elevate the So-lo forest called Cow-Horn. »

P : (215, 25-37; 216; 217; 218; 219, 1-33) : Almost the same, with the differences already listed above. In the Buddha's reply, these differences are noted : The P omits the passage : « Who is staying in the town... up to... he establishes himself in mindfulness. » It omits also : « In the afternoon, he puts back his robe... he spreads his sitting mat. » It mentions also the monk makes a vow not to leave the cross-legged position up to the eradication of the cankers. It adds : without any remainder but omits the assertion that the monk has actually done so. The P adds: he sits with his body erect.

E. — CONCLUSIONS

C: (36*b*, 12–13): « Thus spoke the Buddha. Those monks having heard the Buddha's speech were delighted and abided in ».

P: (219, 34–35): « Thus spoke the Blessed One. Delighted those monks rejoiced at the Blessed One's speech ».

C. S. N° 30

CHINESE : N° 211, Ta-chü-ch'ih-lo-ching (大拘絺羅經) (Tsê vii, 85a-87a).

PĀLI : N° 43, Mahāvedallasutta (T.M.N. i, 292-298).

A. — GIST OF THE C SŪTRA

Elder Shê-li-tzu (P : Sāriputta) approached elder Ta-chü-ch'ih-lo (P : Mahākoṭṭhita) and asked him a series of questions on various subjects, to which elder Ta-chü-ch'ih-lo replied. His replies were praised and accepted by elder Shê-li-tzu.

P : Almost the same. But here, it was elder Mahākoṭṭhita who asked questions to elder Sāriputta.

B. — TITLE OF THE SŪTRA

C : Ta-chü-ch'ih-lo-ching, discourse about elder Ta-chu-ch'ih-lo, which refers to the name of the elder who replied to questions asked by elder Shê-li-tzu.

P : Mahāvedallasutta, discourse on Vedalla, which may refer to the various subjects asked by elder Mahākoṭṭhita.

C. — LOCATION OF THE SŪTRA

C : At Wang-shê town (P : Rājagaha), in the Bamboo grove, at Chia-lan-to park (P : Kalandakanivāpa).

P : At Sāvatthi, in Jetavana, at Anāthapiṇḍikārāma.

D. — CONTENTS OF THE SŪTRA

I. — *Circumstances leading to the deliverance of the discourse :*

C : (85*a*, 1-3) : « At that time, elder Shê-li-tzu, in the evening, got up from his meditation seat, came to elder Ta-chü-ch'ih-lo's place, exchanged greetings with him and sat at one side. Elder Shê-li-tzu said : « Rev. fr. Chü-ch'ih-lo, (I) want to ask (some questions), do you allow me to do so ? » Elder Ta-chü-ch'ih-lo said : « Elder Shê-li-tzu, if you want to ask questions, please do so. Having heard, I shall think over. »

P : (292, 2-7) : Not the same. It was elder Mahākoṭṭhita who got up from his seclusion in the evening, approached elder Sāriputta, exchanged greetings with him and asked the questions.

II. — *Series of questions asked :*

In the C version, there are 32 questions in all and the same number is observed in the P ; but there are only 17 questions which correspond to each other in the 2 versions, while the remaining 15 are not to be found in each other version.

a) 17 corresponding questions : C 3 = P 2; C 4 = P 3; C 5 = P 4; C 6 = P 10; C 7 = P 11 ; C 9 = P 12 ; C 10 = P 13 ; C 11 = P 15; C 12 = P 16 ; C 13 = P 6 ; C 14 = P 8 ; C 16 = P 20 ; C 18 = P 22 ; C 19 = P 24 ; C 20 = P 26 ; C 21 = P 27 ; C 27 = P 32.

b) 15 questions not found in the P version : C 1 ; C 2 ; C 8 ; C 15 ; C 17 ; C 22 ; C 23 ; C 24 ; C 25 ; C 26 ; C 28 ; C 29 ; C 30 ; C 31 ; C 32.

c) 15 questions not found in the C version : P 1 ; P 5 ; P 7 ; P 9 ; P 14 ; P 17 ; P 18 ; P 19 ; P 21 ; P 23 ; P 25 ; P 28 ; P 29 ; P 30 ; P 31.

1) *Questions about good and bad :*

C 1 = P no :

C : (85*b*, 3-5) : Elder Shê-li-tzu asked : « Rev. fr. Chü-ch'ih-lo, demeritorious is called demeritorious ; demeritorious root is called demeritorious root ; what are the demeritorious ? what are the roots of the demeritorious ? Elder Ta-chü-ch'ih-lo replied : « Evil bodily conduct, evil speech, evil thought are called demeritorious. Greed, ill-will and ignorance are the roots of the demeritorious. These are called demeritorious ; these are called roots of the demeritorious. » Elder Shê-li-tzu having heard, uttered praises saying : « Very good, very good, Rev. fr. Chü-ch'ih-lo ». Elder Shê-li-tzu having uttered praises became delighted and abided in.

C 2 = P no :

C : (85*b*, 5-7) : (The way to ask questions, to answer and words of praise at the end of each question are the same for the remaining questions).

Q : Meritorious is called meritorious ; roots of the meritorious are called meritorious. What are the meritorious ? What are the roots of the meritorious ? A : Good bodily conduct, good speech, good thought are called meritorious. No-greed, no ill-will, no-ignorance are the roots of the meritorious. These are called meritorious ; these are called the roots of the meritorious.

2) *Questions about wisdom, right knowledge :*

C 3 = *P* 2 *:*

C : (85*b*, 7-9) : Q : Wisdom is called wisdom ; what is wisdom ? A: Due to such knowledge it is called wisdom. Knowledge of what ? knowledge of this suffering as it really is, knowledge of this origin of suffering as it really is ; knowledge of this cessation of suffering as it really is ; knowledge of this path leading to the cessation of suffering as it really is. Such a knowledge is called wisdom.

P : (292, 17-23) : Almost the same. C : Due to such knowledge it is called wisdom = P : knowing is called knowing. Referring to the 4 noble truths, the P omits : as it really is. In the P version, after elder Sāriputta's answer, elder Mahākoṭṭhita praised saying : « It is good, Rev. fr. » and he rejoiced at what elder Sāriputta had said, thanked him and asked another question.

C 4 = *P* 2 *:*

C : (85*b*, 9-11) : Q : Consciousness is called consciousness. What is consciousness ? A : Cognises, cognises, that is why it is called consciousness. Cognises what ? cognises material form, cognises sound, smell, taste, touch, dharma. Cognises, that is why it is called consciousness.

P : (292, 23-28) : Not the same. Q: Consciousness is called consciousness? in what respect, is it called consciousness ? A: it cognises, it cognises (vijānāti), that is why it is called consciousness. It cognises what ? It cognises happiness, it cognises suffering, it cognises neither happiness nor suffering. Rev. fr., it cognises, it cognises, therefore it is called consciousness.

C. 5 = *P* 4 :

C : (85*b*, 11-13): Q: Wisdom and consciousness, are these 2 dharmas associated together or are they apart? can these 2 dharmas be shown apart? A: These two dharmas are associated together ; these two dharmas cannot be shown apart. Why is it so? What wisdom knows is cognised by consciousness. That is why these two dharmas are associated together, these two dharmas cannot be shown apart.

P: (292, 29-35 ; 293, 1-3): Almost the same. C: can these two dharmas be shown apart? = P: is it possible, having analysed these dhammas again and again to show their differences? C: Why is it so? what wisdom knows is cognised by consciousness. That is why these two dharmas are associated together, these two dharmas cannot be shown apart = P: Rev. fr. these dhammas, wisdom and consciousness, are associated, not dissociated. It is not possible, having analysed these dhammas again and again to show their differences. Rev. fr., what is known is cognised, what is cognised is known ; therefore these dhammas are associated, not dissociated, it is not possible, having analysed these dhammas again and again to show their differences.

C 6 = *P* 10:

C: (85*b*, 13-14): Q:... Knowledge, with the help of what, do you know? A: Knowledge, with the help of wisdom that I know.

P: (293, 34-35): Q: Rev. fr., by what does one know the knowable dhamma? A: Rev. fr., by the eye of wisdom, one knows the knowable dhammas.

C 7 = *P* 11:

C: (85*b*, 14-16): «... Q: What is the meaning of wisdom? what is the excellence of wisdom? what is the merit of wisdom? A: wisdom has disgust as meaning, without desire as meaning, knowledge in accordance with truth as meaning.

P: (293, 36-37): Q: What is the purpose of wisdom? A: the purpose of realizing, the purpose of understanding, the purpose of giving away.

Remarks: Meaning in C should be understood as *purpose.*

C 8 = *P no.*

C: (85*b*, 16-17): Q: What is right view? A: To know suffering as it really is, to know the origin of suffering, the cessation of suffering, the path leading to the cessation of suffering as it really is, is called right view.

C 9 = *P* 12:

C: (85*b*, 17-19): Q: What are the causes? what are the conditions for the arising of right view? A: there are two causes, two conditions for the arising of right view. What are the two? One is to hear from others, the second is to inwardly reflect by oneself. These are called two causes, two conditions for the arising of right view.

P: (294, 1-4): Q: How many conditions are there for the arising of right view? A: There are two conditions for the arising of right view: voice of others and proper reflection.

C 10 = *P* 13:

C: (85*b*, 19-20; 86*a*, 1-3): Q: With how many factors does right view associate to obtain fruit of freedom of mind, fruit of freedom of wisdom, to obtain merits of freedom of mind, merits of freedom of wisdom? A: there are 5 factors to associate with right view to obtain fruit... freedom of wisdom. What are the five? 1) to associate with truth, 2) to associate with moral conduct; 3) to associate with broad hearing; 4) to associate with quietude; 5) to associate with insight.

P: (294, 4-15): Question the same, answer slightly different. A: There are 5 factors to associate with right view to obtain fruit of freedom of mind, advantages of freedom of mind, to obtain fruit of freedom of wisdom, advantages of freedom of wisdom: 1) moral conduct, 2) learning, 3) discussion, 4) quietude (samatha), 5) vipassanā (insight).

In this series of questions, two questions are available only in the P, not in the C version.

P 1 : (292, 8–17) : Q : Weak wisdom is called weak wisdom. In what respect, is it called weak wisdom ? A: He does not know, he does not know, therefore it is called weak wisdom. He does not know what ? he does not know this suffering, does not know this origin of suffering, this cessation of suffering, this path leading to the cessation of suffering. He does not know, he does not know, therefore it is called weak wisdom.

P 5 : (293, 3–8) : Q : That which is wisdom and that which is consciousness, what is the difference between these dhammas ? are these dhammas associated or dissociated ? A : That which is wisdom and that which is consciousness; of these dhammas which are associated not dissociated, wisdom is to be cultivated and consciousness is to be known, this is the difference between them.

3) *Questions about becoming :*

C 11 = P 15 :

C : (86*a*, 3–5) : Q : How does becoming take place in the future ? A: The ignorant worldling is without knowledge, without much learning, covered up by ignorance, bound by the fetter of craving, does not see well learned persons, does not know the noble dharma, is not tamed in the noble dharma. This is called becoming taking place in the future.

P : (294, 17–20) : Question is the same, answer slightly different. A : For the beings who are hindered by ignorance, who are fettered by craving, who enjoy here and there, thus there is again becoming in the future.

C 12 = *P* 16 :

C : (86*a*, 5–6) : Q : How does becoming not take place in the future ? A : If ignorance is destroyed and knowledge arises, then there is cessation of suffering. This is called there is no more becoming in the future.

P : (294, 20–23) : Question is the same, answer slightly different. A : With the removal of ignorance, the arising of knowledge, the cessation of craving, there is no becoming in the future.

In this series of question, one question in P is not available in the C version :

P 14 : (294, 16–17) : Q : How many existences (bhava) are there ? A : there are three existences : kāmabhava, rūpabhava and arūpabhava.

4) *Questions about feelings and perceptions :*

C 13 = *P* 6 :

C : (86*a*, 6–8) : Q : How many feelings are there ? Due to what do they arise ? A: There are 3 feelings ; pleasant feeling, unpleasant feeling, neither pleasant nor unpleasant feeling. Due to strong enjoyment, they arise.

P : (293, 9–13) : Almost the same. Q : Feeling is called feeling. In what respect, is it called feeling ? A : He feels, he feels, therefore it is called feeling. He feels what ? he feels pleasant feeling, he feels unpleasant feeling, he feels neither pleasant nor unpleasant feeling. He feels, he feels, therefore it is called feeling. The P omits the 2nd portion of the question and of the answer.

C 14 = *P* 8 :

C : (86*a*, 8–10) : Q : Feeling, perception and reflection, are these 3 dharmas associated together or dissociated ? Is it possible to show these three dharmas apart ? A : Feeling, perception and reflection, these 3 dharmas are associated together, not dissociated. It is not possible to show these three dharmas apart. Why is it so ? What feeling feels is what perception perceives, is what reflection reflects upon, that is why these three dharmas are associated together, not dissociated ; these dharmas cannot be shown apart.

P : (293, 19–28) : Almost the same. Q : That which is feeling and that which is perception and that which is consciousness, these dharmas are associated together or not associated ? Is it possible, having analysed these dhammas again and again to show their difference ? A : That which is feeling and that which is perception and that which is consciousness, these dhammas are associated together, not dissociated. It is not possible, having analysed these dhammas again and again to show their differences. What one feels is what one perceives ; what one perceives is what one cognises ; therefore these dhammas are associated not dissociated ; and it is not possible having analysed these dhammas again and again to show their differences.

In this series of questions, one question in P is not available in the C version :

P 7 : (293, 13–18) Q : Perception is called perception. In what respect is it called perception ? A : he perceives, he perceives, therefore it is called perception. He perceives what ? he perceives blue colour, he perceives yellow colour, he perceives red colour, he perceives white colour. He perceives, he perceives, therefore it is called perception.

5) *Questions about cessation, five faculties, mind and life :*

C 15 = *P no.*

C : (86*a*, 10–12) : Q : Cessation has what as its object ? A : Cessation has no object.

C 16 = *P* 20 :

C : (86*a*, 12–15) : Q : There are five faculties with different field, with different objects, each receiving its own object, they are eye, ear, nose, tongue and body faculties. These five faculties with different field, with different objects, each receiving its own object, what receives all objects for them? What is their refuge? A: The five faculties are with different field, with different objects, each receiving its own object. They are eye, ear, nose, tongue and body faculties. These five faculties with different field, with different objects, each receiving its own object, mind receives all objects for them, mind is their refuge.

P: (295, 5–17): Almost the same. C: with different pasturage, with different objects = P: nānāvisayāni nānāgocarāni. C: each receives its own object = P: They do not experience the object, the field of each other. C: What receives all objects for them, what is their refuge? = P: What is their refuge? what are the fields of their objects?

C 17 = P *no.*

C: (86*a*, 15–16): Q: Depending on what does the mind dwell? A: Depending on life the mind dwells.

C 18 = *P* 22:

C: (86*a*, 16–17): Q: Depending on what does life dwell? Depending on heat life dwells.

P: (295, 23–25): The same. C: life = P: Āyu. C: heat = P: usmā.

C 19 = *P* 24:

C: (86*a*, 17–20; 86*b*, 1): Q: Life and heat, are these two dharmas associated together or dissociated? Is it possible to show these 2 dharmas apart? A: life and heat, these two dharmas are associated together, not dissociated. It is not possible to show these two dharmas apart. Why is it so? Due to life there is heat; due to heat, there is life. If there is no life, there will be no heat; if there is no heat, there will be no life. Just as dependent on oil, dependent on wick, the lamp is burning. In this lamp, dependent on flame, there is light; dependent on light, there is flame. If there is no flame, there will be no light; if there is no light, there will be no flame. In the same way, dependent on life, there is heat; dependent on heat, there is life. If there is no life, there will be no heat; if there is no heat, there will be no life. That is why these two dharmas are associated, not dissociated; these two dharmas cannot be shown apart.

P: (295, 26–35): Not exactly the same. The question is somewhat different. Q: Now we understand elder Sāriputta's speech that life depends on heat to maintain itself. Now we understand elder Sāriputta's speech that heat depends upon life to maintain itself. How should the meaning of this speech be understood? A: Then I shall give you a simile, intelligent people with the help of a simile understand the meaning of what has been said. Just as when an oil lamp is burning, dependent on flame light appears; dependent on light, flame appears; in the same way, life depends on heat to maintain itself, heat depends on life to maintain itself.

In this series of questions, 3 questions are not available in the C.

P 21 : (295, 18–23) : Q : There are five faculties, such as eye-faculty, ear-faculty, nose-faculty, tongue-faculty, body-faculty. On what do these faculties depend ? A : These five faculties depend on life.

P 23 : (295, 25–26) : A : On what does heat depend ? A : Heat depends on life.

P 25 : (295, 36–37 ; 296, 1–6) : Q : Are these properties of life (Āyusaṅkhārā) the same as these dhammas that should be experienced or are these properties of life different from these dhammas that should be experienced ? A : If these properties of life are the same as those dhammas that should be experienced, then the getting out of the monk who attains the cessation of perception and feeling cannot be shown. As the properties of life are different from the dhammas which should be felt, the getting out of the monk who has attained the cessation of perception and feeling can be shown.

6) *Questions on death, on complete cessation, on no perception :*

C 20 = *P* 26 :

C : (86*b*, 1–4) : Q : How many dharmas are given up when the body is dead and thrown into the cemetery, like a senseless log of wood ? A : 3 dharmas are given up when the body is dead and thrown into the cemetery, like a senseless log of wood. What are the three ? One is life, the second is heat, the 3rd is consciousness. These 3 dharmas are given up when the body is dead and thrown into the cemetery, like a senseless log of wood.

P : (296, 6–11) : Almost the same. Q : How many dhammas are given up, when this body is cast away, thrown away into sleep like a senseless log of wood. The answer is the same.

C 21 = P 27 ; C 22, C 24, C 25, C 26 = P no. (Please see ante, section on Samādhi, page 104 from *C No.* 211 : (*vii*, 86*b*, 4–6) to page 105, up to... then desireless touch (appaṇihita).

C 27 = *P* 32 :

C : (86*b*, 16–18) : Q : Voidness, vowless and signless ; are these 3 dharmas different in meaning and different in letters ? or are they the same in meaning but different in letters ? A : These 3 dharmas are different in meaning and different in letters.

P : (297, 9–37 ; 298, 1–27) : Not exactly the same. C : voidness, vowless and signless = P : Whatever freedom of mind which is immeasurable, whatever freedom of mind which is nothingness, whatever freedom of mind which is substanceless, whatever freedom of mind which is signless. While the C replies simply that they are different in meaning and different in letters, the P says that according to the methods adopted, sometimes they are different in meaning and different in letters, sometimes they are the same in meaning but different in letters. Then the P proceeds to explain that by adopting the practice of four brahmavihāra, the monk obtains freedom of mind which is immeasurable ; by adopting the practice of going beyond all viññāṇañcāyatanaṃ and entering into the ākiñcaññāyatanaṃ, he obtains freedom of mind which is nothingness ; by going to an empty place and pondering over voidness of the self and of what belongs to the self, the monk obtains freedom of mind which is substanceless ; and by not thinking over all signs, by entering into the concentration of mind on signless, he obtains freedom of mind which is signless. Thus this is the method according to which these states are different in meaning and also in letters. Further the P explains that by eradicating rāga, dosa and moha, which are productive of something measurable, obstructive, something productive of the sign, the monk obtains that freedom of mind which is immeasurable, which is nothingness, which is substanceless, which is signless. Thus by this method, these 4 states are of the same meaning but different in letters.

C 28 = *P no.*

C : (86*b*, 18–20) : « How many causes, how many conditions are there to obtain the motionless concentration ? A : There are four causes, four conditions to obtain the motionless concentration. What are the four ? If a monk keeps aloof from sense-desires, from evil, demeritorious dharmas, attains and abides up to the 4th dhyāna, these are called four causes, four conditions to obtain the concentration which is motionless.

C 29 = *P no.*

C : (86*b*, 20 ; 87*a*, 1–3) : Q : How many causes, how many conditions are there to obtain concentration of nothingness ? A : There are three causes, three conditions to obtain concentration of nothingness. What are the three ? If the monk goes beyond all perceptions of material forms up to entering the plane of nothingness and abiding in it, these are called three causes, three conditions to obtain concentration of nothingness.

C 30 = *P no.*

C : (87*a*, 3–5) : A : How many causes, how many conditions are there to obtain concentration of no-perception ? A : There are two causes, two conditions to obtain concentration of no-perception. What are the two ? One is not to think over all perceptions ; the second is to think over the plane of no-perception.

C 31 = *P no.*

C : (87*a*, 5–7) : Q : How many causes, how many conditions are there to dwell into the concentration of no-perception ? A : There are two causes, two conditions to dwell in the concentration of no-perception. What are the two ? One is not to think over all perceptions, the second is to think over the plane of no-perception.

C 32 = *P no.*

C : (87*a*, 7–8) : Q : How many causes, how many conditions are there to emerge from concentration of no-perception ? A : There are 3 causes, 3 conditions to emerge from concentration of no-perception. What are the three ? One is to think over all perceptions, the second is not to think over the plane of no-perception, the 3rd is when this body and the 6 sense-organs associate with life. These are the 3 causes, 3 conditions to cause the emergence from the concentration of no-perception.

In this series of questions, there are 8 questions available in P but not in the C versions.

P 17 : (294, 24–28) : Q : What is the first jhāna stage of concentration? A : When a monk is aloof from sense-desires, aloof from evil, demeritorious dhammas, he enters and abides in the first jhāna which is with initial thoughts, with applied thoughts, which is endowed with joy and happiness born out of seclusion.

P 18 : (294, 28–32) : Q : How many factors are there in the first jhāna ? A : There are five factors in the first jhāna. When a monk obtains the first jhāna, there are initial thoughts, applied thoughts, joy, happiness and onepointedness of mind.

P 19 : (294, 32–37 ; 295, 1–4) : Q : How many factors are got rid of and how many factors are obtained in the first jhāna ? A : In the first jhāna, five factors are eradicated, and five factors are obtained. To the monk who enters the 1st jhāna, sense-desire, ill-will, sloth and torpor, restlessness and worry, doubts are eradicated, initial thoughts, applied thoughts, joy, happiness and onepointedness of mind arise.

P 28 : (296, 24–31) : Q : How many conditions are there to attain freedom of mind which is neither pleasant nor unpleasant ? A : There are four conditions to attain freedom of mind which is neither pleasant nor unpleasant. A monk, having given up pleasant feeling, having given up unpleasant feeling, having reduced former pleasures and sorrows, enters and abides into the 4th jhāna which is pure and endowed with equanimity and mindfulness.

P 29 : (296, 31–35) : Q : How many conditions are there to attain freedom of mind which is signless ? A : There are two conditions to attain freedom of mind which is signless, not to think of all signs and to think of the plane of the signless.

P 30 : (296, 36–37; 297, 1–3) : Q : How many conditions are there to dwell into freedom of mind which is signless ? A : There are 3 conditions to dwell into freedom of mind which is signless, not to think of all signs, to think of the plane of signless and a previous preparation (Pubbe abhisaṅkhāro).

P 31 : (297, 4–8) : Q : What are the conditions to emerge from freedom of mind which is signless ? A : There are two conditions to emerge from freedom of mind which is signless, to reflect on all signs and not to reflect over the plane of the signless.

P 9 : (293, 29–34) : Q : A pure mind-consciousness not connected with five faculties, what can it know ? A : A pure mind-consciousness not connected with five faculties can know the plane of infinite space, the plane of infinite consciousness, the plane of nothingness.

E. — CONCLUSION

C : (87*a*, 8–9) : Thus those two elders praised each other, saying : « Very good, very good, » spoke to each other, were delighted and abided in. Then they got up from their seat and departed.

P : (298, 28–29) : Thus spoke elder Sāriputta. Well pleased, elder Mahākoṭṭhita was delighted in what elder Sāriputta had said.

C. S. N° 31

CHINESE : N° 210, *Fa-lo-pi-ch'iu-ni-ching* (法樂比丘尼經),
(Tsê vii, 83b-85a).

PĀLI : N° 44, Cūḷavedallasuttaṃ (T. M. N. i, 299-305).

A. — GIST OF THE C SŪTRA

Lady-devotee Pi-shê-ch'ü (P : Visākhā) approached bhikṣuṇī Fa-lo (P : Dhammadinnā) and asked her a series of questions on various subjects and to which Bhikṣuṇī Fa-lo replied. Her replies were praised by lady-devotee Pi-shê-ch'ü. Then bhikṣuṇī Fa-lo approached the Buddha and reported her conversation with lady-devotee Pi-shê-ch'ü to him and the Buddha approved all her answers and praised her.

P : Almost the same. But it refers to Visākha as a layman, former husband of Dhammadinnā, and it was Visākha who reported the conversation to the Buddha, and not the nun herself.

B. — TITLE OF THE SŪTRA

C : Fa-lo-pi-ch'iu-ni-ching, discourse on bhikṣuṇī Fa-lo, referring to the name of bhikṣuṇī Fa-lo, to whom lady-devotee Pi-shê-ch'ü asked various questions.

P : Cūḷavedallasutta, discourse on Vedalla, which refers to various subjects asked by Visākha. It bears the same title with the preceding Pāli sutta, with Cūḷa instead of Mahā.

C. — LOCATION OF THE SŪTRA

C : At Shê-wei (Sāvatthi), Shêng-lin (Jetavana), Kei-ku-to park (Anāthapiṇḍikārāma).

P : At Rājagaha, Veluvana, Kalandakanivāpa.

D. — CONTENTS OF THE SŪTRA

I. — *Circumstances leading to the deliverance of the sūtra :*

C : (83*b*, 10-11) : At that time, lady-devotee Pi-shê-ch'ü came to bhikṣuṇī Fa-lo's place, bowed down at her feet, sat at one side and asked :

« Ven., (I) want to ask (some questions), do you allow me to do so?» Bhikṣuṇī Fa-lo replied: « If (you) want to ask questions, please do so. Having heard, I shall think over ».

P: (299, 2-6): It mentions Visākhā as a layman but not Visākhā, the lady-devotee. He asked questions to nun Dhammadinnā straightway, without first asking permission.

II. — *Series of questions asked :*

The 2 versions present many differences about the questions asked. In the C version, there are 30 questions while in the P, there are 34 questions. Corresponding questions in both versions amount to 22, 8 C questions cannot be found in the P version, and 9 P questions cannot be found in the C version. Among the 8 questions not to be found in the P, 6 questions are already found in the previous sūtra Ta-chü-ch'ih-lo-ching. Among the 9 P questions not to be found in the C, 3 questions are already found in the previous C sūtra Ta-chü-ch'ih-lo-ching.

a) 22 *Corresponding questions :* C 1 = P 1; C 2 = P 6; C 3 = P 7; C 4 = P 3; C 5 = P 5; C 6 = P 8; C 7 = P 9; C 9 = P 10; C 12 = P 11; C 17 = P 15; C 18 = P 17; C 19 = P 20; C 20 = P 21; C 21 = P 22; C 22 = P 23 & P 24; C 23 = P 25 & P 26 & P 27; C 24 = P 28; (C 25 = P 28); C 25 = P 29; C 27 = P 30; C 28 = P 31; C 29 = P 32; C 30 = P 34.

b) 8 *C questions not found in the P :* C 8 ; C 10 ; C 11 ; C 13 ; C 14 ; C 15 ; C 16 ; C 26. The following 6 questions are already found in the preceding C and P sūtras : C 10 = C 15 ; C 11 = P 18 ; C 13 = C 20 ; C 14 = C 21 ; C 15 = C 22 ; C 16 = C 23.

c) 9 *P questions not found in the C version :* P 2 ; P 4 ; P 12 ; P 13 ; P 14 ; P 16 ; P 18 ; P 19 ; P 33. Among these nine, 3 questions are already found in the preceding sūtra : P 16 = C 24 ; P 18 = C 25 ; P 19 = C 26. The underlined figures refer to the preceding C and P sūtras.

a) *Questions about one's own body and aggregates :*

C 1 = P 1 :

C : (83*b*, 11-13) : Pi-shê-ch'ü asked : « Ven., one's own body is called one's own body. What is called one's own body ? » Bhikṣuṇī Fa-lo replied : « The W. H. One spoke of the 5 growing aggregates as one's own body, growing aggregates of material form, of feeling, of perception, of mental properties, growing aggregate of consciousness. They are what the W. H. One spoke as five growing aggregates. » Lady-devotee Pi-chê-ch'ü having heard, praised saying : « Very good, very good, Oh Ven. ! » The lady-devotee having praised, was delighted and abided in.

P : (299, 7–16) : Almost the same. The question is the same, the answer is slightly different. C : 5 growing aggregates = P : Pañcupādānakkhandhā. C : These are what the W. H. One spoke as five growing aggregates = P : These 5 upādānakkhandhā were spoken by the Tathāgata as sakkāya.

C 2 = *P* 6 :

C : (83*b*, 13–16) : (The way to ask questions and to answer them is exactly the same in the remaining questions).

Q : How does the view about one's own body arise ? A : The unlearned, ignorant worldling does not see well-learned persons, does not know the ariyan dharma, is not tamed in the ariyan dharma. He sees material forms as soul, sees soul as possessing material forms, sees material forms in the soul, sees soul in material forms (In the same way with the other 4 aggregates). This is called view on one's own body.

P : (300, 4–17) : Almost the same. C : The unlearned, ignorant worldling... in the ariyan dharma = P : The unlearned worldling who does not see the noble ones, who is not versed in the ariyan dhamma, who is not trained in the ariyadhamma, who does not see superman, who is not versed in the superman dhamma, who is not trained in the superman dhamma. C : Soul = Atta.

C 3 = *P* 7 :

C : (83*b*, 16–18) : Q : How does the view about one's own body not come up ? A : (Just the reverse of the preceding answer).

P : (300, 17–30) : Same remarks as in the preceding question.

C 4 = *P* 3 :

C : (83*b*, 18–19 ; 84*a*, 1) : How does one's own body come to be destroyed ? A : The growing aggregates of material forms are eradicated without remainder, given up, thrown out, extinguished, not contaminating (others), cease, stop, vanish. The growing aggregates of feeling, of perception, of mental properties, of consciousness are eradicated without remainder... vanish. This is called the cessation of one's own body.

P : (299, 21–25) : Almost the same. Q : Cessation of one's own body is called cessation of one's own body ; how the Blessed One called cessation of one's own body ? A : The cessation with no attachment remaining, the giving up, the rejection, the emancipation, the doing away, this is called the cessation of one's own body by the Blessed One.

C 5 = *P* 5 :

C : (84*a*, 1–4) : Q : Aggregates are called aggregates. Growing aggregates are called growing aggregates. Are aggregates the same as growing aggregates ? Are growing aggregates the same as aggregates ? Are groving aggregates different from aggregates ? A : There are cases when aggregates are growing aggregates; there are cases when aggregates are not growing aggregates. How aggregates are growing aggregates? When material forms are with defilements, with grasping; when feeling, perception, mental properties, consciousness are with defilements, with grasping, then aggregates are called growing aggregates. How are aggregates not growing aggregates? When material forms are without defilements, without grasping; when feeling, perception, mental properties, consciousness are without defilements, without grasping, then aggregates are not called growing aggregates.

P : (299, 32-35; 300, 1-3): Not exactly the same. Q: Is grasping the same with five aggregates of grasping, or is grasping different from the five aggregates of grasping? A: Grasping is not the same with 5 aggregates of grasping and grasping is not different from the 5 aggregates of grasping. When there are desire and attachment in the 5 aggregates of grasping, then there is grasping. C: Growing aggregates = P: Upādānakkhandhā.

In this series of questions, two P questions are not found in the C version:

P 2: (299, 16-21): Q: The origin of one's own body is called origin of one's own body. How is it called origin of one's own body by the Blessed One? A: Whatever is craving, leading to rebirth, connected with delight and attachment, enjoying this and that, such as craving for sense-desire, craving for becoming, craving for non-becoming. This is called the origin of one's own body by the Blessed One.

P 4: (299, 28-32): Q: The path leading to the cessation of one's own body is called the path leading to the cessation of one's own body. How is it called the path leading to the cessation of one's own body by the Blessed One? A: This noble eightfold path is called the path leading to the cessation of one's own body by the Blessed One, such as right view, right thought, right speech, right action, right livelihood, right exertion, right mindfulness, right concentration.

b) *Questions about the eightfold path :*

C 6 = *P* 8:

C : (84*a*, 4-5): Q: What is the noble eightfold path? A: The noble eightfold path is right view up to right concentration, this is called the noble eightfold path.

P : (300, 31-34): Almost the same. The P enumerates the whole eight.

C 7 = *P* 9:

C : (84*a*, 6-7): Q: Is the noble eightfold path a conditioned dharma? A: The noble eightfold path is a conditioned dharma.

P : (300, 35-36; 301, 1): The same.

C 8 = *P no :*

C : (84*a*, 7–8) : How many groups are there ? A : There are 3 groups : moral-precept-group, concentration-group and wisdom-group.

C 9 = *P* 10 :

C : (84*a*, 8–11) : Q : Does the noble eightfold path include the 3 groups, or the 3 groups include the noble eightfold path ? A : The noble eightfold path does not include the 3 groups, but the 3 groups include the noble eightfold path. Right speech, right action, right livelihood, these three constituents are included in the noble moral precept-group; right mindfulness, right concentration, these two constituents are included in the noble concentration-group; right view, right thought, right means, these 3 constituents are included in the noble wisdom-group. This is why the noble eightfold path does not include the 3 groups, but the 3 groups include the eightfold path.

P : (301, 1–11) : Almost the same, but the form of the question is rather different. Q : Are the 3 groups included in the eightfold path or is the noble eightfold path included in the 3 groups ? One important difference here is that the P includes right exertion (sammāvāyāma) in concentration-group, while the C includes right means in the wisdom-group.

c) *Questions about cessation, first dhyāna and concentration :*

C 10 = *P no :*

C : (84*a*, 11–12) : Q : Has cessation any counterpart ? A : Cessation has no counterpart.

C 11 = *P no :*

C : (84*a*, 12–13) : Q : The first dhyāna has how many factors ? A : The first dhyāna has 5 factors : initial thoughts, applied thoughts, joy, happiness and one-pointedness of mind. This is called the 5 factors of the first dhyāna.

P : Not available here, but already available in the preceding sutta N° 43, P 18.

C 12 = *P* 11 :

C : (84*a*, 13–16) : Q : What is concentration ? What is the sign of concentration ? What is the strength of concentration ? What is the effect (Kung : 功) of concentration ? What is the practice in concentration ? A : If meritorious mind becomes one-pointed, this is called concentration. Four applications of mindfulness are called sign of concentration. The 4 right eradications are called the strength of concentration; the 4 psychic powers are called the effect of concentration. When one trains oneself in these meritorious dharmas, time and again engages oneself in the practice, with exertion, this is called practice in concentration.

P: (301, 11-16): Almost the same. Q: What is concentration ? What is the sign of concentration ? What are the requisites for concentration ? What is the training in concentration ? A: One-pointedness of mind is concentration ; 4 applications of mindfulness are signs of concentration, 4 right exertions are the requisites of concentration; the practice, the training, the continuous practices of these dhammas are called the training in concentration.

d) *Questions about death, concentration of complete cessation, concentration of no-perception :*

Please see ante, section on Samādhi, p. 104 from C N° 211 : (vii, 86b, 4-6) to p. 105, up to... then desireless touch (appaṇihita).

e) *Questions about feelings :*

C 20 = *P* 21 :

C: (84*b*, 10-12): Q: How many feelings are there ? A: There are 3 kinds of feeling, pleasant feeling, unpleasant feeling, neither pleasant nor unpleasant feeling. Depending on what do they come into existence ? Depending on strong enjoyment, they come into existence.

P: (302, 28-30): Almost the same. It omits the last portion: « Dependent on what... come into existence ». C: Strong enjoyment = P: Phassa.

C 21 = *P* 22 :

C: (84*b*, 12-15): Q: What is pleasant feeling? What is unpleasant feeling? What is neither pleasant nor unpleasant feeling? A: When pleasure arises due to strong enjoyment, body and mind enjoy a pleasant and desirable feeling, this is called pleasant feeling. When suffering arises due to strong enjoyment, body and mind suffer an unpleasant, undesirable feeling, this is called unpleasant feeling When neither pleasant nor unpleasant feeling arises due to strong enjoyment, body and mind experience neither pleasant nor unpleasant, neither desirable nor undesirable feeling, this is called neither pleasant nor unpleasant feeling.

P: (302, 30-36 ; 303, 1): Almost the same. The definition here is simpler: Whatever bodily and mental feeling which is pleasant and desirable is called pleasant feeling...

C 22 = *P* 23 & *P* 24:

C: (84b, 15-18): Q: Pleasant feeling, what is its pleasantness? What is its unpleasantness, what is its impermanence, what is its danger, what is its latent tendency? (Same questions for unpleasant feeling and neither pleasant nor . . . . unpleasant feeling). A: Pleasant feeling, when it arises, when it lasts, it is its pleasantness; when it changes, it is its unpleasantness; its impermanence is its danger; desire is its latent tendency. For unpleasant feeling, when it arises, when it lasts, it is its unpleasantness; when it changes, it is its pleasantness; its impermanence is its danger; ill-will is its latent tendency; for neither pleasant nor unpleasant feeling, when it is not known, it is its unpleasantness; when it is not known, it is its pleasantness; its impermanence is its change. Ignorance is its latent tendency.

P 23 : (303, 1-3): Not exactly the same. Here it is simpler. Q: For pleasant feeling, what is pleasant, what is unpleasant? For unpleasant feeling, what is unpleasant, what is pleasant? For neither pleasant nor unpleasant feeling, what is pleasant, what is unpleasant? A: For pleasant feeling, when it lasts, it is pleasant; when it changes, it is unpleasant. For unpleasant feeling, when it lasts, it is unpleasant; when it changes, it is pleasant; for neither pleasant nor unpleasant feeling, when it is known, it is pleasant; when it is not known, it is unpleasant. Here, for neither pleasant nor unpleasant feeling, the C and the P interpretations are not the same.

P 24 : (303, 6-11): As for the latent tendency (anusaya) of the 3 feelings, the answer is the same with the C.

C 23 = *P* 25 + *P* 26 + *P* 27 :

C : (84*b*, 18-20 ; 85*a*, 1-4) : Q: Do all pleasant feelings have desire as its latent tendency? Do all unpleasant feelings have ill-will as its latent tendency? Do all neither pleasant nor unpleasant feelings have ignorance as its latent tendency? A: All pleasant feelings do not have desire as its latent tendency ; all unpleasant feelings do not have ill-will as its latent tendency ; all neither pleasant nor unpleasant feelings do not have ignorance as its latent tendency. How all pleasant feelings have not desire as its latent tendency? When a monk is aloof from desire, is aloof from evil, demeritorious dharmas, attains and abides in the first dhyāna, which is endowed with initial thoughts, with applied thoughts, with joy and happiness born out of seclusion, this is called pleasant feeling which has not desire as its latent tendency. Why is it so? Because this destroys desire. How do all unpleasant feelings not have ill-will as its latent tedency? When one is after happiness of exalted freedom, in his endeavour there arises unpleasant feeling, this is called unpleasant feeling which has not ill-will as its latent tendency. Why is it so? because this destroys ill-will. How all neither pleasant nor unpleasant feelings have not ignorance as its latent tendency? With the cessation of happiness, with the cessation of suffering, with the cessation of former pleasures and sorrows, he attains and abides in the 4th dhyāna which is purified by mindfulness, which is neither pleasant nor unpleasant. This is called neither pleasant nor unpleasant feeling which has not ignorance as latent tendency. Why is it so? Because this destroys ignorance.

P 25, *P* 26, *P* 27 : (303, 11-36 ; 304, 1-7) : The C passage covers up to 3 questions in the P version. The P question N° 25 is the same as the C question N° 23. But it simply answers in the negative. In *P* 26, it is asked what is to be got rid of in pleasant feeling, in unpleasant feeling and in neither pleasant nor unpleasant feeling and the reply is that in pleasant feeling, attachment is to be got rid of, in unpleasant feeling, ill will is to be got rid of, in neither pleasant nor unpleasant feeling, ignorance is to be got rid of. In *P* 27, it is asked if attachment, ill-will and ignorance are to be got rid of respectively in all pleasant feelings, all unpleasant feelings, all neither pleasant nor unpleasant feelings ? The reply is almost the same as in the C. C: Why is it so ? Because this destroys desire = P : Due to this, that attachment is destroyed, there is no latent tendency of attachment here. C : When one is after happiness of exalted freedom, in his endeavour there arises unpleasant feeling, this is called unpleasant feeling which has no ill-will as latent tendency = P : The monk thinks : « Having attained this plane, I will abide in the very plane attained and abided in by the Noble Ones ». To the monk who has made such a vow, displeasure arises on account of this vow ; thus due to this, ill-will is destroyed, there is no latent tendency of ill-will here. As to the reply about neither pleasant nor unpleasant feeling, it is the same as in the C. It adds only: « There is no latent tendency of ignorance here ».

f) *Questions about counterpart : (P : Paṭibhāga) :*

C 24 = *P* 28 :

C : (85*a*, 4-5) : Q : What is the counterpart of pleasant feeling ? A : Unpleasant feeling is the counterpart of pleasant feeling.

P : (304, 8-10) : The same.

C 25 = *P* 29 :

C : (85*a*, 5-6) : Q : What is the counterpart of unpleasant feeling ? A : Pleasant feeling is the counterpart of unpleasant feeling.

P : (304, 10-12) : The same.

C 26 = *P no :*

C : (85*a*, 6-7) : Q : What is the counterpart of pleasant feeling, of unpleasant feeling ? A : Neither pleasant nor unpleasant feeling is the counterpart of pleasant feeling, unpleasant feeling.

C 27 = *P* 30 :

C : (85*a*, 7-9) : Q : What is the counterpart of neither pleasant no unpleasant feeling ? A : Ignorance is the counterpart of neither pleasant noı unpleasant feeling.

P : (304, 12-14) : The same.

C 29 = *P* 32 :

C: (85*a*, 10–11): What is the counterpart of knowledge? A: Nirvāṇa is the counterpart of knowledge.

P: (304, 16–17) : The question is the same but the answer is different. The P replies that freedom is the counterpart of ignorance. Here the P adds another question: « What is the counterpart of freedom? » A: « Nibbāna is the counterpart of freedom ».

C 30 = *P* 34:

C: (85*a*, 11–12): Q: What is the counterpart of Nirvāṇa? A: You want to ask an unlimited question. But what you ask is not beyond my (knowledge). Nirvāṇa has no counterpart, Nirvāṇa has no defect of entanglement, all entanglements have been removed. Due to this meaning (purpose, aim), people practise the brahma-life under the W. H. One.

P: (304, 19–25): The question is the same, but the answer is rather different. A: Your question is beyond limit. It is impossible to grasp the compass of the question. The Brahma-life is for the merger into Nibbāna, for aiming at Nibbāna, for ending into Nibbāna. If you wish it, approach the Blessed One and ask this meaning. What the Blessed One replies, you should bear in mind.

In the P version, there are 3 questions not to be found in the C version. They are N° 12, N° 13, and N° 14.

P 12: (301, 17–18): Q: How many kinds of activities are there? A: There are three kinds of activities: bodily activities, vocal activities, mental activities.

P 13: (301, 19–22): Q: What are bodily activities? What are vocal activities? What are mental activities? A : Breathing in, breathing out are bodily activities; initial thoughts, applied thoughts are vocal activities; perception and feeling are mental activities.

P 14: (301, 22–29): Q: How breathing in, breathing out are bodily activites? How initial thoughts, applied thoughts are vocal activities? How perception and feeling are mental activities? A: Breathing in and breathing out are bodily dharmas, connected with body, therefore they are bodily activities; having first initial thoughts, applied thoughts one breaks out to speak, therefore initial thoughts, applied thoughts are vocal activities. Perception and feeling are psychic factors, they are dhammas connected with mind, therefore they are called mental activities.

III. — *Conversation reported to the Buddha :*

C : (85*a*, 12–18) : Then lady-devotee Pi-shê-ch'ü, having heard Bhikṣuṇī Fa-lo's speech, having well received, well grasped, well recited and well trained, rose from her seat, bowed down at Bhikṣuṇī Fa-lo's feet, went round her three times and departed. Then Bhikṣuṇī Fa-lo, having seen lady-devotee Pi-shê-ch'ü depart not for a long time, came to the Buddha's place, bowed down at the Buddha's feet, sat at one side and reported her whole conversation with lady-devotee Pi-shê-ch'ü to the Buddha. She joined her hands towards the Buddha and said: « W.H. One, I have spoken like that ; I have replied like that. Did I slander the W.H. One? did I speak rightly, did I speak in accordance with the dharma, did I speak following the dharma? Comparing with the dharma, is there (in my speech) anything contrary (to the dharma), anything contestable and faulty? » The W.H. One replied : « Oh bhikṣuṇī, what you have spoken, what you have replied did not slander me. You have spoken rightly, in accordance with the dharma, there is nothing contrary, nothing contestable, nothing faulty. If lady-devotee Pi-shê-ch'ü, with such a sentence, with such a letter comes to ask me, I shall take such a mean'ng, such a sentence, such a letter to reply to lady-devotee Pi-shê-ch'ü. This meaning is what you have spoken. You should bear it in mind. Why is it so? This speech is in accordance with the meaning.

P : (304, 26-36 ; 305, 1-2): Not exactly the same. Here it mentions simply Visākha delighted in bhikkhunī Dhammadinnā's speech, thanked her. In the P, it was layman devotee Visākha who came to the Buddha and reported the whole conversation to him. The P mentions simply that the Buddha praised bhikkhunī Dhammadinnā as being well learned and endowed with great wisdom. And he said that in case lay-devotee came to him with the set of questions, he would reply with the same answers as done by bhikkhunī Dhammadinnā. Then he advised Visākha to abide by this meaning.

B. — CONCLUSIONS

C : (85*a*, 18) : Thus spoke the Buddha. Bhikṣuṇī Fa-lo and the monks, having heard the Buddha's speech, were delighted and abided in.

P : (305, 3-4) : It mentions layman devotee Visākha who was delighted at the Blessed One's speech.

C. S. N° 39

CHINESE : N° 133, *Yu-p'o-li-ching* (優婆利經) (Tsê vi, 55b–59a).

PĀLI : N° 56, Upālisuttaṃ (T.M.N. i, 371–387).

A. — GIST OF THE C SŪTRA

Ch'ang-k'u-hsing (P: Dīghatapassī) had a conversation with the Buddha in which he expounded Ch'in-tzu's (P: Nātaputta) doctrine on punishment and the predominant part played by bodily punishment in any wrong action. On the contrary, the Budhha expounded his doctrine of karma and the predominant part played by mental deed in any wrong action. Ch'ang-k'u-hsing reported this conversation to Ch'in-tzu in the presence of Yu-p'o-li (P: Upāli) a householder. Then Yu-p'o-li, with Ch'in-tzu's approval went to refute the Buddha's views. But the Buddha with some similes converted Yu-p'o-li to his own doctrine and the latter became his disciple. Then Yu-p'o-li went home, proclaimed his new faith, rejected his former faith in the Ni-chien (P: Nigaṇṭhā). Ch'in-tzu, having heard the news, went himself to Yu-p'o-li and being told by the latter of his new conversion, Ch'in-tzu vomitted hot blood and died at Po-ho (P : Pāvā) later on.

P: Almost the same, but omits the death of Nātaputta.

B. — TITLE OF THE SŪTRA

C: Yu-p'o-li-ching, discourse on Yu-p'o-li, which refers to the former disciple of the Ni-chien, who later became the Buddha's disciple.

P: Upālisuttaṃ, which is the same as with the C.

C. — LOCATION OF THE SŪTRA

C: At Nā-nan-t'o, in Po-p'o-li-nai forest.

P: At Nālandā, in Pāvārikambavana.

D. — CONTENTS OF THE SŪTRA

I. — *Conversation between Ch'ang-k'u-hsing and the Buddha :*

C: (55*b* 8–19 ; 56*a*, 1–5): Ch'ang-k'u-hsing came to the Buddha's place, exchanged greetings with the Buddha and sat at one side. The Buddha asked him: «How many deeds does Ni-chien Ch'in-tz'u expound for the getting rid of bad actions ?» Ch'ang-k'u-hsing replied that Ch'in-tzu did not expound deeds for the eradication of bad actions, but he expounded punishment. Then he proceeded to explain that there were three kinds of punishment, bodily punishment, vocal punishment and mental punishment which were not similar and that bodily punishment played the most important part in the eradication of bad deeds. Then the Buddha expounded his own doctrine, on karma (deed) for the eradication of bad actions, on 3 kinds of deed, bodily, vocal and mental, and mental deed played a predominant part in getting rid of bad actions. Both the Buddha and Ch'ang-k'u-hsing repeated three times their own exposition ; then Ch'ang-k'u-hsing departed.

P: (371, 25–29 ; 372 ; 373, 1–28): Almost the same. It adds the Buddha saying to Dīghatapassī: «There is a seat, if you wish, please sit down», and Dīghatapassī took a low seat and sat down. The Buddha's question is slightly different: «How many deeds does Nātaputta, the Nigaṇṭha expound for the performance of a bad action, for the continuance of a bad action.» C: Punishment = P: Daṇḍa. C: Bodily punishment played the most important part in the eradication of bad deeds = P : Bodily punishment produces more demerit. C : Mental deed played a predominant part in getting rid of bad actions = P: Mental deed played a predominant part in performing a bad action. The C interpretation is closer to the Jainas' views.

II. — *Ch'ang-k'u-hsing's report to Ch'in-tzu and Yu-p'o-li's request to go and challenge the Buddha*

C : (56*a*, 5–20 ; 56*b*, 1–5) : Ch'ang-k'u-hsing reported the whole conversation to Ch'in-tzu who praised him as follows : « Very good, very good, you have performed the disciples' duties towards the Teacher. You are of wise actions, intelligent, of sure decision, secure, fearless, having attained mastery, a great arguer, who has obtained the flag of ambrosia, having attained the ambrosia plane and abided in it. Why is it so ? Because you have expounded to recluse Ch'ü-t'an that bodily punishment played the most predominant part in getting rid of bad actions, in not performing bad actions. Vocal punishment is not like that. Mental punishment is the weakest. They cannot compare with bodily punishment which is the strongest» At that time, Yu-p'o-li was in the assembly, along with 500 householders He joined his hands towards Ch'in-tzu and asked Ch'ang-k'u-hsing if really he had thrice pinned recluse Ch'ü-t'an down in such a matter, and to the positive reply of Ch'ang-k'u-hsing, he said that he also could pin dow recluse Ch'ü-t'an in such a matter, to drag him along. Then Yu-p'o-li cited 4 similes to show how he would drag recluse Ch'ü-t'an in his controversy ; just like a strong man who takes hold of a ram by its long fleece and drags it along according to his wish ; just like a strong man who with his hand holding a fleeced cloth, beats it to remove dust ; just like a king-elephant, 60 years old, a proud big elephant with matured tusk, feet and body, in full strength is taken by a strong man to bathe, washing its hip, its back, its belly, its tusk, its head and make it play in the water. While Ch'in-tzu was confident that Yu-p'o-li would succeed in refuting recluse Ch'ü-t'an and urged him to go, Ch'ang-k'u-hsing apprehended the result of such a conversation, saying : « Recluse Ch'ü-t'an knows a conjuring mantra to entice people to become monks, nuns, laymen disciples, laywomen disciples, I am afraid that Yu-p'o-li, the householder will be enticed by recluse Ch'ü-t'an and become his disciple ». Three times Ch'ang-k'u-hsing made known his apprehension, three times Ch'in-tzu allayed Ch'ang-k'u-hsing's fear, saying that there was possibility of recluse Ch'ü-t'an to become Yu-p'o-li's disciple, but there was no possibility of Yu-p'o-li's becoming recluse Ch'ü-t'an's disciple. At the end he allowed Yu-p'o-li to go and challenge the Buddha. Then Yu-p'o-li, the householder bowed his head down at Ch'in-tzu's feet, went round him three times and departed.

P : (373, 29-36 ; 374 ; 375, 1-33) : Almost the same. Nātaputta's praise to Dīghatapassī is as follows : « It is good, it is good that such is the reply given to recluse Gotama by Dīghatapassī, the Nigaṇṭha who knows properly the doctrine of the master and who is a learned disciple. How can a tiny mental punishment be compared with the gross bodily punishment ? The bodily punishment indeed is more to be blamed in the performance, in the continuance of bad actions; mental punishment and vocal punishment are not like that. » In the P version, Upāli repeated Nātaputta's praise to extol Dīghatapassī and expressed his willingness to go and challenge the Buddha. The 4 similes are not exactly the same. The first simile is almost similar. The 2nd simile is different : « Just like a worker in a liquor shop (Soṇḍikākammakara) who sinks a big soṇḍikākilañjaṃ (a mat in the wine-shop) in a deep lake ; he takes hold of its corner and drags it. The 3rd simile is also not the same : « Just like a strong soṇḍikādhutta (a keeper of a liquor shop), who takes hold of a vālaṃ (a hairsieve) by the corner and shakes it, tosses it over and over. The 4th simile refers to an elephant kuñjara, 60 years old, who plunges into a deep pond and plays the game called saṇadhovikam (washing play, saṇa means hemp, which the worker in the wine shop thrashes against water for washing). Dīghatapassī's apprehension is almost the same.

III. — *Conversation between Yu-p'o-li and the Buddha :*

1) *Meeting between Yu-p'o-li and the Buddha :*

C : (56*b*, 5-11) : Then Yu-p'o-li went to the Buddha's place, exchanged greetings with him, sat at one side and started enquirying about the conversation between Ch'ang-k'u-hsing and the Buddha. When he came to know the subject of this conversation, Yu-p'o-li repeated the same praise uttered by him in praise of Ch'ang-k'u-hsing. Then the Buddha asked Yu-p'o-li if he was ready to base his discussion on the truth, then the Buddha would be ready to have a conversation with him. Yu-p'o-li replied in the affirmative and the conversation took place.

P : (375, 34-36; 376, 1-22): Almost the same. C : Exchanged greetings = P : Bhagavantaṃ abhivādetvā.

2) *The Buddha's arguments :*

Ist example : C 1 = P 2 :

C : (56*b*, 11-15): Suppose there is a Ni-chien who comes, who is prone to charity, delights in the practice of charity, does not indulge in any recreation and amusement, absolutely pure and always practises mantras. If while going and coming, he kills lot of big and small creatures, does this killing bring result to him ? Yu-p'o-li replied that if he did it consciously, it was a great crime; if he did it unconsciously, it was no great crime. Then the Buddha asked Yu-p'o-li to think well over before replying as what he spoke now was in contradiction with what he spoke before, what he had spoken before was in contradiction with what he spoke now, and that Yu-p'o-li had promised in the middle of the assembly to base his discussion on truth.

P : (376, 36; 377, 1-16): It mentions also a Nigaṇṭha who is restrained in the 4 restrains (Cātuyāmasaṃvarasaṃvuta), viz. sabbavārivārito (having refused all kinds of (unboiled water), sabbavāriyuto (having used only boiled water or having dispelled evil actions), sabbavāridhuto (having warded off evil actions), sabbavāriphuto (having realized all the restrainsts). This Nigaṇṭha while walking up and down kills many small creatures. The rest is almost the same. Here the P adds: « To what daṇḍa does this cetanā belong ? And to Upāli's reply that it belonged to manodaṇḍa, the Buddha asked Upāli to think well over before replying. The P adds Upāli saying that despite what the Blessed One had said, to him bodily punishment was more to be blamed in the performance and the continuation of evil actions.

2nd example : C 2 = P 1 :

C : (56*b*, 15-18): If there is a Ni-chien who comes, drinking only of boiled water, abstaining from unboiled water, and having no boiled water, wants to drink unboiled water. As he cannot obtain unboiled water, he passes away. What will be his place of rebirth ? Yu-p'o-li replied that there was a heaven called «Mind attached». If this Ni-chien died with a mind attached, he would be born in this heaven called «Mind attached». (The rest about the Buddha's warning is the same as in the first example).

P : (376, 23-36): Almost the same. The P adds that this Nigaṇṭha was very sick (Ābādhiko dukkhito bāḷhagilāno). C: Mind attached = P: Manosattā. The rest is the same as in the previous example.

3rd example : C 3 = P 3 :

C : (56*b*, 18-20; 57*a*, 1-6): Suppose there is a man, holding a knife. He says that in one day, he will kill all the inhabitants of Na-nan-t'o, making a lump of flesh, a heap of flesh of them The Buddha asked Yu-p'o-li if it was possible for this man to do what he intended to do. Yu-p'o-li replied that it was impossible as Na-nan-t'o was a flourishing place with many inhabitants, this man would tire himself out uselessly, without being able to kill all the inhabitants of Na-nan-t'o, making a lump of flesh, a heap of flesh of them. Then the Buddha asked if a recluse, a brāhmaṇa came, who possessed great psychic power, was it possible for him with an irate thought to reduce to ashes the whole Na-nan-t'o? Yu-p'o-li replied that not only one Na-nan-t'o, but even up to 2, 3, 4 Na-nan-t'o, he was able to reduce all the countries, all the inhabitants into ashes with an irate thought. Here Yu-p'o-li was warned by the Buddha as in the previous example.

P : (377, 17-36; 378, 1-12): Almost the same, but with more details. It adds: «In one moment, in one second. Not only one person, but 20, 30, 40, even 50 persons were not able to kill all beings of Nālandā and make a heap, a lump of flesh of them». In the case of a recluse, a brāhmaṇa endowed with psychic power, it is almost the same, it adds: Not only one Nālandā, but 10, 20, 30, 40, 50 Nālandās, this recluse, this brāhmaṇa was able to reduce to ashes with an irate thought.

4th example : C 4 = P 4 :

C : (57*a*, 6-12): The Buddha asked Yu-p'o-li if he has heard about great marsh-troublefree place, licorn-troublefree-place, deer-troublefree place, peace-troublefree place, wilderness-troublefree place, troublefree places they became troublefree places? To the positive reply of Yu-p'o-li, the Buddha asked Yu-p'o-li, who had made these troublefree places become troublefree places? Yu-p'o-li kept silent and the Buddha urged him to reply as it was not the time to keep silent and that he had promised to base the discussion on truth. Yu-p'o-li after a moment of silence replied that not that he wanted to keep silent, but he was thinking of something, he was thinking that, Ni-chien was foolish and ignorant, not knowing anything, had cheated him for a long time, who urged him to come to recluse Ch'ü-t'an and expound the predominant part played by bodily punishment in not performing evil deeds. He himself with his talk with recluse Ch'ü-t'an came to know that due to an angry thought of the deities that those troublefree places became troublefree places.

P : (378, 12-26) : Not exactly the same. The same question was asked by the Buddha to Upāli, but here four forests named Daṇḍaka, Kāliṅga, Mejjha and Mātaṅga were mentioned. In the P, there is no mention of Upāli keeping silent. Here Upāli replied at once that he had heard that these forests, Daṇḍaka, Kāliṅga, Mejjha and Mātaṅga became forest due to an angry thought of the seers of these forests. The rest is the same as in the first example.

III. — *Yu-p'o-li's conversion :*

1) *Yu-p'o-li taking refuge in the Triple Gem for the first time :*

C : (57*a*, 12-13) : Yu-p'o-li said to the Buddha that he had known, he had understood. And he declared his taking refuge in the Triple Gem and asked the Buddha to accept him as a lay-disciple from now on up to his death.

P : (378, 27-35 ; 379, 1-2) : Here Upāli replied that from the very first example he was already satisfied with the explanation given by the Buddha and he pretended to be his adversary in order to hear more about the diverse explanations of the Buddha. Then he praised the Buddha's explanations as being marvellous, excellent in the usual way, declared his taking refuge in the Triple Gem and asked to be accepted as a lay-disciple of the Buddha.

2) *Taking refuge in the Triple Gem for a 2nd time :*

C : (57*a*, 13-20 ; 57*b*, 1-4) : The Buddha advised Y-p'o-li to keep silent, but not to proclaim loudly, as superman considered silence as excellent. Yu-p'o-li, having heard this advice became more pleased and more satisfied with the W.H. One, as if he were to become disciple of other recluses and brāhmaṇas, they would carry flags and banners and proclaim to the whole Na-nan-t'o that he had become a disciple of theirs. But the Buddha advised to keep quiet, not to proclaim anything. Then Yu-p'o-li said that from now on, he would not allow the Ni-chien to enter his house, he would invite only 4 categories of disciples of the W.H. One. But the Buddha said to Yu-p'o-li that the Ni-chien were for a long time respected and revered by Yu-p'o-li and his family, now if they came, Yu-p'o-li should offer them something, according to his capability. Having heard this advice, Yu-p'o-li said that he felt more pleased and more satisfied with the W.H. One, as formerly he had heard the W.H. One proclaiming : « Dāna offered to me and to my disciples will yield great merit ; dāna offered to others, to others' disciples will yield no great merit. » Then the Buddha said that he never said like that ; what he said actually was that Dāna should be offered to every body, according to what pleased our own mind ; Dāna offered to the non-energetic ones would not yield great merit ; dāna offered to the energetic ones would yield great merit. Then Yu-p'o-li said that he vowed not to do anything, he knew to give or not to give to the Ni-chien. Then he declared his taking refuge in the Triple Gem and asked to be accepted as a lay-disciple for a second time.

P : (379, 3-15) : Not exactly the same. Here the Buddha did not advise Upāli to keep silent but advised him to do his actions after wisely pondering over (anuviccakāraṃ) them. To this advice, Upāli declared that he was more pleased with the Blessed One, because if he became disciple of other people, they would hoist flags and proclaim to the whole Nālandā that Upāli was a disciple of theirs. Here the P mentions at once that Upāli declared his taking refuge in the Triple Gem and asked to be accepted as a disciple for the second time. The remaining portion put in this paragraph in the C version is referred to, in the next paragraph, in the P version.

3) *Taking refuge in the Triple Gem for the 3rd time :*

C : (57*b*, 4-10) : Then the W.H. One preached the dharma to Yu-p'o-li, advised, incited, gladdened him, using numberless ways to preach the dharma to him. Having advised, incited, gladdened, the Buddha preached the dharma like the dharmas of (other) Buddhas who first preached the righteous dharmas, which gladdened those who heard them, such as talk on charity, talk on moral precepts, talk on being born in heaven, which deprecated desires as full of dangers, which deprecated birth and death as impure, which praised no-sense-desire as excellent, white and pure. The W.H. One having preached to him such dharma, knew that Yu-p'o-li's mind was glad, satisfied, soft, malleable, uplifted, onepointed, free from doubt, free from hindrance, able, with strength, capable of receiving the right dharma. Then like (other) Buddhas who preached the right essence of the dharma, the W.H. One preached to Yu-p'o-li about suffering, its origin, its cessation, and the path. Just like a white silk (?) that would take dye easily, Yu-p'o-li (sitting) on his very seat perceived the 4 noble truths, suffering, origin, cessation and path. Thus Yu-p'o-li perceived the dharma, obtained the dharma, realized the white and pure dharma, eradicated doubts, overcame uncertainty, without anyone superior to him, having no wavering, already abided in the realization of fruit, became fearless tovards the W.H. One's dharma. Then Yu-p'o-li rose from his seat, paid homage to the W.H. One and declared for the 3rd time his taking refuge in the Triple Gem and his asking to be accepted as a disciple.

P : (379, 16-36 ; 380, 1-13) : The reason that induces Upāli to take refuge for a 3rd time is similar to that one put in the preceding paragraph in the C version. It omits Upāli's declaration that from now on, he would not allow any Nigaṇṭhas to enter his house and that he would receive only 4 categories of Buddha's disciples. Here the Buddha advised Upāli to give alms to the Nigaṇṭhas as his family was a supporter to them for a long time. This advice made Upāli more pleased and satisfied with the Blessed One, as he heard that recluse Gotama had said that dāna should be given tho him and to his disciples, not to others and to others' disciples ;

that dāna offered to him and to his disciples would yield great fruit, dāna offered to others and to others' disciples did not yield great fruit. Here the P omits the Buddha's denial. C: Yu-p'o-li vowed not to do anything, he knew to give or not to give to the Ni-chien = P: Upāli said that he would know the right time for that. In the P version, after Upāli taking refuge in the Triple Gem for a 3rd time, the Buddha preached the dhamma to him. The P omits: « The W. H. One advised, incited, gladdened him... to preach the dharmas to him » C: The Buddha preached the dharmas like the dharmas of (other) Buddhas who first preached the righteous dharmas, which gladdened those who heard them = P: (simply) Bhagavā ānupubbi-kathaṃ kathesi. C: Such as talk on charity... as excellent, white and pure = P: Such as talk on charity, talk on moral practice, talk on heaven, on dangers of sense-desires, on its degradation, its defilements, on advantages of renouncing them. C: The W. H. One, having preached to him such dharma, knew that Yu-p'o-li's mind was glad, satisfied, soft, malleable, uplited, one-pointed, free from doubt, free from hindrance, able, with strength, capable of receiving the right dharma = P: When the Blessed One knew that Upāli's mind was ready, soft, free from hindrances, elated, pleased C: Like (other) Buddhas who preached the right essence of the Dharma, the W H. One preached about suffering, its origin, its cessation, the path = P: Then he preached to Upāli the dhammas that the Enlightened Ones had themselves discovered: Suffering, origin, cessation and path (Sāmukkaṃsikā dhammade-sanā). C: Just like a white silk which would take dye easily, Yu-p'o-li on his very seat perceived the 4 noble truths, suffering, origin of suffering, cessation, path. Thus Yu-p'o-li perceived the dharma, obtained the dharma, realized the white and pure dharma, eradicated doubts, overcame uncertainty, without anyone superior to him, having no wavering, already abided in the realization of fruit, became fearless towards the W. H. One's dharma = P: Just as a clean cloth free from black spots would take dye easily, even so, to the householder Upāli in this very seat, the dhamma-eye which was free from dust, free from stain arose in him: « Whatever was liable to be born was also liable to cease ». Thus householder Upāli had seen the dhamma, had attained the dhamma, had known the dhamma, had gone deep into the dhamma (pariyogāḷhadhammo), had crossed over doubts, had removed uncer-tainty, had attained without any guidance from others, full confidence in the instruction of the Teacher. While in the C version, this attainment of Yu-p'o-li made him declare for the 3rd time, his taking refuge in the Triple Gem, the P version mentions simply that Upāli said to the Blessed One that he had to go to attend to many works.

IV. — *Yu-p'o-li's instruction to his gate-keeper, Ch'in-tzu's visit and Yu-p'o-li's attitude :*

1) *Yu-p'o-li's instruction to his gate-keeper :*

C : (57*b*, 10-13): Yu-p'o-li, having well received and well abided in the W. H. One's preaching, bowed his head at the Buddha's feet, went round him 3 times and went home. There he said to his gate-keeper that now he had become the W. H One's disciple and from now on, the Ni-chien were not allowed to enter his house. Only 4 categories of the Buddha's disciples were invited to enter his house. If the Ni-chien came, the gate-keeper should tell them to wait outside the gate and have alms brought to them.

P : (380, 14-27): Almost the same. While the C uses the general term Ni-chien, the P adds both male and female Nigaṇṭhas.

2) *Ch'in-tzu's visit :*

C : (57*b*, 13-20; 58*a*, 1-11): The news of Yu-p'o-li's attitude reached Ch'ang-k'u-shing who came to Ch'in-tzu, reported the matter to him and complained that Ch'in-tzu did not heed his warnings. But Ch'in-tzu persisted in not believing in such news, saying that there was no possibility of Yu-p'o-li becoming recluse Ch'ü-t'an's disciple, but there was possibility of recluse Ch'u-t'an becoming Yu-p'o-li's disciple. Then he sent Ch'ang-k'u-hsing to go to Yu-p'o-li's house and see things for himself. Ch'ang-k'u-hsing went to Yu-p'o-li's house, found that the rumour was true and reported back again to Ch'in-tzu who even then did not believe him. Ch'in-tzu with 500 Ni-chien came to Yu-p'o-li's house, was met by the gate-keeper who repeated Yu-p'o-li's instructions. Ch'in-tzu said that he did not come for alms but he wanted to see Yu-p'o-li. Then the gate-keeper asked Ch'in-tzu to wait outside the gate and he went in to inform Yu-p'o-li of Ch'in-tzu's visit.

P : (380, 28-36 ; 381 ; 382, 1-25): Almost the same with some minor differences. While the C mentions a great company of 500 Ni-chien, the P says simply with a great assembly of Nigaṇṭhas. The rest is almost the same, with the same differences as seen before.

3) ***Yu-p'o-li's attitude and Ch'in-tzu's reaction :***

a) ***Yu-p'o-li's reception :***

C : (58*a*, 11-19) : When the gate-keeper informed Yu-p'o-li of Ch'in-tzu's visit with 500 Ni-chien, he ordered the gate-keeper to prepare seats in the middle hall. When seats were ready, Yu-p'o-li came to the middle hall, sat cross-legged on the cleanest, highest and most beautiful seat and ordered the gate-keeper to invite Ch'in-tzu and his disciples to come in, saying: The Honoured Yu-p'o-li said: « If your Honoured Ones wish please come in ». When Yu-p'o-li saw Ch'in-tzu enter with his disciples, he said: « Honoured One, there are seats, if you want to sit, please do so ». Then Ch'in-tzu said to Yu-p'o-li why he behaved like that, sitting himself cross-legged like a recluse, without any difference. Yu-p'o-li replied that he had articles, if he wanted to give them, he would give them ; if he did not want to give, he would not give. These seats belonged to him so he said: « There are seats, if you want to sit, please do so ».

P : (382, 25-36 ; 383, 1-20) : Almost the same, with some minor differences. The P adds that formerly when Nātaputta came, Upāli came forward to meet him and reserved the best and highest seat for him, which he dusted with his upper garment. The P omits Nātaputta's reproach to Yu-p'o-li behaving like a recluse and the reply of Yu-p'o-li.

b) *Conversation between Ch'in-tzu and Yu-p'o-li :*

C : (58*a*, 19-20 ; 58*b*, 1-15) : Ch'in-tzu reproached Yu-p'o-li to have been conquered by recluse Ch'ü-t'an, although Yu-p'o-li proposed to conquer Ch'ü-t'an ; just like a man who entered the forest to obtain eyes, but came back with his eyes lost ; or just like a man due to thirst entered a lake but came back still thirsty. Yu-p'o-li quoted a simile to reply to Ch'in-tzu. Suppose there is a brāhmaṇa who has a young and pregnant wife. She asks him to go to the market to buy a toy for his coming child. The brāhmaṇa tells her to wait till she gives birth to a child ; if it happens to be a boy, a toy for boy should be bought ; if it happens to be a girl, a toy for girl should be bought. But 3 times the young wife insists, 3 times the brāhmaṇa tries to reason with her. But he loves his young wife very much, so he asks her what kind of toy he should buy. She tells him to buy a small monkey-toy. When the husband brings a small monkey-toy back from the market, its colour does not please her and she asks her husband to take it to a dyer to have it dyed in yellow colour and to have it beaten so as to make it shine. The dyer says to the husband that this monkey-toy can take a beautiful yellow colour, but it cannot be beaten to make it shine. Then he recites a gāthā :

> « The monkey is able to receive colour, but it cannot be beaten ;
> If it is beaten, it will die ; ultimately, it cannot be beaten.
> This bag of impurities is of bad smell ; the monkey is full of impurities.
> In the same way, the Ni-chien's doctrine cannot be subjected to investigation, cannot be pondered over and contemplated.
> « It can dye the ignorant, but not the wise one ».

Then Yu-p'o-li compared the W. H. One's teachings to a Benares cloth which could take the most beautiful dye and also could be beaten so that it could shine out brilliantly. The Tathāgata's teachings could be subjected to investigation, could be pondered over and contemplated. It could dye the wise, but could not dye the ignorant one.

P : (383, 20-31 ; 384, 10-36 ; 385, 1-31) : Not exactly the same. It adds Nātaputta calling Upāli as becoming mad and foolish to be entangled in the great verbal dispute. The first simile is not the same. It refers to a man who is a gelder (aṇḍahārako ?) and who comes back with his testicles removed. The 2nd simile is the same as in the first simile of the C version. The simile of the brāhmana and his wife is almost the same, but it puts this simile after Nātaputta's accusation of Upāli to be enticed by recluse Gotama, while the C version puts it before. The P adds that the husband is old and aged, that the dyer's name is Rattapāṇi. C : To have it beaten so as to make it shine = P : Ākoṭitapaccākoṭitaṃ ubhatobhāgavimaṭṭhaṃ (beaten round and both sides made smooth). In the P, the dyer does not use a gāthā to reply to the brāmaṇa. He says simply that it can take dye but cannot be beaten round and made smooth both sides. C : The Ni-chien's doctrine cannot be subjected to investigation, cannot be pondered over and contemplated; it can dye the ignorant but not the wise one = P: The doctrine of the foolish Nigaṇṭha is able to dye only the foolish ones, but not the wise ones, cannot stand examination, cannot be polished. In the 2nd simile, the P refers to the same brāhmana who at another time brings Rattapāṇi a pair of new cloth to be dyed and to be beaten and smoothed, while the C refers to an independent simile.

Another accusation from Ch'in-tzu :

C : (58*b*, 15-18) : Ch'in-tzu accused Yu-p'o-li of being enticed by recluse Ch'ü-t'an's enticing mantra. Yu-p'o-li replied that Ch'ü-t'an's mantra was very good, extremely good and it would make his parents, his wife, sons, servants, king of Na-nan-t'o and all beings in the worlds of deities, of Māra, Brahmā, recluses and brāhmaṇas, from human beings up to deities, this enticing mantra would make all of them happy, secure and benefitted for a long time.

P : (383, 32-36 ; 384, 1-9) : Almost the same. C : Being enticed by recluse Ch'ü-t'an's enticing mantra = P : Enticed by the enticing charm of recluse Gotama (āvaṭṭaniyā māyāyāti) C : Very good, extremely good = P : Bhaddikā, kalyāṇī (auspicious, good). The C mentions : his parents, his wife, sons, servants, king of Na-nan-t'o and all beings in the worlds of deities, of Māra, Brahmā, recluses and brāhmaṇas, from human beings up to deities = P : dear blood-relatives, all khattiyas, brāhmaṇas, vessas, suddas, beings of the deva worlds, of Māra world, of Brahma-worlds, recluses, brāhmaṇas, deva and men.

Yu-p'o-li's gāthā : (Please see ante, p. 188, from : C N° 133 : to page 191, ...kiñci yitthaṃ etc)

E. — CONCLUSION

Here the C has its usual conclusion, while the P omits it.

C. S. N° 40

CHINESE : N° 14, Lo-yün-ching (羅 云 經) (Tsê v, 16b-17b).
PĀLI : N° 61, Ambalaṭṭhikā Rāhulovādasuttaṃ (T.M.N. i, 414-420).

A. — GIST ON THE C SŪTRA

The Buddha showed to elder Lo-yün (Rāhula) the danger of intentional lying for a monk and he advised him to reflect well over before performing any bodily, vocal and mental deeds.

P : Almost the same.

B. — TITLE OF THE SŪTRA

C : Lo-yün-ching, Sūtra on Lo-yün, which refers to elder Lo-yün, for whom the discourse is intended.

P : Ambalaṭṭhikā Rāhulovādasutta, discourse on admonition to Rāhula, at Ambalaṭṭhikā, which refers to the discourse delivered by the Buddha to Rāhula at Ambalaṭṭhikā.

C. — LOCATION OF THE SŪTRA

C : The Buddha was staying at Wang-shê town (P : Rājagaha), in the Bamboo grove at Chia-lan-to park (P : Kalandakanivāpa). He came to elder Lo-yün who was staying also at Wang-shê town, in the Hot-spring forest and delivered the discourse to him.

P : Of the same location. But here elder Rāhula was staying at Ambalaṭṭhikā.

Notes : Ambalaṭṭhikā is a royal park on the road between Rājagaha and Nālandā (D.P.P.N. i, 158).

D. — CONTENTS OF THE SŪTRA

1) *The Buddha and elder Lo-yün's meeting :*

C : (16*b*, 6-8) : The Buddha, when night was over, early in the morning, entered Wang-shê town for alms. When he finished his meal, he came over to the Hot-spring forest where elder Lo-yün was. Elder Lo-yün saw the Buddha coming from afar, went out to welcome him, took his robe and bowl, spread the seat and fetched water to wash feet. The Buddha, having washed his feet, sat on Lo-yün's seat.

P : (414, 1–9) : The Buddha here in the evening rose up from his seclusion, came to Ambalaṭṭhikā where elder Rāhula was. Elder Rāhula, seeing the Buddha coming from afar, prepared seat and water for washing feet. The Buddha sat on the prepared seat, then washed his feet. After that, elder Rāhula paid respect to him and sat at one side.

2) *First admonition :*

C : (16*b*, 8–10) : The W.H. One, having taken a little quantity of water which was left over in the vessel, asked Lo-yün if he had seen this little quantity of water ? To Lo-yün's positive answer, the Buddha said that little was the recluseship of one who knowingly told a lie, without shame, without repentance, shameless, remorseless. There was no evil deed, which he could not do. He should learn not to tell a lie even for fun.

P : (414, 10–14) : Almost the same. Here the Buddha said simply that little was the recluseship of one who knowingly told a lie, without shame, like the little quantity of water left over.

3) *2nd admonition :*

C : (16*b*, 10–11) : The Buddha, having thrown away this little quantity of water, asked elder Lo-yün if he had seen this little quantity of water completely thrown away. To Lo-yün's positive answer, the Buddha said that completely thrown away was the recluseship of one who knowingly told a lie... even for fun.

P : (414, 14–19) : Almost the same. Here the Buddha said that thrown away was the recluseship of one, who without shame, knowingly told a lie.

4) *3rd and 4th admonitions :*

C : (16*b*, 11–15) : Then the Buddha overturned the vessel and upturned the vessel and each time, he qualified as overturned and upturned the recluseship of one, who knowingly told a lie... even for fun.

P : (414, 19–28) : Almost the same, with the same remarks. After the 4th admonition, the P adds another admonition. The Buddha pointing out the voidness and the emptiness of the upturned vessel declared that void and empty was the recluseship of one who knowingly told a lie without shame.

5) *5th admonition :*

C : (16*b*, 15–20 ; 17*a*, 1) : Just like a king who possesses a big elephant. When the elephant enters into battle, he uses front legs, hind legs, tail, forehead, back, hip, neck..., ears, tusks, all parts of the body to wage battle, but he protects his trunk. Then the mahout thinks that this elephant still cares for his life. When the elephant uses all parts of his body including his trunk to wage battle, then the mahout thinks that this elephant does not care for his life. The Buddha said that this elephant when it entered the battle would do all kinds of evil deeds. In the same way for one who knowingly told a lie, without shame, without repentance, shameless and remorseless, the Buddha declared that there was no evil deed which he could not do.

P: (414, 29–34; 415, 1–19): Almost the same. The elephant is described as īsādanto (having tusk as big as a pole), ubbūḷhavā (well grown), abhijāto (well born), saṅgāmāvacaro (well frequenting the battle-field). As to the different parts of the body, used by the elephant in the battle, the P omits: forehead, back, hip, neck,...; but adds: front part of the body, hind part of the body, head. C: This elephant still cares for his life = P: This elephant does not throw away his life (apariccattaṃ). Here the admonition of the Buddha is the same as in the C version, except the omission of: Without repentance, shameless and remorseless.

6) *The gāthā:*

C: (17*a*, 2–3): The C version adds a gāthā spoken by the Buddha in this connection:

« A man commits an offence called telling lies;
He does not fear the next world, there is no evil deed which he cannot do.
It is better to swallow an iron ball, which is hot like fire,
Than to infringe the rule and accept charity from the world.
If one is afraid of suffering, having no liking to think of (suffering),
He should not perform evil deeds, secretly or openly.
If demeritorious deeds have been performed, are being performed,
Ultimately, one cannot escape from them,
And also there is no shelter (from them) ».

7) *Reflection before performing bodily, vocal and mental deed:*

a) *Simile of the mirror:*

C: (17*a*, 4–5): The Buddha asked elder Lo-yün what was the use of a mirror? Lo-yün replied that it was for the purpose of seeing one's own face clean or not clean. Then the Buddha advised elder Lo-yün that before performing any bodily deed, he should reflect if this bodily deed was pure or not pure, was for one's own sake of for the sake of others.

P: (415, 20–24): Almost the same. It omits: « To see one's own face clean or not clean. It mentions simply for the sake of looking into it. The Buddha's admonition is: « In the same way, only after much reflection that bodily, vocal and mental deeds should be performed ».

b) *About bodily deed :*

(Please see ante, p. 131, from: *C N°* 14: (*v*, 17*a*, 5-13)... to p. 132,... and of a monastic rule).

9) *A gāthā :*

C : (17*b*, 5-8): (Please see ante p. 183, from « Oh Lo-yün... to... you should not harm others ».

E. — CONCLUSION

Both versions have their usual conclusion, but the C version adds that not only Lo-yün but the monks as well rejoiced at the Buddha's speech.

C. S. N° 54

CHINESE : N° 132, *Lai-cha-ho-lo-ching*, (賴吒和羅經) (Tsê vi, 51b-55b).

PĀLI : N° 82, Raṭṭhapālasuttaṃ (T. M. N. ii, 54-74).

A. — GIST OF THE C SŪTRA

Lai-cha-ho-lo (P : Raṭṭhapāla) having listened to the Buddha's sermon wanted to become a monk, but the Buddha refused as he did not obtain his parents' consent. He went home and by threatening to fast to death, he obtained his parents' consent and became a monk under the Buddha and before long, by exertion, he attained arahantship. Then he came back home to see his parents who tried without success to make him renounce the monk's life. Then he met king Chü-lai-p'o and explained to him the reasons of his adopting a religious life.

P : Almost the same, but with some differences in details.

B. — TITLE OF THE SŪTRA

C : Lai-cha-ho-lo-ching, discourse on Lai-cha-ho-lo, which refers to the young man who became a monk against his parents' wishes.

P : Raṭṭhapālasuttaṃ, discourse on Raṭṭhapāla, which refers to the same person as in the C.

C. — LOCATION OF THE SŪTRA

C : The Buddha was among the Chü-lou-shou (P : Kurus) and stayed at Yü-lu-cha village, in the garden of Pei-t'i-shê-ho.

P : The Buddha was among the Kurus and staying in the market-town of the Kurus called Thullakoṭṭhita.

D. — CONTENTS OF THE SŪTRA

I. — *The Buddha's sermon :*

C : (51*b*, 7-15) : The Buddha was staying at Yü-li-cha village, in the Pei-t'i-shê-ho garden. A great fame spread about recluse Ch'u-t'an in 10 directions : Recluse Ch'ü-t'an was the Tathāgata, without grasping, the perfectly and rightly Enlightened, endowed with wisdom and conduct, the Well-farer, the Knower of the world, the Peerless One, the Tamer of Path and Dharma, Teacher of deities and men, the Buddha, the Protector of all. He, towards this world with the deities, and Māra, Brahmā, recluses and brāhmaṇas, from men up to deities, having realized with his own knowledge, his own realization, attained and abided in. He preached the dharma, which was lovely in the beginning, lovely in the middle, also lovely at the end, endowed with meaning and with letter, showing the completely pure brahma-life. Seeing the Tathāgata, without grasping, the perfectly and rightly Enlightened One, paying respect and making offerings to him would yield quick merit and benefit. Then the brāhmaṇas, the householders of Yü-lu-cha village came to the Buddha's place, some bowed down their head at the Buddha's feet and sat at one side, some said greetings to the Buddha and sat at one side, some joined their hands towards the Buddha and sat at one side, some saw the Buddha from afar, kept quiet and sat down. Then the Buddha, in numberless ways preached the dharma to them, gladdened, excited, aroused them and then kept silent. The brāhmaṇas, the householders of Yü-lu-cha village, being gladdened, excited and aroused by the Buddha, got up from their seats, bowed down at the Buddha's feet, went round him 3 times and departed.

P : (54, 23-27 ; 55, 1-23) : Almost the same. C : Yü-lu-cha village = P : Market-town of Thullakoṭṭhita. It omits : In the Pei-t'i-shê-ho garden. C : The tamer of Path and Dharma = P : Purisadammasārathi. C : The Protector of all = P : Bhagavā. C : Having realized with his own knowledge, his own realization, attained and abided in = P : Sayaṃ abhiññā sacchikatvā pavedeti. C : Endowed with meaning and with letter = P : Sātthaṃ savyañjanam. C : Seeing the Tathāgata, without grasping, the perfectly and rightly Enlightened One, paying respect and making offerings to him would yield quick merit and benefit = P : It is good to see such an Arahant like this. As to the various forms of greetings, the P adds that some having made known their names, their clans, sat down at one side. Here the departure of the brāhmaṇas, the householders is put in the next paragraph, not in the present one.

II. — *Lai-cha-ho-lo's request to become a monk and the Buddha's refusal :*

C : (51*b*, 15-20 ; 52*a*, 1-2) : Lai-cha-ho-lo remained seated, waited for the departure of brāhmaṇas and householders, then he got up from his seat, wore his robe showing one shoulder and said to the Buddha that according to what he understood from the Buddha's preaching, if he stayed as a householder, it was impossible for him to practise the brahma-life, completely and for the whole life. So he requested the Buddha to allow him to adopt a religious life and give him ordination to lead a monk's life. The Buddha refused as Lai-cha-ho-lo did not have his parents' consent and asked him to obtain it.

P : (55, 24-34 ; 56, 1-18) : Almost the same. The P adds a passage in which Raṭṭhapāla was thinking of his decision before announcing it to the Buddha.

III. — *Lai-cha-ho-lo's parents' refusal, his fast and his parents' attempt to induce him to give up his fast :*

C : (52*a*, 1-20 ; 52*b*, 1-2) : Then Lai-cha-ho-lo went home and requested his parents to allow him to embrace the religious life. His parents refused saying that he was their only, dearly loved son. Even if he died, they could not give him up, how could they bear not seeing him, when he was still alive. Lai-cha-ho-lo repeated 3 times his request and 3 times, his parents refused. Then Lai-cha-ho-lo lay down on the ground, refused to get up, did not drink and eat for more than 4 days. His parents implored him to get up and give up his fast, saying that his soft body was used to good seat and couch the whole of his life, how was it that now he did not know suffering. They advised him to get up and to live as a layman in giving charity so as to cultivate merit, as the W H. One's realm was most difficult and to go forth to learn the Dharma was also most difficult. Lai-cha-ho-lo remained silent. Then his parents went first to request their relatives and the great officials, then to request the well-known and learned people who were Lai-cha-ho-lo's friends and companions to advise Lai-cha-ho-lo to give up his fast. They came and were also unsuccessful in their mission. Then they advised Lai-cha-ho-lo's parents to allow him to embrace the religious life, because if he was happy in his religious life, they could see him in his life-time, and if he was unhappy, he would surely die and it served no useful purpose. Lai-cha-ho-lo's parents accepted their advice and gave their consent, on condition that Lai-cha-ho-lo should return to see them after completion of his training in the dharma. The consent was conveyed by his friends and companions to Lai-cha-ho-lo, who was overjoyed, gave up his fast and nourished back his body to normal condition.

P : (56, 19-33 ; 57, 1-26 ; 58 ; 59 ; 60, 1-22) : Almost the same. Here Raṭṭhapāla's parents objected as follows : « You are our only child, dearly loved, used to live in comfort and well cared for, not knowing anything about suffering. Come, eat, drink, indulge in sense-pleasures and perform meritorious deeds. We would not consent to your going forth. If you were to die, we would be unwilling to leave you, how would it be possible for us to allow you to go forth, while you are still living ». Here the P omits mentioning that Raṭṭhapāla fasted up to more than 4 days. His parents' imploration was almost the same with their objections except here they begged him to get up. The P mentions Raṭṭhapāla's parents' approach only to Raṭṭhapāla's friends and companions not to others. The rest is almost the same.

IV. — *Lai-cha-ho-lo's going forth, his attainment of arahantship, his return to see his parents*

C : (52*b*, 2-20 ; 53*a* ; 53*b*, 1-7) : Then Lai-cha-ho-lo approached the Buddha with his parents' authorisation and the Buddha ordained him as a monk. Then the Buddha went to Shê-wei and stayed in Shêng-lin, at Kei-ku-tu park. Lai-cha-ho-lo, after his ordination, dwelt alone and exerted himself in meditation and obtained arahantship. Then after 9 or 10 years, he thought of going to see his parents to fulfil his promise. He approached the Buddha and made known his decision to the Buddha who allowed him to go as the Buddha knew that Lai-cha-ho-lo was beyond any possibility of going back to a lower life. Then Lai-cha-ho-lo went back to his room, put his bedding in order, took his robes and begging bowl and gradually came to Yü-lu-cha village and Pei-t'i-shê-ho garden. Then early in the morning, he took his bowl and entered Yü-lu-cha for alms. He thought that the W. H. One had praised the gradual begging round so he went begging from house to house and came to his father's. At that time, his father was trimming his beard and hair. When he saw Lai-cha-ho-lo, he said : « These bald-headed recluses were given to black (actions), having no offspring, having no lineage, the destructors of my family. I had a dearly loved son, whom we were deeply attached to, but they took him away and ordained him. Do not give anything to eat to him ». Thus Lai-cha-ho-lo did not receive any alms from his own father's house except abuse. At that time, a maid-servant of his father's house filled a basket of rotten and ill-smelling food to throw them away on a refuse-heap. Lai-cha-ho-lo saw her and asked her to put this rotten food into his alms-bowl. While the maid-servant was putting the food into the begging-bowl, she recognised him with the help of two marks : his voice and his hands and feet. Then she came to inform Lai-cha-ho-lo's father who was overcome with joy at the news, and with his left hand holding the robe, with his right hand stroking beard and hair, he came hastily to Lai-cha-ho-lo's place where Lai-cha-ho-lo was eating his rotten food, leaning against the wall. Lai-cha-ho-lo's father asked his son how he could eat this rotten food, as he was of soft body and got used to dainty and delicious food. He asked him also why he did not come to his father's house, when he had reached Yü-lu-cha village. Lai-cha-ho-lo replied that he did come to his parents' house, but he received no alms there except abuse. Then Lai-cha-ho-lo's father begged pardon of his son, respectfully guided him into the house, spread the seat and invited Lai-cha-ho-lo to sit down. After that, he informed Lai-cha-ho-lo's mother of the coming of their son and asked her to prepare food. She gladly had food prepared. Then quickly she had a big heap of coins collected in the middle of the yard (so big), that one man standing at one side and another man sitting at the other side could not see each other. Then she came to Lai-cha-ho-lo and said that this heap of coins was his mother's share, and his father's share was countless and could not be counted by hundreds, by thousands. All this money would be given to Lai-cha-ho-lo, if he would give up the precepts, renounce the religious life, and live in giving charity, performing meritorious deeds, as the W.H. One's realm was most difficult, and to lead a religious life, to be trained in the dharma was most difficult. Then Lai-cha-ho-lo advised her mother to make a new cloth-bag, put all this money into it, have vehicle to carry it to the Ganges and dump it into deep water, as it was due to this money that people experienced grief, suffering, sorrow, despair, lamentation and not happiness. Lai-cha-ho-lo's mother knew that this method could not convince Lai-cha-ho-lo to give up the religious life ; then she came to the former wives of Lai-cha-ho-lo, asked them to bedeck themselves with necklaces and various garments, come to Lai-cha-ho-lo, embrace one of his feet and say : « Oh indiscriminate husband, who are the nymphs, whose beauty beat mine, and for whose sake you embraced the religious life ? » Lai-cha-ho-lo's former wives did as told, but Lai-cha-ho-lo called his former wives as sisters and said that not for any nymph's sake that he embraced the religious fife, but only for the sake of obtaining the Buddha-dharma and now his purpose had been fulfilled. Lai-cha-ho-lo's former wives stood up at one side, and wept saying that they were not Lai-cha-ho-lo's sisters but he called them so. Elder Lai-cha-ho-lo asked his parents to offer him food as it was time already but not to harass him any more. Then his parents got up from their seat, offered water for washing, with their own hands served dainty and delicious food to satisfy elder Lai-cha-ho-lo's hunger. After taking his food, elder Lai-cha-ho-lo preached the dharma to his parents in various ways, gladdened, excited and pleased them. Then he got up from his seat and proclaimed the following gāthā :

> « Look at this bedecked form, with jewels and necklaces, with jade entwining her hair, with violet pencilled eyebrows.
> « This deludes the fool, but not those who have reached the other shore.
> With various beautiful hues, to decorate the foul-smelling body,
> This deludes the fool, but not those who have reached the other shore.
> With variegated scent besmeared the whole body,
> With yellow ochre painting her feet,
> This deludes the fool, but not those who have reached the other shore.
> The body donned with pure and magnificent dress,
> Bedecked like something ephemeral,
> This deludes the fool, but not those who have reached the other shore.
> Having destroyed deer-traps and nets,
> And having broken down the deer-door,
> I have given up the enticing bait,
> How can I find happiness in deer-fetters ? »

P : (60, 23-34 ; 61 ; 62 ; 63 ; 64 ; 65, 1-6) : Not exactly the same. Raṭṭhapāla's ordination and attainment of Arahantship are almost the same. The P adds that the Buddha, half a month after Raṭṭhapāla's ordination, came to Sāvatthi, Jetavana, at Anāthapiṇḍikārāma. It omits Lai-cha-ho-lo thinking of going to see his parents, after 9 or 10 years of his attainment of arahantship. It mentions simply that after his attainment of arahantship, Raṭṭhapāla made known his intention of going to see his parents to the Buddha who consented, after knowing Raṭṭhapāla's mind with his own mind. When Raṭṭhapāla reached Thullakoṭṭhitaṃ, the P adds that he stayed in the deer-park of the Kuru king. While going for alms in Thullakoṭṭhita, Raṭṭhapāla went from house to house, but the P omits Raṭṭhapāla thinking of the Buddha's praise of this way of going for alms When Raṭṭhapāla came to his own house, his father was having his hair combed in the middle of a hall with a door, while the C mentions that he was having his beard and hair trimmed without mentioning in the middle of a hall with a door. While in the C, Lai-cha-ho-lo's father abused the monk as being given to black (actions), having no offspring, having no lineage, the destructors of his own family, the P mentions simply that he said that his only and dearly loved son went forth on account of these bald-headed recluses and thus elder Raṭṭhapāla in the house of his own father did not receive alms, did not receive a refusal but only abuse. C: A maid-servant filled a basket of rotten and ill-smelling food to throw away on a refuse-heap = P: A woman-slave related to Raṭṭhapāla wanted to throw away junket of the previous day. While the C mentions that the maid-servant, having recognised Lai-cha-ho-lo, directly came to inform Lai-cha-ho-lo's father, the P mentions that she informed first Raṭṭhapāla's mother who reported this to her husband. The P adds that, when Raṭṭhapāla's mother was informed of the presence of Raṭṭhapāla, she told the woman-slave that if this were true, she would be no longer a slave. The P omits to mention that Lai-cha-ho-lo's father was overjoyed at the news and with his left hand holding the robe and with his right hand stroking his beard and hair, he came hastily to Lai-cha-ho-lo's place. Here the P adds something new. When Raṭṭhapāla's father saw him sitting against the wall and eating the previous day's junket, he asked: « Is it really that you are eating the previous day's junket ? You should go to your own house ». And Raṭṭhapāla replied that where would be his own house, he who had gone forth from home to a homeless life. He had no home and he had gone to the householder, but he did not receive either alms or refusal but abuse. Then Raṭṭhapāla's father invited him to enter the house, but Raṭṭhapāla refused, saying that he had already taken his meal. Then the father invited him to come for to-morrow meal and he accepted by remaining silent. While in the C, it was Lai-cha-ho-lo's mother who had the money heaped and Lai-cha-ho-lo's former wives to be adorned, in the P, it was Raṭṭhapāla's father who did all this. In the C, the mother attempted twice to win over the Elder, first with heap of money and when this method failed, she asked his former wives to adorn themselves, in the P version, the father had resorted to both methods at the same time. He first had a big heap of gold coins and gold to be collected and hidden behind the screens. Then he asked Raṭṭhapāla's former wives to adorn themselves. When food was ready, he sent word to invite the Elder to come and when Raṭṭhapāla was seated, he uncovered the heap of coins and gold and said to Raṭṭhapāla that one heap belonged to his grand-father, one heap belonged to his mother and another heap belonged to his father. There was possibility for him to enjoy riches and perform meritorious deeds. So he asked his son to give up the training, revert to a lower life, enjoying riches and performing meritorious deeds. Raṭṭhapāla's reply was almost the same as in the C. Now Raṭṭhapāla's former wives came, embraced his feet and said that for what nymph's sake their young lord was adopting the brahma-life ? And Raṭṭhapāla called them sisters and replied in the negative. Then they fell to the ground and fainted after saying that their young lord called them sisters. Here the C is with more details. Then Raṭṭhapāla asked his father to offer him food, but not to annoy him anymore. The P omits Lai-cha-ho-lo's sermon to his parents. It mentions simply that when Raṭṭhapāla had finished his meal, he got up and spoke the verses. The verses in both versions are almost the same, a description of the adorned body, bedecked with ornaments but foul within, such a body deludes the fool, but not those who have reached the other shore. In the 2 last verses, the P is rather different:

« The hunter of the deer sets the trap,
The deer avoid the snare.
Having eaten the bait, they go away,
And the deer-trappers bewail themselves.

Remarks : In the Cingalese edition, but not in the Roman script edition, it inserts that Raṭṭhapāla's father had 2 heaps collected, one of golden coins, one of gold and put the 2 heaps together so that one person standing at one side could not see another man standing the other side and vice-versa. This shows that the Cingalese tradition is close to the Sanskrit tradition.

V. — *Meeting between the elder and king Chü-lao-p'o :*

1) *The king's attempt to induce the Elder to give up his religious life :*

C : (53*b*, 8-20; 54*a*, 1-4): After speaking the verses, Lai-cha-ho-lo with his psychic power flew back to Yü-lu-cha through the air, entered that forest and sat down under Pei-hsi-lei tree (椑醯勒), on his sitting mat. At that time, king Chü-lai-p'o was sitting with his ministers in his palace, speaking about, praising elder Lai-cha-ho-lo and expressing the desire to meet him. Then the king ordered his game-hunter to prepare Yü-lu-cha forest for hunting. When the game-hunter came to Yü-lu-cha forest, he saw the Elder sitting there, so he came to inform the king who at once set out in vehicles to meet the elder. He saw the Elder from afar, got down from the cart and came to meet the Elder. When elder Lai-cha-ho-lo saw the king, he asked him if he wanted to sit down. The king replied that, although this place belonged to him, he would like to be invited by the Elder to sit down. Then elder Lai-cha-ho-lo invited the king to sit down. The king asked the Elder if really he went forth because of shortage of money. If so he was ready to offer him all necessary money so that Lai-cha-ho-lo could disrobe, enjoy sense-pleasures, give charity and perform meritorious deeds, as the Master's doctrine was most difficult and to go forth and be trained in the dharma was also most difficult. Then the Elder replied that the king had used impure things to request him, but not pure things. Being asked by the king how to use pure things to request him but not impure things, the Elder said that he should say that his country's people were secure and happy, without any fear, without any disturbances, without trouble, without being a slave. Then the king said that he wanted to use pure things to request the Elder but not impure things.

P : (65, 7–29; 66, 1–6) : Not exactly the same. Here the P does not mention that the Elder flew back to Yü-lu-cha through the air. He just went back to the deer-park of king of the Kurus, sat down under a certain tree for a day-rest. It does not mention king Chü-lao-p'o sitting with his ministers in his palace, praising the Elder and expressing his desire to see him. It mentions simply that the king of the Kurus ordered his deer-trapper to clear the garden-ground of the park so that he might go and see the lovely ground. The deer-trapper went there, saw the Elder sitting under the root of a tree, came to inform the king who ordered vehicles to be ready and he went there to meet the Elder. When he met elder Raṭṭhapāla, he greeted him and invited the Elder to sit on the elephant-rug (hatthatthara), but the Elder declined and invited the king to sit instead, as he had already his own seat. Here the P omits the attempt of the king to induce elder Raṭṭhapāla to give up the religious life, as seen in the C.

2) *The king's enquiries :*

C : (54*a*, 4–20): King Chü-lai-p'o then said that generally people adopted the religious life through 4 kinds of decadence, due to sickness, due to old age, due to loss of wealth, due to loss of relatives. They have desires, but as they could not enjoy them, they adopted the religious life. But Lai-cha-ho-lo had none of these decadences, so what had he known, what had he seen, and what had he heard that induced him to give up the home-life and to embrace the homeless life ?

P : (66, 7–32 ; 67 ; 68, 1–14) : Almost the same, although the order is slightly different. It puts decadence through old age first, then through sickness and loss of wealth, loss of relatives. While in the C version, the king stated all the 4 decadences first then showed that the Elder had none of them, in the P version, king of the Kurus, after stating one decadence showed at once that the Elder had not such a decadence. The rest is almost the same.

3) *Lai-cha-ho-lo's reply :*

C : (54*a*, 20; 54*b*; 55*a*, 1–14) : The Elder replied that he had known, seen and heard 4 things preached by the Buddha, that he had embraced the holy life : *a*) This world was of no protection, no refuge, *b*) in this world, everything was going to decay, to decadence, *c*) this world was impermanent, all had to depart from it, *d*) this world was always unsatisfied, discontented, being a slave to craving. King Chü-lai-p'o asked how this world was of no protection, no refuge, when he himself had sons, grand-sons, brothers, relatives, elephant-armies, carriage-armies, horse-armies and infantry, who could protect him, when he had heroic and brave princes, athlets, Po-lo-ch'ien-ti'i (鉢邏褰提 ?), Mo-ha-nêng-chia (摩訶能伽 : Mahānāga ?), astrologers, strategists, accountants, well-learned men, skillful debaters, ministers, relatives, mantra-bearers, mantra-knowers ; where there were troubles, dangers, they came to overcome and subdue them. Elder Lai-cha-ho-lo asked the king that when he suffered from wind-disease which he was affected, when he was under acute pain, was it possible for these people to come, protect and defend him. The king was forced to reply in the negative, as due to his own karmas that he had to suffer acute suffering and pain ; so it was proved that this world was of no protection. Then the king asked how in this world, everything was going to decay, to decadence, the Elder asked the king to compare his own agility, his own strength, his own complexion, when he was 24, 25 years of age, and as he was now, the king had to admit that when he was 24, 25 years of age, his agility, his strength and his complexion were invincible, but now he was too old, with faculties too decadent, so this proved that as the Buddha had said, in this world, everything was going to decay, to decadence. Then king Chü-lai-p'o asked the Elder, why the W.H. One said that this world was impermanent, all had to depart from it. The Elder asked the king that when he was dying, struck by impermanence, was it possible for him to take along with him to the other world his prosperous Kuru country, his prosperous inner palace and his prosperous granaries and treasuries. The king had to reply in the negative, saying that he had to go alone, without friends. And this proved that this world was impermanent, all had to depart from it. Then the king asked elder Lai-cha-ho-lo, why the W.H. One said that this world was always unsatisfied, discontented, a slave to craving. Elder Lai-cha-ho-lo asked the king, that although the king had prosperous Kuru country, prosperous inner palace and prosperous granaries and treasuries, but if a trustworthy man came from the North, or from the other 3 directions, or from the other shore of the great ocean, saying that from the direction of his coming, beyond the other shore of the ocean, there was a prosperous country, populous, with lot of wealth and labour, did the king not to attempt to conquer this country and its people, and the king replied in the positive and this proved that this world was always unsatisfied, discontented, a slave to craving.

P : (68, 15-33 ; 69 ; 70 ; 71 ; 72 ; 1-23) : Not exactly the same. The 4 things preached by the Buddha here are in the following order : a) the impermanent world is bound to be carried away, b) the world is no refuge, no protector, c) the world is not oneself, one must go, leaving everything, d) the world is wanting, not satisfied, a slave to craving. Because he had known, seen and heard these four things to be true, so elder Raṭṭhapāla went forth and followed the religious life. To prove that the impermanent world was bound to be carried away, the Elder asked the king what was his strength when he was 20 or 25 years of age, in handling elephants, horses, carriages, bow and sword, how strong were his legs and arms and how expert was he in warfare ? and to compare all this to his present age ? The king had to reply that he was very proficient in handling elephants, horses, carriage, bow and sword, was strong in legs and arms and an expert in matter of warfare, so clever was he as if he had psychic powers ; but now, he was old, worn out, close to the end, of 80 years of age, not master any more of his movements. To prove that the world was no refuge, no protector, elder Raṭṭhapāla showed to the king that although the king had elephant-armies, horse-armies, carriage-armies and infantry to defend him in case of danger, still when he was affected by wind-disease, he could not ask his friends, his relatives to alleviate his pain, to share his suffering. To prove that the world was not oneself, one must go, leaving everything behind, elder Raṭṭhapāla showed to the king that although he had gold coins and gold in abundance underground or on the surface and at present he was able to enjoy the 5 objects of sense-desire, but when he was to leave this world, other people would come in his place and enjoy themselves. To prove that the world was wanting, not satisfied, a slave to craving, elder Raṭṭhapāla showed to the king that although his Kuru country was already prosperous, but if there was any reliable man coming from any of the four directions and informed him that there was a great country there, prosperous, populous, with plenty of elephant-armies, horse-armies, chars-armies and infantry, with plenty of gold, ivory, women, he would surely come and conquer this country.

4) *Lai-cha-ho-lo's gāthā :*

C : (55*a*, 15-20 ; 55*b*, 1) : Then elder Lai-cha-ho-lo uttered these verses :

1) « I saw men in the world,
Wealthy but deluded, not given to charity ;
« Having obtained wealth, they desired for more,
Greedily hoarding, collecting things.

2) « The king, having conquered the earth,
Reigned over it according to his ability;
Not content with this side of the ocean,
He has design over the other side also.

3) King and other people,
With craving not gone, come to die,
With dishevelled hair, wife and sons are crying,
Bewailing, weeping, with suffering hard to subdue.

4) Wrapped in clothes to be buried,
Or (thrown upon) heaped wood to be cremated,
In accordance with the karma, they go to the next world,
Being burnt, they have no enlightened thoughts.

5) After death, wealth cannot follow,
In the same way, wife, children, women-slaves ;
Rich and poor are equal,
The fool and the wise share the same fate.

6) The wise do not nurture grief,
But the fool cherish sorrow,
That is why, wisdom is better,
It helps to obtain right enlightenment.

7) Deeply attached to becoming and becoming,
The fool perform evil deeds,
Towards the dharma, perform un-dharma acts,
Using force to force on others.

8) The unintelligent ones display great effort,
The fool perform many evil deeds,
Being born in the womb, they come to the next world,
Time and again are liable to birth and death.

9) Being born to another life,
They alone perform evil deeds,
Like the robbers, they are bound,
They suffer by their own misdeeds.

10) In this way these living beings,
Are born in the next world.
Due to their own deed,
They suffer by their own misdeeds.

11) Like the ripe fruits they fall by themselves,
Old and young are alike,
They want to adorn and to enjoy themselves,
Their mind is after good and bad material forms.

12) They are bound and harmed by desires,
Due to desire that fear arises,
Oh king, I saw these and realized them,
I know that recluseship is the highest.

P : (72, 26–33 ; 73 ; 74, 1–12) : Almost the same, with more or less details. In the C there are 12 verses, while the P counts up to 13. The last half of the 4th and of the 7th C verses is not available in the P. The 2nd half of the 3rd, the 5th and the 7th of the P are not available in the C. The corresponding verses are as follows : C 1 = P 1 ; C 2 = P 2 ; C 3 = First half P 3 and first half P 4; First half C 4 = Last half P 4; C 5 = P 6 & first half P 8; C 6 = Last half P 8 & first half P 9; First half C 7 = Last half P 9; C 8 = P 10; C 9 & C 10 = P 11; C 11 = First half P 12 & P 13; C 12 = Second half of P 12 & P 13.

C 1 = P 1 : Almost the same, only one line different. C : Having obtained wealth, they desire for more = P : They hanker for more sense-desires.

C 2 = P 2 : Almost the same, only one line different. C : Reigns over it according to his ability = P : Dwelling on a land limited by the sea.

C 3 = First half P 3 & P 4 : C : Bewailing, weeping, with suffering hard to subdue = P : Bewailing, they say : « Alas, he is not undying ».

First half C 4 = Last half P 4 : The C adds : to be buried, while the P mentions only cremation.

C 5 = *P* 6 & *first half P* 8 : Almost the same. The P adds : Heirs take away his wealth but he goes according to his kamma. C : Wealth, children, wife, women-slaves = P : Wealth, children, wife, wealth and kingdom.

C 6 = *Last half P* 8 & *first half P* 9 : C : The wise do not nurture grief, but the fool cherish sorrow = P : The fool lie prostrate, as if stunned by folly, while the wise do not tremble when touched.

First half C 7 = *Last half P* 9 : Almost the same.

C 8 = *P* 10 : Almost the same.

C 9 & *C* 10 = *P* 11 : Almost the same.

C 11 = *First half P* 12 & *P* 13 : C : Like the ripe fruits, they fall by themselves, old and young are alike. They want to adorn themselves and to enjoy themselves, their mind is after good and bad material forms = P : Like fruits fallen from the tree, so are the men, old and young alike at the breaking up of the body. Sense-desires are pleasant, sweet and varied and cause disturbances to the mind.

C 12 = *Second half P* 12 & 13 : Almost the same.

E. — CONCLUSION

While the C mentions that king Chü-lai-p'o rejoiced at elder Lai-cha-ho-lo's speech, the P omits the conclusion.

C. S. N° 60

CHINESE : N° 161, *Fan-mo-ching* (梵摩經) (Tsê vii, 1a-4b).
PĀLI : N° 91, Brahmāyusuttaṃ (T.M.N. ii, 133-146).

A. — GIST OF THE CHINESE SŪTRA

Fan-mo, a brāhmaṇa, having heard the Buddha's fame and wisdom and possessor of the 32 marks of a great man, sent one of his disciples, Yu-to-lo to go and see the Buddha and to ascertain if the report about the Buddha was correct. Yu-to-lo came, saw the 32 marks on the Buddha's body, followed him for a certain time to observe the Buddha's deportment and behaviour. Then he came back and reported the whole matter to brāhmaṇa Fan-mo, who came to see the Buddha in person, observed the 32 marks of a great man, listened to the Buddha's sermon and became a disciple of the Buddha.

P : Almost the same.

B. — TITLE OF THE SŪTRA

C: Fan-mo-ching, discourse on Fan-mo, which refers to the brāhmaṇa who sent a disciple to ascertain the fame and report about the Buddha.

P : Brahmāyusuttaṃ, discourse on Brahmāyu which refers to the same person as in the C.

C. — LOCATION OF THE SŪTRA

C: In the country of Pei-t'o-t'i (P: Videha).

P: The same, in the country of Videha.

D. — CONTENTS OF THE SŪTRA

I. — *The Buddha's fame :*

C : (1*a*, 4-13): At that time, at Mi-sa-lo (P: Mithilā), there was one brāhmaṇa called Fan-mo, of great wealth, of immense properties, with cattle-heads and crops innumerable, with granted households and granaries, rich and plentiful. Mi-sa-lo, together with water, grass and trees was granted by king Wei-shêng-yüan, son of Pei-t'o-t'i of Mo-chieh-t'o (P : Ajātasattu, Videhiputta of Magadha). Brāhmaṇa Fan-mo had a young man called Yu-to-lo (P: Māṇavaṃ Uttaro), brought up by father and mother, living a pure life, up to 7 generations of ancestors, not performing demeritorious deeds. He was learned, of wide knowledge, well versed in the 4 sacred texts, deeply proficient in the science of etymology, in general language, and in the 5 sentences (5 branches of knowledge). He had heard that recluse Ch'ü-t'an, son of the Sakyan clan, had given up the Sakyan clan, shaved off beard and hair, donned the yellow robe, out of faith, gave up the home-life, adopted the homeless life to learn the dharma. He was travelling in Mo-chieh-t'o, along with an assembly of great monks. A great fame spread about that recluse Ch'ü-t'an in 10 directions : Recluse Ch'ü-t'an was the Tathāgata... (See ante page 294-5 up to)... showing the completely pure brahma-life. He had heard also that recluse Ch'ü-tan was endowed with 32 marks of a great man. Those who possessed the 32 marks of a great man had two courses opened to them without fail : If they remained in the family-life, they would become the universal monarch, intelligent, wise, having 4 kinds of armies to rule the world, having stabilised the world due to their own effort, live in accordance with dharma, kings of dharma, possessors of 7 treasures : wheel-treasure, elephant-treasure, horse-treasure, jewel-treasure, woman-treasure, householder-treasure, master-soldier-minister-treasure, father of 1000 sons, handsome, courageous, fearless, subduers of other armies, sovereign of all the lands and even up to great ocean, not resorting to sword and stick, but resorting to dharma to obtain security. If they shave off hair and beard, don the yellow robe, out of faith give up the homelife and adopt the homeless life to be trained in the dharma, they surely become the Tathāgata, the perfectly, rightly enlightened, with fame widely spread in 10 directions.

P : (133, 9-29 ; 134, 1-3) : Almost the same. C : Fan-mo = P : Brahmāyu. The P adds that this brāhmaṇa was old, full of years, of 120 years of age. It omits totally about the great wealth of the brāhmaṇa, wealth granted by the king... about the purity up to 7 generations. C : He was learned, of wide knowledge, well versed in the 4 sacred texts = P : Well versed in the 3 Vedas. C : Deeply proficient in the science of etymology, in general language = P : Well versed in idioms, grammar, worldly knowledge and in the marks of a great man. C : Proficient in the 5 sentences (5 branches of knowledge) = P : Versed in sanighaṇḍuketubhānaṃ sākkharappabhedānaṃ itihāsapañcamānaṃ (vocabularies, rituals, distinction of letters, phonology and the legendary tradition as the 5th). The fame of recluse Gotama is the same as in the previous P suttas. Here the P omits to mention about the 32 marks of a great man, although in the next paragraph, when the brāhmaṇa urged Uttara to go and see recluse Gotama, he mentioned also the 32 marks.

Notes : The P mentions 3 Vedas, while the C mentions 4 vedas ; thus the P traditions are older.

II. — *Fan-mo urged his disciple to go and see recluse Ch'ü-t'an :*

C : (1*a*, 13-20 ; 1*b*, 1-9) : Fan-mo repeated what he had heard about the fame, the qualities and the marks of recluse Ch'ü-t'an to his disciple Yu-to-lo and urged him to go and see whether recluse Ch'ü-t'an was or was not true to what had been reported about him and whether he had the 32 marks of a great man or not, as Yu-to-lo had read in the scriptures about one who was possessor of the 32 marks of a great man.

P : (134, 3-29) : Almost the same. Here the P mentions also the 32 marks and the two only courses open to him. As to the qualities of a universal monarch, both versions are almost the same, with the following differences : The P omits : Intelligent, wise. C : Having stabilised the world due to his own effort = P : Janapadatthāvariyappatto. (Bringer of stability to the country). C : Having four kinds of armies to rule over the vorld = P : Cāturanto vijitāvi (victorious over the 4 directions of the world). For the 7 treasures, the last one only is slightly different : C : Master-soldier-minister treasure = P : Pariṇāyakaratanaṃ (Adviser-treasure). C : With fame widely spread in the 10 directions = P : Loke vivattacchaddo (Having lifted the veil from the world). The P adds Brahmāyu saying that he was a giver of mantras and Uttara was a receiver of mantras. The rest is the same.

III. — *Yu-to-lo's approach to the Buddha :*

C : (1*b*, 9-19) : Then Yu-to-lo approached the Buddha, greeted him and sat at one side. He saw the 30 marks of a great man on the Buddha's body and had doubt about the remaining two : what was hidden was horse-like and the long and large tongue. The Buddha knew Yu-to-lo's doubt and with his psychic power made these two visible to Yu-to-lo. Yu-to-lo saw that what was hidden was horse-like and that the long and large tongue covered the whole face. Then Yu-to-lo knew that recluse Ch'ü-t'an possessed in full the 32 marks of a great man. Then he followed recluse Ch'ü-t'an during 4 months of the summer-season to observe recluse Ch'ü-t'an behaviour and the places he visited. Having done this, he took leave of recluse Ch'ü-t'an and departed.

P : (134, 30-32; 135, 1-24) : Almost the same. C : What was hidden was horse-like = P : Kosohite vatthaguyhe (what was cloth-hid was sheath-cased). As to the long and large tongue, which is said in the C version to cover the whole face, in the P, the Buddha put out his tongue, stroke it forward and backward over his two ears and his two nostrils and covered with his tongue the whole surface of his forehead. C : He followed recluse Ch'ü-t'an during 4 months of the summer-season to observe recluse Ch'ü-t'an's behaviour and the places he visited = P : Young Uttaro for 7 months followed recluse Gotama closely as his shadow to observe recluse Gotama's deportment.

IV. — *Yu-to-lo's report to Fan-mo :*

1) *The 32 marks of a great man :*

(Please see Chapter V on the Buddha, p. 166, from... 4). The 32 marks of a great man... to p. 168, up to... with a level tread.

2) *The Buddha's deportment :*

(Please see ante, p. 168. The Buddha's deportment to p. 172, up to... keeping their eyes on him).

3) *Yu-to-lo's going forth :*

C : (3*a*, 7–9) : Then Yu-to-lo asked permission from the brāhmaṇa to go forth under recluse Ch'ü-t'an and Fan-mo agreed. After that, Yu-to-lo came to the Buddha and asked him to allow him to go forth under him and to receive high ordination and the Buddha made him go forth and gave him high ordination.

P : Not available.

V. — *Meeting between the Buddha and brāhmaṇa Fan-mo :*

1) *Householders and brāhmaṇas' visit to the Buddha :*

C: (3*a*, 9–17) : After the ordination of Yu-to-lo, the Buddha together with the assembly of great monks left Pei-t'o-t'i and gradually came to Mi-sa-lo and stayed at Ta-t'ien-nai forest (P : Makhādevambavana). The Buddha's fame having reached there, Mi-sa-lo's householders and brāhmaṇas together with relatives and acquaintances came out of Mi-sa-lo to the Northern direction and reached Ta-t'ien-nai forest to see the Buddha. Some bowed down at the Buddha's feet and sat at one side, some greeted the Buddha and sat at one side, some joined their hands towards the Buddha and sat at one side, some saw the Buddha from afar, remained silent and sat down. Then the Buddha preached the dharma to them, gladdened, aroused and pleased them, using numberless ways to preach the dharma to them.

P : (140, 29–32 ; 141, 1–13) : It omits Yu-to-lo's ordination. It adds : Some made known their clan and sat down. It omits the Buddha preaching the dharma to them.

2) *Fan-mo's visit and the* 32 *marks of a great man :*

C : (3*a*, 17–20 ; 3*b* ; 4*a*, 1–3) : The Buddha's fame reached Fan-mo who wanted to pay a visit to him. He had lovely vehicles prepared and set out to see the Buddha ; but when he came in sight of the Buddha and seeing him surrounded by countless people listening to the Buddha's sermon, he became afraid, came under a tree and sent a messenger to ask after the Buddha's health and seek permission to see him. The Buddha accepted and Fan-mo approached the Buddha. The householders and brāhmaṇas who had known Fan-mo's virtues and knowledge got up from their seat and made way for him ; but Fan-mo declined and said that he wanted to see the Buddha straight away. Then he came before the Buddha, greeted him and sat at one side. He saw all marks of a great man on the Buddha's body, except two, had doubts over them and in a gāthā, requested the Buddha to overcome these doubts. The Buddha used psychic power to reveal the other two marks to Fan-mo, who saw them and became convinced that the Buddha had possessed the 32 marks of a great man.

P : (141, 14-35 ; 142 ; 143 ; 144, 1-2) : Almost the same, with the same differences as seen in preceding paragraphs. The P does not mention that brāhmaṇa Brahmāyu while approaching the Buddha became afraid and sent a messenger. Here the brāhmaṇa thought it improper for him to see recluse Gotama without asking first the permission. So he sent the messenger. Here also brāhmaṇa Brahmāyu used a gāthā to ask the Buddha, who also used a gāthā to answer him.

3) *The Buddha preaching to Fan-mo :*

C : (4*a*, 3-11) : The Buddha knew that this brāhmaṇa Fan-mo was not a deceiver, a cheat and that only for the sake of knowledge that he asked questions, not for the sake of creating disturbances. He thought it would be better for the Buddha to preach to him the deep A-p'i-t'an (P : Abhidhamma). Then under the form of a gāthā, the Buddha allowed the brāhmaṇa to ask questions for welfare here-now and for happiness in the future. Then Brāhmaṇa Fan-mo asked the following questions, all under gāthā form : « What is Brāhmaṇa ? what is the meaning of the 3 attainments ? Due to what one says one is without grasping (Arahant) ? What is the complete and right enlightenment ? » Then the Buddha, in a gāthā, replied :

« To destroy evil, demeritorious dharmas,
To stand and to dwell on brahma-life,
And to train in the brahma-conduct,
This is called a brāhmaṇa.
A clear knowledge of the past,
A vision of happiness and evil realms,
An eradication of ignorance,
Knowing this, is called a Mu-ni (Sage).
To know well the pure mind,
To eradicate completely lust, malevolence and delusion,
« To attain the 3 knowledges,
Thus are called the 3 attainments.
To be aloof from demeritorious dharmas,
To rightly dwell in the first meaning,
To be the chief object of respect in the world,
Due to this, it is called without grasping.
Helping the deities and human beings,
Giving eyes and destroying quarrels,
Of wide knowledge and becoming eradicated,
This is called right and complete enlightenment ».

P: (144, 3–22): Not exactly the same. The P omits the Buddha thinking that this brāhmaṇa was not a deceiver... to preach the Abhidhamma to him. The permission given by the Buddha is placed in the previous P gāthā already. Here the P adds a passage in which Brahmāyu decided what questions to ask recluse Gotama. Finally he decided to ask questions about the goal of the future state. The questions are not exactly the same in both versions, although some of them are similar, and both are put under the form of a gāthā.

Here the brāhmaṇa asked:

« How is one called brāhmaṇa? How one becomes master of knowledge?
How is one master of 3 knowledges?
How is one called learned?
How is one a perfect One? How one becomes whole?
How is one a sage? How is one called the Awakened One?

The Buddha replied also in the form of a gāthā:

« Who knows his previous birth,
And sees the heaven and sorrowful states,
« He who attains the destruction of births,
He is a sage, who is accomplished in super-knowledge.
He who knows the pure mind, who is free from all attachment,
Who has eradicated birth and death,
He is whole in the brahma-life.
He who knows all states of the mind,
He is called the Awakened One ».

4) *The brāhmaṇa's conversion:*

C: (4*a*, 12–20; 4*b*, 1–14): Then brāhmaṇa Fan-mo got up from his seat and wanted to worship at the Buddha's feet. But at that time, the big assembly of householders and brāhmaṇas shouted loudly that it was marvellous, it was wonderful of recluse Ch'ü-t'an that brāhmaṇa Fan-mo of Mi-sa-lo, who had a lineage of 7 generations of pure ancestors, who was the foremost among householders and brāhmaṇas of Mi-sa-lo and the most learned, the most wealthy, the most aged, of 126 years of age, humbled down and worshipped recluse Ch'ü-t'an. The Buddha, who knew this assembly's mind asked brāhmaṇa Fan-mo to resume his seat. Then the Buddha preached the dharma to him, gladdened, aroused and pleased him, using numberless ways to preach the dharma to him. (Like ante, p. 285... from Having advised, incited, gladdened... (to) ... became fearless towards the W. H. One's dharma). The brāhmaṇa Fan-mo got up from his seat, bowed down his head at the Buddha's feet, declared his taking refuge in the Triple Gem and asked the Buddha to accept him as a layman disciple. Then he invited the Buddha, together with the monks to take food on the next day in his house, and his invitation was accepted. Then the next day, the Buddha, together with the assembly of monks came to the brāhmaṇa's house and were offered food by brāhmaṇa Fan-mo. After the meal, the brāhmaṇa took a lower seat and listened to the Buddha's blessings. The W.H. One blessed him, saying :

« Among sacrifices, fire is the highest,
The penetrating voice is the foundation of all voices.
Among men, king is the supreme chief,
The ocean is longer than rivers.
The moon is brighter than the stars,
But no light can exceed the sun.
The above, the below,
The four alternates and the four directions,
Together with all the worlds,
From mankind up to deities,
Only Buddha was supreme ».

P : (144, 23-31 ; 145 ; 146, 1-7) : Not exactly the same. Here Brahmāyu did actually worship the Buddha, arranging his upper robe upon one shoulder, kissed round the Buddha's feet, stroked them on all sides with his two hands and made known his name. His attitude filled the whole company with awe and wonder. Then the Buddha preached the dhamma to him in the same stereotyped way up to Brahmāyu's attainment of the dhamma-eye. The rest is almost the same as in the C, his taking refuge in the Triple Gem, his inviting the Buddha to a meal, but here there is no mention of the blessings given by the Buddha, who as usual gladdened, aroused and pleased the brāhmaṇa with a dhamma-talk. It adds : At the end of one week, the Buddha set out to tour Videha.

5) *Fan-mo's death and his place of rebirth :*

C : (4*b*, 15-20) : Having stayed for some days at Mi-sa lo, the Buddha set out for Shê-wei and came to Shêng-lin, Kei-ku-tu's park. The news of Fan-mo's death reached him and the monks asked the place of rebirth of Fan-mo. The Buddha replied that he had attained the state of non-returner, not liable to return to this world.

P : (146, 6-20) : Almost the same. It does not mention the Buddha coming to Sāvatthi and staying at Jetavana, Anāthapiṇḍikārāma.

Notes : Miss Horner in her M. L. S., ii, p.332, preferred to read : « na ca maṃ vihesesi » instead of « navamaṃ vihesesi ». Her reading proved to be correct as in the C, such an expression occurs : « For the sake of dharma, he does not trouble me ».

E. — CONCLUSION

While the P mentions that the monks were delighted at the Buddha's speech, the C adds that Fan-mo also was delighted. This shows a great discrepancy in the sense that Fan-mo was already reported dead in the preceding paragraph.

C. S. N° 61

CHINESE : N° 151, *Fan-chih-a-shê-ho-ching* (梵志阿攝惒經): (Tsê vi, 84a-86b).

PĀLI : N° 93, Assalāyanasuttaṃ (T.M.N. ii, 147-157).

A. — GIST OF THE CHINESE SŪTRA

Brāhmaṇa A-she-hô came to challenge the Buddha about his preaching the purity of the 4 castes and to advocate the superiority of the brāhmaṇa caste. The Buddha with various questions, similes and stories convinced A-shê-ho of the hollowness of his claim.

P : Almost the same, with some differences in the questions, similes and stories.

B. — TITLE OF THE SŪTRA

C : Fan-chih-a-shê-ho-ching, discourse on brāhmaṇa A-shê-ho, which refers to the brāhmaṇa who came to challenge the Buddha.

P : Assalāyanasuttaṃ, discourse on Assalāyana, which refers to the same person.

C. — LOCATION OF THE SŪTRA

Both are the same : Sāvatthi, Jetavana, Anāthapiṇḍikārāma.

D. — CONTENTS OF THE SŪTRA

1. — *Circumstances leading to the deliverance of the sūtra :*

C : (84*a*, 18-20; 84*b*, 1-15) : A great number of brāhmaṇas at Chü-sa-lo (P: Kosala) assembled in a school-hall and were discussing recluse Ch'ü-t'an's proclamation of the purity of the four castes, whereas they claimed that the brāhmaṇa caste was the highest, the other castes could not be compared with, the brāhmaṇa-caste was white, the other castes were black ; the brāhmaṇa-caste was pure, the other castes were not pure ; the brāhmaṇa-caste was son of Brahmā, born out of his mouth, created by Brahmā. They thought of someone who was able to go and challenge recluse Ch'ü-t'an. They opted for young A-shê-ho-lo-yen-to, who was pure by birth, up to 7 generations of ancestors, not performing demeritorious deeds. He was learned, of wide knowledge, well versed in the 4 sacred texts, deeply proficient in the law of origination, in general language and in the 5 sentences (5 branches of knowledge). They all came to request A-shê-ho to go and challenge recluse Ch'ü-t'an. A-shê-ho refused, saying that it was impossible to argue with recluse Ch'ü-t'an as he preached the dharma in accordance with dharma. The other brāhmaṇas urged him to go, not to accept defeat without challenge and finally A-shê-ho accepted. Then he, together with those Chü-sa-lo brāhmaṇas, came to recluse Ch'ü-t'an, greeted him, sat at one side, stated his claim about the superiority of the brāhmaṇa-caste and asked recluse Ch'ü-t'an about his opinion.

P: (147, 1-30 ; 148, 1-27): Almost the same. It adds: About 500 brāhmaṇas of various districts came to Sāvatthi for some business. It omits: They assembled in a school-hall, and they referred only to the opinion of recluse Gotama about the purity of the 4 castes. Assalāyana's qualifications are the same as those of Brahmāyu in the Brahmāyusutta, except that Assalāyana was young, of 16 years of age and with head shaven. The P adds: The other brāhmaṇas urged Assalāyana to go and argue with recluse Gotama, saying that a wanderer's life was followed by the good Assalāyana. In the P, the other brāhmaṇas' requests were repeated 3 times, and Assalāyana refused 2 times. Finally Assalāyana accepted by remaining silent in the C version, but in the P, he said that truly recluse Gotama spoke in accordance with the dhamma and it was difficult to argue with those who spoke in accordance with the dhamma, and that he was unable to argue with recluse Gotama. But all the same, he would go as requested. Here the brāhmaṇas' claims are as follows: « The brāhmaṇa-caste is the highest, the other castes are low ; the brāhmaṇa-caste is white, the other castes are black ; the brāhmaṇa-caste is pure, not other castes ; the brāhmaṇas are legitimate sons of Brahmā, born out of his mouth, born of Brahmā, created by Brahmā, heirs of Brahmā ».

II. — *Recluse Chü-t'an's refutations :*

There are 9 refutations and illustrations in both versions, but they are not exactly the same and also not in the same order. The corresponding ones are as follows: C 1=P 2 ; C 2=P no ; C 3=P 5 ; C 4=P 6 ; C 5 & C 6=P 7 ; C 7 & C 9=P 8 ; C 8=P 9. P 1, P 3 and P 4 are not available in the C.

1st refutation : C 1=P 2 :

C: (84*b*, 15-19) : The W.H. One asked A-shê-ho if he had heard about 2 countries, Yü-ni (P : Yonā) and Chien-fu (P : Kamboja), where there were only 2 castes, the master and the slave, master becoming slave and slave becoming master. To A-shê-ho's positive reply, the W.H. One said that if the brāhmaṇas adopted the right way, they would obtain right understanding and self-knowledge in accordance with dharma. In the same way for the Nobles, the householders and the workers. Then A-shê-ho praised recluse Ch'ü-t'an as being marvellous and wonderful, saying that he had understood the simile very quickly ; but the brāhmaṇas had said that the brāhmaṇa-caste was the highest...

P : (149, 4-16) : Almost the same. C : Yü-ni and Chien-fu = P : Yonā, Kamboja. It adds : And other border-countries. The Buddha's conclusion is totally different : « If it is so, oh Assalāyana, from what strength, from what authority, the brāhmaṇas spoke thus : The brāhmaṇa-caste was the highest...

2nd refutation : C 2 = P no.

C : (84*b*, 19-20 ; 85*a*, 1-3) : The W.H. One asked A-shê-ho if only the brāhmaṇas were able not to be grasped by this empty space, not to be bound by, not to be touched and not to be hindered by it. A-shê-ho had to reply that other castes also would enjoy the same. Then the W. H. One stated the same conclusion as in the first refutation.

3rd refutation : C 3 = P 5 :

C : (85*a*, 3-7) : The W.H. One asked A-shê-ho if only the brāhmaṇas were able to practise compassion, without hatred, without enmity, without malevolence, without quarrels and the Nobles, the Householders, the workers could not do so ? A-shê-ho replied that all the 4 castes could do the same. (Same conclusion).

P : (151, 3-17) : Almost the same. It adds : In this country (asmiṃ padese).

4th refutation : C 4 = P 6 :

C : (85a, 7-13) : The Buddha asked A-shê-ho if people of 100 different castes came and one man said that only those who were born noble and brāhmaṇas were able to take the washing beans and go to the water to wash, to take bath, cleaning away dirt and becoming clean and pure; but what about the householders and the workers castes ? A-shê-ho replied that all castes without exception were able to take the washing beans and wash and bathe themselves clean, free of dirt (Same conclusion and remarks from the Buddha).

P : (151, 18-32) : Almost the same. It does not refer to the coming of people of 100 different castes and one man saying that only the nobles and the brāhmaṇas were able to wash away their dirt. Here the Buddha asked Assalāyana whether only the brāhmaṇas (not mentioning the nobles) were able, taking back-scratcher and bath-powder, to go to a river and clean themselves of dust and mud ? C : Washing beans = P : Back-scratcher and bath-powder (Sotthiṃ sināniṃ).

5th and 6th refutations : C 5 & C 6 = P 7 :

C : (85*a*, 13–20 ; 85*b*, 1–7) : The W. H. One asked A–shê–ho : « If there are people of hundred castes who come and one man says : « Please come, only those who are born nobles and brāhmaṇas are able to take very dry Sal wood and sandal-wood, using it as fire generator and drill it round so as to produce fire and keep it ». But other born–householders and workers, if they are to take dry pig–trough, dog–trough and i–lan–t'an wood (P : Elaṇḍakaṭṭha) or other bad wood, using it as a fire–generator and drill it round, are they also able to produce fire and keep it ? » A–shê–ho replied that all these people taking various kinds of wood to make it as fire–generator were able to produce fire. And the fire produced had flame, had colour, had heat and could be served for cooking just as the fire produced by the nobles, the brāhmaṇas using precious wood for producing fire.

P : (151, 33; 152; 153, 1–2) : Almost the same, but with more details. Here it refers to a noble anointed king, who assembled 100 people of different origins. C : Born–nobles and brāhmaṇas taking very dry Sal–wood and sandal–wood = P : People of noble families, of brāhmaṇa–families, of royal families taking the upper portion of a Sal–tree or a tek tree (Sakka), or a salaḷa (kind of sweet–scented tree), or of sandal–wood, or of lotus. C : Born–householders and workers, taking dry pig–trough, dog–trough or i–lan–t'an wood or other bad woods = P : Of caṇḍāla families, hunters, bamboo-workers, cart–wright families, scavengers taking the upper portion of dog-trough (Sāpāna), of pig–trough (Sūkara), of dyeing-trough, or of elaṇḍakaṭṭha (castor–oil plant) ?

7th and 9th refutations : C 7 & C 9 = P 8 :

C : (85*b*, 7–19; 86*a*, 19–20; 86*b*, 1–6) : The W. H. One said to A–shê–ho that people were called according to the families where they were born. Thus from a brāhmaṇa-family, they were called brāhmaṇas, from a noble family, they were called nobles. In the same way with house-holders and workers. Just as fire from stick is called stick–fire, from grass, dung, wood is called grass–fire, dung–fire, wood–fire respectively. But a son from a noble father and a brāhmaṇa mother, resembling either mother or father or not resembling both cannot be called a brāhmaṇa or a noble, but the body is said to belong to himself, as the body is called according to the place of its birth. If a female horse and a male donkey are mated and a mule is born ; the mule cannot be called horse, cannot be called donkey, but only mule. Here the Buddha repeated his own conclusion, and A–shê–ho, his own praise as seen in the previous refutation. Again the W.H. One asked A–shê–ho : « Suppose there is a brāhmaṇa who practises abstinence and charity. He has 4 boys, 2 are learned and 2 are unlearned. To which boys, the brāhmaṇa would give charity first, the best seat, the best washing water and the best food ? » And A–shê–ho replied that he would give to the 2 learned boys. Again the W. H. One asked : « Suppose there is a brāmaṇa who practises abstinence and charity. He has 4 boys, 2 are not learned but laborious and prone to meritorious conduct, 2 are learned but not laborious and prone to demeritorious conduct. To whom the brāhmaṇa would give charity first, the best seat, the best washing water and the best food ? » And A-shê-ho replied that he would give to the 2 unlearned boys, who were laborious and prone to meritorious conduct. Then the W.H One said to A-shê-ho that A-shê-ho first praised learning, then praised observance of moral conduct. The W.H. One had said about the purity of the 4 castes and made it known, A-shê-ho had also said about the purity of the 4 castes and made it known.

P: (153, 12-33 ; 154, 1-25): Not exactly the same. The Pāli puts the 2 refutations together. It omits : People are called according to the families where they are born... called wood-fire respectively. While the C says that a son from a noble father and a brāhmaṇa mother or from a noble mother and a brāhmaṇa father, whether he resembles father or mother or does not resemble them, cannot be called a brāhmaṇa or a noble, and has a class of his own, the P says instead that whatever son was born to a noble girl and a brāhmaṇa youth, or to a noble youth and a brāhmaṇa girl, he would be like his mother and also like his father and he should be called both noble and brāhmaṇa. The simile of the mule is almost the same, but the P does not draw the same conclusion as in the C. Here it is said that because of its crossed birth, it is called a mule and Assalāyana added that here he had observed this difference, but elsewhere, no such difference was seen by him. As for the other refutation, the P does not expressly mention a brāhmaṇa who practises abstinence and charity ; it mentions simply the case of 2 young brothers (not 4) who are of the same mother but not of the same father (C : no), one is clever and well trained (in the Vedas), and the other not. C : To which boys the brāhmaṇa would give charity first, the best seat, the best washing water, the best food — P : To whom first the brāmaṇa should give to eat, offerings for the dead (saddhe), or cereals (thālipāke) or oblations (yaññe), or meals for guests (pāhuṇe). C : 2 are learned but not laborious and prone to demeritorious conduct = P : One is clever and trained (in the Vedas), but of bad moral conduct and evil character. The other is the reverse. The rest is almost the same. One more difference is to be noted here. While in the C, the W. H. One said that A-shê-ho first praised learning then praised observance of moral conduct and that both the W. H. One and A-shê-ho had said about the purity of the 4 castes and made it known, in the P, the Buddha said to Assalāyana that first he had referred to birth, then having left birth, he referred to mantra, having left mantra he referred to the purity of the four castes, just as the Buddha had made known.

8th refutation : C : 8 = P : 9 :

C : (85*b*, 19-20 ; 86*a*, 1-20): The W. H. One related a story to A-shê-ho. Formerly there were many sages who lived together in a high troublefree place. A wrong view came to them that the brāhmaṇa-caste was the highest... Then a sage named A-ssu-lo-t'i-pei-lo (P : Asito Devalo), having known this wrong view, wore the yellow robe, winding a yellow napkin round the head, taking a stick and an umbrella, wearing a white robe, disappeared from his place, and not using the door to enter, he appeared in the secluded house of the sages, and walked up and down, saying: « Where the 7 brāhmaṇa-sages have gone ? » One sage seeing this reported the matter to his friends and asked them to come and curse him. But when they cursed him : « May you become ashes, may you become ashes ! » A-ssu-lo-t'i-pei-lo's complexion became brighter and brighter and his body became more shining. The sages came to ask A-ssu-lo-t'i-pei-lo who was he and when the latter disclosed his identity, the sages asked for forgiveness. Then A-ssu-lo-t'i-pei-lo asked the sages if really a wrong view had occurred to them that the brāhmaṇa-caste was the best... And the sages admitted to have such an opinion. Then he asked these sages if they knew their fathers, grand-fathers up to 7 generations, that they had married brāhmaṇa and non brāhmaṇa ladies ; if they knew that their mothers, grand-mothers up to 7 generations, that they had married brāhmaṇa and non-brāhmaṇa gentlemen ? Then A-ssu-lo asked again if they knew how a pregnancy took place ? They replied that when 3 things came together, there would be conception, the mating of father and mother (the mother's womb), not full and conceivable and the arrival of scented aggregate (P : gandhabba). Then A-ssu-lo asked them if they knew the being who was going to take birth, was it a male or a female, from where did it come, from the noble caste or from the brāhmaṇa caste, or from the householder-caste or from the worker-caste, whether it came from the eastern, or southern, or western or northern directions ? These sages replied that they did not know. A-ssu-lo said that if they did not know about this, how could they claim that the brāhmaṇa-caste was the highest... Then A-shê-ho, being upbraided by the W. H. One adopted a contrite attitude and the Buddha in order to cheer him up proceeded with the 9th refutation.

P : (154, 26-31 ; 155 ; 156 ; 157, 1-16) : Almost the same. Here Asita Devalo was depicted as having hair and beard trimmed, having donned a pair of crimson-coloured robes, having worn sandals with many linings, having taken a staff made of gold and he appeared in the hermitage of the 7 brāhmaṇa-sages. The curse is the same as in the C. Here the more the 7 seers cursed Asita Devala, the more charming became the sage Asita Devala, the more beautiful to look upon, the more lovely. The P adds that the 7 sages thought that formerly when they cursed anybody, their curses took effect immediately, but now their curses had no effect, so their austerity became useless and their brahma-life of no avail. Asita Devala assured them that their austerity dit not become useless and their brahma-life not of no avail. Then he disclosed his identity and the 7 sages approached Asista Devala to honour him. The question about fathers, grand-fathers, mothers, grand-mothers, pregnancy is almost the same. C: (Mother's womb) not full, conceivable = P : Mātā ca utunī hoti (It is the mother's season).

The P omits the question about from where, from what direction the being would come. It adds another question : « This being so, did the 7 sages know who they were ? » And the sages replied in the negative. C : The Buddha said to A-shê-ho that those sages who lived in the forest, in a trouble-free place, being thus well taught and well admonished by A-ssu-lo, could not show the purity of the brāhmaṇa-caste, so how could his teacher be able, who wore the grass-robe ? = P : The Buddha said to Assalāyana that these 7 brāhmaṇa-sages, on being questioned and cross-questioned by the Buddha about their own jātivāda were unable to answer, so how could he, being questioned and cross-questioned by the Buddha about his own jātivāda be able to answer, having the same teacher with them but not Puṇṇa Dabbigāha) (?) In the P, there mentions also the contrite attitude of Assalāyana, but only at the end of the 8th refutation in the P version.

3 refutations not available in the C: P 1, P 3, & P 4 :

P 1 : (148, 29-35 ; 149, 1-3) : The Buddha asked Assalāyana that the brāhmaṇa-wives of the brāhmaṇas were known to have menstruation, conception, to have given birth and to give suck, and the brāhmaṇas were born from their womb, so how could they claim to be the highest ?

P 3 : (149, 17-33 ; 150, 1-10) : The Buddha proved to Assalāyana that not only the nobles, the merchants, the workers but also the brāhmaṇas, if they killed living beings, stole, indulged in wrong sexual intercourse, told lies, slandered, spoke harsh words, used frivolous speech, if they were covetous, malevolent, of wrong views, after their death, they would be born in the sorrowful places, in the Hell.

P 4 : (150, 11-33 ; 151, 1-2) : The Buddha proved to Assalāyana that not only the brāhmaṇas, but also the nobles, the merchants, the workers, if they abstained from killing living beings, from stealing, from indulging in wrong sexual intercourse, telling lies, slandering, speaking harsh works, using frivolous speech, from covetousness, from malevolence, from wrong views, after their death, they all would be born in the happy place, in the heaven.

III. — *A-shê-ho and Chü-sa-lo brāhmaṇas' reactions :*

C : (86*b*, 6-16) : Then A-shê-ho got up from his seat and wanted to worship at the Buddha's feet, but the assembly shouted loudly that recluse Ch'ü-t'an was marvellous, recluse Ch'ü-t'an was wonderful, endowed with great psychic power, with great majesty, with great merit, as he had expounded the purity of the 4 castes and made A-shê-ho also expound the purity of the four castes. The W.H. One, knowing the mind of the assembly asked A-shê-ho to resume his seat, saying that A-shê-ho's mind being pleased was enough. And the W.H. One preached the dharma to him, gladdened, aroused and pleased him. A-shê-ho, bowed down at the W.H.

One's feet, went round him 3 times and departed. Then the brāhmaṇas of Chü-sa-lo blamed A-shê-ho, saying that he came to defeat recluse Ch'ü-t'an but was defeated by him instead. Just as a man in search of eyes entered the forest but came back with his eyes lost ; just as a man, for the sake of drinking entered the lake but came back still thirsty. A-shê-ho told the brāhmaṇas of Chü-sa-lo that he had told them before, recluse Ch'ü-t'an spoke in accordance with the dharma, it was difficult to argue with one who spoke in accordance with the dharma.

P : (157, 17-20) : Not the same. It mentions simply that Assalāyana exclaimed that it was marvellous, it was wonderful, then he asked the Buddha to accept him as a disciple from now on as long as life lasted.

Notes : Miss Horner in her M.L.S. ii, p. 349, note 3, remarked that the usual formula for asking to become a lay-disciple does not appear to occur here in full, and the text does not give abbreviation or omission marks. If we compare with the C text, the C rendering appears to be more reasonable.

E. — CONCLUSION

While the P omits the conclusion, the C has its usual one.

PART FOUR

APPENDIXES.

APPENDIXES 1. — BIOGRAPHY OF SANGHADEVA

Sanghadeva, (Sêng-chia-t'i-p'o : 僧伽提婆) (or Chung-t'ien : 衆天) had Gautama (Ch'ü-t'an : 瞿曇) as surname. He was born in Chi-pin (罽賓 : Kashmir). According to K'ai-yüan-shih-chiao-lü (開元釋教錄) Book 3 and Kao-sêng-chüan (高僧傳) Book 1, he had mastered the 3 Canons and well versed in Abhidharma. He always recited San-fa-tu-lün (三法度論) throughout day and night and considered it to be the gate leading to the attainment of Dharma. He had a sharp and deep intelligence and was of dignified behaviour and very keen on preaching and teaching.

He came to Ch'ang-an (長安) at the end of the reign of Chien-yüan (建元 : 373-384), of the later Tsin (晉 : 384-417). Not long before his coming, Sêng-chia-po-ch'êng (僧伽跋澄 : Sanghabhūti) had translated P'o-hsü-mi (婆須蜜 : Vasumitra's Sangīti śāstra) and T'an-mo-nan-t'i (曇摩難提 : Sk. Dharmanandī) had translated 2 works Ekottarāgama and the Kuang-shuo-san-fa-tu (廣說三法度) of more than 100,000 words, but these translations were not well done. At that time, political troubles occurred and no able person was capable of verifying and correcting the translations and Tao-an (道安) was already dead. Śramaṇa Fa-ho (法和), a friend of Tao-an met Sanghadeva and invited him to come to Lo-yang (洛陽), where he stayed 4 or 5 years to verify the translations. He retranslated the A-p'i-t'an (Abhidharma) and Kuang-shuo-chung-ching (廣說衆經). Then he left Lo-yang, came to the South and was invited to stay at Lu-shan (盧山), by Hui-yüan-fa-shih (惠遠法師), who was the founder of the famous monastery of Lu-shan. There he translated 2 works, A-p'i-t'an-hsin and San-fa-tu-lün in the Prajñā-hall.

In the first year of Long-an (隆安), he came to the capital and was greatly admired by the king and the officials of the Court. The pious Buddhist Wang-hsün (王旬) built a monastery for Sanghadeva, who preached the Abhidharma in that monastery. Wang-hsün invited śramaṇa Shih-hui-chih (釋慧持) and 40 other monks and requested Sanghadeva to translate the Madhyama Āgama and the Ekottarāgama. Śramaṇa Sangharakṣa (Sêng-chia-lo-ch'a) of Chi-pin (Kashmir) held the Sanskrit text in his hand and Sanghadeva translated into Chinese. Śramaṇa Tao-tz'u (道慈) of Yü-chou (豫州) held the brush, Li-pao (李寶) and Tang-hua (唐化) of Wu kingdom wrote down the translation.

At Lu-shan and Chien-k'ang (建康), Sanghadeva had translated 5 works in 118 fasciculi :

1) *Chung-a-ham* of 60 fasciculi or 58 fasciculi, was translated, beginning from the 10th of the 11th month of the first year of Long-an and ended in the 25th of the 6th month of the 2nd year (398). The translation was made in the monastery of Tung-t'ing (東亭).

2) *Ts'êng-i-a-han-ching* of 50 fasciculi. Its translation began on the first month of the 1st year of Long-an. It is a second translation, the first one was done by Dharmanandi.

3) *A-p'i-t'an-hsin-lun* (阿毗曇心論) of 4 fasciculi. Its translation was done in collaboration with Dharma-master Hui-yüan (慧遠), in the 16th year of T'ai-yüan (391). Tao-tz'u (道慈) held the brush, while Sanghadeva dictated the translation.

4) *San-fa-tu-lün* (三法度論) of 2 fasciculi, translated in the 16th year of T'ai-yüan (太元 : 391), at Lü-shan, in collaboration with Dharma-master Wei-yüan (爲遠).

5) *Chiao-shou-pi-ch'iu-ni-fa* (教授比丘尼法) of one fascicule, also translated at Lü-shan. The work was lost.

The first four works, of 117 fasciculi in all, still existed, while the last work was lost.

APPENDIXES 2. — SOME REMARKS ON SANGHADEVA'S TRANSLATION

Sanghadeva translated this work in 398 A.D., thus this translation being an ancient one cannot be judged in the light of terminology fixed by later Chinese translators like Hsüan-Tsang. But Sanghadeva's work vas a commendable one, as it was a pioneering work, done at a time when little was known of the Indian languages and their translation into the Chinese language.

We notice the following characteristics in Sanghadeva's translation :

a) *Archaic terms :* Some terms adopted by Sanghadeva in his translation were discarded by later translators.

Pāli		*Sanghadeva :*	*Later translators :*
Vedanā	:	Chüeh (覺) (1)	Shou (受)
Savitakka	:	Yu-chüeh (有 覺)	Yu - hsin (有 尋)
Savicāra	:	Yu-kuan (有 觀)	Yu - tz'u (有 伺)
Phassa	:	Keng-lo (更 樂) (2)	Ch'ü (觸)
Sammāvāyāma	:	Chêng-fang-pien (正 方 便)	Chêng-ching-chin (正 精 進)
Samudaya	:	Hsi (習) (3)	Chi (集)
Udāna	:	Hsüan-lu (撰 錄)	Wu-wên-tzu-shuo (無 問 自 說)
Upādānakkhandha	:	Shêng-wên (盛 蘊)	Ch'ü-wên (取 蘊)
Purisadammasārathi	:	Tao-fa-yü (道 法 御)	T'iao-yü-chang-fu (調 御 丈 夫)
Aniccatā	:	Wu-shang-fa (無 常 法)	Wu-shang-hsing (無 常 性)
Upādāna	:	Shou (受)	Ch'ü (取)
Saṅkhāra	:	Ssu (思) or Hsing (行)	Hsing (行)

1) In Tse VII, 84a, 2, both Chüeh and Shou are used ; but the term Shou rather qualifies all the 5 aggregates including Chüeh, but does not render the meaning of Vedana along with Chüeh.

2) In some passages, such as VII, 86b, 15-16, Ch'ü also is used for Phassa.

3) In Yüan and Ming editions, Chi is used instead of Hsi.

b) *Wrong interpretation :*

The term *Gayāsīse* which is the name of a locality, is rendered by Saṅghadeva as *Hsiang-ting* (象 頂) meaning elephant-head, thus misinterpreting *Gayā* as *Gaja*. The same can be said of the term *Makhādeva*, which is translated as *Ta-t'ien* (大 天), thus misinterpreting *Makhā* as *Mahā*. Nāga is rendered as dragon instead of elephant. The term *Purisadammasārathi* is rendered by Sanghadeva as *Tao-fa-yü* (道 法 御), Tamer of Path and Dharma, thus the term *damma* is mistaken for *Dhamma*. The later translators preferred the expression *T'iao-yü-fa-shih* (調 御 法 師), which renders the meaning of the Pāli expression. Again the expression *Sahāpi sukhena sahāpi somanassena* is wrongly translated as *Tzu-lo-tzu-hsi* (自 樂 自 喜), meaning with one's own happiness, with one's own pleasure.

c) *Mechanical translation :*

Sometimes we witness a mechanical translation, without bothering about the exact meaning of the term in the context in question. Thus the term *Attha*, which means meaning, purpose, benefit is translated throughout as *I* (義), that is *meaning*. For instance, the term *sāttham* is correctly rendered as *Yu-i* (有 義), with meaning ; but it is rather clumsy and baffling if the term *atthasaṃhita* is rendered as *Yü-i-hsiang-ying* (與 義 相 應): connected with meaning) as seen at *C N°* 191, *vii*, 44*b*, 20. The same can be said of the expressions *atthakāmo* and *anatthakāmo*, meaning wishing for (its) welfare, not wishing for (its) welfare. But the C renders as *ch'iu-i* (求 義) and *pu-ch'iu-i* (不 求 義), meaning seeking its meaning and not seeking its meaning. Another term of curious rendering is *jātarūparajata*, which means gold and silver. The C equivalent is *shêng-sê-hsiang-pao* (生 色 像 寶), *shêng* for *jāta*, *sê* for *rūpa* and *hsiang-pao* for *rajata*. Another curious translation is the term *Mātikā*, translated as *Mu* (母 : Mother) as seen in this passage : « There are monks who are expert in Sūtra, in Vinaya and in Mother » (Tsê vii, 57a, 19). Sometimes the translator just put side by side Chinese words in the same order with the original, without caring as to their meaning as a whole. Thus the well known expression *Yaṃ taṃ ariyā āc'kkhanti, upekkhako satimā sukhavihāri* is translated as *wei-shêng-so-shuo-shêng-so-shê-nien-lo-chu-shih* (謂 聖 所 說 聖 所 捨 念 樂 住 室), which can be translated only with the help of the P text.

d) *Helpful translation :*

In some cases the C translation helps to give a correct interpretation to the Pāli terms. Thus in the famous Upāli gāthā, the presence of the epithet *yakkhassa* in praise of the Buddha is rather puzzling. The C translation : *Who has the highest eyes* supplies the solution. Thus the P *yakkhassa* therefore is clearly *akkhassa* with an initial euphonic y appended to it. The same can be said of the expression *pannadhajassa* in the same gāthā, and which is rendered as banner put down. But the C corresponding expression ***with wisdom born*** offers a more appropriate reading as an epithet qualifying the Buddha. Therefore the P expression *pannadhajassa* should be interpreted as *paññājassa*, in the light of the C term.

e) *Some peculiar translations :*

We remark also some peculiar translations of some terms, the original of which in some cases cannot be the same as in the P. Some of these terms are as follows: P: *appaharite* = C : pure ground. P : *āmisa* = C : food and drink. P: *pisuṇā vācā* = C : double tongue. P: *Ummagga* = C: hsieh-tao (邪道 : wrong path). P: *arañña* = C: wu-shih-ch'ü (無事處). P: *citta* = C: hsin (heart). P: *bandhupādāpacca* = C: tuan-chung-wu-tzu (斷種無子 : Offspring cut off, without son).

The C always renders the term *Viharati* as *yü* (遊) meaning travelling, which is close to the Sanskrit interpretation, but not of the P one, which means staying. Again the term *padakkhiṇaṃ katvā*, having gone round so as to keep the right side turned towards a person, is always rendered in C as *jao-san-tsa* (繞三匝), meaning to move round the person three times. The term *Atta* (Sk. Ātman) is sometimes translated as *soul*, (神) sometimes translated as *self* (O : 我). The usual formula in P is as follows : « *N'etam mama, n'eso'hamasmi, na meso attāti* ». But the C translates as: « *Pi-fei-o-yu, o-fei-pi-yu, i-fei-shih-shên* » (彼非我有我非彼有亦非是神 : That is not mine, I do not belong to that, and also not the soul) (*C N*° 200, *vii*, 65*b*, 13-14).

f) *Akin to Sanskrit interpretation :*

Some Chinese terms show that they are akin to the Sanskrit interpretation rather than to the P interpretation. Thus the term *cattāro sammappadhānā* means the 4 exertions in P. But the C renders as *ssu-chêng-tuan* (正四斷), which means the 4 right eradications, which is close to the Sanskrit *samyakprahāna*. The same can be said of the term *veyyākaraṇa* which means in P as answer, explanation, exposition. But the C corresponding term is *chi-shuo* (記說) meaning prophecies, thus close to the Sanskrit interpretation of the term *vyākaraṇa*, as seen ante p.14, 15.

g) *Some obscure terms :*

There are some C terms which defy understanding and the originals of which cannot be guessed at. Thus in *C. S. N*° 36, elder Ta-mu-chien-lien entered in *ju-ch'i-hsiang-ting* meditation (如其像定) which is difficult to make out its meaning (*C N*° 131, *vi*, 49*b*, 5). Again in the same C.S., such a passage is found : « They thought : Now this recluse in a trouble-free place sat down and passed away. We should collect wood and grass, cover over the whole body and *yeh-wei-chih* (耶維之)» which we might guess as *ḍahati*, meaning to cremate it (*C N*° 131, *vi*, 49*b*, 19). Again the term *fei-p'in* (非品), can be guessed as *nirvāṇa*, *fei* for *nir* and *p'in* for *vāṇa* in the following passage: « The monk is said to cultivate the eradicating basis of psychic power, accomplished in meditation based on wish, which depends on aloofness, on no-desires, on cessation, on giving up, which leads towards fei-p'in ». (*C N*° 206, *vii*, 78*a*, 13-15). But the following expression seems to defy all interpretation. It refers to the enlightenment of the Buddha, under the Bodhi tree as follows: « Knowledge arose; vision arose; *ting-tao-p'in-fa* (定道品法); birth was destroyed; the brahma-life was established; what should be done was done; there would be no more becoming. » (*C N*° 204, *vii*, 74*b*, 20). *Ting* means concentration, *tao* means path, *p'in* means degree, thing and *fa* means dharma. The four words put together defy any guess as to their exact meaning. These 4 words seem to correspond with the expressions: *Ākuppā me vimutti*. Again the expression: « *Sa-yün-jo* (薩云若)» is totally unintelligible in the sentence: « Ni-chien Ch'in-tzu (Nigaṇṭha Nātaputta) is not sa-yün-jo, but he claims to be sa-yün-jo» (*C N*° 196, *vii*, 56*a*, 13). It seems to refer to the term *Sabbaññū* meaning all knowing.

h) *Transliterations and translations :*

The C text mostly uses transliterations to transcribe the original proper names of persons and places, as seen in the following examples: P: *Aggivessana* = C: A-ch'i-shê-na (阿奇舍那); P: *Ajita Kesakambalī* = C: A-i-to-chi-shê-chien-p'o-li (阿夷哆鷄舍劍婆利); P: *Aciravatī* = C: A-i-lo-p'o-t'i (阿夷羅婆提); P: *Kāsi* = C: Chia-shih (加尸); P: *Kimbila* = C: Chin-pi-lo (金毗羅).

Sometimes translations are also found, but not so frequently such as: P: *Jetavana* = C: Shêng-lin (勝林); P: *Migāramātu* = C: Lu-mu (鹿母); P: *Kukkuṭārāma* = C: Chi-yüan (鷄園).

Sometimes mixed transliterations and translations are used such as: P: *Sāriputta* = C: Shê-li-tzu (舍利子), *shê-li* is a transliteration for *Sāri* and *tzu* means *putta*. P: *Mahākassapa* = C: Ta-chia-yeh (大迦葉), *ta* is a translation of the term *Mahā* and *Chia-yeh* is a transliteration of Kassapa. (For fuller details, please refer to infra Appendix N° 10, a glossary of Pāli and Chinese equivalents).

APPENDIXES 3. — SOME REMARKS ON MIDDLE LENGTH SAYINGS

The Chinese text helps to prove the correctness of some of Miss Horner's remarks in her commendable Middle Length Sayings, an English translation of the Pāli Majjhima Nikāya.

Thus in her M L S. ii, p. 332, she prefers to read : « Na ca maṃ vihesesi » instead of « navamam vihesesi ». This is supported by the corresponding C reading : « For the sake of dharma, he does not trouble me ».

Again in the passage : « Saññaṃ idaṃ attena vā attaniyena vā ti » (T.M.N. ii, p. 263, lines 28–29), Miss Horner suggests to read *suññaṃ* instead of *saññaṃ* (M.L.S. iii, p. 49, note 6). Her remarks are corroborated by the following C passage : « The learned ariyan disciple reflects thus : « This world is *void*, void of soul', void of what belongs to the soul' ».

Sometimes the C version helps to show some of her errors in her translation and remarks. Thus in the following P sentence : « Ākaṅkheyya ce bhikkhave bhikkhu : ye me ñātisālohitā petā kālakatā pasannacittā anussaranti tesaṃ taṃ mahapphalaṃ assa mahānisaṃsanti » (i, 33, 21–24), Miss Horner translates : « May this be a great fruit, a great advantage to those of my kith and kin who, their mind pleased recollect the departed who have passed away... » But in Papañcasūdanī, i, 144, it is mentioned that the relatives when they are dead, recollect the monk's good qualities and thereby pass away with their mind pleased » (Tesaṃ tanti Tesaṃ tam mayi pasannacittaṃ vā pasannena cittena anussaraṇaṃ vā). This is supported by the C corresponding passage : « I have relatives. May they on account of me, when they pass away, go to good places up to be born in heaven. » (C N° 105, vi, 29b, 1).

Again in the following passage : « Hoti kho so āvuso samayo yaṃ bāhirā āpodhātu pakuppati, antarahitā tasmiṃ samaye bāhira paṭhavīdhātu hoti ». (i, 185, 27–29), she is of the opinion that the text wrongly reads *āpodhātu* here instead of *paṭhavīdhātu*, (M. L. S. i, 232, Note 1). But the C text shows that the reading of the P is not incorrect. Moreover, there are only 3 calamities, fire–calamity, water–calamity, wind–calamity (Fo–hsüeh–ta–tzu–tion, iii, p.304). In Visuddhi Magga also, there mention only 3 saṃvattā : aposaṃvattā, tejosaṃvattā and vāyosaṃvattā (Chap. 13, para 30). Another instance of Miss Horner's not so happy interpretation is in her M.L S. ii, p. 325, note 6, where she prefers to read *kayasmiṃ* with the Siamese text instead of the text kāyamhā : « The wind cannot make his robe stir », M.A. iii, 393. But the C corresponding passage shows that kāyamhā is used here : « The wind cannot blow out the robe from the body. » Again in the expression : Jālahatthapāda (With hands and feet endowed with net), she prefers to adopt Buddhaghosa's interpretation at M.A. iii, 376, as « The 4 fingers of the Tathāgata's hands and the 5 toes of his feet are of an equal measure » (M.L.S. ii, p. 321, Note 2). But the C mentions clearly as follows : « With webbed fingers and toes like a goose king ».

All the above remarks are not meant as a criticism to her magnificent translation of the Majjhima Nikāya, which is unrivalled so far, but simply as a small contribution to the excellent work done by this great scholar.

APPENDIXES 4. — CLASSIFICATION OF 222 SŪTRAS OF THE CMA ACCORDING TO VARGAS, FASCICULI AND DAYS OF RECITAL

A. — 18 VARGAS OR CHAPTERS

CHAPTER I : *Ch'i-fa* (七法 : *Sapta dharmāḥ*) : 10 *sūtras* :

1) Shan-fa-ching, 2) Chou-tu-shu-ching, 3) Ch'êng-yü-ching, 4) Shui-yü-ching, 5) Mu-chi-yü-ching, 6) Shan-jên-wang-ching, 7) Shih-chien-fu-ching, 8) Ch'i-jih-ching, 9) Ch'i-ch'ê-ching, 10) Lou-chin-ching.

CHAPTER II : *Yeh-hsiang-ying* (業相應 : *Karmasamyukta*) : 10 *sūtras* :

11) Yen-yü-ching, 12) Ho-p'o-ching, 13) Tu-ching, 14) Lo-yün-ching, 15) Ssu-ching, 16) Ch'ieh-lan-ching, 17) Ch'ieh-mi-ni-ching, 18) Shih-tzu-ching, 19) Ni-kan-ching, 20) Po-lo-lao ching.

CHAPTER III : *Shê-li-tzu-hsiang-ying* (舍利子相應 : *Sāriputrasamyukta*) : 11 *sūtras* :

21) Têng-hsin-ching, 22) Ch'êng-chiu-chiai-ching, 23) Chih-ching, 24) Shih-tzu-hou-ching, 25) Shui-yü-ching, 26) Ch'ü-ni-shih-ching, 27) Fan-chih-t'o-jan-ching, 28) Chiao-hua-ping-ching, 29) Ta-chü-hsi-lo-ching, 30) Hsiang-chi-yü-ching, 31) Fên-pieh-shêng-ti-ching.

CHAPTER IV : *Wei-ts'êng-yu-fa* (未曾有法 : *Adbhutadharma*) : 10 *sūtras* :

32) Wei-ts'êng-yu-fa-ching, 33) Shih-che-ching, 34) Po-chü-lo-ching, 35) A-hsiu-lo-ching, 36) Ti-tung-ching, 37) Chan-po-ching, 38) Yu-ch'ieh-chang-che-ching, 39) Yu-ch'ieh-chang-che-ching, 40) Shou-chang-che-ching, 41) Shou-chang-che-ching.

CHAPTER V : *Hsi-hsiang-ying* (習相應 : *Samudaysamyukta*) : 16 *sūtras* :

42) Ho-i-ching, 43) Pu-ssu-ching, 44) Nien-ching, 45) Ts'an-k'uei-ching, 46) Ts'an-k'uei-ching, 47) Chiai-ching, 48) Chiai-ching, 49) Kung-ching-ching, 50) Kung-ching-ching, 51) Pên-chi-ching, 52) Shih-ching, 53) Shih-ching, 54) Chin-chih-ching, 55) Nieh-p'an-ching.

CHAPTER VI : *Wang-hsiang-ying* (王相應 : *Rājasamyukta*) : 14 *sūtras* :

56) Mi-hai-ching, 57) Chi-wei-pi-ch'iu-shuo-ching), 58) Ch'i-pao-ching, 59) San-shih-êrh-hsiang-ching, 60) Ssu-chou-ching, 61) Niu-fên-yü-

ching, 62) P'in-pei-so-lo-wang-ying-fo-ching, 63) Pei-p'o-ling-ch'i-ching, 64) T'ien-shih-ching, 65) Wu-niao-yü-ching, 66) Shuo-pên-ching, 67) Ta-t'ien-nai-lin-ching, 68) Ta-shan-chien-wang-ching, 69) San-shih-yü-ching, 70) Chüan-lün-wang-ching, 71) Pai-ssu-ching.

CHAPTER VII : *Ch'ang-shou-wang* (長壽王 : *Dīrghāyurāja*) : 15 *sūtras* :

72) Ch'ang-shou-wang-pên-ch'i-ching, 73) T'ien-ching, 74) Pa-nien-ching, 75) Ching-pu-tung-tao-ching, 76) Yu-ch'ieh-chih-lo-ching, 77) So-chi-ti-san-tsu-hsing-tzu-ching, 78) Fan-t'ien-ch'ing-fo-ching, 79) Yu-shêng-t'ien-ching, 80) Chia-ch'ih-na-ching, 81) Nien-shên-ching, 82) Chih-li-mi-li-ching, 83) Chang-lao-shang-tsun-shui-mien-ching, 84) Wu-tz'u-ching, 85) Chên-jên-ching, 86) Shuo-ch'u-ching.

CHAPTER VIII : *Wei-pin* (穢品 : *Aṅgaṇavarga*) : 10 *sūtras* :

87) Wei-p'in-ching, 88) Ch'iu-fa-ching, 89) Pi-ch'iu-ch'ing-ching, 90) Chih-fa-ching, 91) Chou-na-wên-chien-ching, 92) Ch'ing-pai-lien-hua-yü-ching, 93) Shui-ching-fan-chih-ching, 94) Hei-pi-ch'iu-ching, 95) Chu-fa-ching, 96) Wu-ching.

CHAPTER IX : *Yin-p'in* (因品 : *Nidānavorga*) : 10 *sūtras* :

97) Ta-yin-ching, 98) Nien-ching, 99) K'u-yin-ching, 100) K'u-yin-ching, 101) Ts'êng-shang-hsin-ching, 102) Nien-ching, 103) Shih-tzu-hou-ching, 104) Yu-t'an-p'o-lo-ching, 105) Yüan-ching, 106) Hsiang-ching.

CHAPTER X : *Lin-p'in* (林品) : *Vanavarga*) : 10 *sūtras* :

107) Lin-ching, 108) Lin-ching, 109) Tzu-kuan-hsin-ching, 110) Tzu-kuan-hsin-ching, 111) Ta-fan-hsing-ching, 112) A-nu-po-ching, 113) Chu-fa-pên-ching, 114) Yu-t'o-lo-ching, 115) Mi-wan-yü-ching, 116) Ch'ü-t'an-mi-ching.

CHAPTER XI : *Ta-p'in* (大品 : *Mahāvarga*) : 25 *sūtras* :

117) Jou-juan-ching, 118) Lung-hsiang-ching, 119) Shuo-ch'u-ching, 120) Shuo-wu-ch'ang-ching, 121) Ch'ing-ch'ing-ching, 122) Chan-po-ching, 123) Sha-mên-êrh-shih-i-ching, 124) Pa-nan-ching, 125) P'in-ch'iung-ching, 126) Hsing-yü-ching, 127) Fu-t'ien-ching, 128) Yu-p'o-sai-ching, 129) Yüan-chia-ching, 130) Chiao-t'an-mi-ching, 131) Hsiang-mo-ching, 132) Lai-cha-ho-lo-ching, 133) Yu-p'o-li-ching, 134) Shih-wên-ching, 135) Shan-shêng-ching, 136) Shang-jên-ch'iu-ts'ai-ching, 137) Shih-chien-ching, 138) Fu-ching, 139) Hsi-chih-tao-ching, 140) Chih-pien-ching, 141) Yü-ching.

CHAPTER XII : *Fan-chih-pin* (梵志品 : *Brāhmaṇavarga* : 20 *sūtras* :

142) Yü-shih-ching, 143) Shang-ko-lo-ching, 144) Suan-shu-mu-chien-lien-ching, 145) Ch'ü-mê-mu-chien-lien-ching, 146) Hsiang-chi-yu-ching,

147) Wên-tê-ching, 148) Ho-k'u-ching, 149) Ho-yü-ching, 150) Yü-shou-ko-lo-ching, 151) A-shê-ho-ching, 152) Ying-wu-ching, 153) Hsü-hsien-t'i-ching, 154) P'o-lo-p'o-t'ang-ching, 155) Hsü-ta-to-ching, 156) Fan-po-lo-yen-ching, 157) Huang-lü-yüan-ching, 158) T'ou-na-ching, 159) A-ch'ieh-lo-ho-na-ching, 160) A-lan-na-ching, 161) Fan-mo-ching.

CHAPTER XIII : *Kên-pên-fên-pieh-p'in* (根本分別品): *Mūlavibhaṅgavarga*) : 10 *sūtras* :

162) Fên-pieh-liu-chieh-ching, 163) Fên-pieh-liu-ch'u-ching, 164) Fên-pieh-kuan-fa-ching, 165) Wên-ch'üan-lin-t'ien-ching, 166) Shih-chung-ch'an-shih-tsun-ching, 167) A-nan-shuo-ching, 168) I-hsing-ching, 169) Chü-lou-shou-wu-cheng-ching, 170) Ying-wu-ching, 171) Fên-pieh-ta-yeh-ching.

CHAPTER XIV : *Hsin-p'in* : (心品 : *Cittavarga*) : 10 *sūtras* :

172) Hsin-ching, 173) Fou-mi-ching, 174) Shou-fa-ching, 175) Shou-fa-ching, 176) Hsing-shan-ching, 177) Shuo-ching, 178) Lieh-shih-ching, 179) Wu-chih-wu-chu-ching, 180) Ch'ü-t'an-mi-ching, 181) To-chieh-ching.

CHAPTER XV : *Shuang-p'in* : (雙品 : *Yamakavarga*) : 10 *sūtras* :

182) Ma-i-ching, 183) Ma-i-ching, 184) Niu-chiao-so-lo-lin-ching, 185) Niu-chiao-so-lo-lin-ching, 186) Ch'iu-chieh-ching, 187) Shuo-chih-ching, 188) A-i-na-ching, 189) Shêng-tao-ching, 190) Shao-k'ung-ching, 191) Ta-k'ung-ching.

CHAPTER XVI : *Ta-p'in* (大品 : *Mahāvarga*) : 10 *sūtras* :

192) Chia-lou-wu-t'o-i-ching, 193) Mou-li-p'o-ch'ün-na-ching, 194) Po-t'o-ho-li-ching, 195) A-shih-pei-ching, 196) Chou-na-ching, 197) Yu-p'o-li-ching, 198) T'iao-yü-ti-ching, 199) Ch'ih-hui-ti-ching, 200) A-li-cha-ching, 201) Ch'a-ti-ching.

CHAPTER XVII : *Pu-li-to-p'in* (晡利多品 : *Potaliyavarga*) : 10 *sūtras* :

202) Ch'ih-chai-ching, 203) Pu-li-to-ching, 204) Lo-mo-ching, 205) Wu-hsia-fên-chieh-ching, 206) Hsin-wei-ching, 207) Chien-mao-ching, 208) Chien-mao-ching, 209) Pei-mo-na-hsiu-ching, 210) Fa-lo-pi-ch'iu-ni-ching, 211) Ta-chü-hsi-lo-ching.

CHAPTER XVIII : *Li-p'in* (例品 : *Sanvidahanavarga*) : 11 *sūtras* :

212) I-ch'ieh-chih-ching, 213) Fa-chüang-yen-ching, 214) Pei-ho-t'i-ching, 215) Ti-i-tê-ching, 216) Ai-shêng-ching, 217) Pa-ch'êng-ching, 218) A-na-lü-t'o-ching, 219) A-na-lü-t'o-ching, 220) Chien-ching, 221) Chien-yü-ching, 222) Li-ching.

B. — 60 FASCICULI

FASC. 1-2 : CHAPTER I : Ch'i-fa-p'in : 10 sūtras.
FASC. 3-4 : CHAPTER II : Yeh-hsiang-ying-p'in : 10 sūtras.
FASC. 5-7 : CHAPTER III : Shê-li-tzu-hsiang-ying-p'in : 11 sūtras.
FASC. 8-9 : CHAPTER IV : Wei-ts'êng-yu-fa-p'in : 10 sūtras.
FASC. 10 : CHAPTER V : Hsi-hsiang-ying-p'in : 16 sūtras.
FASC. 11-16 : CHAPTER VI : Wang-hsiang-ying-p'in : 14 sūtras.
FASC. 17-21 : CHAPTER VII : Ch'ang-shou-wang-p'in : 15 sūtras.
FASC. 22-23 : CHAPTER VIII : Wei-p'in : 10 sūtras.
FASC. 24-26 : CHAPTER IX : Ying-p'in : 10 sūtras.
FASC. 27-28 : CHAPTER X : Lin-p'in : 15 sūtras.
FASC. 29-34 : CHAPTER XI : Ta-p'in : 25 sūtras.
FASC. 35-41 : CHAPTER XII : Fan-chih-p'in : 20 sūtras.
FASC. 42-44 : CHAPTER XIII : Kên-pên-fên-pieh : 10 sūtras.
FASC. 45-47 : CHAPTER XIV : Hsin-p'in : 10 sūtras.
FASC. 48-49 : CHAPTER XV : Shuang-p'in : 10 sūtras.
FASC. 50-54 : CHAPTER XVI : Ta-p'in : 10 sūtras.
FASC. 55-58 : CHAPTER XVII : Pu-li-to-p'in : 10 sūtras.
FASC. 59-60 : CHAPTER XVIII : Li-p'in : 11 sūtras.

C. — 5 DAYS OF RECITAL

1st DAY :	Chapter I to 1st half of Chapter VI =	64	sūtras
2nd DAY :	2nd half of Chapter VI to Chapter X =	52	—
3rd DAY :	Chapter XI to 1st half of Chapter XII =	35	—
4th DAY :	2nd half of chapter XII to 1st half of Chapter XV	35	—
5th DAY :	2nd half of chapter XV to Chapter XVIII =	36	—

APPENDIXES 5. — CORRESPONDING TITLES AND LOCATION OF SŪTRAS BETWEEN THE CHINESE AND PĀLI CORRESPONDING SŪTRAS

C. S. N° 1 : C N° 100, *Hsiang-ching.* On perceptions.

Shê-wei, Shêng-lin, Kei-ku-tu park (Sāvatthi, Jetavana, Anāthapiṇḍikārāma).

P N° 1, *Mūlapariyāyasutta.* On the fundamentals.

Ukkaṭṭhā, Subhagavana, at the foot of a Sālarāja tree.

C. S. N° 2 : C N° 10, *Lou-chin-ching.* On the extinction of cankers.

In the Chü-lou-shou, at the market town of Chien-mo-sê-t'an (Kurus, Kammassadamma).

P N° 2, *Sabbāsavasutta.* On all cankers.

Sāvaṭṭhi, Jetavana, Anāthapiṇḍikārāma.

C. S. N° 3 : C N° 88, *Ch'iu-fa-ching.* On seekers of dharma.

Chü-so-lo, Wu-so-lo, village, North of T'i-shê-ho forest (Kosala, Pañcasālā, Siṃsapāvana).

P N° 3, *Dhammadāyādasutta.* On heirs of the Dhamma.

Sāvatthi, Jetavana, Anāthapiṇḍikārāma.

C. S. N° 4 : C N° 87, *Wei-p'in-ching.* On kinds of blemishes.

P'o-ch'i-shou, T'o mountain, in the fearful forest (Bhagga, Suṃsumāragiri, Bhesakalāvana), Deer park.

P N° 5, *Anaṅgaṇasutta.* On no blemishes.

Sāvatthi, Jetavana, Anāthapiṇḍikārāma.

C. S. N° 5 : C N° 105, *Yuän-ching.* On wishes.

Shê-wei, Sheng-lin, Kei-ku-tu park (Sāvatthi, Jetavana, Anāthapiṇḍikarama).

P N° 6, *Ākaṅkheyyasutta.* On what one may wish.

Sāvatthi, Jetavana, Anāthapiṇḍikārāma.

C. S. N° 6 : C N° 93, *Shui-ching-fan-chih-ching.* On brāhmaṇa Shüi-ching.

Yu-pei-lo, on the bank of Ni-lien-jan, under the A-yeh-ho-lo-ni-chü-lei tree (Uruvelā, Nerañjarā, Ajapālanigrodha).

P N° 7, *Vatthūpamasutta.* On the simile of the cloth.

Sāvatthi, Jetavana, Anāthapiṇḍikārāma.

C. S. N° 7 : C N° 91, *Chou-na-wên-chien-ching.* On Chou-na asking about views.

Chü-shê-mi, in Ch'ü-shih-lo (Kosambī, Ghositārāma).

P N° 8, *Sallekhasutta.* On destruction.

Sāvatthi, Jetavana, Anāthapiṇḍikārāma.

C. S. N° 8 : C N° 98, *Nien-ch'u-ching.* On application on mindfulness.	P N° 10, *Satipaṭṭhānasutta.* On intent application of mindfulness.
Among the Chü-lou-shou, in the township called Chien-mo-sê-t'an (Kurus, Kammassadamma).	Among the Kurus, in the township of the Kurus called Kammassadamma.
C. S. N° 9 : C N° 103, *Shih-tzu-hou-ching.* On the lion's roar.	P N° 11, *Cūḷasīhanādasutta.* On the lion's roar (Lesser).
Among the Chü-lou-shou, in the township called Chien-mo-sê-t'an (Kurus, Kammassadamma).	Sāvatthi, Jetavana, Anāthapiṇḍikārāma.
C. S. N° 10 : C N° 99, *K'u-yin-ching.* On the aggregates of suffering.	P N° 13, *Mahādukkhakkhan-dhaS.* On the aggregate of suffering (Greater).
Shê-wei, Shêng-lin, Kei-ku-tu-park, (Sāvatthi, Jetavana, Anāthapiṇḍikārāma).	Sāvatthi, Jetavana, Anāthapiṇḍikārāma.
C. S. N° 11 : C N° 100, *K'u-yin-ching.* On the aggregate of suffering.	P N° 14, *CūḷadukkhakknandhaS.* On the aggregate of suffering (Lesser).
Among the Shih-chi-shou, at Chia-wei-lo-wei, in the Ni-chü-lei grove (Sakkas, Kapilavatthu, Nigrodha).	Among the Sakkas, at Kapilavatthu, in the Nigrodha grove.
C. S. N° 12 : C N° 89, *Pi-ch'iu-ch'ing-ching.* On the invitation to the monk.	P N° 15, *Anumānasutta.* On inference.
Wang-shê-town, Bamboo-grove, Chia-lan-to park (Rājagaha, Veluvana, Kalandakanivāpa).	Among the Bhaggas, at Suṃsumāragiri, Bhesakalāvana, in the Deer park.
C. S. N° 13 : C N° 206, *Hsin-wei-ching.* On mental depravities.	P N° 16, *Cetokhilasutta.* On mental obstructions.
Shê-wei, Shêng-lin, Kei-ku-tu-park (Sāvatthi, Jetavana, Anāthapiṇḍikārāma).	Sāvatthi, Jetavana, Anāthapiṇḍikārāma.
C. S. N° 14 : C N° 107, *Lin-Ching.* On forest.	P N° 17, *Vanapatthasutta.* On forest-grove.
Shê-wei, Shêng-lin, Kei-ku-tu park (Sāvatthi, Jetavana, Anāthapiṇḍikārāma).	Sāvatthi, Jetavana, Anāthapiṇḍikārāma.
C. S. N° 15 : C N° 115, *Mi-wan-yü-ching.* On the simile of the honey-ball.	P N° 18, *Madhupiṇḍikasutta.* On honey-ball.
Among the Shih-chi-shou, at Chia-wei-lo-wei (Sakkas, Kapilavatthu).	Among the Sakkas, at Kapilavatthu, in the Nigrodha grove.

C. S. N° 16 : C N° 102, *Nien-ching*. On thoughts.	P N° 19, *Dvedhāvitakkasutta*. On twofold thoughts.
Shê-wei, Shêng-lin, Kei-ku-tu park (Sāvatthi, Jetavana, Anāthapiṇḍikārāma).	Sāvatthi, Jetavana, Anāthapiṇḍikārāma.
C. S. N° 17 : C N° 101, *Tsêng-shang-hsin-ching*. On high and noble thoughts.	P N° 20, *Vitakkasanthānasutta*. On the form of thoughts.
Shê-wei, Shêng-lin, Kei-ku-tu park (Sāvatthi, Jetavana, Anāthapiṇḍikārāma).	Sāvatthi, Jetavana, Anāthapiṇḍikārāma.
C. S. N° 18 : C N° 193, *Mou-li-p'o-ch'ün-na-ching*. About Mou-li-p'o-ch'ün-na.	P N° 21, *Kakacūpamasutta*. On the simile of the saw.
Shê-wei, Shêng-lin, Kei-ku-tu-park (Sāvatthi, Jetavana, Anāthapiṇḍikārāma).	Sāvatthi, Jetavana, Anāthapiṇḍikārāma.
C. S. N° 19 : C N° 200, *A-li*-cha-*ching*. About A-li-cha.	P N° 22, *Alagaddūpamasutta*. On the simile of the serpent.
Shê-wei, Shêng-lin, Kei-ku-tu park (Sāvatthi, Jetavana, Anāthapiṇḍikārāma).	Sāvatthi, Jetavana, Anāthapiṇḍikārāma.
C. S. N° 20 : C N° 9, *Ch'i-shê-ching*. On 7 chariots.	P N° 24, *Rathavinītasutta*. On trained chariots.
Wang-shê-town, Bamboo grove, then Shê-wei, Shêng-lin, Kei-ku-tu park (Rājagaha, Veluvana, then Sāvatthi, Jetavana, Anāthapiṇḍikārāma).	Rājagaha, Veluvana, Kalandakanivāpa; then Sāvatthi, Jetavana, Anāthapiṇḍikārāma.
C. S. N° 21 : C N° 178, *La-shih-ching*. On the hunter.	P N° 25, *Nivāpasutta*. On the bait.
Wang-shê-town, Bamboo-grove, Chia-lan-to park (Rājagaha, Veluvana, Kalandakanivāpa).	Sāvatthi, Jetavana, Anāthapiṇḍikārāma.
C. S. N° 22 : C N° 204, *Lo-mo-ching*. On Lo-mo.	P N° 26, *Ariyapariyesanasutta*. On the ariyan quest.
Shê-wei, Lu-tzu-mu's palace (Sāvatthi, Migāramātu's palace).	Sāvatthi, Jetavana, Anāthapiṇḍikārāma, then Pubbārāma, Migāramātu's palace.
C.S. N° 23 : C N° 146, *Hsiang-chi-yu-ching*. On the simile of the Elephant-foot-print.	P N° 27, *Cūḷahatthipadopamasutta*. On the simile of the Elephant-foot-print (Lesser).
Shê-wei, Shêng-ling, Kei-ku-tu park (Sāvatthi, Jetavana, Anāthapiṇḍikārāma).	Sāvatthi, Jetavana, Anāthapiṇḍikārāma.

C. S. N° 24 : C N° 30, *Hsiang-chi-yü-ching*. On the simile of the Elephant-foot-print (Same location as the preceding sūtra).	P N° 28, *Mahāhatthipadopamasutta*. On the simile of the Elephant-foot-print (greater). (Same location as the preceding sutta).
C. S. N° 25 : C N° 185, *Niu-chioh-so-lo-lin-ching*. On the So-lo forest called Horn of the Cow.	P N° 31, *Cūḷa-Gosiṅgasutta*. On Gosiṅga, the Horn of the Cow (Lesser).
Na-mo-t'i-shou, Chien-ch'i monastery (Nādikā, Giñjakāvasatha).	Nādikā, Giñjakāvasatha.
C. S. N° 26 : C N° 184, *Niu-chioh-so-lo-lin-ching*. On the So-lo forest called Horn of the Cow.	P N° 32, *Mahā-Gosiṅgasutta*. On Gosiṅga, the Horn of the Cow (Greater).
P'o-ch'i-shou, Niu-chioh-so-lo forest (Bhagga, Gosiṅgasalavana).	Gosiṅgasalavanadāya.
C. S. N° 27 : C N° 201, *Ch'a-ti-ching*. Discourse on Ch'a-ti.	P N° 38, *MahātaṇhāsaṅkhāyaS*. On destruction of craving, (Greater).
Shê-wei, Shêng-lin, Kei-ku-tu park (Sāvatthi, Jetavana, Anāthapiṇḍikārāma).	Sāvatthi, Jetavana, Anāthapiṇḍikārāma.
C. S. N° 28 : C N° 182, *Ma-i-ching*. On the Horse-Market-town.	P N° 39, *Mahāassapurasutta*. On Assapura (Greater).
Ying-ch'i, Ma-i market-town, Ma-lin monastery (Aṅga, Assapura, Assavana).	Among the Aṅgas, Assapura.
C. S. N° 29 : *C* N° 183, *Ma-i-ching* On the Horse-market-town. (Same location as in preceding sūtra).	P N° 40, *Cūḷaassapurasutta*. On Assapura (Lesser). (Same location as above).
C. S. N° 30 : C N° 211, *Ta-chü-hsi-lo-ching*. Discourse on elder Ta-chü-hsi-lo.	P N° 43, *Mahāvedallasutta*. Discourse on Vedalla (Greater).
Wang-shê-town, Bamboo-grove, Chia-lan-to park (Rājagaha, Veluvana, Kalandakanivāpa).	Sāvatthi, Jetavana, Anāthapiṇḍikārāma.
C. S. N° 31 : C N° 210, *Fa-lo-pi-ch'iu-ni-ching*. Discourse on nun Fa-lo.	P N° 44, *Cūḷavedallasutta*. Discourse on Vedalla (Lesser).
Shê-wei, Shêng-lin, Kei-ku-tu park (Sāvatthi, Jetavana, Anāthapiṇḍikārāma).	Rājagaha, Veluvana, Kalandakanivāpa.
C. S. N° 32 : C N° 174, *Shou-fa-ching*. Discourse on receiving the dharma.	P N° 45, *Cūḷadhammasamādānas*. Discourse on undertaking the Dhamma (Lesser).
Shê-wei, Shêng-lin, Kei-ku-to park.	Sāvatthi, Jetavana, Anāthapiṇḍikārāma.

C. S. N° 33 : C N° 175, *Shou-fa-ching*. Discourse on receiving the dharma.

(Same location as above).

P N° 46, *Mahādhammasamādāna S*. Discourse on undertaking the Dhamma (Greater).

(Same location as above).

C. S. N° 34 : C N° 185, *Ch'iu-chieh-ching*. Discourse on quest for knowledge.

Among the Chü-lou-shou, at Chien-mo sê-t'an (Kurus, Kammassadamma).

P N° 47, *Vīmaṃsakasutta*. Discourse on investigation.

Sāvatthi, Jetavana, Anāthapiṇḍikārāma.

C. S. N° 35 : C N° 78, *Fan-t'ien-ch'ing-fo-ching*. Discourse on Brahmā's invitation to the Buddha.

Shê-vei, Shêng-lin, Kei-ku-tu park.

P N° 49, *Brahmanimantaṇika S*. Discourse on Brahmā's invitation to the Buddha.

Sāvatthi, Jetavana, Anāthapiṇḍikārāma.

C. S. N° 36 : C N° 131, *Hsiang-mo-ching*. Discourse on overpowering Māra.

P'o-ch'i-shou, T'o mountain, Fearful forest, Deer park (Bhagga, Suṃsumāragiri, Bhesakalāvana).

P N° 50, *Māratajjaniyasutta*. Discourse on censuring Māra.

Among the Bhaggas, Suṃsumāragiri, Bhesakalāvana, Deer-park.

C. S. N° 37 : C N° 217, *Pa-shêng-ching*. Discourse on eight towns.

Pei-shê-li, on the bank of Monkey river, at the upper terrace of a mansion (Vesali = Pei-shê-li).

P N° 52, *Aṭṭhakanagarasutta*. Discourse on eight towns.

Vesāli, Beluvagāmaka.

C. S. N° 38 : C N° 203, *Pu-li-to-ching*. Discourse on Pu-li-to.

Na-nan-ta, Po-ho-li-nai park (Nālandā, Pāvārikambavana).

P N° 54 *Potaliyasutta*. Discourse on Potaliya.

Aṅguttarāpa, in the market-town called Āpana.

C. S. N° 39 : C N° 133, *Yu-p'o-li-ching*. Discourse on Yu-p'o-li.

Na-nan-t'o, Po-p'o-li-nai forest (Nālandā, Pāvārikambavana).

P N° 56, *Upālisutta*. Discourse on Upāli.

Nālandā, Pāvārikambavana.

C. S. N° 40 : C N° 14, *Lo-yün-ching*. Discourse on Lo-yün.

The Buddha was staying at Wang-shê-town, Bamboo-grove, Chia-lan-to park. He came to see elder Lo-yün, at Wang-shê town, in the Hot-spring forest. (Rājagaha, Veluvana, Kalandakanivāpa).

P N° 61, *Ambalaṭṭhikārāhulovādasutta*. Discourse on admonition to Rāhula, at Ambalaṭṭhikā.

The Buddha was staying at Rājagaha, Veluvana, Kalandakanivāpe. He came to see elder Rāhula at Ambalaṭṭhikā.

C. S. N° 41 : C N° 221, *Chien-yü-ching*. Discourse on the simile of the arrow.

Shê-wei, Shêng-lin, Kei-ku-tu park.

P N° 63, *Cūḷamālunkyasutta*. Discourse on Māluṅkyaputta (Lesser).

Sāvatthi, Jetavana, Anāthapiṇḍikārāma.

C. S. N° 42 : C N° 205, *Wu-hsia-fên-chieh-ching*. Discourse on 5 factors binding to a lower existence.

(Same location as above).

P N° 64, *Mahāmālunkyasutta* Discourse on Māluṅkya (Greater).

(Same location as above).

C. S. N° 43 : C N° 194, *Po-t'o-ho-li-ching*. Discourse on Po-t'o-ho-li.
(Same location as above).

P N° 65, *Bhaddālisutta*. Discourse on Bhaddāli.
(Same location as above).

C. S. N° 44 : C N° 192, *Chia-lou-wu-t'o-i-ching*. Discourse on Wu-t'o-i.

Among the Ying-chia, at A-ho-na, Chien-jo monastery (Among the Aṅgas, at Āpaṇa).

P N° 66, *Laṭukīkopamasutta*. Discourse on the simile of the quail.

Aṅguttarāpa, in the market-town of Āpaṇa.

C. S. N° 45 : C N° 77, *So-chi-ti-san-tso-hsing-tzu-ching*. Discourse on 3 sons of family at So-chi-ti.

So-chi-ti, in the Blue forest (So-chi-ti = P : Sāketa).

P N° 68, *Naḷakapānasutta*. Discourse at Naḷakapāna.

Among the Kosalas, at Naḷakapāna in Palāsa forest.

C. S. N° 46 : C N° 26, *Ch'ü-ni-shih-ching*. Discourse about Ch'ü-ni-shih.

Wang-shê town, Bamboo grove, Chia-lan-to park.

P N° 69, *Gulissānisutta*. Discourse on Gulissāni.

Rājagaha, Veluvana, Kalandakanivāpa.

C. S. N° 47 : C N° 195, *A-shih-pei-ching*. Discourse on A-shih-pei.

First at Chia-shih (Kāsi) then at Chia-lo-lai, in the North of T'i-shê-ho village (Siṃsapāvana).

P N° 70, *Kīṭagirisutta*. Discourse on Kīṭagiri.

First at Kāsi, then Kīṭagiri, in the market-town of Kāsi.

C. S. N° 48 : C N° 153, *Hsü-hsien-t'i-ching*. Discourse on Hsü-hsien-t'i.

Among the Chü-lou-shou, in the house of P'o-lo-p'o (Kurus, Bhāradvājagotta).

P N° 75, *Māgandiyasutta*. Discourse on Māgandiya.

Among the Kurus, in Kammassadamma, in the firehouse of Bhāradvājagotta.

C. S. N° 49 : C N° 207, *Chien-mao-ching*. Discourse on Chien-mao.	P N° 77 *MahāsakulūdāyīS*. Discourse on Sakulūdāyī, (Greater).
First at Wang-shê-town, Bamboo-grove, Chia-lan-to park. Then to the Peacock forest (Rājagaha, Veluvana, Kalandakanivāpa, Moranivāpa).	First at Rājagaha, Veluvana, Kalandakanivāpa. Then to Moranivāpa, Paribbājakārāma.
C. S. N° 50: C N° 179, *Wu-chih-wu-chu-ching*. Discourse on Wu-chih-wu-chu.	P N° 78, *Samaṇamaṇḍikasutta*. Discourse on Samaṇamaṇḍika.
Shê-wei, Shêng-lin, Kei-ku-tu park.	Sāvatthi, Jetavana, Anāthapiṇḍikārāma.
C. S. N° 51 : C N° 208, *Chien-mao-ching*. Discourse on Chien-mao.	P N° *Cūḷasakulūdāyīsutta*. Discourse on Sakulūdāyī (Lesser).
First at Wang-shê-town, Bamboo-grove, Chia-lan-to park, then to Peacock feeding ground (Moranivāpa).	Rājagaha, Veluvana, Kalandakanivāpa, then to Moranivāpa.
C. S. N° 52 : C N° 209, *Pei-mo-na-hsiu-ching*. Discourse on Pei-mo-na-hsiu.	P N° 80, *Vekhanassasutta*. Discourse on Vekhanassa.
Shê-wei, Shêng-lin, Kei-ku-tu park.	Sāvatthi, Jetavana, Anāthapiṇḍikārāma.
C. S. N° 53 : C N° 63, *Pei-p'o-ling-chi-ching*. Discourse on Pei-p'o-ling-chi.	P N° 81, *Ghaṭīkārasutta*. Discourse on Ghaṭīkāra
Among the Chü-so-lo (Kosalas).	Among the Kosalas.
C. S. N° 54 : C N° 132, *Lai-cha-ho-lo-Ching*. Discourse on Lai-cha-ho-lo.	P N° 82, *Raṭṭhapālasutta*. Discourse on Raṭṭhapāla.
Among the Chü-lou-shou, at Yü-lu-cha, in the North of T'i-shê-ho (Kurus, Thullakoṭṭhita, Siṃsapāvana).	Among the Kurus, at Thullakoṭṭhita.
C. S. N° 55 : C N° 67, *Ta-t'ien-nai-lin-ching*. Discourse on Forest Ta-t'ien-nai.	P N° 83, *Makhādevasutta*. Discourse on Makhādeva.
Pei-t'o-t'i Mi-sa-lo, Ta-t'ien-nai forest (Videha, Mithilā, Makhādevambavana).	Mithilā, in the forest of Makhādevambavana.
C. S. N° 56 : C N° 216, *Ai-chêng-ching*. Discourse on born of attachment.	P N° 87, *Piyajātikasutta*. Discourse on born of attachment.
Shê-wei, Shêng-lin, Kei-ku-tu park.	Sāvatthi, Jetavana, Anāthapiṇḍikārāma.

C. S. N° 57 : C N° 214, *Pei-ho-t'i-ching*. Discourse on Pei-ho-t'i.
(Same location as above).

P N° 88, *Bāhitikasutta*. Discourse on Bāhitika.
(Same location as above).

C. S. N° 58 : C N° 213, *Fa-chuäng-yen-ching*. Discourse on ornaments of the Dharma.
Among the Shih-chi-shou, at Mi-lou-li market-town (Sakkas, Medaḷumpa).

P N° 89, *Dhammacetiyasutta*. Discourse on respects to Dhamma.
Among the Sakkas, at Medaḷumpa market-town.

C. S. N° 59 : C N° 212, *I-ch'ieh-chih-ching*. Discourse on embracing knowledge. At Yü-t'ou-sui-jo, in P'u-chi-tzu forest (Ujuññā, Kaṇṇakatthala.

P N° 90, *Kaṇṇakatthalasutta*. Discourse on Kaṇṇakatthala. At Ujuññā, Kaṇṇakatthala, in the Deer-park.

C. S. N° 60 : C N° 161, *Fan-mo-ching*. Discourse on Fan-mo.
In the country of Pei-t'o-ti (Videha.)

P N° 91, *Brahmāyusutta*. Discourse on Brahmāyu.
In the country of Videha.

C. S. N° 61 : C N° 151, *Fan-chih-a-shê-ho-ching*. Discourse on brāhmaṇa A-shê-ho.
Shê-wei, Shêng-lin, Kei-ku-tu park.

P N° 93, *Assalāyanasutta*. Discourse on Assalāyana.
Sāvatthi, Jetavana, Anāthapiṇḍikārāma.

C. S. N° 62 : C N° 150, *Yü-shou-ko-lo-ching*. Discourse on Yü-shou-ko-lo.
Wang-shê town, Bamboo grove, Chia-lan-to park (Rājagaha, Veluvana, Kalandakanivāpa).

P N° 96, *Esukārīsutta*. Discourse on Esukārī.
Sāvatthi, Jetavana, Anāthapiṇḍikārāma.

C. S. N° 63 : C N° 27, *Fan-chih-t'o-jan-ching*. Discourse on brāhmaṇa To-jan.
Wang-shê town, Bamboo grove, Chia-lan-to park.

P N° 97, *Dhānañjānisutta*. Discourse on Dhānañjāni.
Rājagaha, Veluvana, Kalandakanivāpa.

C. S. N° 64 : C N° 152, *Ying-wu-ching*. Discourse on Ying-vu.
Wang-shê town, Bamboo grove, Chia-lan-to park.

P N° 99, *Subhasutta*. Discourse on Subha.
Sāvatthi, Jetavana, Anāthapiṇḍikārāma.

C. S. N° 65 : C N° 19, *Ni-kan-ching*. Discourse on Ni-kan.
Among the Shih-chi-shou, at T'ien-i market-town (Sakkas, Devadaha).

P N° 101, *Devadahasutta*. Discourse on Devadaha.
Among the Sakkas, in the market-town called Devadaha.

C. S. N° 66 : C N° 196, *Chou-na-ching*. Discourse on Chou-na.
Among the P'o-ch'i, at Shê-mi village (Bhaggas ?, Sāmagāma).

P N° 104, *Sāmagāmasutta*. Discourse on Sāmagāma.
Among the Sakkas, at Sāmagāma.

C. S. N° 67 : C N° 75, *Ching-pu-tung-tao-ching*. Discourse on the pure and unshakable path.	P N° 106, *Āṇañjasappāyasutta*. Discourse on the unshakable and suitable (path).
Among the Chü-lou-shou, at Chien-mo-sê-t'an market-town (Kurus, Kammassadamma).	Among the Kurus, at the market-town of Kammassadamma.
C. S. N° 68 : C N° 144, *Suan-shu-mu-chien-lien-chieng*. Discourse on Suan-shu-mu-chien-lien.	P N° 107, *Gaṇaka-Moggallānasutta*. Discourse on Gaṇaka Mogallāna.
Shê-wei, Eastern-park, Lu-tzu-mu palace (Sāvatthi, Pubbārāma, Migāramātu's palace).	Sāvatthi, Pubbārāma, Migāramātu's palace.
C. S. N° 69 : C N° 145, *Ch'ü-mê-mu-chien-lien-ching*. Discourse on Ch'ü-mê-mu-chien-lien.	P N° 108, *Gopaka-Moggallānasutta*. Discourse on Gopaka-Moggallāna.
After the Buddha's Parinirvāṇa, elder A-nan was staying at Wang-shê-town (Rājagaha).	After the Buddha's Parinibbāna, elder Ānanda was staying at Rājagaha, Veluvana, Kalandakanivāpa.
C. S. N° 70 : C N° 187, *Shuo-chih-ching*. Discourse on speaking about knowldge.	P N° 112, *Chabbisodhanasutta*. Discourse on six cleansing ways.
Shê-wei, Shêng-lin, Kei-ku-tu park.	Sāvatthi, Jetavana, Anāthapiṇḍikārāma.
C. S. N° 71 : C N° 85, *Chên-jên-ching*. Discourse on true men.	P N° 113, *Sappurisasutta*. Discourse on supermen.
(Same location as above).	(Same location as above).
C. S. N° 72 : C N° 181, *To-chieh-ching*. Discourse on many elements.	P N° 115, *Bahudhātukasutta*. Discourse on many elements.
(Same location as above).	(Same location as above).
C. S. N° 73 : C N° 189, *Shêng-tao-ching*. Discourse on the Noble Path.	P N° 117, *MahācattārīsakaS*. Discourse on 40 great qualities.
Among the Chü-lou-shou, at Chien-mo-sê-t'an market-town (Kurus, Kammassadamma).	Sāvatthi, Jetavana, Anāthapiṇḍikārāma.
C. S. N° 74 : C N° 81, *Nien-shên-ching*. Discourse on contemplation on the Body.	P N° 119, *Kāyagatāsatisutta*. Discourse on contemplation on the body.
In Ying-ch'i country, at A-ho-na-chien-ni (Aṅga, Āpaṇa ?).	Sāvatthi, Jetavana, Anāthapiṇḍikārāma.

C. S. *N°* 75: C N° 168, *I-hsing-ching*. Discourse on activities of mind.	P N° 120, *Saṅkhāruppatisutta*. Discourse on activities of mental factors.
Shê-wei, Shêng-lin, Kei-ku-tu park.	Sāvatthi, Jetavana, Anāthapiṇḍikārāma.
C. S. *N°* 76: C N° 190, *Hsiao-k'ung-ching*. Discourse on lesser voidness.	P N° 121, *Cūḷasuññatasutta*. Discourse on lesser voidness.
Shê-wei, Eastern park, Lu-tzu-mu palace (Sāvatthi, Pubbārāma, Migāramātu's palace).	Sāvatthi, Pubbārāma, Migāramātu's palace.
C. S. *N°* 77: C N° 191, *Ta-k'ung-ching*. Discourse on greater voidness.	P N° 122, *Mahāsuññatasutta*. Discourse on greater voidness.
Among the Shih-chi-shou, at Chia-wei-lo-wei, Ni-chü-lei park (Sakkas, Kapilavatthu, Nigrodha).	Among the Sakkas, at Kapilavatthu, in Nigrodha park.
C. S. *N°* 78: C N° 32, *Wei-ts'êng-yu-fa-ching*. Discourse on wonderful dharmas.	P N° 123, *Acchariyabbhutadhammasutta*. Discourse on wonderful dhammas.
Shê-wei, Shêng-lin, Kei-ku-tu park.	Sāvatthi, Jetavana, Arāthapiṇḍikārāma.
C. S. *N°* 79: C N° 34, *Po-chü-lo-ching*. Discourse on Po-chü-lo.	P N° 124, *Bakkulasutta*. Discourse on Bakkula.
After the Buddha's Parinirvāṇa, elder Po-chu-lo was staying at Wang-shê-town, Bamboo grove, Chia-lan-to park.	Elder Bakkula was staying at Rājagaha, Veluvana, Kalandakanivāpa.
C. S. *N°* 80: C N° 198, *T'iao-yü-ti-ching*. Discourse on foundation for taming.	P N° 125, *Dantabhūmisutta*. Discourse on foundation for taming.
(Same location as above).	(Same location as above).
C. S. *N°* 81: C N° 173, *Fou-mi-ching*. Discourse on Fou-mi.	P N° 126, *Bhūmijasutta*. Discourse on Bhūmija.
(Same location as above).	(Same location as above).
C. S. *N°* 82: C N° 79, *Yu-shêng-t'ien-ching*. Discourse on existence of higher heavens.	P N° 127, *Anuruddhasutta*. Discourse on Anuruddha.
Shê-wei, Shêng-lin, Kei-ku-tu-park.	Sāvatthi, Jetavana, Anāthapiṇḍikārāma.
C. S. *N°* 83: C N° 72, *Ch'ang-shou-wang-pên-ch'i-ching*. Discourse on king Ch'ang-shou's previous birth.	P N° 128, *Upakkilesasutta*. Discourse on blemishes.
Chü-shê-mi, Ch'ü-shih-lo-park (Kosambī, Ghositārāma).	At Kosambī, Ghositārāma.

C. S. N° 84 : C N° 199, *Ch'ih-hui-ti-ching*. Discourse on the fool and the wise.	P N° 129, *Bālapaṇḍitasutta*. Discourse on the fool and the wise.
Shê-wei, Shêng-lin, Kei-ku-tu park.	Sāvatthi, Jetavana, Anāthapiṇḍikārāma.
C. S. N° 85 : C N° 64, *T'ien-shih-ching*. Discourse on the Heaven messenger.	P N° 130, *Devadūtasutta*. Discourse on the Heaven messenger.
Shê-wei, Shêng-lin, Kei-ku-tu park.	Sāvatthi, Jetavana, Anāthapiṇḍikārāma.
C. S. N° 86 : C N° 167, *A-nan-shuo-ching*. Discourse on A-nan's speech.	P N° 132, *Ānanda-Bhaddeka-rattasutta*. Discourse on Ānanda-Bhaddekaratta.
(Same location as above).	(Same location as above).
C. S. N° 87 : C N° 165, *Wên-ch'üan-lin-t'ien-ching*. Discourse on the Heaven of the hot-spring grove.	P N° 133, *Mahākaccāna-BhaddekarattaS*. Discourse on Mahākaccāna - Bhaddekaratta.
Wang-shê-town, Bamboo grove, Chia-lan-to park.	Rājagaha, Tapodārāma.
C. S. N° 88 : C N° 166, *Shih-chung-ch'an-shih-tsun-ching*. Discourse on the excellence of the meditation-hall of the Sakkas.	P N° 134, *Lomasakaṅgiya-Bhaddekarattasutta*. Discourse on Lomasakaṅgiya-Bhaddekaratta.
Shê-wei, Shêng-lin, Kei-ku-tu park.	Sāvatthi, Jetavana, Anāthapiṇḍikārāma.
C. S. N° 89 : C N° 170, *Ying-wu-ching*. Discourse on the parrot.	P N° 135, *Cūḷakammavibhaṅ-gasutta*. Discourse on the analysis of action (Lesser).
(Same location as above).	(Same location as above).
C. S. N° 90 : C N° 171, *Fên-pieh-ta-yeh-ching*. Discourse on the great analysis of action.	P N° 136, *Mahākammavibhaṅ-gasutta*. Discourse on the analysis of action (Greater).
Wang-shê town, Bamboo grove, Chia-lan-to park.	Rājagaha, Veluvana, Kalanda-kanivāpa.
C. S. N° 91 : C N° 163, *Fên-pieh-liu-ch'u-ching*. Discourse on the analysis of the 6 sense-organs.	P N° 137, *Saḷāyatanavibhaṅ-gasutta*. Discourse on the analysis of the 6 sense-organs.
Shê-wei, Shêng-lin, Kei-ku-tu park.	Sāvatthi, Jetavana, Anāthapiṇ-ḍikārāma.

C. S. N° 92 : C N° 164, *Fên-pieh-kuan-fa-ching*. Discourse on the analysis of discrimination of Dharmas.	P N° 138, *UddesavibhaṅgaS*. Discourse on the analysis of propounding.
(Same location as above).	(Same location as above).
C. S. N° 93 : C N° 169, *Chü-lou-shou-wu-cheng-ching*. Discourse on no quarrels among the Chü-lou-shou (Kurus).	P N° 139, *Araṇavibhaṅgasutta*. Discourse on the analysis of no-quarrels.
Among the P'o-ch'i-shou, at Chien-mo-sê-t'an market-town (Bhagga, Kammassadamma).	Sāvatthi, Jetavana, Anāthapiṇḍikārāma.
C. S. N° 94 : C N° 162, *Fên-pieh-liu-chieh-ching*. Discourse on the analysis of the 6 elements.	P N° 140, *Dhātuvibhaṅgasutta*. Discourse on the analysis of elements.
In Mo-chieh-t'o, at Wang-shê town (Magadha, Rājagaha).	In Magadha, at Rājagaha.
C. S. N° 95 : C N° 31, *Fên-pieh-shêng-ti-ching*. Discourse on the analysis of the noble truths.	P N° 141, *Saccavibhaṅgasutta*. Discourse on the analysis of Truths.
Among the Chü-lou-shou, at Chien-mo-sê-t'an (Kurus, Kammassadamma).	Bārāṇasī, Isipatana, Migadāya.
C. S. N° 96 : C N° 180, *Ch'ü-t'an-mi-ching*. Discourse on Ch'ü-t'an-mi.	P N° 142, *DakkhiṇavibhaṅgaS*. Discourse on the analysis of donations.
Among the Shih-chi-shou, at Chia-vei-lo-wei, in Ni-chü-lei grove (Sakkas, Kapilavatthu, Nigrodha).	Among the Sakkas, at Kapilavatthu, Nigrodhārāma.
C. S. N° 97 : C N° 28, *Chiao-hua-ping-ching*. Discourse on admonition to the sick person.	P N° 143, *AnāthapiṇḍikovādaS*. Discourse on admonition to Anāthapiṇḍika.
Shê-wei, Shêng-lin, Kei-ku-tu park.	Sāvatthi, Jetavana, Anāthapiṇḍikārāma.
C. S. N° 98 : C N° 86, *Shuo-ch'u-ching*. Discourse on speech about places.	P N° 148, *Chachakkasutta*. Discourse on six sets of six.
(Same location as above).	(Same location as above).

APPENDIXES 6. — LIST OF 22 PĀLI SŪTTAS IN THE PMN WHICH CANNOT BE TRACED IN THE CMA AND IN OTHER AGAMAS (1)

1) P N° 30, Cūḷa Saropamasutta
2) P N° 36, Mahā Saccakasutta
3) P N° 41, Sāḷeyyakasutta
4) P N° 42, Velañjakasutta
5) P N° 51, Kandarakasutta
6) P N° 55, Jīvakasutta
7) P N° 57, Kukkuravatikasutta
8) P N° 58, Abhayarājakumārasutta
9) P N° 60, Apaṇṇakasutta
10) P N° 71, Tevijja-Vacchagottasutta
11) P N° 85, Bodhirājakumārasutta
12) P N° 94, Ghoṭamukhasutta
13) P N° 95, Caṅkīsutta
14) P N° 98, Vāseṭṭhasutta
15) P N° 100, Saṅgāravasutta
16) P N° 102, Pañcattayasutta
17) P N° 103, Kintīsutta
18) P N° 105, Sunakkhattasutta
19) P N° 111, Anupadasutta
20) P N° 114, Sevitabbāsevitabbasutta
21) P N° 118, Ānāpānasatisutta
22) P N° 131, Bhaddekarattasutta.

We remark that the P sutta N° 85, Bodhirājakumārasutta has its corresponding sūtra in the isolated Wu fên-lü, which belongs to the Vinayapiṭaka and the P sutta N° 118, Ānāpānasatisutta, in the isolated sūtra Chih-ching.

(1) According to *C.A.P.N.*

APPENDIXES 7. — LIST OF 19 SŪTRAS IN THE CMA WHICH CANNOT BE TRACED IN THE PMN AND IN OTHER NIKĀYAS [1]

1) C N° 7, Shih-chien-fu-ching
2) C N° 39, Yu-ch'ieh-chang-che-ching
3) C N° 44, Nien-ching
4) C N° 54, Chin-chih-ching
5) C N° 55, Nieh-p'an-ching
6) C N° 60, Ssu-chou-ching
7) C N° 62, P'in-pi-so-lo-wang-ying-fo-ching
8) C N° 65, Wu-niao-yü-ching
9) C N° 69, San-shih-yü-ching
10) C N° 80, Chia-ch'ih-na-ching
11) C N° 92, Ch'ing-pai-lien hua-yü-ching
12) C N° 147, Wên-tê-ching
13) C N° 159, A-ch'ieh-lo-ho-na-ching
14) C N° 176, Hsing-ch'an-ching
15) C N° 177, Shuo-ching
16) C N° 197, Yu-p'o-li-ching
17) C N° 218, A-na-lü-t'o-ching
18) C N° 219, A-na-lü-t'o-ching
19) C N° 222, I-i-ching.

The C sūtra N° 197 Yu-p'o-li-ching has its Pāli equivalent in the Pāli Mahāvagga (6,1-8). The C sūtra N° 62 has its Pāli equivalent in Pāli Mahāvagga (1,4-1).

(1) According to the *C.A.P.N.*

APPENDIXES 8. — GIST OF THE 19 SŪTRAS IN THE CMA WHICH CANNOT BE TRACED IN THE PMN AND IN OTHER NIKĀYAS

1) *C N° 7, Shih-chien-fu-ching (v, 9b–10b):*

The Buddha explained 7 kinds of merit in the world, that is the donation by male and female members of clans and families to the Order of monks a) rooms and lodgings, b) seats, carpets, mattresses, sleeping mat, c) all kinds of new and clean robes, d) food, e) to send gardener, servant to attend upon the monks, f) when there were wind, rain, cold, snow, to come in person to the monastery and offer donation, g) after the monks ending their food (to see to it that), they would not suffer from wind, rain, cold, snow, from getting wet their clothes, day and night, they could practise meditation and contemplation with security. Then the Buddha explained 7 kinds of merit which were supermundane, that is, the faithful male and female members of clans and families became overjoyed, a) when they heard that the Tathāgata, the Tathāgata's disciples were travelling in such a place, b) when they heard that the Tathāgata, the Tathāgata's disciples wanted to go from that place to this place, c) when they heard that the Tathāgata, the Tathāgata's disciples had already come from that place to this place, d) having heard that, they with a pure heart came to see and pay homage to them, e) to offer donations, gifts to them, f) having offered gifts and donations, they took the 3 refuges in the Triple Gem, g) and to receive precepts. The Buddha explained further that these actions yielded innumerable, countless meritorious fruits, like the water of the 5 big rivers of Jambudīpa.

2) *C N° 39, Yu-ch'ieh-chang-che-ching (v, 53a–54a):*

Not long after the Buddha's demise, there was at Pei-shê-li (P: Vesāli), a householder who used to give charity to all people and every 5 days he invited the monks for food. One day, he lost one of his ships and Ven. A-nan was sent by the monks to dissuade him from giving charity any more. Householder Yü-ch'ieh told Ven. A-nan that he gave charity to fulfil his universal monarch's vow. He explained that the village poor man's vow was to become a village rich man; the village rich man's vow was to become a district rich man; the district rich man's vow was to become the richest man in the town; the town rich man's vow was to become the respected and honourable man in the town; the town respected and honourable man's vow was to become minister of the country; the country-minister's vow was to become a small king; the small king's vow was to become a universal monarch; a universal monarch's vow was to adopt a religious life, become a monk, realize the truth and attain arahantship. Thus he gave great charity so as to fulfil his universal monarch's vow. Then Yü-ch'ieh added that he had another 4 accomplishments : a) When he came to the monastery, he always paid homage to the monk, sat with them, discussed the Dharma with them and never looked down upon any monk, b) when he was offering dāna to the monks, there was a deity, who stayed in the air and told him : « This one is an arahant, this one is a would-be arahant ; this one is a non-returner, this one is a would-be non-returner; this one is an once-returner, this one is a would-be once-returner ; this one is a stream-attainer, this one is a would-be stream-attainer ; this one is a diligent one, this one is not a diligent one». But he did not have any distinction among the monks when he offered dāna to them ; c) when he was offering dāna to the monks, there was a deity who stayed in the air and told him that there were the Tathāgata, without grasping, the completely and rightly Enlightened One, the Dharma well preached by the W. H. One, and the noble Order of the Tathāgata. But he did not believe that deity, did not follow that deity's advice and wish ; but with his pure wisdom, he knew that there were the Tathāgata... and the noble Order of the Tathāgata ; d) he aloof from desire, from demeritorious dharmas attained and abided in up to the 4th dhyāna.

3) *C N° 44, Nien-ching (v, 57a) :*

The Buddha told the monks that if the monk was forgetful and without right knowledge, then this was harmful to right mindfulness, right knowledge. Absence of mindfulness, absence of right knowledge were harmful to protection of faculties, protection of precepts, no-remorse, delight, joy, calmness, happiness, concentration, true vision, true knowledge, disgust, absence of desire, emancipation. Absence of emancipation was harmful to Nirvāṇa. If the monk was not forgetful and with right knowledge, then this was origination for mindfulness, for right knowledge. Mindfulness and right knowledge were origination for protection of faculties... emancipation. Emancipation was origination for Nirvāṇa.

4) *C N° 54, Chin-chih-ching, (v, 60b-61a) :*

The Buddha told the monks that with knowledge, with vision, one could obtain extinction of cankers, not without knowledge, without vision. Due to knowledge and vision of suffering, of the origination of suffering, of the cessation of suffering, of the path leading to the cessation of suffering in accordance with truth that one obtained the extinction of cankers. Then the Buddha enumerated a series of 24 dharmas in succession, showing that the 1st dharma had the 2nd dharma as origin, the 2nd dharma had the 3rd dharma as origin and so on up to the 24th dharma. The 24 dharmas are as follow : 1) Absolute knowledge, 2) freedom, 3) absence of desire, 4) disgust, 5) true vision, true knowledge, 6) concentration, 7) happiness, 8) calmness, 9) joy, 10) delight, 11) no-remorse, 12) protection of precepts, 13) protection of faculties, 14) right mindfulness, right knowledge, 15) right consideration, 16) belief or faith, 17) consideration of patience, 18) recital, 19) receiving and hearing the dharma, 20) consideration of the meaning of the dharma, 21) the ear-sphere, 22) listening to good dharma, 23) approach, and 24) to honour, to attend upon. Then the Buddha explained these 24 dharmas in the reverse order and in the negative way.

5) *C N° 55, Nieh-p'an-ching* (*v*, 61*a*-61*b*) :

The Buddha enumerated a series of 29 dharmas in succession, showing that the 1st dharma had the 2nd dharma as origin, the 2nd dharma had the 3rd dharma as origin and so on up to the 29th dharma. The 29 dharmas are as follows: 1) Nirvāṇa, 2) freedom, 3) absence of desire, 4) disgust, 5) true vision, true knowledge, 6) concentration, 7) happiness, 8) calmness, 9) joy, 10) delight, 11) no-remorse, 12) protection of precepts, 13) protection of faculties, 14) right mindfulness, right knowledge, 15) right consideration, 16) faith, 17) suffering, 18) old age and death, 19) birth, 20) becoming, 21) grasping, 22) craving, 23) feeling, 24) strong enjoyment, 25) 6 sense-spheres, 26) name and form, 27) consciousness, 28) mental activities, 29) ignorance. Then the Buddha explained these dharmas in the reverse way, due to ignorance, there are mental activities, ... and so on up to Nirvāṇa.

6) *C N° 60, Ssu-chou-ching* (*v*, 64*a*-65*a*) :

The Buddha confirmed elder A-nan's thoughts that in this world very few people died with their desires satisfied, very few people died with mind disgusted with desires. Then the Buddha related one of his former lives when he vas a universal monarch ruling over 4 continents, 1) over Yen-fu (閻浮 : Jambudipa) continent where he had immense wealth, innumerable people, 7.000 sons, with jewels raining dow during 7 days up to knee-deep, 2) over the Western continent of Ch'ü-t'o-ni (瞿陀尼 : Aparagoyāna), 3) over the Eastern continent of Fu-p'o-pei-t'o-t'i (弗婆鞞陀提 : Pubbavideha), 4) over the continent of Yü-tan-yüeh (鬱單曰 : Uttarakuru). Although he ruled over these 4 continents, he was not satisfied. Then he went to Thirty-three heaven and there intoxicated by his resemblance with Ti-shih (P : Inda), except the eyes, he wanted to usurp Indra's throne, and due to that he fell down again to the continent of Jambudīpa. Then he recognised and made known that if he would die, he died with an unsatisfied mind. The Buddha proceeded to explain that now it was different as he had become a Tathāgata, fully and rightly enlightened and had ended all kinds of suffering.

7) *C N° 62, P'in-pi-p'o-lo-wang ying-fo-ching* (*v*, 66*a*-67*b*) :

This sūtra has its P equivalent in Mahāvagga, i, 4-i., about the invitation of king Bimbisāra of Magadha to the Buddha.

8) C N° 65, *Wu-niao-yü-ching* (*v*, 73*b*–75*b*) :

The Buddha used 7 similes, of an otter, of a chiu-mo (究暮 : a kind of bird of prey), of a vulture, of a bird who ate vomitted food, of a wolf, of a crow and of a calf to advise the monks not to behave like the 6 former animals and birds (that is to receive requisites for life from the laity but not of pure conduct), but to follow the example of the calf that is to get rid of the 5 hindrances to engage in meditation and to obtain arahantship.

9) C N° 69, *San-shih-yü-ching* (*v*, 83*b*–85*a*) :

The Buddha used 30 similes of various articles and men possessed by the king or the king's minister to advise the monks and the nuns to be endowed with 30 qualities required from those who had gone forth. They are : 1) Moral percepts as ornaments, 2) fulfilment of moral precepts to protect the brahma-life as the 5 insignia, 3) protection of the 6 faculties, as palace-guard, 4) right mindfulness as gate-keeper, 5) quiet mind as pure, full bathing pond, 6) wise companion as bath-attendant, 7) observance of precepts as perfume smearing the body, 8) shame and scrupulousness as beautiful dress, 9) the 4 dhyānas as seat, 10) right mindfulness as a barber, 11) joy as tasty and excellent food, 12) taste of dharma as delicious drinks, 13) 3 meditations on empty space, on vowlessness, on signlessness as various garlands of beautiful flowers, 14) deities' house, brahma-house, noble's house as towers, palaces, 15) wisdom as housekeeper, 16) 4 applications of mindfulness as four kinds of taxes, 17) 4 right eradications as kinds of armies, 18) 4 psychic powers as 4 kinds of carriages, 19) concentration and insight as ornaments to the carriages, 20) right mindfulness as charioteer, 21) one's own mind as lofty banner, 22) the noble eightfold path as straight and even road, 23) wisdom as officer of the army, 24) wisdom as principal audience-hall, 25) mounting the high and supreme palace of wisdom as king and king's minister ascending the high palace, 26) the attainment of 4 kinds of noble clans as the expert in clans and dynasties, 27) right mindfulness as an able doctor, 28) unobstructive meditation as well decorated and cushioned couch, 29) unshakable freedom of mind as famous jewel, 30) contemplation of one's own mind to purity the body, as the king, the king's minister taking bath and smearing perfume over the body to purify their body.

10) C N° 80, *Chia-ch'ih-na-ching* (*v*, 110*a*–122*b*) :

Ven. A-na-lü-t'o (P : Anuruddha) told Ven. A-nan that his 3 robes were torn and in a bad state and he requested Ven. A-nan to order the monks to prepare 3 robes for him. Then elder A-nan ordered the monks to assemble and prepare the robes for Ven. A-na-lü-t'o. The Buddha saw this and asked elder A-nan why A-nan did not inform him so that he also could come to help in making the robes. Then the Buddha came to the assembly and lent a hand in preparing the robes for elder A-na-lü-t'o along with 800 monks present and the robes were finished with-in one day. Then the W. H. One having a backache, lay down before the assembly for a little rest and asked Ven. A-na-lü-t'o to deliver a speech on Chia-ch'ih-na (Kathina) to the monks and Ven. A-na-lü-t'o did as told. A-na-lü-t'o showed the reason of his embracing the religious life, his observance of the moral precepts, his getting rid of the 5 hindrances, his practice of meditation, his attainment of the 4 dhyānas, psychic powers, divine ear, knowledge of others' mind, knowledge of former births, knowledge of births and deaths, knowledge of the 4 noble truths, of the cankers as they really were. Then Ven. A-na-lü-to asked the monks if they had any doubt about his attainment of these 6 high knowledges, they might ask him and he would reply to all. Then the Buddha, his ache being abated, got up from his sleeping position, sat cross-legged, praised A-nu-lü-t'o and enjoined him to preach the Chia-ch'ih-na dharma to the monks and advised the monks to practise the Chia-ch'ih-na dharma.

11) *C N°* 92, *Ch'ing-pai-lien-hua-yü-ching* (*vi*, 12*a*-12*b*) :

The Buddha told the monks that there were dharmas which could be destroyed by body, such as demeritorious bodily actions, there were dharmas which could be destroyed by mouth such as demeritorious vocal actions ; there were dharmas wihch could not be destroyed by body and by mouth, such as quarrel, dispute, hatred, greed, craftiness, flattery, shamelessness, scrupulousness, evil desires, evil views which could not be destroyed by body and mouth, but only by wisdom.

12) *C N°* 147, *Wên-tê-ching*, (*vi*, 80*a*-80*b*) :

The Buddha enumerated to brāhmaṇa Shêng-wên 14 merits to be obtained by the Buddha's religious disciples and lay-disciples due to their much learning and practice : 1) Not to be afflicted and overcome by grief, if their business was not prosperous, 2) not to be afflicted and overcome by grief, if they were separated from what they had affection, 3) to consider wealth as impermanent and thinking of adopting the homeless life and learn the dharma, 4) to adopt the homeless life and learn the dharma, 5) to bear with forbearance, hardship and difficulties of all kinds, 6) to bear unhappiness, with forbearance and not to be affected by unhappiness, 7) to bear fearfulness with forbearance and not to be affected by fear, 8) not to be affected by thoughts of desire, malevolence, harming, 9) to be aloof from evil, demeritorious dharmas, to attain and dwell in the 4 dhyānas, 10) to attain the state of stream-attainer, 11) to attain the state of once-returner, 12) to attain the state of no-returner, 13) to attain freedom (due) to quietude, free from material forms, to attain immaterial state, 14) to obtain the 6 higher knowledges and the attainment of arahantship.

13) *C N°* 159, *A-ch'ieh-lo-ho-na-ching* (*vi*, 98*b*-99*a*) :

Brāhmaṇa A-ch'ieh-lo-ho-na asked the Buddha a series of questions, beginning first with : « Upon which foundation stood the Vedic texts » and consequently up to Nirvāṇa, which was the 16th dharma. The Buddha replied with a series of 17 dharmas, beginning with *man*, which was said to be the foundation upon which the Vedic texts stood, and so on up to *Nirvāṇa*, the consequent dharma being the foundation upon which the preceding dharma stood, except for the 6th dharma, *the space*, which had no foundation as due to moon and sun that space came to exist; except also for the Nirvāṇa, which had no foundation. The 17 dharmas are as follows : 1) Men, 2) crop, 3) earth, 4) water, 5) wind, 6) space, 7) sun and moon, 8) the 4 kings-heavens, 9) the 33-heaven, 10) the Yen-mo heaven, 11) Tusitā heaven, 12) the Ho-lo-t'ien, 13) T'a-hua-lo-t'ien, 14) the Brahmaloka, 15) the Great Brahma, 16) forbearance and kindness, 17) Nirvāṇa.

14) *C N° 176, Hsing-ch'an-ching (vii, 24a-26a) :*

The Buddha explained to the monks, 4 kinds of people practising meditation, those who were retrogressive in their meditation but thought that they were progressive, those who were progressive in their meditation but thought that they were retrogressive; those who were retrogressive in their meditation but knew that they were retrogressive; those who were progressive in their meditation and knew that they were progressive.

15) *C N° 177, Shuo-ching (vii, 26a-27b):*

The Buddha explained to the monks the doctrine on four kinds of speech. There was a monk who practised and attained the 1st dhyāna, but he did not hold on to this practice, did not think of its characteristic, but harboured thoughts connected with desire. That monk should know that he gave rise to the 1st dhyāna which would not stand fast, would not progress, and he would retrograde. If there was a monk who practised and attained the 1st dhyāna, but held on to this practice, thought of its characteristic, established his mind on this dharma and made it onepointed, that monk should know that he gave rise to that dharma which was not retrogressive, not progressive ; he would not become disgusted, but would be steadfast and his concentration would last long. Again there was a monk who practised and attained the 1st dhyāna. He did not hold on to this practice, did not think of its characteristic, but harboured thoughts connected with the 2nd dhyāna and wishing to progress further. That monk should know that he gave rise to that dharma, but did not retrograde, did not stand in one place, did not become disgusted ; but that dharma made him progress further and before long he would obtain the 2nd dhyāna. Again there was a monk who practised and attained the 1st dhyāna, did not hold on to that dharma, did not think of its characteristic, but harboured thoughts connected with extinction, calmness, absence of desire, that monk should know that he gave rise to that dharma, but did not retrograde, did not stand in one place, did not progress ; but that dharma made him disgusted and before long, he would obtain the cessation of cankers. In the same way with the 2nd dhyāna, 3rd dhyāna, 4th dhyāna up to the state of neither perception nor non-perception.

16) *C N° 197, Yu-p'o-li-ching (vii, 57b–58b) :*

This sūtra has its Pāli equivalent, not in the Nikāyas, but in Mv. IX, 6-1-8.

17) *C N° 218, A-na-lü-t'o-ching (vii, 95b) :*

The monks asked Ven. A-na-lü-t'o how a monk was said to die as a noble ? Ven. A-na-lü-t'o replied that when a monk practised and attained up to the 4th dhyāna, he was said to die as a noble but he died not as absolutely noble. But the monk who obtained the divine ear, the knowledge of others' mind, the knowledge of previous births, the knowledge of births and deaths, the extinction of cankers, freedom of mind, freedom of wisdom, arahantship, was said to die with a noble mind, and this was supreme, absolute.

18) *C N° 219, A-na-lü-t'o-ching (vii, 95b-96a) :*

The monks asked Ven. A-na-lü-t'o how a monk was said to die without distress ? Ven. A-na-lü-t'o replied that when a monk had straightforward view and obtained precepts loved by the noble ones, when a monk practised the 4 applications of mindfulness, when a monk practised the four illimitables, when a monk practised the dhyāna of the arūpa-world up to the plane of neither perception nor non-perception, they would die without distress, but not absolutely without distress. Only the monks who knew how to extinguish the bodily touch, and with wisdom eradicated all the cankers, they would die absolutely without distress.

19) *C N° 222, Li-ching (vii, 97b-100b) :*

The Buddha told the monks that to eradicate or to know separately the 12 constituents (P : nidāna) of the dependent origination, one should practise the 4 applications of mindfulness, the 4 right eradications, the 4 psychic powers, the 4 dhyānas, the five faculties, the 5 powers, the 7 factors of wisdom, the noble eightfold path, the 10 all pervading spheres (Sk. Kṛṣṇāyatana) and the 10 dharmas of the non-learners (P : Asekha).

APPENDIXES 9. — REMAINS OF 2 SŪTRAS OF THE SANSKRIT MADHYAMA ĀGAMA UNEARTHERD IN CENTRAL ASIA

UPĀLI SŪTRA (1)

1a–c stood on the proceding folio.

2a *Āryasya bhāvitātmanaḥ prāp*tiprāptasya vyākaraṇeṣu/

2b Smṛtimato vipaśyasya anabhinata *sya no apanatasya*/

2c *Aniñjyasya vaśiprāptasya Bhagavatas tasya śrāvaka Upālī*//

3a–c Apparently missed out.

4a *Niṣabhasya* aprameyasya gaṁbhīrasya maunaprāptasya/

4b Ksemaṁkarasya vedi*naḥ dharmastha-sya saṁvṛtātmanaḥ*/

4c *Dāntasya niṣprapañcasya Bhagavatas tasya śrāvaka* Upālī//

5a Nāgasya prāntaśayānasya kṣīṇasamyojanasya mu*ktasya*/

5b *Pratimantrakasya dhantasya prajñā-dhvajasya vītarāgasya*/

5c *Anāvṛtta*kasya Śakrasya Bhagavatas tasya śrāvaka Upālī//

6a Samyaggatasya dhyā*yinaḥ ananugatāntarasya śuddhasya*/

6b *Asmitasya alpahīnasya praviviktasya agraprāp*tasya/

6c Viśāradasya nipuṇasya Bhagavatas tasya śrāvaka Upālī

7a *Snātakasya pradīpasya praśrabdhasya viditavedasya*/

7b *Śīlavṛd*dhasya śamita-vairasya

7c Vīrasya viprasannasya Bhagavatas tasya śrāva*ka Upālī*//

8a *Śāntasya bhūriprajñasya mahāprajñasya vītalobhasya*/

8b *Āhavanīyasya akṣasya apratipudgalasya* atulasya/

8c Saṁgātigasya padakasya Bhagavat*as tasya śrāvaka Upālī*//

9a *Asaṁśavasya kuśalasya vainayikasya sārathivarasya*/

9b *Anuttarasya dharma*rucirasya niṣkāṁkṣasya prabhāsakarasya/

9c Māyācchido hy amāyasya Bhag*avatas tasya śrāvaka Upālī*/ (2)

10a *Tṛṣnācchido hi Buddhasya vītadhūmasya anupralip*tasya/

10b Tathāgatasya Sugatasya uttamapudgalasya amamasya/

10c Yaso*graprāptasya mahato Bhagavatas tasya śrāvaka Upālī*/

11*a* Missing.

11b Pūrvam avitarkitam avadad Upāli/

11c Purato nigranthapariṣadaḥ varṇam varṇam *Buddhasya* (prose, about 17 syllables missing)

Mālā tadyathā bhadanta dakṣo mālākāro vā mālākārāntevāsī vā vici.

---

(1) M.R.E.T. pp 30-41.

(2) The italic lines are restituted passages done by Hoernle.

1.6, *tram mālām grathnīvāt nānāpuṣpāṇaṃ mahāpuṣpārāśim evam eva* tasya Bhagavatas Tathāgatasyārhataḥ samyak-sambuddhasy = ananda x.

SUKA SŪTRA (1)

FOLIO 56. OBVERSE

1) (VII) śakyāt kuśala-mūlādvicchandanam alpa-śakyānām pudgalānāṃ paribhavaḥ ime daśa dharmā alpa-śakya-

2) Samvartanīyāḥ (VIII) Daśa dharmā mahā-śakyā-samvartanīyāh katame daśa anirṣyukaḥ parasya lābha-satkāra-

3) Slokair āttamanatā parasya kīrtiśabda-ślokair āttamanatā: ryatra-pradānam bodhicittôtpādaḥ.

4) Tathāgata: biṃba-karaṇam mātāpitṛṇāṃ pratyudgamanaṃ āryāṇāṃ pratyudgamanaṃ alpa-śakyāt kuśa-

5) la-mūlād vicchandanam mahāśakye kuśala-mūle samādāpanam im daśa dharmā mahāśakya-saṃvartanī-

FOLIO. 56. REVERSE

1) yāḥ (IX) Daśa dharmā nīcakula-saṃvartanīyāḥ katame daśa amātṛjñatā apitṛjñatā aśrāmaṇyatā

2) abrahmaṇyatā kūle na jyeṣṭhânupālakatvam āsanādi na pratyutthānam āsane na nimantraṇam

3) mātāpitror aśuśruṣā āryāṇām aśuśruṣā nīca-kula-jātānāṃ pudgalānām antike pari-

4) bhavaḥ ime daśa dharma nīcakula-saṃvartanīyā (X) Daśa dharmā ucca-kula-saṃvartanīyāḥ katame daśa:

5) mātṛjñatā pitṛjñatā śrāmaṇyatā brāhmaṇyatā kule jyeṣṭhânupālakatvam āsanāt pratyut*thā*

FOL. 57. OBVERSE

1) nam āsanen=âbhinimaṃtraṇam mātāpitroḥ śuśrūṣā āryāṇāṃ śuśrūṣā nīca-kula-jātānāṃ pu-

2) dgalānāṃ aparibhavaḥ ime daśa dharmā ucca-kula-saṃvartanīyāḥ (XI) Daśa dharmā alpabhoga-saṃva-

---

(1) M.R.E.T. pp. 48-50.

3) rtanīyāḥ katame daśa adattâdānam adattâdāna : samādāpanam adattâdānasya–

4) ca varṇa-vāditā, adattâdānena āttamanatā mātāpitṛṇāṃ vṛttyupacchedaḥ āryāṇaṃ vṛtyupa–

5) cchedaḥ parasya alābhena āttamanatā parasya lābhenan = âttamanatā parasya lābh–ântarā–

FOL. 57. REVERSE

1) yo durb*hikṣā*-yācanā ca ime daśa dharmā alpa–bhoga–saṃvartanīyāḥ (XII) Daśa dharmā mahābhoga–saṃvarta–

2) nīyāḥ katame daśa dānaṃ adattādāna–vairamaṇam adattâdānavairamaṇasya varṇavāditā.

3) adattâdāna--vairama–ṇena āttamanatā parasya alābhena anāttamanatā parasya.

4) lābhena āttamanatā parasya lābhôdyogaḥ dānasy = âbhyanumodanam dān–âdhimuktānāṃ pudga–

5) lānām saṃpraharṣaṇaṃ subhikṣāyācanā ca ime daśa dha–rmā mahābohga : saṃvartanīyāḥ.

APPENDIXES 10. — PĀLI-CHINESE-ENGLISH EQUIVALENTS

Akusala : Pu–shan (不 善): Demeritorious.

Aggivessana : A–ch'i–shê–na (阿 奇 舍 那): Probably name of a brahmin clan.

Aṅga : Yang–ch'i (鴦 騎): One of the 16 great countries.

Aṅgamagadha : Yang–chia–mo–chieh–t'o (鴦 迦 摩 竭 陀): A country's name.

Aṅgirasa : Ying–i–lo–p'o (應 疑 羅 婆): One of the 10 ancient seers.

Acavanadhamma : Pu–chung–fa (不 終 法): Not subject to death.

Acīravata : A–i–na–ho–t'i (阿 夷 那 和 提): Name of a novice.

Aciravatī : A–i–lo–p'o–t'i (阿 夷 羅 婆 提): One of the five big rivers.

Acchariyābbhutadhamma · Wei–ts'êng–yu–fa (未 曾 有 法): Marvellous quality.

Ajapālanigrodha : A–yeh–ho–lo–ni–chü–lei (阿 耶 恕 羅 尼 拘 類): Name of a tree, on the bank of Nerañjarā.

Ajātasattu Vedehiputta : Wei–shêng–yüan (未 生 怨): Bimbisāra's son.

Ajita Kesakambalī : A–i–to–chi–shê–chien–p'o–li (阿 夷 哆 雞 舍 劍 婆 利): One of the 6 heretical Teachers of the Buddha's time.

Ajjatagge : Ts'ung–chin–jih–shih (從 今 日 始): From now onwards.

Ajjhatta vūpasama : Nei–chih (內 止): Inner repose, inner peace.

Ajjhatta sampasādana : Nei–ching (內 靜): Inner tranquillity.

Ajjhattikā paṭhavīdhātu : Nei–ti–chieh (內 地 界): Inner earth–element.

Aññaṃ jīvaṃ aññaṃ sarīraṃ : Ming–i–shên–i (命 異 身 異): Life and body are not the same.

Aṭṭhaka : Yeh–cha (夜 吒): One of the 10 ancient ṛṣiṣ of the brahmins.

Aṭṭhādasa manopavicārā : Shih–pa–i–hsing (十 八 意 行): 18 mental ranges.

Atimāna : Kuo–man (過 慢): Over–pride.

Atimuttaka : A–t'i–mou–to (阿 提 牟 哆): Acacia flovers.

Atīta addhāna : Kuo–ch'ü (過 去): The past.

Attabyābādha : Tzu–hai (自 害): Self–harm.

Adinnādāna : Pu–yü–ch'ü (不 與 取): Taking what is not given.

Adukkha asukha : Pu–k'u–pu–lo (不 苦 不 樂): Without suffering, without happiness.

Adhicitta : Tsêng–shang–hsin (增 上 心): Lofty mind.

Anaṅgaṇa : Wu–wei (無 穢): Without blemishes.

Anantavā loko : Shih–wu–ti (世 無 底): The world is infinite.

Anariyapariyesana : Fei–shêng–ch'iu (非 聖 求): The unariyan quest.

Anāgata addhāna : Chiang–lai (將 來): The future.

Anāthapiṇḍika : Kei-ku-tu (給孤獨): One of the Buddha's disciples.

Anāvattidhamma : Pu-t'ui-fa (不退法): Not liable to return to a lower life.

Anicca : Wu-ch'ang (無常): Impermanence.

Aniṭṭha akanta amanāpa dhamma : Pu-hsi-pu-ai-pu-k'o-fa (不喜不愛不可法): Joyless, desireless, unlovely dhamma.

Anibbānasaṃvattanika : Pu-tê-nieh-p'an (不得涅槃): Unable to attain Nibbāna.

Animittā cetovimutti : Wu-hsiang-hsin-chieh-t'o (無相心解脫): Freedom of mind on signless.

Anuttara : Wu-shang-shih (無上士): The Peerless One.

Anuruddha : A-na-lü-t'o (阿那律陀): First cousin of the Buddha and one of his eminent disciples.

Anusaya : Sui-mien (隨眠): Latent tendency.

Anekapariyāya : Wu-liang-fang-pien (無量方便): In various ways.

Antavā loko : Shih-yu-ti (世有底): The world is finite.

Andhavana : An-t'o-lin (安陀林): A grove to the South of Sāvatthi

Apāpuraṇa : Yao (鑰): A key.

Appamāṇā cetovimutti: : Wu-liang-hsin-chieh-t'o (無量心解脫): Boundless emancipation of mind.

Abbhutadhammā : Wei-ts'êng-yu-fa (未曾有法): Wonderful dhammas.

Abhijjhā : T'an-tz'u (貪伺): Covetousness, lust.

Abhidhamma : A-p'i-t'an (阿毗曇): Abhidhamma.

Abhiya Kaccāna : Chên-chia-chan-yen (眞迦旃延): or Sabhiya Kaccāna, a monk who was formerly a paribbājaka.

Amatadundubhī : Kan-lu-ku (甘露鼓): The ambrosia drum.

Amūḷhavinaya : Pu-ch'ih-chih-chêng-lü (不癡止諍律): Acquittal on the ground of restored sanity.

Ayoniso manasikāra : Hsieh-ssu-wei (邪思惟): Wrong consideration.

Arañña : Wu-shih-ch'u (無事處): A forest. C: A place free of troubles.

Arahaṃ : A-lo-han (阿羅漢): The Perfect One.

Ariṭṭha : A-li-cha (阿黎吒): Name of a monk who was a former vulture-trainer.

Ariya : Shêng (聖): Noble.

Ariyadhamma : Shêng-fa (聖法): The noble dhamma.

Ariyapariyesana : Shêng-ch'iu (聖求): The noble quest.

Ariya aṭṭhaṅgika magga : Pa-shêng-tao (八聖道): The noble eightfold path.

Avijjānusaya : Wu-ming-shih (無明使): Ignorance tendency.

Avijjāsavā cittaṃ vimuccittha : Wu-ming-lou-hsin-chieh-t'o (無明漏心解脫): Mind emancipated from canker of ignorance.

Avijjāsava : Wu-ming-lou (無明漏): Canker of ignorance.

Avitakkaṃ avicāraṃ samādhijaṃ pītisukhaṃ : Wu-chüeh-wu-kuan-ting-shêng-hsi-lo (無覺無觀定生喜樂).

Later translation : Wu-hsin-wu-tz'u-ting-shêng-hsi-lo (無尋無伺定生喜樂) : Joy and happiness arisen out from meditation, without initial thoughts, without discursive thoughts.

Asassata loka : Shih-wu-yu-ch'ang (世無有常) : The world is impermanent.

Asita Devala : A-ssu-lo-t'i-pei-lo (阿私羅提稗邏) : A ṛṣi.

Asura : A-hsiu-lo (阿修羅) : A titan.

Assaji : A-shih-pei (阿濕貝) : The 5th of the pañcavaggiya monks.

Assāda : Wei (味) : Taste.

Assapura : Ma-i (馬邑) : A city in the kingdom of Aṅga.

Assaratana : Ma-pao (馬寶) : Horse-jewel.

Assalāyana : A-shê-ho-lo-yen-to (阿攝积羅延多) : A young brahmin.

Assavana : Ma-lin (馬林) : Name of a forest.

Assasati : Ju-hsi (入息) : Inhaling.

Ahiri : Wu-ts'an (無慚) : Shamelessness.

Ā

Ākāsānañcāyatana : Wu-liang-k'ung-ch'u (無量空處) : Sphere of infinite space.

Ākiñcaññāyatana : Wu-so-yu-ch'u (無所有處) : Sphere of nothingness.

Āgama : A-han-mo (阿含慕) : Religion, scripture.

Ādikalyāṇa : Ch'u-miao (初妙) : Excellent in the beginning.

Ādīnava : Huan (患) : Danger.

Āneñjasappāyā paṭipadā : Ching-pu-tung-tao (淨不動道) : Way of pure immovability.

Ānanda : A-nan (阿難) : One of the foremost Buddha's disciples.

Āpodhātu : Shui-chieh (水界) : Water-element.

Ābhassara : Chi-kuang-t'ien (極光天) : The radiant God.

Āmisa : Yin-shih (飲食) : Of the flesh, material C : food and drink.

Āyatiṃ dukkhavipāka : Tang-lai-shou-k'u-pao (當來受苦報) : Unhappy result in the future.

Āyatiṃ sukhavipāka : Tang-lai-shou-lo-pao (當來受樂報) : Happy result in the future.

Āraddhaviriya : Ching-chin (精進) : Energy, exertion.

Ārāma : Yüan (園) : Park.

Ārogyaparamā lābhā : Wu-ping-ti-i-li (無病第一利) : No sickness is the highest gain.

Āḷāra Kālāma : A-lo-lo-chia-lo-mo (阿羅羅加羅摩) : One of the Gotama's teachers, before his enlightenment.

Āvuso : Hsien–che (賢者) : Reverend friend.
Āsava : Lou (漏) : Canker.

I

Iṭṭhā kantā manāpā dhammā : Hsi–ai–k'o–fa (喜愛可法) : Joyful, desirable, lovely dhammas.
Itivuttaka : Tz'u–shuo (此說) : Thus it is said.
Itthiratana : Nü–pao (女寶) : Women–jewel.
Iddhipāda : Ju–i–tsu (如意足) : Psychic power.
Inda : Ti–shih (帝釋) : Lord, God Indra.
Indriyesu guttadvāra : Shou–hu–chu–kên (守護諸根) : Control of faculties.
Isidatta : Hsien–yü (仙餘) : A chamberlain of king Pasenadi.
Isipatana : Chu–t'ien–chu–ch'u (諸天住處) : Place where the Buddha first preached the Dhamma.

U

Ujañña : Yü–t'ou–sui–jo (鬱頭隨若) : Name of a place.
Uttara : Yu–to–lo (優多羅) : A pupil of Brahmāyu.
Uttarāsaṅga : Yu–to–lo–sêng (優多羅僧) : Upper robe.
Udāyī : Wu–t'o–i (烏陀夷) : Name of a monk.
Uddaka Rāmaputta : Yu–t'o–lo–lo–mo–tzu (鬱陀羅羅摩子) : One of Gotama's Teachers before his enlightenment
Uddhacca–kukkucca : Tao–hui (悼悔) : Restlessness, remorse.
Upaka : Yu–t'o (優陀) : Name of an ājīvaka.
Upananda : P'o–nan (婆難) : Commander–in–chief of Magadha.
Upāyāsa : Nao (惱) : Despair.
Upāli : Yu–p'o–li (優婆離) : A former follower of Nātaputta.
Upāsaka : Yu–p'o–sê (優婆塞) : Layman–disciple.
Upāsikā : Yu–p'o–ssu (優婆私) : Lay–woman–disciple.
Upekkhako satimā sukhavihārī : Shê–nien–lo–chu–shih (捨念樂住室) : Dwelling in happiness, with equanimity, with mindfulness.
Upekkhāsatiparisuddhi : Shê–nien–ch'ing–ching (捨念清淨) : Purity of mindfulness which comes of equanimity.
Upekkhāsambojjhaṅga : Shê–chüeh–chih (捨覺支) : Equanimity as factor of wisdom.
Uppala : Ch'ing–lien–huo (青蓮花) : Blue lotus.
Uruvelā : Yü–pei–lo (鬱鞞羅) : Name of a place, where the 3 Kassapa brothers stayed.

E

Ekatta : I (一): Oneness.

Ekantasukha : I-hsiang-lo (一向樂): Absolute happiness.

Ekapuṇḍarīka : Pên-t'o-li (奔陀利): Name of an elephant.

Ekaṃ disaṃ pharitvā : Pien-man-i-fang (遍滿一方): Having suffused in one direction.

Ekaṃ samayaṃ : I-shih (一時): At one time.

Ekasālaka Mallikāya ārāma : I-so-lo-mo-li-yüan (一娑羅末利園): Name of a park.

Ekālopika : I-k'ou (一口): One mouthful.

Ekāsanabhojana : I-tso-shih (一坐食): One-sessioner's practice.

Ekāhika : Jih-i-shih (日一食): One meal a day.

Evaṃ jānato evaṃ passato : Ju-shih-chih-ju-shih-chien-i (如是知如是見已): Having known thus, having seen thus.

Esukārī : Yü-shou-ko-lo (鬱瘦歌羅): Name of a brahmin.

O

Ottappa : Kuei (愧): Scrupulousness.

Opapātika : Hua-shêng (化生): Spontaneous birth.

Orambhāgiyāni saṃyojanāni : Hsia-fên-chieh (下分結): Fetters binding to a lower existence.

Oḷārika · Ts'u (粗): Coarse.

K

Kakusandha : Chüeh-li-chü-hsün-ta (覺礫拘筍大): The first of the five Buddhas in the past.

Kaṅkhāvitaraṇavisuddhi : I-ching (疑淨): Purity of removing doubts.

Kataṃ karaṇīyaṃ : So-tso-i-pan (所作已辦): What should be done is done.

Kapilavatthu : Chia-wei-lo-wei (加維羅衛): Capital of the Sākyans.

Kabaliṅkāra āhāra : T'uan-shih (摶食): Food made into a ball.

Kamboja : Chien-fu (劍浮): One of the 16 countries.

Kammassadamma : Chien-mo-sê-t'an (劍磨瑟曇): A township of the Kurus.

Karavīka : Chia-lo-p'i-chia (迦羅毗伽): Indian cuckoo.

Karuṇā : Pei (悲): Compassion.

Kalandakanivāpa : Chia-lan-to-yüan (迦蘭哆園): A woodland in Veluvana.

Kassapa : Chia-yeh (迦葉): One of the Buddha's great disciples.

Kāmaguṇā : Yü-kung-tê (欲功德): Strands of desire.

Kāmavitakka: Yü-nien (欲念): Thought of desire.

Kāmāsava : Yü-lou (欲漏): Canker of desire.

Kāmāsavā cittaṃ vimucittha : Yü-lou-hsin-chieh-t'o (欲漏心解脫): Emancipation of mind from canker of desire.

Kāmupādāna: Yü-shou (欲受): Grasping of desire.

Kāyadaṇḍa : Shên-fa (身罰): Bodily punishment.

Kāyaviññāṇa : Shên-shih (身識): Body-consciousness.

Kāyasakkhī : Shên-chêng-che (身證者): Body-realizer.

Kāyassa bhedā : Shên-huai (身壞): At the breaking of the body.

Kāyindriya : Shên-kên (身根): Body-faculty.

Kālī : Hei-pên (黑本): Maid-servant of Videhikā.

Kāsāyāni vatthāni acchādetvā : Chu-chia-so-i (著袈裟衣): Having donned the yellow robe.

Kāsi : Chia-shih (加尸): One of the 16 great countries.

Kikī : Chia-pei (頰鞞): King of Benares at Buddha Kassapa's time.

Kimbila : Chin-p'i-lo (金毗羅): Name of a monk.

Kukkuṭārāma : Chi-yüan (鷄園): Hen-park.

Kuru : Chü-lou-shou (拘樓瘦): One of the 16 great countries.

Kullūpama : Fa-yü (栰喩): Parable of the raft.

Kusala : Shan (善): Meritorious.

Kesamassuṃ ohāretvā : T'i-ch'ü-hsü-fa (剃除鬚髮): Having shaved hair and beard.

Kodha : Wei or hui (恚): Anger.

Koravya : Chü-lao-p'o (拘牢婆): The descendent of Kuru.

Kosakāhāra : Chü-shih-shih (拘施食): A bowl of food.

Kosambi : Chü-shê-mi (拘舍彌): Capital of the Vatsas or Vaṃsas.

Kosala : Chü-so-lo (拘娑羅): A country's name.

Kosohita vatthaguyha : Yin-ma-ts'ang (陰馬藏): What is cloth-hid is sheath-cased.

KH

Khattiyakula : Sha-li-tsu-hsing (殺利族性): Warrior's clan.

Khayadhammatā : Chin-fa (盡法): Liable to extinction.

Kharigata : Chien-hsing (堅性): Hardness.

Khīṇā jāti : Shêng-i-ching (生已盡): Birth is destroyed.

G

Gaṇaka Moggallāna : Suan-shu-mu-chien-lien (算數目揵連): A brahmin teacher.

Gaddhabādhi : Chia-t'o-p'o-li (伽陀婆梨): A vulture-trainer.

Gandha : Hsiang (香): Smell.

Gandhabba : Hsiang-yin (香 陰): Heavenly musician, said to preside over child-conception. C : Perfume aggregate.

Gayāsīsa : Hsiang-ting (象 頂): A hill near Gayā. C : Elephant head, with Gayā read as Gaja.

Gahapatiratana : Chü-shih-pao (居 士 寶): Householder-jewel.

Gāthā : Chieh (偈): Verse.

Giñjakāvasatha : Chien-ch'i (揵 祁): A brick-hall at Nādika.

Giribbaja : Yen-shan (巖 山): A name for Rājagaha.

Gulissāni : Ch'ü-ni-shih (瞿 尼 師): A monk who used to live in forest.

Geyya : Ko-yung (歌 詠): Metrical verse.

Goghātakasūnā : T'u-niu-ch'u (屠 牛 處): Slaughter-house.

Gotama : Ch'ü-t'an (瞿 曇): The Buddha's name.

Gotamī : Ch'ü-t'an-mi (瞿 曇 彌): Mahā Pajāpatī Gotamī, the Buddha's step-mother.

Gopaka Moggallāna : Ch'ü-mê-mu-chien-lien (瞿 默 目 揵 連): A brahmin-minister of Ajātasattu.

Gosiṅgasālavana : Miu-chioh-so-lo-lin (牛 角 娑 羅 林): Name of a forest, where dwelt Anuruddha, Nandiya and Kimbila.

C

Cakkaratana : Lün-pao (輪 寶): Wheel-jewel.

Cakkavattī : Chüan-lün-wang (轉 輪 王): A universal monarch.

Cakkhundriya : Yen-kên (眼 根): Eye-faculty.

Cakkhuviññāṇa : Yen-shih (眼 識): Eye-consciousness

Cañkī : Shang-chia (商 伽): A mahāsāla brahmin.

Catuttha jhāna : Ti-ssu-shan (第 四 禪): The 4th Jhāna.

Catuttham jhānaṃ upasampajja vihāsiṃ : Tê ti-ssu-shan ch'êng chiu-yü (得第四禪成就遊): Having attained the 4th jhāna, I dwelt upon.

Catunnaṃ mahābhūtānaṃ upādāya rūpaṃ : Ssu-ta-so-tsao-sê (四大所造色): Material form derived from 4 great elements.

Cattāri ariyasaccāni : Ssu-shêng-ti (四聖帝): 4 noble Truths.

Cattāro mahābhūtā : Ssu-ta (四 大): The 4 elements.

Candana Devaputta : Pan-na (般那): A deva, vassal of the 4 Regent Gods.

Cāgādhiṭṭhāna : Shih-ch'u (施處): Resolution of generosity.

Cittavisuddhi : Hsin-ching : (心淨): Purity of mind.

Cittekaggatā : I-hsin (一心): One-mindedness.

Cīvara : I (衣): Robe.

Cutūpapātañāṇa : Shêng-szu-chih (生死智): Knowledge of birth and death.

Cunda : Chou-na (周那): A worker in metal living in Pāvā or name of a monk.

Cetaso ekodibhāva : I-hsin (一心) : One-mindedness
Cetopariyañāṇa : T'a-hsin-chih (他心智) : Knowledge of others' mind
Cetovimutti : Hsin-chieh-t'o (心解脫) : Freedom of mind.

CH

Cha : Liu (六) : Six.
Chaṭṭha : Ti-liu (第六) : Sixth.
Chanda : Yü (欲) : Wish, impulse, will.

J

Jaṭilaka : Pien-fa (編髮) : Matted hair.
Jambudīpa : Yen-fu (閻浮) : Country of rose-apples, i. e. India.
Jayasena : Ch'i-p'o-hsien-na (耆婆先那) : A prince's name.
Jarāmaraṇa : Lao-ssu (老死) : Old age and death.
Jāgariyaṃ anuyutta : Chêng-chih (正知) : Well-awareness.
Jāṇussoṇi : Shêng-wên (生聞) : A Mahāsāla brahmin.
Jātaka : Shêng-ch'u (生處) : Birth-stories; C : Birth-place.
Jāti : Shêng (生) : Birth.
Jānato : I-chih (以知) : From knowledge.
Jigacchā : Chi (饑) : Hunger.
Jivhāviññāṇa : Shê-shih (舌識) : Tongue-consciousness.
Jivhindriya : Shê-kên (舌根) : Tongue-faculty.
Jetavana : Shêng-lin (勝林) : A park in Sāvatthi.
Jotipāla : Yu-to-lo-tzu (優多羅子) : The Bodhisatta born as a brahmin of Vehaliṅga in Kassapa Buddha's time.

JH

Jhāna : Shan (禪) : Concentration of mind; meditation.

Ḍ

Ḍaṃsa : Mêng (虻) : Gad-fly.

T

Taṇhā : Ai (愛) : Craving.
Tatiyaṃ jhānaṃ : Ti-san-shan (第三禪) : The 3rd stage of meditation.
Tatiyaṃ jhānaṃ upasampajja vihāsiṃ : Tê-ti-san-shan-ch'êng-chiu-yü (得第三禪成就遊) : Having attained the 3rd stage of meditation, I abided in.

Tatthaparinibbāyī : Yü-pi-êrh-pan-nieh-p'an (於彼而般涅槃): From there, he would attain Nibbāna.

Tathāgata : Ju-lai (如來): An epithet of the Buddha.

Tapodārāma : Wên-ch'üan-lin (温泉林): A grove near lake Tapodā.

Taṃ jīvaṃ taṃ sarīraṃ : Ming-chi-shih-shên (命即是身): Life and body are the same.

Tayo khandhā : San-chü-wên (三聚蘊): Three aggregates.

Tassapāpiyyasikā : Ying-yü-chün-chih-chêng-lü (應與君止諍律): Punishment given to him, the offender.

Tāvatiṃsa : San-shih-san-t'ien (三十三天): Name of a heavenly abode.

Tibbadosajātika : Chung-cho-ch'ên (重濁嗔): Born with sharp ill-will.

Tibbamohajātika : Chung-cho-ch'ih (重濁癡): Born with sharp delusion.

Tibbarāgajātika : Chung-cho-yü (重濁欲): Born with sharp attachment.

Tiracchānakathā : Ch'u-shêng-lun (畜生論): Animal talk.

Tiracchānayoni : Ch'u-shêng (畜生): Animal kingdom. C : Animal.

Tusitadeva : Tou-shuai-to-t'ien (兜率哆天): Name of a heavenly abode.

Teja : Huo (火): Fire, heat.

Todeyyaputta : Tou-t'i-tzu (都題子): Name of a brāhmaṇa.

TH

Thīnamiddha : Shui-mien (睡眠): Sloth and torpor.

Thullavajja : T'ou-lo-chê (偸羅柘): A grave offence.

D

Dasama gahapati aṭṭhakanāgara : Ti-shih-chü-shih-pa-ch'êng (第十居士八城): Name of a householder.

Dānakathā : Shuo-shih (說施): Speech on charity.

Diṭṭhadhammasukhavihāra : Hsien-fa-lo-chü (現法樂居): Dwelling in happiness here-now.

Diṭṭhānusaya : Chien-shih (見使): Inclination to speculation.

Diṭṭhippatta : Chien-tao (見到): One who has formed right or wrong view.

Diṭṭhivisuddhi : Chien-ching (見淨): Purity of view.

Diṭṭhupādāna : Chien-shou (見受): Grasping of view.

Diṭṭhe va dhamme sayaṃ abhiññāya sacchikatvā : Yü-hsien-fa-chung-tzu-chih-tzu-tso-chêng (於現法中自知自作證): Having known, having realized by oneself here-now.

Dibbasota : T'ien-êrh (天耳): Divine ear.

Dīghatapassī : Ch'ang-k'u-hsing (長苦行): Name of a Jaina.

Dīghāyu : Ch'ang-shêng (長生): Dīghīti's son.

Dīghīti : Ch'ang-shou (長 壽): Name of a king.

Dīgha Kārāyana : Ch'ang-tso (長 作): King Pasenadi's minister.

Dukkha : K'u (苦): Suffering.

Dukkhakkhandha : K'u-yin (苦 陰): Aggregate of suffering.

Dukkhanirodha : K'u-mieh (苦 滅): Cessation of suffering.

Dukkhasamudaya : K'u-chi (苦 集): Origination of suffering.

Dukkhassa pahāna : K'u-mieh (苦 滅): Extinction of suffering.

Duggati : O-ch'u (惡 處): Evil place.

Dutiya jhāna : Ti-êrh-shan (第 二 禪): 2nd stage of meditation.

Dutiyaṃ jhānaṃ upasampajja vihāsiṃ : Tê-ti-êrh-shan-ch'êng-chiu-yü (得第二禪成就遊): Having attained the 2nd stage of meditation, I dwelt upon.

Dūsī : O-ngo (惡 我): Māra's name.

Devadaha : T'ien-i (天 邑): A township of the Sākyans.

Devadūta : T'ien-shih (天 使): Heavenly messenger.

Domanassa : Yu (憂): Grief.

Dosa : Ch'ên (嗔): Ill-will, hatred.

DH

Dhamma : Fa (法): Norm, truth, mental object.

Dhammacetiya : Fa-chuang-yen (法 莊 嚴): Memorial in honour of the Dhamma.

Dhammadāyāda : Ch'iu-fa (求 法): Heir of the dhamma.

Dhammadinnā : Fa-lo (法 樂): Name of a bhikkhunī. Sometimes written Dhammanandī, hence the C translation Fa-lo.

Dhammādāsa : Fa-ching (法 鏡): Mirror of Dhamma.

Dhammānupassī : Fa-nien-ch'u (法 念 處): Contemplation of dhamma.

Dhānañjāni : T'o-jan (陀 然): A brahmin of Taṇḍulapāladvāra in Rājagaha.

N

Na ehibhadantika : Pu-lai-tsun (不 來 尊): He is not one to whom people say: « Please come, Ven. Sir! »

Na tiṭṭhabhadantika : Pu-chu-tsun (不 住 尊): He is not one to whom people say: « Please stand still, Ven. Sir! »

Naḷakāra : Na-lo-ko-lo (那 羅 哥 邏): The Bodhisatta, born as deva in Tāvatiṃsa.

Na hoti Tathāgato paraṃ maraṇā : Ju-lai-yu-chung (如 來 有 終): The Tathāgata does not exist after death.

Nātaputta : Ch'in-tzu (親 子): The leader of the Nigaṇṭhā.

Nādika : Na-mo-t'i (那摩提) : Name of a place, a l cality in the Vajji country, between Koṭigāma and Vesāli.

Nānaṭṭhā : I i (異義) : Of different meaning.

Nānāgocarāni : I-hsing (異行) : Of different pasturage.

Nānābyañjana : I-wên (異文) : Of different terminology.

Nānāvisayāni : I-ching-chieh (異境界) : Of different object.

Nāparaṃ itthattāyāti abbhaññāsiṃ : Pu-kêng-shou-yu-chih-ju-chên (不更受有知如眞) : I knew that there was no more becoming.

Nālandā : Na-tan-t'o (那難陀) : A famous centre of Buddhist learning, near Rājagaha.

Nāḷijaṅgha : Na-li-yang-chia (那利鴦伽) : A brahmin, wh m Mallikā sent to the Buddha.

Nigaṇṭha : Ni-chien (尼揵) : The Jainas.

Nigrodha : Ni-chü-lei (尼拘類) : Name of a tree.

Nibbāna : Nieh-p'an (涅槃) : Cooling, final bliss.

Nimi : Ni-mi (尼彌) : The Bodhisatta born as king of Mithilā.

Nimitta : Hsiang (相) : Characteristic, mental image.

Nimmāṇaratī deva : Hua-lo-t'ien (化樂天) : A class of deities.

Niraya : Ti-yü (地獄) : the Hell.

Nisīdana : Ni-shih-t'an (尼師檀) : Mat to sit on.

Nissaraṇa : Ch'u-yao (出要) : Escape.

Nihitadaṇḍa nihitasattha : Ch'i-shê-tao-chang (棄捨刀丈) : With stick laid down, with weapon laid down. C : With knife and stick laid down.

Nekkhammavitakka : Wu-yü-nien (無欲念) : Thought of no-desire.

Nerañjarā : Ni-lien-jan, Ni-lien-shan (尼連然) (尼連禪) : Name of a river, on the bank of which, the Buddha sat in meditation, prior to his Enlightenment.

Nevasaññānāsaññāyatana : Fei-hsiang-fei-fei-hsiang-ch'u (非想非非想處) : Plane of neither perception nor non-perception.

Neva hoti na na hoti Tathāgato paraṃ maraṇā : Ju-lai-i-fei-chung-i-fei-pu-chung (如來亦非終亦非不終) : The Tathāgata neither exists nor not exists after death.

P

Pakudha Kaccāyana : Pi-fu-chia-tan (彼復迦旃) : Head of one of the 6 heretical sects of the Buddha's time.

Paccaya : Yüan (緣) : Condition.

Paccayaṃ paṭicca : Yin-yüan-ku (因緣故) : Dependent upon.

Paccuppannasukha : Hsien-lo (現樂) : Present happiness.

Pajāpati : Shêng-chu (生主) : Lord of Beings.

Pañca orambhāgiyāni : Wu-hsia-fên-chieh (五下分結) : Five fetters binding to a lower existence.

Pañcakaṅga : Wu-chih-wu-chu (五支物主): The chamberlain of Pasenadi, a devoted follower of the Buddha.

Pañca nīvaraṇāni : Wu-kai (五蓋): Five hindrances.

Pañcasālā : Wu-so-lo (五娑羅): A brahmin village of Magadha.

Paññādhiṭṭhāna : Chêng-hui-ch'u (正慧處): Resolution based upon wisdom.

Paññānirodhika : Mieh-hui (滅慧): Tending to the destruction of wisdom.

Paññāvimutti : Hui-chieh-t'o (慧解脫): Freedom of mind.

Paṭighānusaya : Wei-shih (恚使): Hatred tendency.

Paṭiññāya kāretabbā : Ying-yü-tzu-fa-lu-chih-chêng-lü (應與自發路止諍律): Verdict to be given according to acknowledgement.

Paṭipadāñāṇadassanavisuddhi : Tao-chi-chih-chien-ching (道跡知見淨): Purity by knowledge and vision of the path.

Paṭibhāga : Tui (對): Counterpart.

Paṭivāta : Hsiang-fêng (向風): Against the wind.

Paṭisevana : Yung (用): Use.

Paṭhamaṃ jhānaṃ upasampajja viharati : Tê-ch'u-shan-ch'êng-chiu-yü (得初禪成就遊): Having attained the 1st jhāna, he dwells in.

Paṭhavī : Ti (地): Earth, the solid element.

Pattacīvara : I-po (衣鉢): Bowl and robe.

Pamāda : Fang-i (放逸): Negligence.

Parabyābādha : Hai-t'a (害他): Harmful to others.

Parideva : Pei (悲): Lamentation.

Parināyakaratana : Chu-ping-ch'ên-pao (主兵臣寶): Adviser jewel. C: Officer-soldier-minister-jewel.

Paribbājakārāma : I-hsüeh-yüan (異學園): Park of wanderers.

Pariyosānakalyāṇa : Hou-miao (後妙): Excellent at the end.

Parivajjana : Li (離): Avoidance.

Parisuddha ājīva : Ming-hsing-ch'ing-ching (命行清淨): Of pure livelihood.

Parisuddha kāyasamācāra : Shên-shing-ch'ing-ching (身行清淨): Of pure bodily conduct.

Parisuddha pariyodāta : Ch'ing-ching (清淨): Purity.

Parisuddha manosamācāra : I-hsing-ch'ing-ching (意行清淨): Of pure mental conduct.

Parisuddha vacīsamācāra : K'ou-hsing-ch'ing-ching (口行清淨): Of pure vocal activities.

Pavaḍḍhati : Tsêng-kuang (增廣): Increase.

Pavivitta : Hsien-chü (閑居): Living secluded.

Pasenadi Kosala : Chü-so-lo-wang-po-ssu-ni (拘薩羅王波斯匿): Pasenadi, king of Kosala.

Passat I-chien (以見): For vision.

Passaddhisambojjhaṅga : Hsi–chüeh–chih （息覺支）: Serenity as factor of wisdom.

Passasati : Ch'u–hsi（出息）: Breathing out, exhaling.

Pahātabba : Tuan（斷）: Should be eradicated.

Pahīyati : Mieh（滅）: To vanish, to pass away.

Pahūtajivhatā : Kuang–ch'ang–shê（廣長舌）: A large tongue.

Pācīnavaṃsadāya : Pan–na–man–shê–szu（般那蔓闍寺）: A park in the Cetiya–kingdom.

Pāṭaliputta : Po–lo–li–tzu（波羅利子）: Capital of Magadha.

Pāṇātipāta : Sha–shêng（殺生）: Killing living beings.

Pātimokkha : Chieh–t'o（解脫）: Code of monastic rules.

Pāpaka : O（惡）: Evil.

Pāpikā icchā : O–yü（惡欲）: Evil desire.

Pāvā : Po–ho（波和）: A city of the Mallas.

Pāvārikambavana : Po–p'o–li–nai–lin（波婆離捺林）: A mango–grove at Nālandā.

Pāsaṃsa : K'o–ch'êng（可稱）: Praiseworthy.

Piṇḍapāta : Yin–shih（飲食）: Alms–food. C: Food and drink.

Piṇḍapāta atirekadhomma : Ts'an–shih（殘食）: Remaining food.

Pipāsā : K'o（渴）: Thirst.

Pilotika : Pei–lu（卑盧）: A paribbājaka.

Pisuṇāvācā : Liang–shê（兩舌）: Slanderous speech. C: Double tongue.

Pītiyā virāgā : Li–hsi–yü（離喜欲）: Aloof from delight and desire.

Pītisambojjhaṅga : Hsi–chüeh–chih（喜覺支）: Delight as factor of wisdom.

Pukkusāti : Fu–chia–lo–so–li（弗迦羅娑利）: A young monk whom the Buddha met at the house of Bhaggava. the potter.

Puṇṇa Mantānīputta : Man–tz'u–tzu（滿慈子）: A monk who belongs to a brahmin family of Donavatthu, near Kapilavatthu.

Puṇṇikā : Pu–ni（不尼）: A salave–girl of Pokkharasāti.

Puthujjana : Fan–fu（凡夫）: The worldling.

Punabbasuka : Fu–na–p'o–hsiu（弗那婆修）: Follower of Punabbasu, one of the Chabbaggiyas.

Pubbārāma : Tung–yüan（東園）: A park outside the Eastern gate of Sāvatthi.

Pubbenivāsānussati : Su–nien–chih（宿念智）: Knowledge of previous births.

Pubbe somanassadomanassāṇaṃ atthagamā : Hsi–yu–pên–i–mieh（喜優本已滅）: With former pleasant and unpleasant feelings subsided already.

Purāṇa : Su–chiu（宿舊）: A chamberlin of Pasenadi.

Purāṇā dutiyikā : Pên–fu（本婦）: Former wife.

Purisadammasārathi : Tao–fa–yü（道法御）: Charioteer for men to be tamed. C: Tame of path and dharma. Later translators preferred : Tiao–yü–chang–fu（調御丈夫）: (Of the same meaning with the Pāli).

Pūraṇakassapa : Pu-lan-chia-yeh（不蘭迦葉）: One of the 6 heretical teachers.

Pettivisaya : Ngo-kuei（餓鬼）: Hungry ghost.

Pokkharasāti : Fu-chia-so-so-lo（弗袈娑娑羅）: A mahāsāla brahmin of great wealth and learning.

Potaliputta : Pu-lo-t'o-tzu（哺羅陀子）: Name of a paribbājaka.

Potaliya : Pu-li to（哺利多）: A householder of Āpaṇa.

PH

Pharusavācā : O-k'ou（惡口）: Harsh speech.

Phassa : Kêng-lo（更樂）: Touch. C : Strong enjoyment. Later translators preferred Ch'u（觸）: Touch, contact.

Phoṭṭhabba : Ch'u（觸）: Touch, contact.

B

Bakkula : Po-chü-lo（薄拘羅）: A monk born in the family of a councillor of Kosambī.

Bārāṇasī : Po-lo-nai（波羅捺）: Capital of Kāsi janapada.

Bālakaloṇakāragāma : P'o-lo-lou-lo（婆羅樓羅）: A locality near Kosambī.

Bāhiti : Pei-ho-t'i（鞞訶提）: A kind of cloth.

Bāhirā paṭhavī dhātu : Wai-ti-chieh（外地界）: External earth.

Bāhukā nadī : To-shui-ho（多水河）: A river to which sacrifices were offered.

Bimbisāra : P'in-pei-so-lo（頻鞞娑羅）: King of Magadha.

Beluvāhāra : Pei-lo-shih（鞞羅食）: Eating one beluvā food.

Brahmadatta : Fan-mo-ta-to（梵摩達哆）: King of Kāsi. He captured Kosala, murdered its king Dīghīti.

Brahmā : Fan-t'ien（梵天）: Chief of Brahmā-loka.

Brahmāyu : Fan-mo（梵摩）: A brahmin in Mithilā, foremost in his knowledge of the Vedas.

Brāhmaṇa : Fan-chih（梵志）: One of the four castes.

Brāhmaṇakulaputta : Fan-chih-tsu-hsing-tsu（梵志族姓子）: Son of brāhmaṇa-family.

BH

Bhagavā : Shih-tsun（世尊）: The Blessed One. C : The World Honoured One.

Bhagavaṃ nettika : Shih-tsun-wei-fa-chu（世尊爲法主）: The Blessed One is the Leader. C : The World Honoured One is the Lord of the Dharma.

Bhagavaṃ mūlaka : Shih-tsun-wei-fa-pên (世尊爲法本): The Blessed One is the root. C: The World Honoured One is the root of the Dharmas.

Bhagu : P'o-ho, P'o-chiu (婆和, 婆咎): A famous sage of old.

Bhaggā : P'o-ch'i-shou (婆奇瘦): Name of a tribe and a country, the capital of which was Suṃsumāragiri.

Bhaddāli : Pa-t'o-ho-li (跋陀和利): Name of a monk.

Bhaddekaratta : Pa-ti-lo-ti (跋地羅帝): a) A descriptive title of a monk with certain qualifications, b) Stanzas describing such a monk.

Bhava : Yu (有): Becoming.

Bhavarāgānusaya : Yu-shih (有使): Tendency of craving for becoming.

Bhavāsava : Yu-lou (有漏): Canker of becoming.

Bhavāsavā cittaṃ vimuccittha : Yu-lou-hsin-chieh-t'o (有漏心解脫): The mind is free from canker of becoming.

Bhāgineyya : Shêng-nan (生男): Nephew.

Bhāradvāja : P'o-ssu-cha (婆私吒): Name of a brahmin clan.

Bhāradvājagotta : P'o-lo-p'o (婆羅婆): Name of a clan.

Bhikkhu : Pi-ch'iu (比丘): The monk.

Bhikkhunī : Pi-ch'iu-ni (比丘尼): The nun.

Bhuttāvī : Yin-shih-ch'i (飲食訖): One who has eaten.

Bhūnahu : Huai-pai-ti (壞白地): A fætus-killer.

Bhūmija : Fu-mi (浮彌): A monk, uncle of prince Jayasena.

Bhesakalāvana : Pu-lin (怖林): A grove in the Bhagga country.

M

Makhādeva : Ta-t'ien (大天): A king, son of Sāgaradeva. C: Great deity, interpreting Makhā as Mahā.

Makhādevambavana : Ta-t'ien-nai-lin (大天捺林): A mango-grove in Mithilā where Makhādeva lived in meditation.

Makkhali Gosāla : Mo-hsi-chia-li-ch'ü-shê (摩息迦利瞿舍): One of the six heretical teachers.

Magadha : Mo-chieh-t'o (摩竭陀): One of the four chief kingdoms of India, at the time of the Buddha.

Maggāmaggañāṇadassanavisuddhi : Tao-fei-tao-chih-chien-ching (道非道知見淨): Purity of knowledge and vision as to the path and non-path.

Macchera, Macchariya : Chien (慳): Stinginess.

Majjhimā paṭipadā : Chung-tao (中道): The Middle-Path.

Majjhe kalyāṇa : Chung-miao (中妙): Excellent in the middle.

Maṇiratana : Chu-pao (珠寶): Gem-jewel.

Mana : I (意): Mind.

Manindriya: I-kên (意根): Faculty of mind.

Manokamma: I-yeh (意業): Mental action.

Manodaṇḍa: I-fa (意罰): Mental punishment.

Manoviññāṇa: I-shih (意識): Mind-consciousness.

Manosañcetanāhāra: I-nien-shih (意念食): Mental food.

Mallikā: Mo-li (末利): Chief queen of Pasenadi.

Mahanta ñātiparivaṭṭa: To-ch'in-tsu (多親族): Big circle of relatives. C: Many relatives.

Mahākaccāna: Ta-chia-chan-yen (大迦旃延): One of the most eminent disciples of the Buddha.

Mahākassapa: Ta-chia-yeh (大迦葉): One of the Buddha's most eminent disciples.

Mahākoṭṭhita: Ta-chü-ch'ih-lo (大拘絺羅): One of the foremost disciples of the Buddha.

Mahācunda: Ta-chou-na (大周那): Name of a monk.

Mahānāma Sakka: Shih-mo-ho-nan (釋摩訶男): A sākyan rāja, son of Amitodana.

Mahāpajāpati: Mo-ho-po-lo-shê-po (摩訶簸羅闍鉢): An eminent Therī, the Buddha's step-mother.

Mahāpurisalakkhaṇāni: Ta-jên-chih-hsiang (大人之相): Marks of a great man.

Mahābhogakkhandha: To-ts'ai-wu (多財物): Great aggregate of properties. C: Lot of properties.

Mahāmoggallāna: Ta-mu-chien-lien (大目揵連): One of the chief disciples of the Buddha, foremost in psychic powers.

Maṃsapesi: Jou-luan (肉臠): Sliced meat, piece of flesh.

Mā pacchā vippaṭisārino ahuvattha: Wu-ling-hou-hui (無令後悔): So you would not feel remorse later on.

Mā pamādattha: Wu-tê-fang-i (勿得放逸): Do not be negligent.

Māgandiya: Hsu-hsien-t'i (鬚閑提): A paribbājaka.

Mātuthañña: Mu-ju (母乳): Mother's milk.

Māna: Man (慢): Pride.

Mānānusaya: Man shih (慢使): Tendency of pride.

Māyā: Ch'i-kuang (欺誑): Crafty, deceitful.

Māra pāpimā: Mo-po-hsūn (魔波旬): Māra, the Evil One.

Māranivāpa: Mo êrh (魔餌): Bait of Māra.

Māravisaya: Mo-ching-chieh (魔境界): Māra's realm.

Māluṅkyaputta: Man-t'ung-tzu (鬘童子): Son of the assessor of the king of Kosala, his mother being Māluṅkya.

Migāramātā: Lu-tzu-mu (鹿子母): Another name of Visākhā.

Micchādiṭṭhi: Hsieh-chien (邪見): Wrong view.

Mithilā: Mi-sa-lo (彌薩羅): The Capital of Videha country.

Muditā : Hsi (喜) : Sympathy in others' welfare.

Musāvāda : Wang-yen (妄 言) : Speaking lies.

Mettā : Tz'u (慈) : Benevolence, amity.

Mettā sahagatena cetasā : Hsin-yü-tz'u-chü (心 與 慈 俱) : Mind endowed with friendliness, with benevolence.

Medaḷumpa or *Medatalumpa :* Mi-lou-li (彌 婁 離) : A sākyan village, 3 leagues from Saṅgaraka.

Moghapurisa : Yü-ch'ih (愚 癡) : Foolish man.

Mora : K'ung-ch'üeh (孔 雀) : Pea-cock.

Moranivāpa : K'ung-ch'üeh-lin (孔 雀 林) : Pea-cock forest, a grove in Veḷuvana, at Rājagaha.

Moliyaphagguna : Mou-li-p'o-ch'ün-na (牟 利 破 群 那) : A monk always friendly with the nuns.

Moha : Ch'ih (癡) : Ignorance.

Y

Yathā divā tathā rattiṃ ; yathā rattiṃ tathā divā : Ju-chou-yeh-i-jan ; ju-yeh-chou-i-jan (如 晝 夜 亦 然, 如 夜 晝 亦 然) : Like the day, the night is the same ; like the night, the day is the same).

Yathābhūtaṃ : Ju-chên (如 眞) : As it really is.

Yama : Yen-wang (閻 王) : The ruler of the kingdom of death.

Yamataggi : Yeh-p'o-t'o-chien-ni (夜 婆 陀 揵 尼) : A sage of old, one among the originators of the Vedic hymns.

Yaṃ taṃ ariyā ācikkhanti : Wei-shêng-so-shuo (謂 聖 所 說) : That is what the Noble Ones call.

Yaṃ p'icchaṃ na labhati taṃ pi dukkhaṃ : Ch'iu-pu-tê-k'u (求 不 得 苦) : Not obtaining what one desires is suffering.

Yāmā devā : Yen-mo-t'ien (焰 摩 天) : A class of deities.

Yebhuyyasikā : Ying-yü-chan-chuan-chih-chêng-lü (應 與 展 轉 止 諍 律) : Decision of the majority. C : Gradual way of settling the dispute.

Yojana : Yu-yen (由 延) : A league.

Yonā : Yü-ni (餘 尼) : A country and its people, probably iohians, the Baktrian Greeks.

Yoniso manasikāra : Chêng-ssu-wei (正 思 惟) : Right reflection, right consideration.

R

Raṭṭhapāla : Lai-cha-ho-lo (賴 吒 和 羅) : A monk, chief of those who had left the world through faith.

Rattin-divā : I-jih-i-yeh (一 日 一 夜) : One day and one night.

Rammaka : Lo-mo (羅摩): A brahmin whose hermitage was in Sāvatthi, near the Pubbakoṭṭhaka.

Rasa : Wei (味) : Taste.

Rāga : T'an (貪) : Lust.

Rāgadosamoha : Yin-nu-ch'ih (婬怒癡) : Lust, ill-will, delusion.

Rāgānusaya : Yü-shih (欲使) : Tendency of lust.

Rājagaha : Wang-shê-ch'êng (王舍城) : A city, capital of Magadha.

Rāhula : Lo-yün (羅云) : Only son of Gotama Buddha.

Rūpa : Sê (色) : Material forms.

Revata : Li-yüeh-to (離越哆) : An arahant who loved solitude.

L

Lokavidū : Shih-chien-chieh (世間解) : Knower of the world.

Lobha : T'an (貪) : Greed.

Lomasakaṅgiya : Lu-i-ch'iarg-ch'i (盧夷強耆) : An arahant.

V

Vacīkamma : K'ou-yeh (口業) : Vocal action.

Vacīdaṇḍa : K'ou-fa (口罰) : Vocal punishment.

Vacchāyana : P'o-ts'o (婆蹉) : Name of Pilotika's clan.

Vajjī : Pa-ch'i (跋耆) : One of the 16 mahājanapadas.

Vayadhammatā : Shuai-fa (衰法) : Subject to decay.

Vassakāra : Yü-shih (雨勢) : A brahmin, Ajātasattu's chief minister.

Vassika : P'o-shih-hua (婆師花) : A kind of flower.

Vājirī : P'o-i-li (婆夷利) : Daughter of Pasenadi.

Vāpa : Fêng (風) : Wind.

Vāmaka : P'o-mo (婆摩) : One of the great sages held in estcem by the brahmins.

Vāmadeva : P'o-mo-t'i-p'o (婆摩提婆) : One of the great sages held in esteem by the brahmins.

Vāseṭṭha : P'o-lo-p'o (婆羅婆) : Name of an old ṛṣi held in high esteem for his knowledge.

Vigatūpakkilesa : Wu-fan (無煩) : Without distress.

Vighātapakkhika : To-fan-nao (多煩惱) : Associated with trouble. C : Of much trouble.

Vicikicchānusaya : I-shih (疑使) : Tendency of doubt.

Vijjācaraṇasampanna : Ming hsing-tsu (明行足) : Endowed with wisdom and conduct. C : Complete in wisdom and conduct.

Viññāṇañcāyatana : Wu-liang-shih-ch'u (無量識處) : Plane of infinite consciousness.

Viḍūḍabha : Pei-liu-lo (鞞留羅) : Son of Pasenadi and Vāsabhakhattiyā.

Vitakkavicāraṃ vūpasamā : Chüeh-kuan-i-hsi (覺觀已息) : With the calming down of initial and applied thoughts. Later translators preferred : Hsin-tz'u-i-hsi (尋伺已息).

Videha : Pei-t'o-t'i (鞞陀提) : One of the 2 important principalities of the Vajjian confederacy.

Vidhura : Ying (音) : One of the 2 chief disciples of Kakusandha Buddha.

Vipariṇāmadhammatā : Pien-i-fa (變易法) : Subject to change.

Vipariṇāmadhamma : Mieh-fa (滅法) : Liable to cessation.

Vipassanā : Kuan (觀) : Insight.

Vimuttasmiṃ vimuttan ti ñāṇaṃ ahosi : Chieh-t'o-i-pien-chih-chieh-t'o (解脫已便知解脫) : Having been emancipated, he knew that he was emancipated.

Viriyasambojjhaṅga : Ching-chin-chüeh-chih (精進覺支) : Exertion as factor of wisdom.

Vivicca akusalehi dhammehi : Li-o-pu-shan-chih-fa (離惡不善之法) : Aloof from evil, demeritorious dhammas.

Vivicc'eva kāmehi : Li-yü (離欲) : Aloof from desires.

Vivekajaṃ pītisukhaṃ : Li-shêng-hsi-lo (離生喜樂) : Joy and happiness arisen from aloofness.

Visākhā : P'i-shê-ch'ü (毗舍佉) : The chief among the female lay-disciples of the Buddha.

Vihiṃsāvitakka : Hai-nien (害念) : Thought of harming.

Vītaccika vītadhūma : Wu-yen-yen (無烟燄) : Without flame, without smoke. C : Without smoke and flame.

Vītamissā cakkhusotaviññeyyā dhammā : Tsa-yen-êrh-chih-fa (雜眼耳知法) : Mixed states cognisable through eye, through ear.

Vusitaṃ brahmacariyaṃ : Fan-hsing-i-li (梵行已立) : The brahma-life has been fulfilled.

Vekhanassa : Pei-mo-na-hsiu (鞞摩那修) : A paribbājaka, teacher of Sakuludāyī.

Vedanānupassī : Chüeh-nien-ch'u (覺念處) : Contemplation on feelings. Later translators preferred : Shou-nien-ch'u (受念處).

Vedalla : Kuang-chieh (廣解) : One of the aṅgas. C : detailed explanation.

Vedehikā : Pi-t'o-t'i (鞞陀提) : A lady of Sāvatthi, wrongly reputed for her gentleness.

Vebhaliṅga or *Vehaliṅga* : Pei-p'o-ling-ch'i (鞞婆陵耆) : A township where lived Ghaṭīkāra, friend of Jotipāla.

Veyyākaraṇa : Chi-shuo (記說) : Exposition, one of the 9 aṅgas. C : Prophecies, one of the 12 aṅgas.

Vesāli : Pei-shê-li (鞞舍離) : A city, capital of the Licchavī.

Vessāmitta : Pi-shê-mi-to-lo (毗奢蜜哆邏) : A celebrated sage of old.

Vehapphala : Kuang-kuo-t'ien (廣果天): One of the Brahmā-worlds of the Rūpaloka.

Vyāpādavitakka : Wei-nien (恚念): Thought of hatred.

S

Sakadāgāmi : I-lai (一來), Or Ssu-t'o-han (斯陀含): Once-Returner.

Sakuludāyī : Chien-mao (箭毛): A famous paribbājaka.

Sakka : Shih-chi-shou (釋罽瘦): Chief of the Devas.

Sakkāyadiṭṭhi : Shên-chien (身見): Heresy of individuality.

Saggakathā : Shuo-shêng-t'ien-fa (說生天法): Speech about heaven.

Saṅkiliṭṭhā cakkhusotaviññeyyā dhammā : Wei-wu-yen-êrh-chih-fa (穢汙眼耳知法): Blemished dhammas cognised by eye, by ear.

Saṅghāṭi : Sêng-chia-li (僧伽梨): One of the 3 robes.

Saccādhiṭṭhāna : Chên-ti-ch'u (眞諦處): Determination on truth.

Sañjaya Ākāsagotta : Hsiang-chi-hsiang-tzu (想吉祥子): Name of a person.

Sañjaya Belaṭṭhiputta : P'o-jo-pi-lo-ch'ih-tzu (婆若鞞羅遲子): One of the six heretical teachers.

Sañjīva : Hsiang (想): One of the two disciples of Buddha Kakusandha.

Saññāvedayitanirodha : Hsiang-chih-mieh-ting (想知滅定): Cessation of perception and feeling.

Satipaṭṭhāna : Nien-ch'u (念處): Application of mindfulness.

Sativinaya dātabba : Ying-yü-i-chih-chêng-lü (應與憶止諍律): Verdict to be given with the help of memory.

Satisambojjhaṅga : Nien-chüeh-chih (念覺支): Mindfulness as factor of wisdom.

Sato ca sampajāno : Chêng-nien-chêng-chih (正念正知): Mindfulness and thoughtfulness. C: right mindfulness, right knowledge.

Satta adhikaraṇāni : Ch'i-chih-chêng (七止諍): 7 ways of settling disputes.

Satthā devamanussānaṃ : T'ien-jên-shih (天人師): Master, Teacher of deities and men.

Sadda : Shêng (聲): Sound.

Saddhānusārī : Yu-hsin-hsing (有信行): Faith-follower.

Saddhāvimutti : Yu-hsin-chieh-t'o (有信解脫): Freed through faith.

Santāvihārā : Hsi-chieh-t'o (息解脫): Peaceful dwellings, state of peacefulness.

Santuṭṭha : Chih-tsu (知足): Contentment.

Sappurisa : Chên-jên (眞人): True man, superman.

Sappurisadhamma : Shang-jên-fa (上人法): Dhamma of the superman.

Sabyañjana : Yu-wên (有文): With the letter.

Samaṇa : Sha-mên (沙門): Recluse.

Samaṇamaṇḍikāputta : Sha-mên-wên-ch'i-tzu (沙門文祁子) : A name for the paribbājaka Uggāhamāna.

Samatha : Chih (止) : Quietude.

Samādhikkhandha : Ting-chü (定聚) : Meditation-group.

Samādhijaṃ pītisukhaṃ : Ting-shêng-hsi-lo (定生喜樂) : Joy and happiness arisen from meditation.

Samādhisambojjhaṅga : Ting-chüeh-chih (定覺支) : Meditation as factor of wisdom

Samiddhi : San-mi-t'i (三彌提) : A monk belonging to a householder's family of Rājagaha

Samudaya : Chi (集) : Origination. Old translation : Hsi (習) : Practice.

Samphappalāpa : I-yü (綺語) : Frivolous talk.

Sammā ājīva : Chêng-ming (正命) : Right livelihood.

Sammākammanta : Chêng-yeh (正業) : Right action.

Sammādiṭṭhi : Chêng-chien (正見) : Right view.

Sammāpaññā : Chêng-chih (正智) : Right wisdom.

Sammāvācā : Chêng-yü (正語) : Right speech.

Sammā vāyāma : Chêng-fang-pien (正方便) : Right exertion. C : Right means. Later translators preferred : Chêng-ching-chin (正精進), of the same Pāli meaning.

Sammāsaṅkappa : Chêng-ssu-wei (正思惟) : Right consideration, right thinking.

Sammāsati : Chêng-nien (正念) : Right mindfulness.

Sammāsamādhi : Chêng-ting (正定) : Right concentration.

Sammāsambuddha : Têng-chêng-chüeh (等正覺) : Perfectly Enlightened.

Sammukhāvinaya dātabba : Ying-yü-mien-ch'ien-chih-chêng-lü (應與面前止諍律) : Verdict to be given in presence of.

Sassataloka : Shih-yu-ch'ang (世有常) : The world is eternal.

Sahāpi sukhena sahāpi somanassena : Tzu-lo-tzu-hsi (自樂自喜) : Along with happiness, with pleasure. C : with one's own happiness, with one's own pleasure.

Saṃyojana : Chieh-shih (結使) : Fetter.

Saṃsaṭṭha : Ho (合) : Mixed up with, associated with.

Sāketa : Chi-ti (鷄帝) : A town in Kosala.

Sāṭheyya : Yü-ch'an (諛諂) : Craftiness.

Sāti Kevaṭṭaputta : Ch'a-ti-chi-ho-to-zu (嗏帝鷄和哆子) : A monk son of a fisherman.

Sāttha : Yu-i (有義) : With meaning, with profit.

Sāmagāma : Shê-mi (舍彌) : A sākyan village.

Sāriputta : Shê-li-tzu (舍利子) : The chief disciple of the Buddha.

Sāvatthi : Shê-wei (舍衛) : The capital town of Kosala.

Sirivaḍḍha : Shih-li-a-ch'a (尸利阿荼) : A minister of Pasenadi.

Sīla : Chiai (戒) : Moral conduct, moral code.

Sīlakathā : Shuo-chiai (說戒) : Speech on moral precept.

Sīlakkhandha : Chiai-chü (戒 聚) : Morality-group.

Sīlabbataparāmāsa : Chiai-ch'ü (戒 取) : Belief in mere rules and rituals. C : Grasping of rules.

Sīlavisuddhi : Chiai-ching (戒 淨) : Purity of moral conduct.

Sukhañ ca kāyena paṭisaṃvedesiṃ : Êrh-shên-chüeh-lo (而 身 覺 樂) : And I experienced bodily happiness.

Sukhassa pahānā : Lo-mieh (樂 滅) : With the cessation of happiness.

Sukhuma : Hsi (細) : Subtle.

Sugata : Shan-shih (善 逝) : The Well-Farer.

Suṇātha, sādhukaṃ manasikarotha : Ti-t'ing, shan-ssu-nien-chih (諦 聽 善 思 念 之) : Listen and well consider.

Sutta : Chêng-ching (正 經) : Principal discourse.

Suddhodana : Pai-ching (白 淨) : Father of Gotama Buddha.

Supinaka : Mêng or mung (夢) : Dream.

Subha : Ying-wu (鸚 鵡) : A young man called Todeyyaputta.

Subhakiṇṇā : Pien-ching-t'ien (遍 淨 天) : Lustrous devas.

Subha māṇava Todeyyaputta : Ying-wu-mo-na-tu-t'i-tzu (鸚 鵡 摩 納 都 提 子) : A young man called Todeyyaputta.

Subhūti : Hsü-pu-t'i (須 菩 提) : Name of a monk.

Suṃsumāragiri : T'o-shan (鼉 山) : A city in the Bhagga country.

Senāsana : Ch'uang-ju (床 褥) : Dwelling, lodging. C : Bed and mattress.

So evaṃ samāhite citte : Pi-ju-shih-ting-hsin (彼 如 是 定 心) : He, with such a concentrated mind.

Soka : Ch'ou (愁) : Grief.

Sokaparidevadukkhadomanassupāyāsa : Ch'ou-ch'i-t'i-k'u-yu-k'u-ao-nao (愁 戚 啼 哭 憂 苦 懊 惱) : Grief, lamentation, suffering, distress, despair.

Sotaviññāṇa : Êrh-shih (耳 識) : Ear-consciousness.

Sotāpanna : Hsü-t'o-yüan or yü-liu (須 陀 洹 , 預 流) : Stream-attainer,

Sotindriya : Êrh-kên (耳 根) : Ear-faculty.

Somā Sakulā : Hsien-yüeh (賢 月) : Both are sisters and queens of Pasenadi.

H

Hatthi : Hsiang (象) : Elephant.

Hatthipada : Hsiang-chi (象 跡) : Elephant-foot-print.

Hadaya : Hsin (心) : Heart.

Hiri : Ts'an (慚) : Sense of shame.

Hirikopīna : Ts'an-kuei (慚 愧) : Shame.

Hetu : Yin (因) : Cause.

Hoti ca na ca hoti Tathāgato paraṃ maraṇā : Ju-lai-chung-pu-chung (如 來 終 不 終) : The Tathāgata exists and does not exist after death.

Hoti Tathāgato paraṃ maraṇā : Ju-lai-pu-chung (如 來 不 終) : The Tathāgata exists after death.

INDEX OF SOME DOCTRINAL TERMS

A

B

C

D

E

F

H

I

J

K

M

N

O

P

R

S

T

V

W

INDEX OF CHINESE TERMS

A

C

F

Fa-chuang-yen-ching 法莊嚴經.
Fa-hsing 法行.
Fa-lo-pi-ch'iu-ni-ching 法樂丘比尼經.
Fan-chih-p'in 梵志品.
Fan-chih-t'o-jan-ching 梵志陀然經.
Fan-mo 梵摩.
Fan-mo-ching 梵摩經.
Fan-mo-ta-to 梵摩達哆.
Fan-t'ien-ch'ing-fu-ching 梵天請佛經.
Fên-pieh-kuan-fa-ching 分別觀法經.
Fên-pieh-liu-chieh-ching 分別六界經.
Fên-pieh-liu-ch'u-ching 分別六處經.
Fên-pieh-ta-yeh-ching 分別大業經.
Fou-mi-ching 浮彌經.
Fu-tien-ching 佛田經.
Fü-hsüeh-ta-tzu-tien 佛學大辭典.

H

Ho-i-ching 何義經.
Ho-p'o-ching 恕破經.
Hsi-yü-chi 西遊記.
Hsiang-a-na-han 向阿那含.
Hsiang-ching 想經.
Hsiang-hsü-t'o-yüan 向須陀洹.
Hsiang-mo-ching 降魔經.
Hsiang-ssu-t'o-han 向斯陀含.
Hsiao 小
Hsao-k'ung-ching 小空經.
Hsiao-wu 孝武.
Hsin-chieh-t'o 心解脫.
Hsin-hsing 信行.
Hsin-wei-ching 心穢經.
Hsing-pan-nieh-p'an 行般涅槃.
Hsü-t'o-yüan 須陀洹.
Hsü-t'o-yüan-hsiang 須陀洹向.
Hsüeh-jen 學人.
Hsü-hsien-t'i 鬚閑提.
Hsüan-tsang 玄莊.
Hu-fa 護法.
Hui-chieh-t'o 慧解脫.

I

I-chung 一種.
I-hsing-ching 意行經.

J

Jou-juang-ching 柔軟經.

K

Kei-ku-tu 給孤獨.
Kên-pên-fên-pieh-p'in 根本分別品.
K'u-yin-ching 苦陰經.
Kuan-shih-yin 觀世音.

L

Lai-cha-ho-lo 賴吒恕羅.
Li-ching 例經.
Li-p'in 例品.
Li-yüeh-to 離越哆.
Lieh-shih-ching 獵師經.
Lin-ching-ti-êrh 林經第二.
Lin-p'in 林品.
Lo-mo-ching 羅摩經.
Lou-chin-ching 漏盡經.
Lu-tzu-mu 鹿子母.
Lung-an 隆安.

M

Ma-i-ching 馬邑經.
Ma-ha-nan 摩訶男.
Man-tung-tzu 鬘童子.
Man-tz'u-tzu 滿慈子.
Mi-lou-li 彌婁離.
Mi-wan-yü-ching 蜜丸喩經.
Mou-li-p'o-chün-na-ching 牟犂破群那經.
Mu-chi-yü-ching 木積喩經.

N

Na-mo-t'i 那摩提.
Na-nan-t'o 那難陀.
Nan-t'i-po-lo 難提波羅.
Ni-chien 尼揵.
Ni-chü-lei 尼拘類.
Ni-kan-ching 尼乾經.
Ni-lien-jan 尼連然.
Ni-shih-t'an 尼師檀.
Nien-ching 念經.
Nien-ch'u-ching 念處經.
Niu-chiao-so-lo 牛角娑羅.
Niu-chiao-so-lo-lin-ching 牛角娑羅林經.

P

P'in-pi-so-lo-wang-ying-fo-ching 頻鞞娑邏王迎佛經.
P'o-chiu 婆裘.
P'o-ch'i-shou 婆奇瘦.
P'o-p'o-li-nai 婆婆離捺.
P'o-t'o-ho-li 跋陀和利.
P'o-t'o-ho-li-ching 跋陀和利經.
Pa-ch'êng-ching 八城經.
Pa-ti-lo-ti 跋地羅帝.
Pei-ho-t'i-ching 鞞訶提經.
Pei-mo-na-hsiu 鞞摩那修.
Pei-p'o-ling-ch'i-ching 鞞婆陵耆經.
Pei-t'o-t'i 鞞陀提.
Po-ho 波和.
P'o-lo-p'o 婆羅婆.
Po-ssu-ni 波斯匿.
Pu-li-to 哺利多.
Pu-li-to-ching 哺利多經.
Pu-li-to-p'in 哺利多品.
Pu-t'ui-fa 不退法.
Pu-tung-fa 不動法.

S

San-mi-t'i 三彌提.
Sêng-chia-li 僧伽梨.
Shan-fa 善法.
Shan-fa-ching 善法經.
Shan-jen-wang-ching 善人往經.
Shang-liu-sê-chiu-ching 上流色究竟.
Shê-li-tzu 舍利子.
Shê-li-tzu-hsiang-ying-p'in 舍利子相應品.
Shê-mi 舍彌.
Shê-wei 舍衛.
Shên-chêng 身證.
Shêng-chin-fa 昇進法.
Shêng-lin 勝林.
Shêng-wên 生聞.
Shih-che-ching 侍者經.
Shih-chi-shou 釋羈瘦.
Shih-chien-fu-ching 世間福經.
Shih-chung-ch'an-shih-tsun-ching 釋中禪室尊經.
Shih-tsun 世尊.
Shih-tzu-hou-ching 師子吼經.
Shou-fa-ching 受法經.
Shuang-p'in 雙品.
Shui-chin-fan-chih-ching 水淨梵志經.
Shui-yü-ching 水喩經.

T

W

Y